Charging Against Wellington

*Napoleon's Cavalry
in the Peninsular War 1807–1814*

Contents

Illustrations

Plates may be found between pages 156 and 157

List of Tables

Tables

Foreword

'*Procella equestris*' – a hurricane of cavalry – is how French General Count Maximilan Sebastien Foy described Napoleon's imperial squadrons in his uncompleted 1827 *Histoire de la guerre de la péninsule sous Napoléon*. In capable hands the Napoleonic mounted storm could be swift, sweeping, spectacular. At times it was devastating. When opportunity offered, the emperor's cavalry, in small numbers or great, demonstrated decisive power at battles like Medina de Rio Seco in July 1808 and Medellin in March 1809. At Maria in June 1809 a single Polish squadron unhinged the Spanish defence and at Ocaña, five months later, the cavalry under Sebastiani played a key role in perhaps the largest Napoleonic battlefield capture to date – Marshal Soult reported 26,000 Spanish prisoners.

The Anglo-Portuguese army, too, shared discomfiture at the hands of imperial troopers, as at the Coa River in 1810 and at Fuentes de Oñoro and Albuera in 1811. Small wonder that French cavalry in numbers worried Arthur Wellesley, commander of the British expeditionary force. *Charging Against Wellington* traces how France's hurricane of horsemen was organised and led through the harsh war fought across the Iberian Peninsula and southern France from 1807 to 1814.

France's cavalry were also called upon to assist in a relentless and widespread 'little war', *el guerrilla*, which often required regiments to be dispersed in isolated, self-reliant detachments to pacify or garrison a locality, act as escorts, or conduct mobile operations against partisans (*guerrillas*). 'When we marched from one province to another,' wrote Sublieutenant Albert Jean Michel de Rocca, a Swiss in the 2nd Hussars, in his 1814 memoir of Iberian service,

> the partisans immediately reorganised the country we had
> abandoned in the name of Ferdinand VII, as if we were never to go
> back, and punished very severely every one who had shewn any

kind of zeal for the French. Thus the terror of our arms gave us no influence around us. As the enemy was spread over the whole country, the different points that the French occupied were all more or less threatened; their victorious troops, dispersed in order to maintain their conquests, found themselves, from Irun to Cadiz, in a state of continual blockade; and they were not in reality masters of more than the ground they actually trod upon.

Portuguese and Spanish resistance to France's sustained effort to occupy and pacify the Peninsula required frequent redistribution of the Emperor's cavalry and changes of command structure. The very geographic breadth and duration of the Peninsular War, as well as its remoteness from imperial headquarters, however, challenged not only the capacity of Napoleon and his staff to track and record his army's evolving position and field-organisation, but generations of subsequent historians to elucidate it accurately.

Robert Burnham's study of French imperial cavalry untangles the tale clearly. Divided into three sections, *Charging Against Wellington* guides the reader through the arm's organisational commitment in the Peninsula, supported by over 250 tables and 80 biographical sketches of the generals who commanded it.

Part One, with 57 organisational tables, charts the regimental com-position and leadership of France's cavalry brigades and divisions, as well as their assignments to divisional, army corps, and army commands throughout the war. Its four chapters traverse the conflict's arc, from creeping invasion, beginning in late October 1807, to an attempted conquest which, by 1810, was supported by 40,000 troopers, to the difficulties of occupation and pacification, followed by 'the long retreat'that ended in southern France in April 1814. Meeting the shifting needs of each of these phases, and the unique military requirements of each region of the Iberian Peninsula, required frequent changes in command structures and regimental assignments.

Part Two analyses, as a group, the generals who commanded cavalry formations during the six and a half years of the Peninsular War, and includes compact biographies of each of them. A rapid battlefield-glance (*coup-d'œil*), impulsive determination, combined with youthful vigour, good eyesight, ringing voice, athletic dexterity, and a centaur's agility, were all necessities for an outstanding cavalry general, observed General Foy in his *History*, but above all: a prodigal supply of bravery. Unfortunately, bravery (and disease) exacted a heavy toll: only 57 per cent of the cavalry generals survived their service in the Peninsula alive, unwounded, and uncaptured. Moreover, a war largely waged far from the

immediate gaze of the emperor lacked opportunities for noticed glory and
ensuing advancement. Nevertheless, while some cavalry generals exposed
their leadership deficiencies (nine were relieved for cause), others, such as
Delort, Milhaud, Montbrun, Tour-Maubourg and Watier, proved themselves to be highly capable.

Part Three of *Charging Against Wellington* presents a tabular outline
of key data – including which squadrons of a regiment were present and
when, major commands to which assigned, battles in which they fought
– for each of the 54 French, 2 foreign auxiliary, and 11 allied cavalry
regiments serving the Emperor in the Peninsula, as well as for some 25
provisional cavalry regiments formed for service there. By 1812 half of
all French cavalry regiments had sent one or more squadrons to Spain or
Portugal. Yet with over 500,000 square kilometres of Iberian Peninsula to
secure against an hostile population supported by the British army and
Royal Navy, and competing wars in eastern and central Europe, there
simply were never enough horsemen.

Charging Against Wellington neatly catalogues and describes the
service of the Emperor's cavalry so that its organisation can be explored
and traced from almost any level, and its generals placed in the context of
their commands and accomplishments. Synthesising as it does a wealth
of data, Robert Burnham's study will reward both the casual enthusiast
of the Peninsular War and the researcher or scholar seeking to follow the
threads or patterns of organisation and leadership of Napoleon's mounted
arm during that long and costly campaign.

Howie Muir
Nevada City, California

Acknowledgements

This book grew out of camaraderie that developed on the Napoleon Series website (www.napoleon-series.org). I first met Tony Broughton via the site in 1996 over the years we have a developed a close friendship. We originally were going to write this book together, but he had another commitment and was unable to actively help me with the writing. Fortunately, for someone who was not actively helping me, he was able to put in many hours! Tony has studied Napoleonic history for many decades and is an expert on the French military of the era. In addition to providing advice and direction on how to proceed with the book, Tony gave me free access to his personal library, which has thousands of books on Napoleonic history. The focus of his library is the French army and it is probably contains the largest collection of the French regimental histories in private hands. Some of these books are so hard to find that they not available elsewhere except in the rare book collections of national libraries. Although giving access to his library may not seem like much, Tony and I live on opposite sides of the Atlantic Ocean, so giving me access really meant that any time I needed to check a source in his library, it was Tony who pulled the book, looked to see if would be useful, and then copied and sent to me the relevant information. He cheerfully did this more times than I can count. I am not sure I could have completed this book without his help! Ron McGuigan, who co-authored two other books with me, was also very helpful with this one. He spent many hours helping me find information on a wide variety of topics. He also pored over the manuscript to ensure I got the facts right . . . and let me know when I did not! Then there is Howie Muir. Apart from writing the Foreword, Howie went line-by-line through the manuscript, making many suggestions on how to make the text clearer and like Ron, made sure my facts were right. Howie's suggestions and corrections were always right on the money and made this a much better book! As well as Tony, Ron and Howie, individuals from nine different countries, who contribute to the Napoleon Series on a regular basis, also freely provided assistance to me. Steven Smith once again showed his mastery at finding information on the internet. I knew that he had superb skills in winnowing out obscure sources in English and French, but he demonstrated an equal ability in German, Italian and Polish! Jack Gill was also forthcoming with information on a wide range of German topics, such as the Westphalian, Nassau and Berg cavalry, and French provisional regiments. Tom Devoe spent many hours compiling invaluable information on the Nassau and Westphalian cavalry, and Guy Dempsey helped with the Berg and Hanoverian cavalry. From Italy, Virgilio Ilari provided me with several papers that he wrote on the Italian experience during the Peninsular War, while Aleksander Sazanow, who lives in Poland, helped with the Polish lancers. Others include Dominique Timmermans, Alain Chappet, Trygve Smidt, Paul Dawson, Terry Crowdy, John Cook, Thomas Hemmann, Anthony Gray, Mark Webb, and Frank McReynolds. It is a quite a crew and the most amazing thing about it is that of the eighteen people I have mentioned above, I have only ever met Howie Muir and Jack Gill! I am still waiting to meet Ron McGuigan, with whom I have co-authored two books, but have only talked to once. As for Tony Broughton who spent hundreds of hours working on this book with me, I have neither met nor spoken to him. Perhaps we will be able to change that in the next year! I would be remised if I did not mention David McCracken. He serves as the moderator of the Napoleon Series History Forum. His dedication to the thankless job of managing the Forum allowed me to time to write this book. There are several other individuals who were very helpful. I refer to them as my research assistants: Nadya Muchoney, a student at Boston College, and my son Jonathan Burnham who studies at George Mason University. They were the ones I turned to for help in finding and copying sections from long-out-of-print books. I was always surprised with what they were able to find! My son Stuart also freely gave of his time helping me by photocopying sources at the Library of Congress. His tour of duty as a cavalry officer on a remote outpost in Iraq had to be eerily similar to that of a French dragoon officer in southern Spain in 1811.

Finally, I have to thank my wife Denah, who once again cheerfully gave up the kitchen table for my writing over the past eight months. When I told her that all I had left to do was write the Acknowledgement, she got very excited and then asked if that meant I would be clearing off the table!

Bob Burnham

Introduction

I considered our cavalry so inferior to that of the French, from want of order, although I consider one squadron a match for two French squadrons, I should not have liked to see four British opposed to four French; and as the numbers increased, and order of course became more necessary, I was more unwilling to risk our cavalry without having a greater superiority of numbers.[*]

The Duke of Wellington to Lord W. Russell, 31 July 1826

There are three great works in English that cover the French attempt to bring Spain and Portugal into Napoleon's empire. The first, written a few decades after the Peninsular War ended, is Sir William Napier's six-volume *History of the War in the Peninsula and in the South of France*. Seventy-five years later, at the beginning of the twentieth century, the first volume of Sir Charles Oman's *History of the Peninsular War* was published. Fifteen years later, in 1922, he finished the seventh and final volume. Between 1899 and 1930 Sir John Fortescue published his 20-volume *History of the British Army*. Five of those volumes focused on the British army in the Peninsular War. All three of these works were groundbreaking for their time and do a superb job covering the war. However they do have their limitations. The first is that they are Anglocentric. The authors write from the British perspective, drawing heavily on British sources. Furthermore, they tended to focus on the campaigns and battles where the British army was involved. That is not to say that the campaigns of the French and Spanish armies are ignored in the histories, but they do not receive the same depth of coverage that the campaigns of Wellington's army do. The second limitation is that the histories were written almost 100 to 150 years ago. Since those years, sources have been discovered that were not available then.

Although those three histories will give the reader a very good overview of the Peninsular War, they often gloss over minor details that can leave the reader puzzled. This is very apparent when concerning

---

[*] Wellington, *General Orders*, vol. 8, p. 334.

French orders of battle, especially regarding simple things such as which regiment was assigned to which brigade and even who commanded the brigade. This was not a deliberate oversight; it resulted from the level of complexity in the organisation of the French armies in the Peninsula, and applied equally to the French cavalry. There were two types of cavalry regiment assigned to the Peninsula. The first comprised provisional regiments formed by combining squadrons from several regiments into one temporary regiment. Sometimes, instead of using squadrons from two or three regiments, the provisional regiment would consist of single companies from seven or eight different regiments. Unfortunately for the reader, Charles Oman would often list just the parent regiments and not tell the reader that the regiments in question were only at squadron strength and that they were actually part of a provisional regiment. The second type assigned to the Peninsula was the regular cavalry regiment: 24 dragoon regiments, 7 hussar regiments and 16 chasseur regiments. The strength of these regiments varied throughout the years depending on the number of squadrons assigned to it. Some regiments would have four squadrons present, while others would only have one. It was not uncommon for a regiment to have four squadrons in country, but only two operating with the regimental headquarters. The other two would be assigned to a different army. Oman often would explain to the reader that they were part of a provisional regiment, but at times he did not. To muddle things even further, and to make things even more difficult to track, some histories showed individual regiments serving simultaneously both in the Peninsula and in Germany, especially in 1809 and 1813. The impending war with Austria compelled Napoleon to order 3rd and 4th Squadrons going to Spain in 1809 as replacements for their regiments diverted to the Grande Armée being built in Germany. Something similar happened in 1813, when Napoleon started withdrawing officers and non-commissioned officers from regiments in Spain to help rebuild the Grande Armée. The cadre would return to France, gather up the new soldiers in the regimental depot and form them into new squadrons. A regiment could have its first two squadrons in Spain and its 3rd and 4th Squadrons in Germany.

My goal in writing *Charging Against Wellington* is not to write another history of the Peninsular War, but to clear up misconceptions and inaccuracies about the French cavalry serving there. This book focuses on three interrelated topics. The first section looks at the organisation of the cavalry during the six years of the war: how the organisation evolved through the years depending on the geographic location of the brigade and division and how Napoleon used it as a pool of experience regiments to rebuild his shattered cavalry in central Europe. The second section examines the leadership of the cavalry at the brigade and division level. Over 80 cavalry generals served in the Peninsula; some were quite effective, while others are rightfully forgotten. For each of those generals, a short biography is provided with an emphasis on the general's service in the Peninsula and how well they led their troops. The third section consists of a history of each regiment's service in the Peninsula: when they arrived, who they were assigned to, what their unit composition was, and when they left the Peninsula.

The French cavalry in the Peninsular War

The Peninsular War can be divided into four distinct phases, during which the mission and organisation of the cavalry was different from what it was in the previous or following phases.

Phase one: the build-up (October 1807–November 1808)

Napoleon thought that he could control Spain and Portugal with a minimum number of troops without having to commit the main French army, which was still deployed in garrisons in Eastern Europe. Five corps were created, but he had few regiments to spare to man them. The First Corps to be created was commanded by General Junot and its infantry in it consisted mostly of the 3rd battalions of regiments already in the east. The Second Corps created was commanded by General Dupont and it was formed by the Legions of Reserve. The Third and Fourth Corps were filled with provisional regiments, while the Fifth Corps had a French division of eight 3rd and 4th battalions, plus a weak division of Italian and Neapolitan regiments.

Four of the five corps would have a cavalry division assigned to it, but like the infantry the cavalry destined to support the corps was in a similar situation. Its leadership at division level was excellent and included Generals Grouchy, Fresia and Kellermann. However, except for General Lasalle, the cavalry brigade commanders were not like the experienced younger generals who led the cavalry in the Grande Armée in Germany and Poland: they tended to be much older and had little experience at brigade command. This in itself would not have been a problem if they had had experienced regimental commanders. But they did not. In June 1808 15 of the 20 line cavalry regiments were provisional regiments, commanded by either junior colonels or senior majors. Of the other five regiments, one was Italian, one was Neapolitan and one was Polish, which had been created three months before. The French forces did include some experience cavalry including 1,300 men of the Imperial Guard and General Lasalle's Brigade of the 10th and 22nd Chasseurs. In June the total cavalry numbered about 12,000 men.

The French initially moved into northern Spain on the pretext of invading Portugal. The Spanish supported them and by November 1807 General Junot had occupied Lisbon. Also in November General Dupont and his corps crossed into northern Spain, without the permission of the Spanish government. In January 1808 another French corps marched to the border and occupied the provinces of Biscay and Navarre, while General Dupont moved to Burgos. In February the French and Italians occupied Barcelona. In March a fifth French corps, commanded by Marshal Bessières, crossed into Spain and Marshal Murat was ordered to Spain as the commander of the 100,000 French troops there. In April Napoleon convinced King Ferdinand, the Spanish king, to come to France for talks that would resolve their differences.

By early May the Spanish people had had enough and on 2 May the people of Madrid rose in revolt. This rebellion was put down after some fierce fighting, but the insurrection spread to the countryside. King Ferdinand was taken prisoner upon his arrival in France and forced to abdicate on 6 May. Napoleon appointed his brother Joseph, the new king of Spain. When news of French treachery reached Spain, the people were determined to oust the French invaders and six long years of war began.

After some initial successes including the occupation of Portugal, the French forces in Spain and Portugal were in serious trouble. The inexperienced leaders and troops were confronted by hostile forces everywhere they went. Although General Junot's Corps had succeeded in capturing Lisbon, they were at the end of lengthy lines of communication that could not be protected. By May they were isolated and had no contact with the rest of the French army. In June General Dupont invaded Andalusia, hoping to capture the Spanish government that had fled to Seville. Like General Junot in Portugal he found that his lines of communication became more tenuous as he advanced. It was not too long before he found himself cut off from the rest of the French army. By the end of August both General Junot and General Dupont had been forced to surrender their corps. The insurrection spread rapidly as the news of General Dupont's defeat and surrender came wide known. General Dupont's surrender made Madrid undefendable and the French had to evacuate the city. By September the French controlled the major cities in northern Spain but little else.

By August Napoleon realised that he had miscalculated and that it would require more than inexperienced troops to control the Iberian Peninsula. In early September orders were given to shift 200,000 troops from Eastern Europe to Spain.

Phase two: the invasion and conquest of Spain (November 1808–June 1810)

By late October the majority of the French units were in place to begin the conquest of Spain. In early November the invasion had begun and on 3 December Madrid had surrendered. By mid-December, the French armies were deployed in a massive arc across northern Spain from Barcelona to the east, Madrid in the south, and the Asturias in the west. A British expeditionary force under General Moore advanced into north-western Spain in late November and Napoleon was forced to divert to his attention from operations against the Spanish to destroying this threat to his flank. Once Napoleon shifted his focus to the British, General Moore realised that he could not defeat the French and ordered a retreat to Corunna in an effort to save his army. Napoleon left the pursuit of the British to Marshal Soult and turned his talents to consolidating his gains in Spain.

By mid-January 1809 it became very obvious to Napoleon that war with Austria was on the horizon and that he could not afford to tie himself down in Spain, so the rest of the month was spent reorganising his forces and planning the conquest of the rest of Spain. He left Spain in late January and never returned. Although much of the command structure remained intact when Napoleon left, he ordered the Imperial Guard to return to France and more importantly he took eleven cavalry generals with him.

For the rest of 1809 the war in Spain went well for the French, despite a tactical defeat by the British at Talavera in July and by the Spanish at Tamames in October. On 18 November, in the vicinity of Ocaña, 7,000 French and Spanish cavalry fought the largest cavalry battle of the war. The Spanish were forced to retreat after taking heavy casualties. The next day the rest of the French army caught up to their cavalry and destroyed the main Spanish army at Ocaña. The few Spaniards to escape fled south. By the end of 1809 the French had conquered most of central Spain and were deployed along the Tagus River. In early January 1810 a French army under Marshal Soult began the invasion of southern Spain and by the end of July most of the major cities in Spain had been captured except for those along the coast, such as Alicante, Cadiz and Tarifa, and those in Valencia and Murcia. The exception to this was the fortress city of Badajoz. This did not mean that the country was pacified, but the French controlled the cities and much of the population.

During this phase the French cavalry in Spain expanded from less than 10,000 men to over 40,000. By February 1809 there would be five dragoon divisions and 14 brigades of light cavalry. In addition to quadrupling the amount of cavalry sent into Spain, this invasion force represented an increase in the quality and cohesiveness of the cavalry. These regiments were not provisional regiments, hastily put together, but hardened veterans of the campaigns of 1806 and 1807 in Germany and Poland. They had proven themselves on numerous battlefields against the Prussians, Saxons and Russians. They believed in themselves and they trusted their leaders. They were led by some of the most renowned cavalry commanders of the age and those leaders at both the division and brigade level were experienced.

Phase three: occupation (spring 1810–July 1812)
The beginning of 1810 saw the French army change from an army of conquest to an army of occupation. Except for the British in Portugal and small scattered Spanish forces, little systematic resistance remained. The French focus was now on securing their gains by pacifying the countryside. They changed the organisation of their forces to reflect this new mission. Throughout most of 1809 the French commanders were under the nominal control of King Joseph in Madrid. However, over the next year the French forces would be organised into six armies based on geographic location. The commanders of these armies were usually marshals and they reported directly to Napoleon, not to King Joseph. About the same time Napoleon ordered the creation of military governments in the provinces along the main French lines of communications. Eventually there would be seven military governments and their main purpose was to co-ordinate the pacification efforts in the provinces.

During the late summer the newly formed Army of Portugal, under command of Marshal Massena, invaded Portugal in an attempt to evict the British from the country. They would disappear deep into Portugal and would not return for six months. After having found that Lisbon was protected by the impregnable Lines of Torres Vedras, the Army of Portugal retreated and reappeared along the Spanish–Portuguese border in March 1811. It was a force that had been whittled down by disease and hunger. The British army, commanded by the Duke of Wellington, pursued them to the border. From 3–5 May Marshal Massena fought the British at Fuentes de Oñoro, but in the end was not able to force them away from the border. In June Marshal Massena was replaced in command by Marshal Marmont. The new commander had been given permission by Napoleon to reorganise the Army of Portugal, which he did. In the process he abolished the corps structure and organised all of the army's cavalry into a single dragoon division and two brigades of light cavalry.

In Andalusia Marshal Soult spent 1810 and 1811 consolidating his hold on the south. He continued to besiege Cadiz and in March 1811 took the fortress of Badajoz. The cavalry would be busy over the next three months fighting numerous skirmishes and battles in the vicinity of Badajoz. On 16 May a bloody battle was fought at Albuera. This battle was fairly indecisive, with both armies taking horrendous casualties, and the French were forced to retreat. The French cavalry performed superbly during the battle, destroying a British brigade that they caught in the open. In the end British also retreated and the border remained relatively quiet for another ten months. Marshal Soult was given permission to reorganise the Army of the South in December 1811. He disbanded the corps structure and placed the light cavalry brigades in a single division.

In June 1811 Napoleon ordered the creation of nine lancer regiments. Rather than raising new regiments, six dragoon regiments were redesignated as lancers. The seventh and eighth regiments were to be formed from the 1st and 2nd Vistula Legion Lancers, while the ninth regiment would be formed from the 30th Chasseurs. Five of the dragoon regiments were serving in Spain; they were ordered back to France. Three of the regiments were assigned to the Army of Portugal, while two were in the Army of the South. The departing regiments would not be replaced. The 1st Vistula Legion Lancers was renamed the 7th Lancers, but they remained in southern Spain.

The rate of attrition among the cavalry generals between 1810 and July 1812 was heavy. Six generals had been killed in action or died from wounds, three had been captured, three were so seriously wounded they had to return to France and six had been relieved of their commands for either corruption, insubordination, or incompetence. Another two were so worn out from previous wounds and campaigning they were allowed to retire.

Twenty cavalry colonels were promoted to general of brigade during the same period; 11 of them were promoted on 6 August 1811! Many of them had been serving as acting brigade commanders. Yet even all of these promotions did not alleviate the shortage of generals. In 1811, in anticipation of war with Russia, Napoleon began recalling cavalry generals serving in Spain for service with the Grande Armée. By March 1812 22 cavalry generals had left. These included four generals of division (Generals Houssaye, Lorge Montbrun, and Tour-Maubourg), as well as seven experienced brigade commanders and 11 of the generals of brigade who were promoted in 1811. To offset these losses Napoleon sent two generals to Spain and kept six of the newly promoted generals with their commands.* But there was still a net loss of 34 general officers in a space of 30 months.

Phase four: the long retreat (July 1812–April 1814)
The first five months of 1812 did not go well for the French. The border fortresses of Ciudad Rodrigo and Badajoz were captured by the British

---

* One of these generals was Vital Chamorin who was killed before he found out that he had been promoted!

and in January and April, respectively, and the pontoon bridge across the Tagus River at Almaraz, was destroyed on 19 May. The loss of the bridge cut the Army of the South's shortest line of communication with the north and would add several hundred kilometres to any movement between the Army of the South and the other armies in Spain. In June Wellington's army moved into central Spain and, for the first time in four years, the French would be on the defensive. On 22 July the Army of Portugal was mauled by the British and Portuguese at Salamanca. Within a month Madrid had been liberated and the great French supply depot at Burgos was under siege.

The events in central Spain, forced the Army of the South to lift the siege of Cadiz and evacuate Andalusia. Marshal Soult was able to co-ordinate a counter-offensive and forced Wellington and his army back to the Portuguese border. The year ended with the French armies deployed in similar positions that they were in at the end of 1809. They were formed in a wide arc running from Barcelona in the east, along the Tagus River in the south and up to Bayonne the north-west.

Things only got worse. Napoleon lost 400,000 men during his invasion of Russia and needed men and horses to rebuild the Grande Armée. This drawing of men from Spain at the same time as the British, Spanish and Portuguese were getting stronger sealed the fate of the Napoleonic kingdom in Spain. The 7th Lancers were the first to be ordered out in January, and then the Lancers of Berg and three squadrons from the Westphalian Lancers were recalled in February. By May seventeen other regiments were ordered to send the cadres of their 3rd and 4th squadrons back to their depots. Once there they became the nucleus of new units that would be sent to the Grande Armée in Germany. In June Napoleon sent for another 17 cavalry regiments from his forces in the Peninsula. This time the whole regiment departed not just the cadre. This reduced the cavalry in the Peninsula by over 5,000 men, leaving less than 10,000 troopers in country. The timing could not have been worse.

In May the Duke of Wellington went on the offensive again and on 21 June 1813 decisively beat the combined Armies of the Centre, Portugal and the South at Vitoria. The remnants of the three armies retreated into France. The only French troops left in Spain were isolated garrisons across the north and the Army of Aragon in the east. Marshal Soult, who had been recalled to France in mid-January, was sent back to the Peninsula with orders giving him command of the new Army of Spain – which included all units of the Armies of the Centre, the North, Portugal, and the South. He combined the cavalry into two divisions, but they would see little action for the rest of the war.

In January 1814 Napoleon drew on the Army of Spain and Army of

Aragon once again for more cavalry. Over 5,300 men in twelve regiments were sent. Unlike the previous withdrawals, the call was for General Trelliard's Division, plus General Sparre's and General Delort's Brigades. By the time word of Napoleon's abdication reached the Marshals Soult and Suchet, the Peninsular cavalry numbered less than 4,000 men . . . a far cry from the 40,000 sabres that invaded Spain in November 1808.

Some notes on *Charging Against Wellington*
Locations Whenever possible, I have tried to include the regiment's location. This reflects where the regimental headquarters or cantonment was during the relevant period, but it does not necessarily mean the whole regiment was there at the time. During much of the Peninsular War a regiment would only spend a small portion of its time in operations against an organised enemy army. Most of the time the regiment would be assigned to a specific geographic area trying to keep the countryside pacified against the pervasive guerrilla presence. Often it was tasked to provide a company or a squadron to support an infantry unit's counter-insurgency operations. When not supporting the infantry, the regiment was called upon to protect convoys, to be escorts for a general officer, to forage and to make their own security sweeps. So on any given date, the regiment might have all its squadrons present in the cantonment, but it was far more likely to have at least one of its subordinate elements absent.

Dates The French armies in Spain were often over 1,500 kilometres from Paris, so if an army commander requested permission to do something, it could take months for approval to arrive. In most cases the date given is the date when an event such as the assumption of command, the arrival of a unit or an attachment or detachment actually occurred. These dates may differ from the dates given in other sources, for those sources often use the official date of an event, the one that Napoleon approved. For example, in September 1810 Marshal Massena appointed Colonel Ornano commander of the 3rd Brigade of the 2nd Dragoon Division. The army then invaded Portugal and was out of touch with Paris for several months. In March 1811 Colonel Ornano was then appointed commander of the Army of Portugal's Dragoon Division's 2nd Brigade. It would not be until June that official confirmation of his appointment from Paris reached him – nine months after he first assumed command! Because of the distance, sometimes word arrived too late. Colonel Chamorin, the commander of the 26th Dragoons, was promoted to general of brigade on 13 May 1811. He never received word of his promotion for he was killed in action seven weeks prior on 25 March. Word of his death had not reached Paris before his promotion was announced.

Provisional regiments From the very beginning of the war in 1807 to the autumn of 1811, the French army in Spain relied on provisional cavalry regiments. Napoleon ordered the creation of these regiments because his commands moving into Spain needed cavalry and most of his cavalry was committed elsewhere. The best of these provisional regiments were made up of one or two squadrons from two different regiments. Yet often the provisional regiments were filled by tasking multiple regiments to provide single companies. In most cases a regiment would consist solely of dragoons, chasseurs or hussars. Yet the men for the provisional cuirassier regiments were drawn from the cuirassier and carabinier regiments, and it was not unusual to have hussars mixed in with the chasseurs. In addition to providing men, companies or squadrons to a provisional regiment, the regiment might also be ordered to provide their second colonel or a chief of squadrons to command the regiment.

These provisional regiments were flawed from the beginning. Napoleon usually told his cavalry regiments to provide the men from the regimental depot and not from the squadrons deployed on active service. The depots usually had two kinds of men in them: new recruits and men the regimental commander did not want to take to war with him. Additionally the best of the non-commissioned officers and junior officers were with the war squadrons. The leaders in the depot were either newly promoted or not of the highest calibre. If they were, the regimental commander would have found a way to take them with him. Thus when the provisional regiments were formed, they often lacked a leavening of seasoned junior officers and sergeants a normal regiment would have.

The performance of the regiments was mixed. The provisional cavalry regiments in General Dupont's Corps were abysmal. The young troops died because there few veterans to teach them how to take care of themselves while on campaign. Discipline was lax and the rapacious behaviour of the troops towards the Spaniards was one of the reasons why the countryside rose in rebellion against them. In June 1808 the provisional regiments in Dupont's Corps sacked Cordova, one of the great religious centres of Spain. This so enraged the Spanish that it doomed the men of Dupont's Corps. The Spanish peasant fought the French with a passion never encountered before by a French army. French atrocities were met with even greater brutality and soon no part of Spain was safe for the French unless they were there in strength. Unfortunately for all concerned, this proved to be a pattern that would be repeated countless times over the next six years. Yet other provisional regiments performed superbly and were formally incorporated into the French army. The 3rd Provisional Cuirassiers became the 13th Cuirassiers in December 1808, while the 3rd Provisional Chasseurs became the 29th Chasseurs in August 1809. In September 1811 elements of the recently disbanded 1st

Provisional Light Cavalry became the nucleus of the newly formed 31st Chasseurs.

In this study provisional regiments are abbreviated by 'Prov.', for example, 1st Prov. Chasseurs

March regiments A march regiment was a temporary command organised to move replacements from the French army's depot at Bayonne to their regiments in Spain. They were often used to protect convoys being sent to Spain. It was not supposed to be a fighting command and it was not expected to be used as such unless it came under attack while performing its escort duties. March regiments dispersed as soon as they reached their destination. Since they were temporary formations, I have not incorporated them into this study.

Who was in command? After Napoleon left the Peninsula in 1809, there began a steady drain of general officers from the Peninsula. This was understandable in 1809 since the war with Austria was looming and Napoleon needed leaders for his troops in Germany. But even after the war with Austria ended, the number of generals leaving the Peninsula or who had become casualties exceeded the number of generals either being transferred to the armies in Spain or being promoted from the forces there. Compounding the problem was the creation of new commands and administrative positions – such as provincial and military governments – that were filled by generals. The real shortage was felt at brigade level. Many of the dragoon divisions had at least one brigade commander who was not a general. Sometimes it was even worse. In June 1810 General Tour-Maubourg's 1st Dragoon Division had no general officers to command its three brigades! In most cases the senior regimental commander in the brigade would be given command of the brigade when there was no general available. Although this solved the brigade's problem, it just passed the problem down to the regiment, because it created a hole in the regimental command structure that had to be filled by the senior squadron commander. His place would then have to be filled by the senior company commander. This could lead to a dangerous shortage of officers at the regimental level if the regiment took casualties. In July 1812 after the battle of Salamanca the senior surviving officer in the 6th Dragoons was a lieutenant!

In the pages below I have differentiated between general officers and colonels commanding a brigade, by showing a colonel's name in italics. For example: 2nd Brigade (*Saint-Genies*)

Tactical flexibility Napoleon's armies were always noted for their flexible command arrangements. It was not unusual for a combined arms force of infantry, cavalry, and artillery, to be put together for a specific mission and then disbanded once the mission was accomplished. The

French armies in Spain were no exception. During 1809 regiments and brigades were often attached to different divisions and corps for a specific campaign. The unit was usually returned to his parent organisation, but not always. For example, in the autumn of 1810 General Bron commanded the 1st Brigade of the 4th Dragoon Division, which was attached to the Army of the South for the conquest of Andalusia. The division was ordered to return to La Mancha, but General Bron's Brigade was still conducting operations in south-west Spain. General Marizy commanded the 1st Brigade of the 5th Dragoon Division and had been attached to the 5th Corps for the same operation. About the same time, the 5th Dragoon Division was disbanded. By October the campaigning season was nearing its end for the year. General Bron and his brigade was reassigned to the 1st Dragoon Division of the Army of the South, while General Marizy's Brigade was transferred to the 4th Dragoon Division.

Throughout much of the Peninsular War, the French spent more time fighting a vicious guerrilla war than a war against conventional armies. This required a force that was small enough that could manoeuvre quickly to respond to take the fight to the insurgents or to respond quickly enough to guerrilla attacks. Divisions were often not flexible enough for the mission, so the job fell to the brigades and regiments. In the Armies of the Centre, and the North, cavalry regiments were often not assigned to a cavalry brigade, but were directly attached to an infantry division. This was especially true in the Army of Aragon and the Army of Catalonia. In the following chapters regiments that were not assigned to a cavalry brigade or cavalry division are listed as 'Unattached'.

Spelling of names   One of the problems I encountered in my research was the different spelling for an individual's name. For example, General Pierre Watier's name was also spelled Wathier, Wathiez and Wattier, depending on the source. To minimise confusion I have used Georges Six's *Dictionnaire Biographique des Généraux and Amiraux Français de la Révolution et de l'Empire (1792–1814)* as the standard for the spelling of an individual's name.

Names of battles   The name of a battle is often dependent on the nationality of the source. For example, the British call the battle that took place on 22 July 1812 'Salamanca', but to the French it is 'Les Arapiles' and to the Spanish 'Los Arapiles'. In order to be consistent, I have used the spellings that Sir Charles Oman used in his *History of the Peninsular War*.

Spelling of locations   Names of cities and villages posed a problem, since very few of the sources agree on the spelling of many small towns and villages. In an effort to aid the reader locate a town or village, I have used the modern spelling as found on Google maps.

Cadres   The cadre of a regiment or a squadron comprised the officers, senior non-commissioned officers, the staff and musicians. The junior non-commissioned officer and the common soldier were not included. This distinction was important. When a regiment's effective strength fell to a point that they were too weak to perform their duties, the cadre of the 3rd Squadron would be sent back to the regimental depot to rebuild its strength and bring forward replacements. The junior non-commissioned officers and common soldier would not return to the depot. Instead they sent them to the other two squadrons to bring them up to strength.

Part I

Organisation of the French Cavalry
in the Peninsula

Chapter One

The Build-up (July 1807–October 1808)

On 29 July 1807 Napoleon ordered the formation of a 20,000-man army for possible deployment to Portugal. Four days later he ordered that the army be expanded to 30,000 men and to be concentrated at Bayonne. It would be called the 1st Corps of Observation of the Gironde and it would be commanded by General Jean Junot. The corps would have three infantry divisions and one cavalry division. The infantry divisions would consist mostly of 3rd and 4th battalions from infantry regiments serving with the Grande Armée in eastern Europe. The cavalry would be commanded by General François Kellermann and would consist of two brigades. These brigades were commanded by Generals Pierre Margaron and Antoine Maurin. The brigades each had two provisional regiments that were formed from the 4th Squadrons of the 1st, 3rd, 5th, 9th and 15th Dragoons, and the 4th Squadron of the 26th Chasseurs. The strength of the cavalry division on 19 August was 2,140 men and horses.

Table 1.1   The Cavalry Division of the 1st Corps of Observation of the Gironde, August 1807

Brigade	Regiment	4th Squadrons	Strength	Men sick	Unfit horses
1st	1st Prov.	26th Chasseurs	240	38	77
(Margaron)	2nd Prov.	1st Dragoons	350	59	59
		3rd Dragoons 300	85	13	
2nd	3rd Prov.	4th Dragoons	300	27	—
(Maurin)		5th Dragoons	300	75	44
	4th Prov.	9th Dragoons	350	46	30
		15th Dragoons	300	68	83
Total			2,140	398	306

The Peninsular War began on 18 October 1807, when the lead elements of General Junot's 1st Corps of Observation of the Gironde crossed into Spain at Irun. Instead of gunfire they were met with an honour guard of Spanish troops that would escort them across northern Spain, where the first column would arrive in Salamanca on 9 November. The corps was organised into 16 columns, with the cavalry forming the 13th, 14th, 15th, and 16th Columns.

Table 1.2   Deployment of the Cavalry Division of the 1st Corps of Observation of the Gironde, October 1807

Column	Composition	No. of men	No. of horses
13th	Division HQ and 1st Prov. Cavalry Regiment	228	247
14th	2nd Prov. Cavalry Regiment	556	596
15th	3rd Prov. Cavalry Regiment	510	523
16th	4th Provisional Cavalry Regiment	564	586

Only one column marched across the border per day and the cavalry did not begin entering Spain until 30 October. The division HQ and the 1st Provisional Cavalry Regiment arrived in Salamanca on 23 November.

Table 1.3   The march of the cavalry across Spain, October–November 1807

Location	Col. no. 13 dates in city	Col. no. 14 dates in city	Col. no. 15 dates in city	Col. no. 16 dates in city
Bayonne	28 Oct.	29 Oct.	30 Oct.	31 Oct.
Saint Jean de Luz	29 Oct.	30 Oct.	31 Oct.	1 Nov.
Irun	30 Oct.	31 Oct.	1 Nov.	2 Nov.
Astigarraga	31 Oct.	1 Nov.	2 Nov.	3 Nov.
Tolosa	1 Nov.	2 Nov.	3 Nov.	4 Nov.
Zumarraga	2 Nov.	3 Nov.	4 Nov.	5 Nov.
Mondragon	3 Nov.	4 Nov.	5 Nov.	6 Nov.
Vitoria	4–5 Nov.	5–6 Nov.	6–7 Nov.	7–8 Nov.
Miranda	6 Nov.	7 Nov.	8 Nov.	9 Nov.
Pancorbo	7 Nov.	8 Nov.	9 Nov.	10 Nov.
Briviesca	8 Nov.	9 Nov.	10 Nov.	11 Nov.
Monasterio	9 Nov.	10 Nov.	11 Nov.	12 Nov.
Burgos	10–11 Nov.	11–12 Nov.	12–13 Nov.	13–14 Nov.
Celada	12 Nov.	13 Nov.	14 Nov.	15 Nov.
Villodrigo	13 Nov.	14 Nov.	15 Nov.	16 Nov.

Table 1.3   continued

Location	Col. no. 13 dates in city	Col. no. 14 dates in city	Col. no. 15 dates in city	Col. no. 16 dates in city
Torquemada	14 Nov.	15 Nov.	16 Nov.	17 Nov.
Duenas	15 Nov.	16 Nov.	17 Nov.	18 Nov.
Valladolid	16–17 Nov.	17–18 Nov.	18–19 Nov.	19–20 Nov.
Tordesillas	18 Nov.	19 Nov.	20 Nov.	21 Nov.
Naval del Rey	19 Nov.	20 Nov.	21 Nov.	22 Nov.
Torrecilla	20 Nov.	21 Nov.	22 Nov.	23 Nov.
Bavilafuente	21 Nov.	22 Nov.	23 Nov.	24 Nov.
Toro	22 Nov.	23 Nov.	24 Nov.	25 Nov.
Salamanca	23 Nov.	24 Nov.	25 Nov.	26 Nov.

On 19 November the 1st Corps of Observation of the Gironde crossed the border into Portugal.

As the 1st Corps of Observation of the Gironde was moving across Spain, the 2nd Corps of Observation of the Gironde was being formed and would be commanded by General Pierre Dupont. Initially the corps had only the 4th Squadron of the 10th Dragoons assigned to it as cavalry support. In early November the Corps of Observation of the Ocean Coast began to be organised and it would be commanded by Marshal Bon Adrien Moncey. Unlike the 2nd Corps, this corps would have over 4,000 cavalry in two divisions, each of two brigades. General Grouchy's Division would have two dragoon regiments and two hussar regiments, while General Fresia's Division would have two heavy cavalry regiments and two chasseur regiments. Like the 1st Corps, these regiments were provisional regiments and consisted of companies from five or six different regiments. Different regiments were tasked to provide a chief of squadrons to command the regiments. In early December Marshal Moncey was ordered to send General Fresia and his division to the 2nd Corps. By 1 January, the three French corps had over 5,100 cavalry in the Peninsula.

Table 1.4   French Cavalry in Spain and Portugal, late January 1808

Division	1st Brigade	Regiments	Strength	Location
Junot Corps				
Kellerman		Division HQ	4	Belem
	Margaron	Brigade HQ	3	Belem
		1st Prov. Cavalry*	241	Belem

---

* 1st Provisional Cavalry, consisting of the 26th Chasseurs, had 43 replacements in the rear and 15 men in the hospital on 1 January.

Division	1st Brigade	Regiments	Strength	Location
		2nd Prov. Cavalry	327*	Belem
	Maurin	Brigade HQ	2	Lisbon
		3rd Prov. Cavalry	410†	Lisbon
		4th Prov. Cavalry	373‡	Lisbon
Total			1,360	

Dupont Corps

Division	1st Brigade	Regiments	Strength	Location
Fresia		Division HQ	1	Vitoria
	Boussart	Brigade HQ	1	Vitoria
		6th Prov. Dragoons	620§	Vitoria
	Rigaud	Brigade HQ	1	Logroño
		1st Prov. Cuirassiers	534¶	Logroño
		2nd Prov. Cuirassiers	500**	Logroño
	Duprés	Brigade HQ	1	Santo Domingo
		1st Prov. Chasseurs	412	Santo Domingo
		2nd Prov. Chasseurs	537	Santo Domingo
Total			2,607	

Moncey Corps

Division	1st Brigade	Regiments	Strength	Location
Grouchy		Division HQ	4	Vitoria
	Pryvé	Brigade HQ	1	Vitoria
		1st Prov. Dragoons	393††	Vitoria
		2nd Prov. Dragoons	351‡‡	Vitoria
	Watier	Brigade HQ	3	Vitoria

* 2nd Provisional Cavalry, consisting of 158 men from the 1st Dragoon Regiment, had 100 replacements in the rear and 35 men in the hospital on 1 January, and 169 men from the 3rd Dragoons, which had 91 replacements in the rear and 34 men in the hospital on 1 January.

† 3rd Provisional Cavalry had 206 men from the 4th Dragoons, which had 45 replacements in the rear and 18 men in the hospital on 1 January, and 204 men from the 5th Dragoons, which had 34 replacements in the rear and 32 men in the hospital on 1 January.

‡ 4th Provisional Cavalry had 200 men from the 9th Dragoons, which had 81 replacements in the rear and 91 men in the hospital on 1 January, and 173 men from the 15th Dragoons, which had 101 replacements in the rear and 23 men in the hospital on 1 January.

§ 6th Provisional Dragoons included the 4th Squadron, 10th Dragoons which had 310 men present for duty with another 14 replacements in the rear and 15 men in the hospital on 1 January.

¶ 1st Provisional Cuirassiers had 40 men in the rear on 1 January.

** 2nd Provisional Cuirassiers had 104 men in the rear on 1 January.

†† 1st Provisional Dragoons had 25 in the rear and 16 men in the hospital on 1 January.

‡‡ 2nd Provisional Dragoons had 13 in the rear and 9 men in the hospital on 1 January.

Table 1.4   continued

Division	1st Brigade	Regiments	Strength	Location
		1st Prov. Hussars	351[*]	Vitoria
		2nd Prov. Hussars	367[†]	Vitoria
Total			*1,470*	
Total cavalry in the Peninsula			**5,437**	

In early December a Division of the Western Pyrenees was formed. It would be the predecessor of the Corps of Observation of the Western Pyrenees. It had two brigades of cavalry commanded by Generals August Caulaincourt and Joseph Lagrange, plus four companies of the 22nd Chasseurs. The corps would enter Spain in late March and in April 1808 it had a cavalry strength of about 2,200 men.

Table 1.5   Strength of cavalry, Corps of the Western Pyrenees, 23 April 1808

Brigade	Regiments	Strength	Location
Lagrange	Brigade HQ	2	Aranda
	Chasseur March Regiment	197[‡]	Aranda
	Hussar March Regiment	366[§]	Aranda
Total		*565*	
Caulaincourt	Brigade HQ	3	Burgos
	Cuirassier March Regiment	279[¶]	Burgos
	Dragoon March Regiment	460[**]	Lerma and Valladolid
	1st March Squadron	426[††]	Burgos
	2nd March Squadron	336	Burgos
	4th March Squadron	131[‡‡]	Ernani
Total		*1,635*	
Combined total		**2,200**	

---

[*] 1st Provisional Hussars had 12 men in the rear and 8 men in the hospital on 1 January.
[†] 2nd Provisional Hussars had 7 men in the rear and 7 men in the hospital on 1 January.
[‡] Chasseur March Regiment had 1 man in the rear and 11 men in the hospital.
[§] Hussar March Regiment had 30 men in the hospital
[¶] Cuirassier March Regiment had 8 men in the rear and 15 men in the hospital.
[**] Dragoon March Regiment had 155 men in the rear and 8 men in the hospital.
[††] 1st March Squadron had 15 men in the rear and 9 men in the hospital.
[‡‡] 4th March Squadron had 2 men in the hospital.

About the same time in March Marshal Bessières and his Corps of Observation of the Pyrenees entered Spain. It had only one regiment of light cavalry, the 22nd Chasseurs. In early May it was joined by the 10th Chasseurs and a march squadron of cuirassiers. This brigade, commanded by General Lasalle, had a strength of about 1,100 men.

Table 1.6   Strength of cavalry, Corps of the Pyrenees, early May 1808

Brigade	Regiments	Strength	Location
Lasalle	10th Chasseurs	469	Tolosa
	22nd Chasseurs	439*	Vitoria and Tolosa
	March Squadron of Cuirassiers	153	Tolosa
Total		1,061	

In late December 1807 Napoleon ordered the formation of the Corps of Observation of the Eastern Pyrenees, which would be commanded by General Philibert Duhesme. It would have a brigade of provisional cavalry regiments led by General Bessières and an Italian cavalry brigade commanded by General Schwarz. The division entered Spain in early February and occupied Catalonia and Barcelona. In April the Corps had a strength of 1,782 cavalry.

Table 1.7   Strength of cavalry, Corps of the Eastern Pyrenees, 23 April 1808

Brigade	Regiments	Strength	Location
Bessières	Brigade HQ	1	Barcelona
	3rd Prov. Cuirassiers	423†	Barcelona
	3rd Prov. Chasseurs	483‡	Barcelona
Total		907	
Schwarz	Brigade HQ	1	Hospitalet
	1st Italian Prov.§	902	Hospitalet
Total		903	
Combined total		1,810	

---

* 22nd Chasseurs had 30 men in the rear and 14 in the hospital.

† 3rd Provisional Cuirassiers had 61 men in the rear and 12 men in the hospital on 30 April.

‡ 3rd Provisional Chasseurs had 19 men in the hospital on 30 April.

§ On 24 March 1st Provisional Italian Regiment was redesignated as 2nd Italian Chasseurs and the 2nd Neapolitan Chasseurs.

On 18 February 1808 Napoleon ordered his Imperial Guard to send a division to Spain, under the command of General Lepic. The division had 4,800 men, of which 1,340 were cavalry. Each Imperial Guard cavalry regiment was tasked to send a squadron. The division left France in late March and a month later was in Madrid. Attached to the Guard cavalry were two squadrons of the Berg Light Horse.

Table 1.8   Imperial Guard Cavalry in Spain, April 1808

Regiment	Present for duty	In the rear	Hospitalised	Total
Chasseurs and Mamelukes	225	70	16	311
Polish Light Horse	307	88	13	408
Dragoons	90	132	4	226
Horse Grenadiers	202	3	14	219
Gendarmes	87	87	1	175
Berg Light Horse	300*	??	??	300
Total	*1,211*	*380*	*48*	*1,639*

On 2 May the people of Madrid rebelled against the French and soon the rest of the country followed. Before long, the French had their hands full trying to subdue northern Spain. Many of the cities of Spain were in open revolt, including Saragossa and Barcelona, while throughout Spain the provinces became very dangerous for isolated French troops. It would be almost six years before peace would reign in Spain.

On 21 May General Rigau returned to France and his brigade was dissolved. The 1st Provisional Cuirassiers were given to General Watier's Brigade, while the 2nd Provisional Cuirassiers were transferred to Marshal Moncey's Corps, but not assigned to a brigade. About the same time, the cavalry in General Dupont's Corps was reorganised. General Fresia was kept in command of the cavalry, however. Generals Caulaincourt's and Lagrange's brigades were dissolved and the men in the march regiments were turned over to their regiments. General Caulaincourt was assigned to the army's headquarters, while General Lagrange was assigned to General Dupont's Corps. On 12 June the 1st Vistula Legion Lancers arrived in Spain and were assigned to the forces under Marshal Lannes that were besieging Saragossa. The Imperial Guard Cavalry would be commanded by General Lasalle, who also was the commander of a light cavalry brigade. By mid-June, the French had over 12,000 cavalry in Spain and Portugal.

---

* Two squadrons of the Berg Light Horse were attached to the Guard Cavalry Brigade. Estimated strength was 150 men.

Table 1.9 Organisation of the French cavalry in Spain and Portugal, June 1808

Division	Brigade	Regiment	Strength	Location
Bessières Corps				
Lasalle		Chasseurs and Mamelukes	321	Madrid
		Polish Light Horse	737	Madrid
		Empress Dragoons	252	Madrid
		Horse Grenadiers	219	Madrid
		Gendarmes	85	Madrid
		Berg Light Horse	300	Madrid
Total			*1,914*	
		10th Chasseurs	469	Santander
		22nd Chasseurs	460	Santander
Total			*929*	
Junot Corps				
Kellermann	Margaron	1st Prov. Cavalry	244	Lisbon
		2nd Prov. Cavalry	497	Lisbon
	Maurin	3rd Prov. Cavalry	511	Belem
		4th Prov. Cavalry	502	Belem
Total			*1,754*	
Dupont Corps				
Fresia	Boussart	6th Prov. Dragoons	620	Cordova
	Pryvé	1st Prov. Dragoons	434	Cordova
		2nd Prov. Dragoons	373	Cordova
	Duprés	1st Prov. Chasseurs	412	Cordova
		2nd Prov. Chasseurs	537	Cordova
	Independent	2nd Prov. Cuirassiers	604	Cordova
Total			*2,980*	
Moncey Corps				
Grouchy	Watier	1st Prov. Hussars	597	Cuenca
		2nd Prov. Hussars	721	Cuenca
		1st Prov. Cuirassiers	778	Getaffe
Total			*2,096*	
Duhesme Corps				
	Bessières	3rd Prov. Cuirassiers	409	Barcelona
		3rd Prov. Chasseurs	416	Barcelona
Lechi	Schwarz	2nd Italian Chasseurs	504	Hospitalet
		2nd Neapolitan Chasseurs	391	Hospitalet
Total			*1,720*	
Lannes Corps				
		1st Vistula Legion Lancers	717	Saragossa
Total French cavalry in Spain and Portugal			*12,110*	

In mid-June General Maurin, commander of one of General Kellermann's cavalry brigades, was captured by Portuguese guerrillas and turned over to the British Royal Navy on 19 June.

General Dupont's Corps moved into Andalusia in the beginning of June to bring it under control by capturing Cordova and Seville. The French took and sacked Cordova on 7 June and General Dupont spent the next ten days resting his force. He soon realised that he could not accomplish his mission with the small force that he had. On 19 June he left Cordova heading north to make contact with the French forces in La Mancha. By mid-July the countryside had risen against his army and after being defeated at Bailen on 19 July, General Dupont surrendered his army. The officers and men of the six provisional cavalry regiments in his corps went into captivity and would not return to France until 1814. In north-east Spain the 1st Squadron of the 28th Chasseurs arrived in Barcelona to support General Duhesme's Corps of Eastern Pyrenees in July.

In August a British expeditionary force landed in Portugal. Shortly after landing, they beat General Junot and his corps at Roliça and Vimeiro. Believing that his situation was hopeless, Geneal Junot signed the Convention of Cintra, which permitted him to evacuate Portugal to France aboard British ships. In the space of five weeks the French position in the Peninsula had a major reversal of fortune – two of its five corps had surrendered. Among those who surrendered were 10 of the 20 line cavalry regiments amounting to almost 4,700 men or 40 per cent of all the cavalry in the Peninsula. After the four regiments in General Junot's Corps were returned to France in October, they were disbanded and the men sent back to their parent units.

Expanding the Army

By the beginning of August, Napoleon realised that the situation in Spain had deteriorated to a point that would require his intervention. On 5 August 1808 he ordered the Minister of War to begin moving troops from Eastern Europe back France for duty in Spain. The 1st Corps, commanded by Marshal Victor, was to move from Brandenburg to Mainz. The 6th Corps, commanded by General Marchand, was to move from Silesia to Mainz, while Marshal Mortier's 5th Corps was to march from Silesia to Bayreuth. General Tour-Maubourg's 1st Dragoon Division was to march from Silesia to Mainz. General Milhaud's 3rd Dragoon Division was to depart Hamburg and move to Wesel. General Houssaye's 4th Dragoon Division was ordered to Mainz. From Mainz, the troops would march to Bayonne in 50 stages.[*]

---

[*] Balagny, *Campagne de l'Empereur Napoléon*, vol. 1, pp. 3–4.

In the Decree of 7 September 1808 Napoleon set up the Army of Spain, consisting of eight corps, the Imperial Guard and the Cavalry Reserve.

Table 1.10   Command structure of the French cavalry designated for service in Spain, 7 September 1808

Division	Brigade	Regiment	Location
Reserve Corps			
Imperial Guard		Chasseurs	France and Spain
		Dragoons	France and Spain
		Grenadiers	France and Spain
		Gendarmes	France and Spain
		Polish Light Horse	France and Spain
		Berg Light Horse	France and Spain
Reserve Corps			
1st Dragoon (Tour-Maubourg)	1st (Perreimond)	1st Dragoons	France
		2nd Dragoons	France
	2nd (Oullenbourg)	4th Dragoons	France
		14th Dragoons	France
	3rd (Digeon)	20th Dragoons	France
		26th Dragoons	France
Reserve Corps			
2nd Dragoon (Milet)	1st (*Grézard*)	3rd Dragoons	France
		6th Dragoons	France
	2nd (Carrié)	10th Dragoons	France
		11th Dragoons	France
Reserve Corps			
3rd Dragoon (Milhaud)	1st (Debelle)	8th Dragoons	France
		12th Dragoons	France
	2nd (Barthélemi)	16th Dragoons	France
		21st Dragoons	France
Reserve Corps			
4th (Houssaye)	1st (Marizy)	17th Dragoons	France
		27th Dragoons	France
	2nd (Davenay)	18th Dragoons	France
		19th Dragoons	France

Table 1.10   continued

Division	Brigade	Regiment	Location
Reserve Corps			
5th Dragoons (Lorge)	1st (Vialannes)	13th Dragoons	France
		22nd Dragoons	France
	2nd (Fournier)	15th Dragoons	France
		25th Dragoons	France
1st	Montbrun	2nd Hussars	France
		4th Hussars	France
		Hanoverian Chasseurs	France
		5th Chasseurs	France
2nd Corps			
Light Cavalry (Lasalle)		10th Chasseurs	Spain
		22nd Chasseurs	Spain
		26th Chasseurs	France
		9th Dragoons	France
3rd Corps			
	Watier	1st Prov. Hussars	Spain
		2nd Prov. Hussars	Spain
		1st Prov. Cuirassiers	Spain
		1st Vistula Legion Lancers	Spain
4th Corps			
	Maupetit	5th Dragoons	France
		3rd Dutch Hussars	Holland
		Nassau Light Horse*	Nassau
		Westphalian Light Horse	Westphalia
5th Corps			
	Bessières	3rd Prov. Cuirassiers	Spain
		3rd Prov. Chasseurs	Spain
	Schwarz	2nd Italian Chasseurs	Spain
		2nd Neapolitan Chasseurs	Spain
	Fontane	1st Italian Chasseurs	France
		Napoleon Dragoons	France
	Unattached	24th Dragoons	France
		28th Chasseurs	Spain

* One squadron only.

Division	Brigade	Regiment	Location
6th Corps			
	Colbert	3rd Hussars	France
		15th Chasseurs	France

General Milet was appointed its provisional commander of the 2nd Dragoon Division in November 1807, after its commander, General Grouchy was sent to Spain. No one was appointed commander of the 1st Brigade, so Colonel Grézard, commander of the 3rd Dragoon Regiment would lead the brigade into Spain. General Montbrun, the commander of the 1st Corps's Light Cavalry Brigade, was relieved from command in late September, when he missed the brigade's deployment into Spain because he was still on his honeymoon. He was replaced by General Beaumont.

On 2 October Napoleon ordered two additional corps to be added to the forces going to Spain. Marshal Mortier's Corps was on its way from Germany and it would be designated the 5th Corps. The old 5th Corps, which was commanded by General Gouvion Saint-Cyr, was redesignated the 7th Corps. General Junot's Corps, which was returning from Portugal, courtesy of the British Royal Navy, would become the 8th Corps.

Table 1.11 Command structure of the French cavalry designated for service in Spain, 2 October 1808

Corps	Brigade	Regiment	Location
5th	Delaage	10th Hussars	France
		21st Chasseurs	France
8th	?	1st Hussars	France
		27th Chasseurs	France

Chapter Two

The Invasion and Conquest of Spain
(November 1808–March 1810)

The troops began to filter into Spain and by 15 November all the corps except for the 5th and 8th Corps were there. However, only the 1st and 3rd Dragoon Divisions had crossed the border. General Houssaye's 4th Dragoon Division had just arrived in Bayonne, while the 2nd and 5th Dragoon Divisions were still marching through France. Although the structure of the corps and the dragoon divisions was in place prior to their deployment to Spain, once a unit crossed the border both their internal composition and their superior headquarters could change. As the campaign progressed, brigades and regiments were often detached from one command and attached to another, in response both to the strategic and tactical situation. For example, Debelle's Brigade from the 3rd Dragoon Division was attached to the 2nd Corps. Debelle only took the 8th Dragoon Regiment with him but was given the Auxiliary Chasseur Regiment that was part of the 2nd Corps, to round out his brigade. General Franceschi was also assigned to the 2nd Corps and given a brigade, by combining regiments from the 1st and 2nd Corps. General Beaumont's Brigade was attached to the army reserve. Further to the east, Marshal Jean Lannes had an independent command that consisted of Marshal Moncey's 3rd Corps, an infantry division and General Colbert's Light Cavalry Brigade from the 6th Corps and General Digeon's Brigade from the 1st Dragoon Division. The following table shows the organisation of the cavalry in Spain at the commencement of the campaign.

Table 2.1   French cavalry in Spain, 15 November 1808

Division	Brigade	Regiment	Effective strength	
			Men	Horses
Reserve Corps				
Imperial Guard		Chasseurs	710	844

Division	Brigade	Regiment	Effective strength	
			Men	Horses
		Dragoons	665	801
		Grenadiers	651	769
		Gendarmes	179	207
		Polish Light Horse	715	845
		Berg Light Horse	76	84
Total of Imperial Guard Cavalry			**2,996**	**3,550**
1st Dragoon (Tour-Maubourg)	1st (Perreimond)	1st Dragoons	479	516
		2nd Dragoons	714	770
Total			*1,193*	*1,286*
	2nd (Oullenbourg)	4th Dragoons	532	583
		14th Dragoons	659	703
Total			*1,191*	*1,286*
	Gendarmes		45	51
Total for the 1st Dragoon Division		**2,429**	**2,623**	
3rd Dragoon (Milhaud)	2nd (Barthélemi)	12th Dragoons	469	514
		16th Dragoons	364	395
		21st Dragoons	386	427
Total			*1,219*	*1,336*
Total for the 3rd Dragoon Division			*1,219*	*1,336*
1st Corps				
	Beaumont	2nd Hussars	715	780
		4th Hussars	769	780
Total			*1,484*	*1,560*
2nd Corps				
Light Cavalry (Lasalle)		10th Chasseurs	482	503
		22nd Chasseurs	512	545
		9th Dragoons	543	576
Total			*1,537*	*1,624*
	Franceschi	Hanoverian Chasseurs	416	407
		5th Chasseurs	708	783
Total			*1,124*	*1,190*
	Debelle	8th Dragoons	566	607
		Auxiliary Chasseurs	375	300
Total			*941*	*907*

Table 2.1 continued

Division	Brigade	Regiment	Effective strength Men	Horses
4th Corps				
	Maupetit	5th Dragoons	523	457
		Dutch Hussars	385	403
		Westphalian Light Horse	428	428
		Nassau Light Horse	123	123
Total			*1,459*	*1,411*
		26th Chasseurs	490	522
7th Corps				
	Bessières	3rd Prov. Cuirassiers	?	?
		3rd Prov. Chasseurs	?	?
	Schwarz	2nd Italian Chasseurs	?	?
		2nd Neapolitan Chasseurs	?	?
Pino	Fontane	1st Italian Chasseurs	600	550
		Napoleon Dragoons	550	500
		24th Dragoons	668	?
		28th Chasseurs	?	?
Lannes	Watier (3rd Corps)	1st Prov. Hussars	261	301
		2nd Prov. Hussars	236	257
		1st Vistula Legion Lancers	704	646
		Cavalry of the Mar.	293	400
		1st Prov. Cuirassiers	413	457
Total			*1,907*	*2,061*
	Colbert (6th Corps)	3rd Hussars	574	618
		15th Chasseurs	651	670
		Gendarmes	26	29
Total			*1,251*	*1,317*
	3rd (Digeon)	20th Dragoons	579	633
		26th Dragoons	729	781
Total			*1,308*	*1,414*

In late November General Franceschi was given command of a light cavalry brigade consisting of the 22nd Chasseurs and the Hanoverian Chasseurs. His brigade replaced General Lasalle's Division which received the 5th Chasseurs from the 1st Corps and the Polish Lancers from the 3rd Corps. General Beaumont's Brigade was detached from the 1st Corps and attached to the 6th Corps. General Digeon's Dragoon Brigade was detached from the 1st Dragoon Division and also attached to the 6th Corps. By the beginning of December General Houssaye's 4th Dragoon Division of 2,500 men and General Lorge's 5th Dragoon Division of 2,900 men, as well as the 5th Corps, had arrived in Spain.

By mid-December the French army had concentrated on Madrid. Three of the dragoon divisions were screening the capital in wide arc ranging from Tarancon in the east to Toledo in the south to Talavera in the south-west. The 5th Dragoon Division had just arrived in Spain and was in the vicinity of Burgos. General Lasalle's Division had extended the screen further south-west to Almaraz. Generals Debelle and Franceschi were on the right flank of the army, north-west of Madrid at Sahagun and Valladolid respectively. General Watier's Brigade was in the north-east at Alagon, in the vicinity of Saragossa. The Imperial Guard Cavalry, as well as Maupetit's, Colbert's and Beaumont's brigades, were in Madrid, while the 7th Corps's cavalry was marching on Barcelona. The 5th Corps had begun to arrive in Spain and General Boussart assumed command of its light cavalry brigade on 18 December. It was located at Miranda. The 4th Hussars were transferred from the 1st Corps to the 3rd Corps. The 1st Corps Light Cavalry Brigade received the 26th Chasseurs in their place.

Table 2.2   Location of French cavalry in Spain, mid-December 1808

Division	Brigade	Regiment	Strength	Location
Reserve Corps				
Imperial Guard		Chasseurs	914	Madrid
		Dragoons	779	Madrid
		Grenadiers	748	Madrid
		Gendarmes	263	Madrid
		Polish Light Horse	574	Madrid
		Berg Light Horse	109	Madrid
Total of Imperial Guard Cavalry			*3,387*	
1st Dragoon (Tour-Maubourg)	1st (Perreimond)	1st Dragoons	?	Villanueva del Cardete
		2nd Dragoons	?	Tarancon

Table 2.2   contd

Division	Brigade	Regiment	Strength	Location
	2nd (Oullenbourg)	4th Dragoons	?	Aranjuez
		14th Dragoons	?	Aranjuez
Total for the 1st Dragoon Division			*3,737*	
3rd Dragoon (Milhaud)	2nd (Barthélemi)	12th Dragoons	446	Talavera
		16th Dragoons	324	Talavera
		21st Dragoons	341	Talavera
Total for the 3rd Dragoon Division			*1,111*	
4th Dragoons (Houssaye)	2nd (Davenay)	18th Dragoons	?	Escorial
		19th Dragoons	?	Escorial
Total for the 4th Dragoon Division*			*2,423*	
5th Dragoons (Lorge)	1st (Viallanes)	13th Dragoons	777	Burgos
		22nd Dragoons	681	Burgos
Total			*1,458*	
	2nd (Fournier)	15th Dragoons	529	Burgos
		25th Dragoons	635	Burgos
Total			*1,164*	
Total for the 5th Dragoon Division			*2,622*	
Light Cavalry (Lasalle)	Bordessoulle	9th Dragoons	501	Almaraz
		10th Chasseurs	465	Almaraz
	Montbrun	5th Chasseurs	459	Almaraz
		1st Vistula Legion Lancers	633	En route
Total			*2,058*	
Franceschi		22nd Chasseurs	512	Valladolid
		Hanoverian Chasseurs	416	Medina de Rio Seco
Total			*928*	
1st Corps				
	Marizy	17th Dragoons	?	Toledo
		27th Dragoons	?	Toledo

* Includes the 1st Brigade, which was attached to the 1st Corps.

Division	Brigade	Regiment	Strength	Location
2nd Corps				
	Debelle	8th Dragoons	402	Sahagun
		Auxiliary Chasseurs	252	Sahagun
Total			654	
3rd Corps				
	Watier	13th Cuirassiers	1,069	Alagon
		4th Hussars	760	Alagon
		1st Prov. Hussars	?	Alagon
		2nd Prov. Hussars	?	Alagon
4th Corps				
	Maupetit	5th Dragoons	460	Madrid
		Westphalian Light Horse	428	Madrid
		Dutch Hussars	336	Madrid
		Nassau Light Horse	123	Madrid
Total			1,347	
5th Corps				
	Boussart	10th Hussars	?	Miranda
		21st Chasseurs	?	Miranda
6th Corps				
	Colbert	3rd Hussars	450	Madrid
		15th Chasseurs	450	Madrid
Total			900	
	Beaumont	2nd Hussars	715	Madrid
		26th Chasseurs	?	Madrid
	Digeon	20th Dragoons	?	Madrid
		26th Dragoons	?	Madrid
7th Corps				
	Bessières	3rd Prov. Cuirassiers	?	Catalonia
		3rd Prov. Chasseurs	?	Catalonia
Lechi	Schwarz	2nd Italian Chasseurs*	572	Catalonia
		2nd Neapolitan Chasseurs†	477	Catalonia
Total			1,049	

---

* Effective strength based on 1 January 1809 strength report.
† Effective strength based on 6 January 1809 strength report.

Table 2.2	contd			
Division	*Brigade*	*Regiment*	*Strength*	*Location*
Pino	Fontane	1st Italian Chasseurs[*]	520	Catalonia
		Napoleon Dragoons[†]	530	
Total			*1,050*	
	Unattached	24th Dragoons	?	Catalonia
		28th Chasseurs	?	Barcelona

On 19 December Napoleon received word of the British advance into Spain that threatened his lines of communication with France. Two days later the 40,000 French soldiers concentrated in Madrid were in motion to intercept the British. The force included the Imperial Guard, the 2nd and 6th Corps and the 4th and 5th Dragoon Divisions. Several changes in the organisational occurred over the next several weeks. The 1st Provisional Cuirassiers were formally established as the 13th Cuirassiers. On 21 December the commander of the 2nd Brigade of the 4th Dragoon Division, General Davenay was relieved from his command for insubordination to General Houssaye. He was replaced by General Caulaincourt. The following day Davenay was given command of an independent brigade, consisting of the 3rd Dutch Hussars and the 3rd and 4th Provisional Dragoon Regiments. About the same time, the two light cavalry brigades in the 2nd Corps were formed into a division and its command was given to General Franceschi, who was also one of the brigade commanders. The other brigade was commanded by General Debelle, whose force was mauled by the British at Sahagun on 21 December. By the end of December, the 2nd Dragoon Division and the 8th Corps had arrived in Bayonne and were making final preparations for moving into Spain. On 29 December General Lefebvre-Desnouettes, commander of the Chasseurs of the Imperial Guard, was captured by the British at the combat of Benavente.

January 1809 saw additional changes. Shortly after it moved into Spain, Napoleon ordered the disbanding of the 8th Corps. The 1st Hussar Regiment was assigned to General Debelle's Brigade in place of the Auxiliary Chasseurs, which had taken heavy casualties at Sahagun. The Auxiliary Chasseurs was placed on garrison duty in Leon. The 27th Chasseurs, which had been brigaded with the 1st Hussars when they were part of the 8th Corps, was assigned to Madrid. On 3 January General Colbert, the commander of the 6th Corps Light Cavalry Brigade was killed at Cacabellos while pursuing the retreating British Army. He was replaced the next day by General Lorcet. On 7 January, due to their heavy

[*] Effective strength based on 1 January 1809 strength report.
[†] Effective strength based on 1 January 1809 strength report.

casualties, Napoleon ordered the dragoon regiments to send the cadres of their 3rd Squadrons back to France. The troopers were to be incorporated into the other squadrons. In most cases, however, the regiments avoided implementing this order until late spring. On 9 January General Kellermann assumed command of the 2nd Dragoon Division. On the 11th the Berg Light Horse was disbanded and the men were incorporated into the Imperial Guard Chasseurs and on the 16th Napoleon ordered the disbanding of the 1st and 2nd Provisional Hussar Regiments. The order to disband however was not implemented until March. General Bessières's Brigade was dissolved and he was given command of the 1st Brigade of General Souham's Infantry Division.

Table 2.3 Location of French cavalry in Spain, mid-January 1809

Division	*Brigade*	*Regiment*	*Location*
Reserve Corps			
Imperial Guard		Chasseurs	Valladolid
		Dragoons	Valladolid
		Grenadiers	Valladolid
		Gendarmes	Valladolid
		Polish Light Horse	Valladolid
1st Dragoon (Tour-Maubourg)	1st (Perreimond)	1st Dragoons	Tribaldos
		2nd Dragoons	Tribaldos
	2nd (Oullenbourg)	4th Dragoons	Tribaldos
		14th Dragoons	Tribaldos
	3rd (Digeon)	20th Dragoons	Madrid
		26th Dragoons	Tembleque
2nd Dragoon (Kellermann)	1st (Milet)	3rd Dragoons	Zamora
		6th Dragoons	Zamora
	2nd (Carrié)	10th Dragoons	Soria Province
		11th Dragoons	Soria Province
3rd Dragoon (Milhaud)	2nd (Barthélemi)	12th Dragoons	Madrid
		16th Dragoons	Madrid
		21st Dragoons	Madrid
4th Dragoon (Houssaye)	1st (Marizy)	17th Dragoons	Galicia
		27th Dragoons	Galicia

Table 2.3   contd

Division	Brigade	Regiment	Location
	2nd (Caulaincourt)	18th Dragoons	Galicia
		19th Dragoons	Galicia
5th Dragoons	1st (Viallanes) (Lorge)	13th Dragoons	Betanzos
		22nd Dragoons	Betanzos
	2nd (Fournier)	15th Dragoons	Mondonedo
		25th Dragoons	Betanzos
Light Cavalry (Lasalle)	1st (Montbrun)	9th Dragoons	Talavera
		1st Vistula Legion Lancers	Talavera
	2nd (Bordessoulle)	5th Chasseurs	Talavera
		10th Chasseurs	Talavera
	Davenay	3rd Dutch Hussars	Zamora
		3rd Prov. Dragoons	Zamora
		4th Prov. Dragoons	Zamora
		Auxiliary Chasseurs	Leon
		27th Chasseurs	Madrid
1st Corps			
	Beaumont	2nd Hussars	Madrid
		26th Chasseurs	Madrid
		Westphalian Light Horse	Madrid
2nd Corps			
Franceschi	*Desfossés*[*]	22nd Chasseurs	Galicia
		Hanoverian Chasseurs	Galicia
	Debelle	8th Dragoons	Galicia
		1st Hussars	Galicia
3rd Corps			
	Watier	4th Hussars	Saragossa
		13th Cuirassiers	Saragossa
		1st Prov. Hussars	Saragossa
		2nd Prov. Hussars	Saragossa
		1st Vistula Legion Lancers[†]	Saragossa

[*] Colonel François Michel dit Desfossés, commander of the 22nd Chasseurs.

[†] One company of the 1st Vistula Legion Lancers were attached to the 3rd Corps and

Division	Brigade	Regiment	Location
4th Corps			
	Maupetit	5th Dragoons	Salamanca
		Nassau Light Horse	Salamanca
5th Corps			
	Boussart	10th Hussars	Saragosa
		21st Chasseurs	Saragosa
6th Corps			
	Lorcet	3rd Hussars	Galicia
		15th Chasseurs	Galicia
7th Corps			
Lechi	Schwarz	2nd Italian Chasseurs	Catalonia
		2nd Neapolitan Chasseurs	?
Pino	Fontane	1st Italian Chasseurs	Catalonia
		Napoleon Dragoons	?
	Unattached	24th Dragoons	Catalonia
		28th Chasseurs	Barcelona
		3rd Prov. Cuirassiers	Barcelona
		3rd Prov. Chasseurs	Catalonia

February–July 1809

In January 1809 Napoleon realised that war with Austria was imminent and spent two weeks in Valladolid finalising plans for the conquest of Spain and determining which troops and commanders would be needed elsewhere. The Imperial Guard was told to concentrate in preparation for redeployment to Germany. Napoleon also identified key commanders in Spain that he wanted to take with him. General Montbrun was the first to leave, departing for France on 23 January. Within five months eleven cavalry generals had left Spain for service in other theatres of operation. Particularly hard hit was General Lasalle's Light Cavalry Division. All three generals assigned to it were gone by the end of April. General

---

were serving as an escort for General Suchet.

Christophe Merlin, an aide-de-camp to King Joseph, took command of the division.

Table 2.4   Cavalry generals who departed Spain January–June 1809

Name and command or position	*Date left*	*Sent to*
Louis Montbrun		
1st Brigade, Lasalle's Division	Jan. 1809	Germany
Jean Arrighi		
Empress Dragoons	Mar. 1809	Germany
Etienne Bordessoulle		
2nd Brigade, Lasalle's Division	Mar. 1809	Germany
André Bron de Bailly		
Army Headquarters	Mar. 1809	Germany
Archange Davenay		
Prov. Cavalry Brigade	Mar. 1809	Italy
Auguste Lamotte		
4th Dragoons*	21 Mar. 1809	Germany
Louis Lepic		
Horse Grenadiers of the Guard	Mar. 1809	Germany
Antoine Lasalle		
Light Cavalry Division	Apr. 1809	Germany
Pierre Watier		
Cavalry Brigade, 3rd Corps	Jun. 1809	Germany
Anne Trelliard		
Cavalry Depot at Aranda, Spain	May 1809	Germany
André Perreimond		
1st Brigade, 1st Dragoon Division	10 Jun. 1809	France

Compounding the loss of these generals was General Maupetit, commander of the 4th Corps's Cavalry Brigade, who returned to France with poor health caused by his numerous wounds over the years. Additionally General Franceschi, commander of the 2nd Corps's Light Cavalry Division, was captured by Spanish guerrillas in June. He was replaced by General Pierre Soult, the younger brother of Marshal Soult. On 24 June General Vialannes, commander of the 1st Brigade of the 5th Dragoon Division, requested permission to return to France owing to poor health. On the 29th he was replaced by General Jean Cambacérès, who had commanded the cavalry depot at Palencia. To offset the loss of these 14 generals, General Charles Beaurgard was sent to Spain in June

---

* Auguste Lamotte was promoted to general of brigade on 21 March 1809 and sent to Germany.

and replaced General Boussart as the commander of the 5th Corps's Light Cavalry Brigade. General Boussart took command of the 3rd Corps's Cavalry Brigade.

In addition to the upheaval among commanders, several organisational changes also occurred. The cavalry of the Imperial Guard departed for France in mid-March. The 9th Dragoon Regiment was reassigned from Lasalle's Light Cavalry Division in April to General Franceschi's Light Cavalry Division, but by the beginning of July they were assigned to the 1st Dragoon Division. The 20th Dragoons were detached from the 1st Dragoon Division and assigned to the 3rd Dragoon Division.

By the end of June the French were located in three distinct geographic areas: in north-west Spain, in the provinces south of Madrid and in north-east Spain. In March Marshal Soult invaded Portugal from northern Spain with his 2nd Corps, plus the 4th and 5th Dragoon Divisions and General Franceschi's Light Cavalry Division. Marshal Ney and his 6th Corps were given the task of securing the long lines of communications running through Galicia. Marshal Mortier's 5th Corps and General Kellermann's 2nd Dragoon Division were responsible for the lines of communications from Valladolid back to the French border. The French were able to capture Oporto in late March, but their invasion stalled due to unsecured supply lines caused by the uprising of the population against the French invaders. In May a British army, commanded by the future Duke of Wellington, counter-attacked and forced the French out of Oporto and causing them to flee back towards Spain. By the end of June, the French had been pushed out of Portugal. Marshal Soult's headquarters was at Salamanca while Marshal Ney's headquarters was located in Leon and Marshal Mortier's at Valladolid.

Table 2.5   Organisation of French cavalry in north-west Spain, 1 July 1809

Division	Brigade	Regiment	Location
2nd Dragoon (Kellermann)	1st (Milet)	3rd Dragoons	Salamanca
		6th Dragoons	Salamanca
	2nd (Carrié)	10th Dragoons	Carrion de los Condes
		11th Dragoons	Palencia
4th Dragoons (Houssaye)	1st (Marizy)	17th Dragoons	Benavente
		27th Dragoons	Benavente
	2nd (Caulaincourt)	18th Dragoons	Benavente

Table 2.5   continued

Division	Brigade	Regiment	Location
		19th Dragoons	Benavente
5th Dragoons (Lorge)	1st (Cambacérès)	13th Dragoons	Puebla de Sanabria
		22nd Dragoons	Benavente
	2nd (Fournier)	15th Dragoons	Valladolid
		25th Dragoons	Lugo
2nd Corps			
Light Cavalry (Soult)	1st (*Desfossés*)	22nd Chasseurs	Zamora
		Hanoverian Chasseurs	Zamora
	2nd (Debelle)	8th Dragoons	Zamora
		1st Hussars	Zamora
5th Corps			
	Beaurgard	10th Hussars	Valladolid
		21st Chasseurs	Salamanca
6th Corps			
	Lorcet	3rd Hussars	Galicia
		15th Chasseurs	Galicia

The French cavalry in central Spain was also struck hard by the departure of generals in the spring. In May General Merlin, the aide-de-camp to King Joseph, was appointed the commander of General Lasalle's Light Cavalry Division, while Adjutant Commandant Strolz, another aide-de-camp to King Joseph, took command of its 1st Brigade. The 2nd Brigade was commanded by Adjutant Commandant Ormancey. In July General Cavrois was moved from the headquarters of the 2nd Corps to take command of the 2nd Brigade of the 1st Dragoon Division, while General Oullenbourg took command of the 3rd Brigade. He replaced General Digeon, who was reassigned as the commander of the 2nd Brigade of the 3rd Dragoon Division. The 1st Brigade of the 3rd Dragoon Division was now commanded by General Barthélemi, who had commanded the 2nd Brigade. The 1st Dragoon Division was commanded by its senior regimental commander, Colonel Paul Dermoncourt, of the 1st Dragoon Regiment.

Several regiments that had been operating independently or whose parent unit had been disbanded were reassigned. When General Maupetit returned to France in June, his brigade was disbanded. The 5th Dragoons were assigned to the 1st Brigade of the 3rd Dragoon Division. The 3rd Dutch Hussars were also transferred to the same division, but not assigned to a brigade. The Westphalian Light Horse went to General Merlin's

Light Cavalry Division. The 9th Dragoons and the 5th Chasseurs were reassigned from General Merlin's Division. The 9th Dragoons being given to the 3rd Brigade of the 1st Dragoon Division and the 5th Chasseurs to General Beaumont's Light Cavalry Brigade.

By early June the French army in central Spain was deployed in a broad arc south of Madrid running from Alcantara in the west to Toledo in the east. The 1st Corps had been reinforced with the 1st Dragoon Division and the 1st Brigade of the 3rd Dragoon Division, while General Merlin's Light Cavalry Division were operating in the south-west. The 4th Corps, with the 3rd Dragoon Division were operating in the south-east in the vicinity of Toledo. Most of the French cavalry was deployed south of the Tagus River, but retreated north when the British and Spanish armies began their offensive that would end at Talavera in late July.

Table 2.6 Organisation and location of French cavalry in central Spain, 1 July 1809

Division	Brigade	Regiment	Location
Reserve Corps			
1st Dragoon (Tour-Maubourg)	1st (Dermoncourt)*	1st Dragoons	Talavera
		2nd Dragoons	Talavera
	2nd (Cavrois)	4th Dragoons	Toledo
		9th Dragoons	Toledo
	3rd (Oullenbourg)	14th Dragoons	Almaraz
		26th Dragoons	Almaraz
3rd Dragoon (Milhaud)	1st (Barthélemi)	5th Dragoons	Almaraz
		12th Dragoons	Almaraz
	2nd (Digeon)	16th Dragoons	Almagro
		20th Dragoons	Almagro
		21st Dragoons	Almagro
		3rd Dutch Hussars	Madridejos
1st Corps			
	Beaumont	2nd Hussars	Between Toledo and Talavera
		5th Chasseurs	Between Toledo and Talavera
		27th Chasseurs	Madrid

* Colonel Paul Dermoncourt, commander of the 1st Dragoons.

Table 2.6 continued

Division	Brigade	Regiment	Location
4th Corps			
Light Cavalry (Merlin)	1st (*Strolz*)	10th Chasseurs	Granatula
		26th Chasseurs	Granatula
	2nd (*Ormancey*)	1st Vistula Legion Lancers	Granatula
		Westphalian Light Horse	Granatula
	Unattached	Nassau Light Horse	?

In eastern Spain the French had succeeded in capturing Saragossa by the end of February. In April the commander of the 3rd Corps Light Cavalry Brigade, General Watier, had been recalled to France for duty in Germany. He was replaced by General Boussart. Most regiments were attached to the infantry brigades and did not operate as part of a cavalry brigade.

Table 2.7 Organisation of French Cavalry in Eastern Spain, 15 July 1809

	Brigade	Regiment	Location
3rd Corps	Boussart	4th Hussars	Aragon
		13th Cuirassiers	Aragon
7th Corps		1st Italian Chasseurs	Barcelona
		Napoleon Dragoons	Palamos
		2nd Italian Chasseurs	Videbras
		2nd Neapolitan Chasseurs	Gerona
		24th Dragoons	Catalonia
		28th Chasseurs	Gerona
		3rd Prov. Cuirassiers	Barcelona
		3rd Provisional Chasseurs	Catalonia

After the battle of Talavera (27–28 July) and the pushing of the British and Spanish armies away from central Spain in August, the French cavalry underwent more changes. In early August General Debelle was relieved of his command and recalled to France. No general was sent to replace him and his brigade would be commanded by Colonel Alexandre d'Ermenonville, commander of the 8th Dragoons. On 7 September General Caulaincourt, commander of the 2nd Brigade of the 4th Dragoon Division, was promoted to general of division and returned to France. As with Debelle, no general was sent as a replacement for him and Colonel

Jean Saint-Genies, commander of the 19th Dragoons, took command. Also in September General Noirot took command of the 1st Brigade of the 3rd Dragoons, replacing General Barthélemi, who became the governor of Santander. The French would spend September and the first part of October resting and rebuilding their strength.

Table 2.8 Location of French cavalry in Spain, October 1809

Corps	Division	Brigade	Location
	1st Dragoon (Tour-Maubourg)		Madridejos
	2nd Dragoon (Kellermann)		Salamanca
	3rd Dragoons (Milhaud)		Ocaña
	4th Dragoons (Houssaye)		Plasencia
	5th Dragoons (Lorge)		Talavera
1st		Beaumont	Toledo
2nd	Light Cavalry (Soult)		Talavera
3rd		Boussart	Aragon
4th	Light Cavalry (Merlin)		Aranjuez
5th		Beaurgard	Toledo
6th		Lorcet	Salamanca
7th		All regiments	Catalonia

With the war with Austria over Napoleon began to focus his attention on Spain again. He gave orders for the creation of a new 8th Corps that would be commanded by General Junot. Napoleon also wanted to expand the cavalry in Spain, but had no regiments to send, other than six provisional dragoon regiments. He did not believe these regiments would be enough, so he ordered the creation of six more. Twenty-four of the 25 dragoon regiments in Spain were tasked to provide their 3rd and 4th Squadrons to fill the provisional regiments.* Additionally, some regiments had to provide their second colonels to be the commander of these regiments. Initially the regiments were to be the cavalry for the 8th Corps and would be formed into two divisions, with Generals Caulaincourt and Fouler as the division commanders. Generals Sainte-Croix, Poinsot, Bron, Lamotte and Bessières (who was transferred from the 7th Corps) would be the brigade commanders.

On 30 October Napoleon wrote two letters to the Minister of War, General Clarke, outlining his plans for further expansion of the cavalry in Spain. His goal was to bring the effective strength of each chasseur, hussar and cuirassier regiment to 1,500 men. Two divisions were to be formed the

---

* Only the 24th Dragoons had not been required to provide squadrons for the provisional dragoon regiments.

1st Reserve Division to be commanded by General Loison and the 2nd Reserve Division by General Reynier. General Loison's Division would have two brigades of infantry and the 1st and 2nd Marching Regiments of Cavalry. General Reynier's Division would have three brigades of infantry and the 3rd and 4th Marching Regiments of Cavalry. Napoleon's idea was to task all the regiments in Germany for replacements for the regiments in Spain. These detachments would be formed into marching regiments and the regiments would be commanded by second colonels. Once in Spain the regiments would be broken up and the men sent to their parent regiments. Those men belonging to regiments stationed in Germany would be assigned to those units in Spain that had similar uniforms. The 1st Reserve Division was expected to enter Spain at the end of November, while the 2nd Reserve Division would arrive there in early January. When the divisions did arrive, the march regiments were broken up and the men sent to their parent regiments.

The French command underwent several changes in late October and early November. On 17 October General Paris took command of the light cavalry brigade of the 5th Corps. On 7 November General Digeon, commander of the 2nd Brigade of the 3rd Dragoon Division was reassigned as the commander of the cavalry of General Loison's Reserve Division. He was replaced by Colonel Vial, the commander of the 16th Dragoons. General Oullenbourg, the commander of the 2nd Brigade of the 1st Dragoon Division, was allowed to return to France due to health conditions on the same day. He would be replaced by Colonel Bouvier des Eclaz, commander of the 14th Dragoons. On 18 November the largest cavalry battle of the Peninsular War was fought near Ocaña, during which General Paris was killed. He was replaced by Colonel Subervie, the commander of the 10th Chasseurs. The next day the Spanish army under General Areizaga was crushed at Ocaña and forced to retreat from central Spain. During the battle Colonel Vial, the new commander of the 3rd Dragoon Division's 2nd Brigade, was killed, 12 days after taking command. After the battle the fighting was done for the year, with the French in nominal control of much of Spain.

Although the French would spend the next few months resting, refitting and reorganising their units, they also spent considerable time subduing a hostile population that had risen up in arms when the Spanish armies began their autumn campaign. Several major changes occurred in the organisation of the French forces in December. General Perreimond, who returned to Spain in September, took command of the 4th Corps's Light Cavalry Brigade. This brigade was only a shadow of what it had been six months before. The Westphalian Light Horse had been reassigned to General Laval's German Division and was located in

Segovia, while the 26th Chasseurs were sent to back to Madrid, where it joined the 3rd Dutch Hussars, which had also been ordered there. Before Ocaña General Beaurgard, commander of the 5th Corps's Light Cavalry Brigade, replaced General Cambacérès in command of the 1st Brigade of the 5th Dragoon Division. The 5th Division also lost General Fournier-Sarlovèse, commander of the 2nd Brigade, when he returned to France on 19 December. In the 2nd Dragoon Division, General Carrié had been seriously wounded at Alba des Tormes on 28 November 1809 and his brigade was temporarily commanded by Colonel Jean-Baptiste Dommanget, of the 10th Dragoons. Colonel Corbineau, the commander of the 20th Dragoons, took command of the 2nd Brigade of the 3rd Dragoon Division. By the end of December, there was a serious shortage of generals to command the cavalry brigades. Eight of the 20 cavalry brigades were commanded by the brigade's senior regimental commander.

Table 2.9   Organisation of the French Cavalry, mid-December 1809

Division	Brigade	Regiment	Location
1st Dragoon (Tour-Maubourg)	1st (*Dermoncourt*)[*]	1st Dragoons	Madridejos
		2nd Dragoons	Madridejos
	2nd (Cavrois)	4th Dragoons	Madridejos
		9th Dragoons	Madridejos
	3rd (*Bouvier des Eclaz*)[†]	14th Dragoons	Ciudad Real
		26th Dragoons	Ciudad Real
2nd Dragoon (Kellermann)	1st (Milet)	3rd Dragoons	Cantalapiedra
		6th Dragoons	Cantalapiedra
	2nd (*Dommanget*)[‡]	10th Dragoons	Leon
		11th Dragoons	Zamora[§]
3rd Dragoon (Milhaud)	1st (Noirot)	5th Dragoons	Cuenca
		12th Dragoons	Cuenca

[*] Colonel Paul Dermoncourt, commander of the 1st Dragoons.
[†] Colonel Joseph Bouvier des Eclaz, commander of the 14th Dragoons.
[‡] Colonel Jean-Baptiste Dommanget, commander of the 10th Dragoons.
[§] The 11th Dragoons spent December conducting a route reconnaissance in the Douro and Tormes River valleys to see which one would provide the best route for an invasion force to move into Portugal.

Table 2.9   continued

Division	Brigade	Regiment	Location
	2nd (*Corbineau*)*	16th Dragoons	Aranjuez
		20th Dragoons	Aranjuez
		21st Dragoons	Aranjuez
4th Dragoons (Houssaye)	1st (Marizy)	17th Dragoons	Cebolla
		27th Dragoons	Cebolla
	2nd (*Saint-Genies*)†	18th Dragoons	Cebolla
		19th Dragoons	Cebolla
5th Dragoons (Lorge)	1st (Beaurgard)	13th Dragoons	Madrid
		22nd Dragoons	Madrid
	2nd (*Ornano*)‡	15th Dragoons	Alba de Tormes
		25th Dragoons	Alba de Tormes
Madrid Reserve		3rd Dutch Hussars	Madrid
		26th Chasseurs	Madrid
		27th Chasseurs	Madrid
1st Corps			
	Beaumont	2nd Hussars	Villanueva-de-los-Infantes
		5th Chasseurs	
2nd Corps			
Light Cavalry (Soult)	1st (*Desfossés*)	22nd Chasseurs	Zamora
		Hanoverian Chasseurs	Zamora
	2nd (*d'Ermenonville*)§	8th Dragoons	Zamora
		1st Hussars	Zamora
3rd Corps			
	Boussart	4th Hussars	Aragon
		13th Cuirassiers	Aragon
4th Corps			
	Perreimond	10th Chasseurs	Ocaña

---

* Colonel Jean Corbineau, commander of the 20th Dragoons.
† Colonel Jean Saint-Genies, commander of the 19th Dragoons.
‡ Colonel Antoine d'Ornano, commander of the 25th Dragoons.
§ Colonel Alexandre d'Ermenonville, commander of the 8th Dragoons.

Division	Brigade	Regiment	Location
		1st Vistula Lancers	Madridejos
	Independent	Nassau Light Horse	?
		Westphalian Light Horse	?
5th Corps			
	*Steenhaudt**	10th Hussars	La Mancha[†]
		21st Chasseurs	La Mancha
6th Corps			
	Lorcet	3rd Hussars	Salamanca
		15th Chasseurs	Salamanca
7th Corps			
	Unattached	2nd Italian Chasseurs	Gerona
		1st Italian Chasseurs	Fornells
		Napoleon Dragoons	Fornells
		24th Dragoons	Vich
		3rd Prov. Chasseurs	Vich
		28th Chasseurs	?
		3rd Prov. Cuirassiers	Barcelona
		3rd Prov. Chasseurs	Catalonia
		2nd Neapolitan Chasseurs[‡]	Besalu

* Colonel Charles-François Steenhaudt, commander of the 21st Chasseurs.
† The 5th Corps's Light Cavalry Brigade were in cantonments in Consuegra, Madridejos and Orgaz.
‡ One squadron only. The 2nd Neapolitan Chasseurs had withdawn to Carcassone.

Chapter Three

Occupation
(Spring 1810–July 1812)

By early 1810 most of the Spanish armies had been defeated and everything north of Andalusia except for Valenica was under nominal French control. By June even Andalusia had fallen and the Spanish government was under siege in Cadiz. The French would spend the next two and half years consolidating and protecting their conquered territories in Spain. A major effort was also made to evict the British from Portugal by invading the country in September 1810. To facilitate the consolidation Napoleon took two major steps the creation of military governments and the dissolution of the Army of Spain and the creation of the six independent armies.

Protecting lines of communication with France
Before Napoleon departed Spain in 1809, he designated one major supply line to all the provinces in Spain, except for Catalonia and Aragon. This supply line began at Bayonne and went to Burgos. From there it either proceeded east to Saragossa or south-west to Valladolid and then on to Madrid. Once Andalusia was conquered, the lines of communication proceeded south-east to Toledo and then to Seville or from Madrid to Talavera, across the pontoon bridge at Almaraz and then on to Seville. Fortified resting points were set up about a day's march for a soldier on foot. There he could receive provisions to cover his next stage of the trip. The trip for an infantryman marching from Bayonne to Madrid was almost 700 kilometres long and would take 22 days, if the soldier did not stop longer than a night in any place.

Table 3.1   French supply routes in Spain from Bayonne to Valladolid, 1809 (483 km in 15 days)

From Bayonne to:	km	Provisions
Irun	43	Bread and meat for a day

From Bayonne to:	km	Provisions
Hernani	32	Bread and meat for a day
Tolosa	19	Bread and meat for a day
Villareal	39	Bread and meat for a day
Mondragon	32	Bread and meat for a day
Vitoria	34	Bread and meat for a day
Miranda	34	Bread and meat for two days
Pancorbo	26	—
Briviesca	26	Bread and meat for a day
Burgos	43	Bread and meat for four days
Celada	26	—
Villodrigo	26	—
Torquemada	32	Bread and meat for two days
Duenas	32	—
Valladolid	39	—

Table 3.2   French supply routes in Spain from Valladolid to Madrid, 1809 (212 km in 7 days)

From Valladolid to:	km	Provisions
Valdestillas	26	Bread and meat for three days
Olmedo	26	—
Santa Maria de la Nieva	39	—
Segovia	30	Bread and meat for a day
Saint-Ildefonse	13	Bread and meat for 20 days
Guardarrama	39	—
Madrid	39	—

Table 3.3   French supply routes in Spain from Bayonne to Saragossa, 1809 (468 km in 15 days)

From Bayonne to:	km	Provisions
Irun	43	Bread and meat for a day
Hernani	32	Bread and meat for a day
Tolosa	19	Bread and meat for a day
Villareal	39	Bread and meat for a day
Mondragon	32	Bread and meat for a day
Vitoria	34	Bread and meat for a day
Miranda	26	Bread and meat for a day
Haro	21	Bread and meat for a day
Logrono	11	Bread and meat for two days

Table 3.3   continued

From Bayonne to:	Km	Provisions
Calahorra	47	Bread and meat for a day
Alfaro	47	Bread and meat for a day
Tudela	26	Bread and meat for two days
Mallen	26	Bread and meat for a day
Alagon	39	Bread and meat for a day
Saragossa	26	—

In most campaigns in central Europe, once the enemy's army was defeated the local population stayed pacified, but in Spain it was different. No area was deemed safe unless the French occupied it in strength. Convoys, stragglers and isolated detachments were constantly attacked. With supply lines of 700 kilometres or more,[*] the French had to divert a large number of troops to protect them. On 8 February 1810 Napoleon decreed the formation of military governments in the provinces of Catalonia, Aragon, Navarre and Biscay. Three months later, on 29 May, military governments were also authorised for the provinces of Burgos, Valladolid, Palencia and Toro. By the end of the year a seventh government would be formed in Salamanca. The governments' primary mission was to ensure their provinces stayed pacified and to raise contributions from the local population to support the French armies in Spain. Not surprisingly, four of the military governments were in the northern provinces that were astride the French supply line to France. Additionally, the war was draining the French treasury and Napoleon was determined to make the Spanish people pay for the cost of maintaining the army. The number one mission of these governors was to support the new French armies, who would provide the necessary troops to the governor. The military governors were authorised not only to level monetary contributions, but also to requisition needed supplies and food. He was the ultimate authority in the province and could name and fire any civil functionaries within the province.

Table 3.4   French military governments in Spain, 1810

Government	Provinces	Governor	Army assigned to
1st	Catalonia	Marshal MacDonald	Army of Catalonia
2nd	Aragon	General Suchet	Army of Aragon
3rd	Navarre	General Dufour	Army of Spain
4th	Biscay	General Thouvenot	Army of Spain
5th	Burgos	General Dorsenne	Army of Spain

[*] The supply line from Cadiz to Bayonne was over 1,300 kilometres long!

Government Provinces		Governor	Army assigned to
6th	Valladolid,		
	Palencia and Toro	General Kellermann	Army of Spain
7th	Salamanca	General Thiebault	Army of Portugal

Depending on the province, the military government had a variety of forces to support it. In the autumn of 1810 the 6th Military Government under General Kellermann had two dragoon brigades and an infantry division.

For most parts, the military governors performed as expected. General Suchet's was especially effective, while General Kellermann's rule was noted for its corruption and his refusal to support the Army of Portugal.

The creation of the armies

The year also saw the disbanding of the Army of Spain. Until early 1810, all the French forces were supposedly operating under the command of King Joseph, who had Marshal Soult as his chief-of-staff. They still retained the name of the Army of Spain, but in reality it did not exist, except in the mind of King Joseph. The individual corps commanders took their direction from Napoleon, who was as much as 1,500 kilometres away in Paris. Napoleon recognised that owing to the geography of the country the commanders had to be able to operate without constantly deferring to a central command authority. In the spring of 1810 Napoleon set up separate armies based on their geographical locations. These armies were designed to operate independently and their commanders reported directly to Paris. They did not work for King Joseph in Madrid. As long as the armies were facing only poorly organised Spanish forces, this was not an issue, for the different French armies usually defeated them with little or no help from the other armies. However, by mid-1811, when the British were back along the Portuguese–Spanish border, coordination between the commands was critical. A unified strategy was needed, yet too often the army commanders' focus was on the problems in their own area of operations and not the overall strategic situation.

Table 3.5   The creation of French armies in Spain, 1810 and 1811

Army	Commander	When Created
Army of Portugal	Marshal André Massena	17 Apr. 1810
Army of Aragon	General Louis Suchet	May 1810
Army of Catalonia	Marshal Etienne MacDonald	May 1810
Army of the Centre	King Joseph	29 Sep. 1810
Army of the South	Marshal Jean Soult	15 Jul. 1810
Army of the North	Marshal Bessières	Jan. 1811

Arrival of the 8th Corps and the Provisional Dragoon Brigades

In early January 1810 General Junot's 8th Corps began arriving in Spain. They had a two-fold mission, to reinforce the units in western Spain and to protect the French supply lines that ran through northern Spain. Originally they were supposed to be organised into two divisions, but General Fouler never assumed command of his division. All five brigades were initially part of General Caulaincourt's Division.

Table 3.6   Organisation of the Provisional Dragoon regiments, January 1810

Brigade	Commander	Regiments	Date Entered Spain
1st	Sainte-Croix	1st	Jan. 1810
		2nd	Jan. 1810
		3rd	Jan. 1810
2nd	Gardanne	4th	31 Jan. 1810
		5th	31 Jan. 1810
3rd	Bessières	6th	Jan. 1810
		7th	Jan. 1810
4th	Bron	8th	Jan. 1810
		9th	Jan. 1810
		10th	Jan. 1810
5th	Lamotte	11th	23 Jan. 1810
		12th	23 Jan. 1810

On 8 February 1810 Napoleon ordered General Gardanne's Brigade to be sent to Valladolid and upon arrival, it and the regiments within it, were to be disbanded. The 3rd and 4th Squadrons of 3rd, 6th, 10th and 11th Dragoon Regiments, which had formed the 4th and 5th Provisional Dragoon Regiments were sent to their parent regiments in the 2nd Dragoon Division. General Lamotte's Brigade was also disbanded and the 11th and 12th Provisional Dragoon Regiments dissolved and the 3rd and 4th Squadrons joined their regiments in Madrid (the 13th and 22nd Dragoons) and Alba de Tormes (the 15th and 25th Dragoons). On the 28th General Caulaincourt received permission to return to France owing to poor health. In May General Gardanne took command of the 3rd Brigade of the 2nd Dragoon Division, replacing Colonel Ornano, who had been commanding it since the previous November. General Lamotte would eventually take command of the 6th Corps's Light Cavalry Brigade.

The three remaining provisional dragoon brigades were assigned to General Kellermann's 2nd Dragoon Division in March and stayed with it when General Trelliard assumed command on 17 April. General

Kellermann would become the governor of the newly formed 6th Military Government in late May. In June Generals Bessières's and Bron's Brigades were transferred to the 6th Military Government, which was located in Valladolid. They would be responsible for protecting the long supply lines back to France. General Sainte-Croix's Brigade was assigned to the 8th Corps and would join the Army of Portugal.

In late December 1809, in preparation for the upcoming campaigns in Andalusia and Portugal, King Joseph and Marshal Soult reorganised the cavalry in the Army of Spain, attaching the dragoon divisions to the different corps. By May 1810 three new armies had also been organised: the Armies of Aragon, Portugal and Catalonia. The Army of Portugal, which had been formed on 17 April, was commanded by Marshal Massena. General Louis Montbrun was given overall command of the Army of Portugal's cavalry, which consisted of the 2nd Dragoon Division, commanded by General Trelliard, the 2nd Corps's Light Cavalry Division, the 6th Corps's Light Cavalry Brigade and the 8th Corps's Provisional Dragoon Brigade. General Cavrois transferred from the 1st Dragoon Division to take command of the 2nd Brigade of General Trelliard's 2nd Dragoon Division.

In early January 1810 the 27th Chasseurs were assigned to General Perreimond's Light Cavalry Brigade in the 4th Corps. In the spring the 1st Dragoon Division was attached to the 1st Corps in support of the siege of Cadiz. The 3rd Dragoon Division was attached to the 4th Corps and operating in south-east Spain in the vicinity of Grenada. Throughout much of the spring, the 4th Dragoon Division was attached to the 2nd Corps for operations in western Extremadura. However, at the beginning of May, the 2nd Corps was ordered north to join the Army of Portugal. The 4th Dragoon Division did not go with it and would spend May and June along the Spanish–Portuguese border near Badajoz. General Lorge's 5th Dragoon Division was broken up in April. Its 1st Brigade was assigned to the 5th Corps and combined with the Corps's light cavalry brigade to form a new division. General Marizy, who had commanded the 1st Brigade in the 4th Dragoon Division, became the division commander, while General Briche commanded the Light Cavalry Brigade. He replaced General Beaurgard, who was killed in action at Valverde on 19 February. The division's dragoon brigade was commanded by Colonel Reiset of the 13th Dragoons. The 2nd Brigade of the 5th Dragoon Division was reassigned to General Trelliard's Dragoon Division and became its 3rd Brigade. General Gardanne was appointed its commander on 29 May. General Digeon would replace General Marizy as the commander of the 1st Brigade of the 4th Dragoon Division.

Except for the 2nd Dragoon Division, all of the cavalry divisions were short of general officers to command its brigades. Neither of the brigades in the 2nd Corps's Light Cavalry Division had general officers commanding them, nor did the three brigades in the 1st Dragoon Division. The other three cavalry divisions were better off, but all were short a general officer to command one of its brigades.

In the Army of Catalonia the regiments were often broken up into company-size detachments in support of counter-insurgency operations. The locations given for the regiments were where the regimental head-quarters were at the time. When not supporting operations, the subordinate elements of the regiments were often dispersed throughout the countryside protecting the lines of communication. During the winter the 28th Chasseurs were transferred to north-western Spain and would be assigned to General Bonet's Division operating in the Asturias. On 12 February the 1st Neapolitan Chasseurs arrived in Spain to support the 7th Corps. In May the 2nd Italian Chasseurs departed Spain to return to Italy.

In January Napoleon ordered the Imperial Guard to send two divisions into northern Spain to help secure the supply lines. By June these troops included a cavalry brigade, commanded by General Lepic. The brigade had two composite Guard cavalry regiments and the Lancers of Berg. The cavalry of the 1st and 2nd Reserve Divisions were kept in northern Spain for a few months, but were disbanded and the men sent to their various regiments by June.

Table 3.7 Organisation of the French cavalry, June 1810

Division	*Brigade*	*Regiment*	*Location*
Army of Portugal			
2nd Dragoon (Trelliard)	1st (Milet)	3rd Dragoons	Ciudad Rodrigo
		6th Dragoons	Ciudad Rodrigo
	2nd (Cavrois)	10th Dragoons	Ciudad Rodrigo
		11th Dragoons	Ciudad Rodrigo
	3rd (Gardanne)	15th Dragoons	Ciudad Rodrigo
		25th Dragoons	Ciudad Rodrigo
2nd Corps			
Light Cavalry (Soult)	1st (*Desfossés*)	22nd Chasseurs	Lobon
		Hanoverian Chasseurs	Lobon
	2nd (*d'Ermenonville*)	8th Dragoons	Merida
		1st Hussars	Lobon

Division	Brigade	Regiment	Location
6th Corps			
	Lorcet	3rd Hussars	Marialba
		15th Chasseurs	Marialba
8th Corps			
	Sainte-Croix	1st Prov. Dragoon	San Felices
		2nd Prov. Dragoon	Gallegos
		3rd Prov. Dragoon	Gallegos
Army of Aragon			
3rd Corps			
	Boussart	4th Hussars	Mequinenza?
		13th Cuirassiers	Mequinenza?
Army of Catalonia			
7th Corps			
		1st Neapolitan Chasseurs	Figueras
		2nd Neapolitan Chasseurs	Figueras
		1st Italian Chasseurs	Besalu
		Napoleon Dragoons	Massanet
		3rd Prov. Chasseurs	Vich
		24th Dragoons	Vich
		3rd Prov. Cuirassiers	Barcelona
		3rd Prov. Chasseurs	Catalonia
Army of Spain			
1st Corps			
1st Dragoon (Tour-Maubourg)	1st (*Dermoncourt*)	1st Dragoons	Vicinity of Cadiz
		2nd Dragoons	Vicinity of Cadiz
	2nd (*Quenot*)*	4th Dragoons	Vejer de la Frontera
		9th Dragoons	Medina Sidonia
	3rd (*Bouvier des Eclaz*)	14th Dragoons	Arcos de la Frontera
		26th Dragoons	Cordova
	Beaumont	2nd Hussars	Arcos de la Frontera
		5th Chasseurs	

---

* Colonel Mathieu Quenot, commander of the 9th Dragoons.

Table 3.7   continued

Division	Brigade	Regiment	Location
4th Corps			
3rd Dragoon (Milhaud)	1st (Noirot)	5th Dragoons	Grenada
		12th Dragoons	Grenada
	2nd (*Corbineau*)	16th Dragoons	Grenada
		20th Dragoons	Grenada
		21st Dragoons	Grenada
	Perreimond	10th Chasseurs	Antequera
		27th Chasseurs	Antequera
		1st Vistula Lancers	Baza
5th Corps			
Cavalry (Marizy)	1st (*Reiset*)*	13th Dragoons	Aceuchal
		22nd Dragoons	Zafra
	2nd (Briche)	10th Hussars	Seville
		21st Chasseurs	Seville
4th Dragoons (Houssaye)	1st (Digeon)	17th Dragoons	Calamonte
		27th Dragoons	Calamonte
	2nd (*Saint-Genies*)	18th Dragoons	Arroyo de San Servan
		19th Dragoons	
Reserve		3rd Dutch Hussars†	Madrid
		26th Chasseurs	Madrid
German		Westphalian Light Horse	Segovia
		Nassau Light Horse	Manzanares
6th Military Government	3rd Prov. Dragoon (Bessières)	6th Prov. Dragoons	Medina del Campo
		7th Prov. Dragoons	Medina del Campo
	4th Prov. Dragoon (Bron)	8th Prov. Dragoons	Zamora

* Colonel Marie Reiset, commander of the 13th Dragoons.
† The 3rd Dutch Hussars had one squadron, the other squadrons having returned to Holland in January.

Division	Brigade	Regiment	Location
		9th Prov. Dragoons	Salamanca
		10th Prov. Dragoons	Benavente
Imperial Guard	Lepic	Heavy Cavalry*	Burgos
		Light Cavalry†	Burgos
		Lancers of Berg	Burgos
		28th Chasseurs	Asturias

The Army of Portugal spent the first part of the summer of 1810 besieging Ciudad Rodrigo in preparation for the invasion of Portugal. During that time General Lamotte took command of the 6th Corps's Light Cavalry Brigade. General Lorcet transferred from it to the 1st Brigade of the 2nd Dragoon Division, replacing General Milet who was reassigned to the 6th Military Government. On 15 July the 1st, 4th and 5th Corps were formed into the Army of the South. It would spend the summer attempting to secure Andalusia and capture Cadiz. The 4th Dragoon Division returned to La Mancha and was in the vicinity of the Tagus River. Its 1st Brigade, commanded by General Digeon, did not return to La Mancha with the division, but stayed in the vicinity of Cordova. General Lorge, the former commander of the 5th Dragoon Division was sent to Madrid and made the governor of La Mancha and commander of the Confederation of the Rhine Division – also known as the German Division. In November General Watier arrived in the north with a brigade consisting of 1st Provisional Light Cavalry Regiment and two squadrons of the 9th Hussars (which had been in Spain since the summer).

After the fall of Ciudad Rodrigo in late July the Army of Portugal began its invasion and spent August besieging and capturing Almeida. By September the French Army was deep into Portugal and would fight at Bussaco on the 27th of the month. General Gardanne was left behind as the commandant of Ciudad Rodrigo. He would have the 10th Dragoons as part of his garrison. Colonel Ornano, commander of the 25th Dragoons, would command the brigade in his place. General Poinsot took command of the 3rd Provisional Dragoon Brigade, replacing General Bessières, who was assigned to the 6th Military Government. General Cambacérès, who was working in the 2nd Corps's Headquarters, returned to France. In August General Fournier returned to Spain with a brigade comprised of

---

* Included two squadrons of the Empress Dragoons and one squadron of Horse Grenadiers.

† Included two squadrons of Polish Lancers, one squadron of Chasseurs, a company of Velites and a company of Mamelukes.

the 3rd and 4th Squadrons of the 7th, 13th and 20th Chasseurs, which had about 1,500 men.* They were assigned to the Salamanca area and had the mission of protecting the lines of communication. They would replace General Bron's 4th Provisional Dragoon Brigade, which was disbanded by the end of October. Only the 3rd and 4th Squadrons of the 15th Dragoons would reinforce the Army of Portugal. The other squadrons rejoined their regiments in the Armies of the Centre and of the South.

Elsewhere in Spain, on 22 August the 3rd Provisional Chasseurs were redesignated as the 29th Chasseurs. General Schwarz, who served as a cavalry brigade commander in eastern Catalonia, surrendered to Spanish forces on 14 September. On 29 September the Army of the Centre was officially formed and was responsible for the defence of La Mancha. King Joseph would keep command of this army for himself. On 30 September the cadre of the remaining squadron of the 3rd Dutch Hussars was ordered to return to Holland and the troopers were reassigned to the 1st Hussars.

In early October General Digeon became the governor of the province of Cordova. He was replaced in command of the 1st Brigade of the 4th Dragoon Division, by General Bron. On 10 October Colonel Bouvier des Eclaz was promoted to general of brigade. The next day General Sainte-Croix was killed by a cannonball while conducting a reconnaissance in Portugal. Later that month General Marizy's Dragoon Brigade was ordered to La Mancha and was transferred to the Army of the Centre. On 15 November the brigade was assigned to the 4th Dragoon Division. In exchange for General Marizy's Brigade, the 1st Brigade of the 4th Dragoon Division, commanded by General Bron, which was still in southern Spain, was transferred to the Army of the South.

By the end of 1810 most of Spain had been occupied except for the coastal cities in Andalusia, Murcia, Galicia and, Valencia; while the fortress city of Badajoz was still in Spanish hands. Whether it was pacified is opened to debate. The Army of Portugal had pulled back from the Lines of Torres Vedras that were protecting Lisbon and was in the general vicinity of Santarem. The Army of Aragon was in garrisons throughout the provinces, while the Army of Catalonia occupied Barcelona and the coastal towns. The cavalry of the Army of the Centre was in cantonments along the Tagus River, while the cavalry of the Army of the South was deployed in a wide arc ranging from Grenada in the east to Cadiz in the south to Badajoz in the west. In the north four brigades of cavalry were helping secure the vital lines of communication with France.

---

* This brigade is sometimes referred to as the 2nd Provisional Light Cavalry Regiment.

Table 3.8   Organisation of the French cavalry, November 1810

Division	Brigade	Regiment	Location
Army of Portugal			
2nd Dragoon (Trelliard)	1st (Lorcet)	3rd Dragoons	Santarem
		6th Dragoons	Santarem
	2nd (Cavrois)	11th Dragoons	Santarem
	3rd (*Ornano*)	15th Dragoons	Alcoentre
		25th Dragoons	Alcoentre
	Gardanne	10th Dragoons	Ciudad Rodrigo
2nd Corps			
Light Cavalry (Soult)	1st (Desfossés)	22nd Chasseurs	Santarem
		Hanoverian Chasseurs	Santarem
	2nd (*d'Ermenonville*)	8th Dragoons	Santarem
		1st Hussars	Santarem
6th Corps			
	Lamotte	3rd Hussars	Leiria
		15th Chasseurs	Leiria
8th Corps			
	?	1st Prov. Dragoon	Alcanena
		2nd Prov. Dragoon	Alcanena
		3rd Prov. Dragoon	Alcanena
	Fournier	7th Chasseurs	Almeida
		13th Chasseurs	Almeida
		20th Chasseurs	Almeida
Army of Aragon			
3rd Corps			
Boussart	4th Hussars		Mequinenza?
		13th Cuirassiers	Ulldecona
Army of Catalonia			
7th Corps			
		1st Italian Chasseurs	Besalu
		Napoleon Dragoons	Massanet
		29th Chasseurs[*]	?
		24th Dragoons	Vich
		3rd Prov. Cuirassiers	Barcelona

---

[*] The 29th Chasseurs were broken up into company-size detachments.

Table 3.8 continued

Division	Brigade	Regiment	Location
		1st Neapolitan Chasseurs	Figueras
		2nd Neapolitan Chasseurs	Figueras
Army of the Centre			
4th Dragoons (Houssaye)	1st (Marizy)	13th Dragoons	Navalmoral
		22nd Dragoons	Navalmoral
	2nd (*Saint-Genies*)	18th Dragoons	Mora
		19th Dragoons	Toledo and Segovia
Madrid Reserve		26th Chasseurs	Madrid
German		Westphalian Light Horse	Segovia
		Nassau Light Horse	Manzanares
Army of the South			
1st Corps			
1st Dragoon (Tour-Maubourg)	1st (*Dermoncourt*)	1st Dragoons	Vicinity of Cadiz
		2nd Dragoons	Vicinity of Cadiz
	2nd (*Quenot*)	4th Dragoons	Vejer de la Frontera
		9th Dragoons	Medina Sidonia
	3rd (Bouvier des Eclaz)	14th Dragoons	Ecija
		26th Dragoons	Cordova
	Bron	17th Dragoons	Cordova
		27th Dragoons	Cordova
	Beaumont	2nd Hussars	Seville
		5th Chasseurs	Arcos de la Frontera
4th Corps			
3rd Dragoon (Milhaud)	1st (Noirot)	5th Dragoons	Baza
		12th Dragoons	Grenada
		16th Dragoons	Seville
	2nd (*Corbineau*)	20th Dragoons	Seville
		21st Dragoons	Seville

Division	Brigade	Regiment	Location
	Perreimond	10th Chasseurs	Baza
		27th Chasseurs	Baza
		1st Vistula Lancers	Baza
5th Corps			
	Briche	10th Hussars	Seville
		21st Chasseurs	Seville
Army of Spain			
6th Military	3rd Prov.	6th Prov.	
Government	Dragoon (Poinsot)	Dragoons	Leon
		7th Prov. Dragoons	Medina del Campo
Imperial Guard	Lepic	Heavy Cavalry	Burgos
		Light Cavalry	Burgos
		Lancers of Berg	Burgos
	Watier	9th Hussars	Pamplona
		1st Prov. Light Cavalry	Asturias
	Unattached	28th Chasseurs	Asturias

1811

In January 1811 the Army of the North was formed and Marshal Bessières was appointed its commander. It mission was to protect the supply lines to France by keeping the countryside pacified. Marshal Bessières had under his command four of the seven military governments.

Table 3.9 French military governments assigned to the Army of the North, January 1811

Government	Provinces	Governor
3rd	Navarre	General Dufour
4th	Biscay	General Thouvenot
5th	Burgos	General Dorsenne
6th	Valladolid, Palencia and Toro	General Kellermann

Most of the troops assigned to the military governments served as garrisons in the cities and towns that were along the main supply routes. Each of them had at least an infantry division and various gendarme legions. Additionally, two of the four governments had at least one cavalry brigade assigned to it or located within its province.

Table 3.10   Cavalry Brigades in the Army of the North, January 1811

Government	Brigade	Regiments	Location
	Watier	1st Prov. Light Cavalry	Asturias
		9th Hussars	Pamplona
	Unattached	28th Chasseurs	Asturias
5th	Lepic	Guard Heavy Cavalry	Burgos
		Guard Light Cavalry	Burgos
		Lancers of Berg	Burgos
6th	3rd Prov. Dragoon (Poinsot)	6th Prov. Dragoons	Leon
		7th Prov. Dragoons	Medina del Campo

In April General Milet was sent from the 6th Military Government to take command of the province of Avila. In May the 6th Military Government also lost General Bron, who was given command of the 1st Brigade of General Tour-Maubourg's 1st Dragoon Division in the Army of the South. On 20 May General Kellermann, the Governor of the 6th Military Government was relieved of his command for corruption and sent home to France.

In the Army of the Centre General Marizy, commander of the 3rd Brigade of the 4th Dragoon Division, was on his way back to France when he was ambushed by Spanish guerrillas on 8 February. He died from his wounds the next day. He was replaced by Colonel Marie Reiset, the commander of the 13th Dragoons.

In March Marshal Massena decided to withdraw the Army of Portugal back to the Spanish border in order to resupply and reorganise it. The army had been living off the country for six months and was in terrible shape, especially its horses. Between 16 September 1810 and 1 March 1811, the cavalry and artillery loss 4,597 horses. Over half were lost by the artillery. The cavalry reported losing 2,217 mounts. The worse losses were in the Hannover Chasseurs who had 362 horses killed or died of illness. The five dragoon regiments of General Trelliard's Dragoon Division lost only 458 horses in the same period![*]

---

[*] Koch, *Mémoirs de Massena*, vol. 7, p. 590.

Table 3.11 Loss of horses in the cavalry of the Army of Portugal, 16 September 1810–1 March 1811

Corps	Division or brigade	Regiment	16 Sept.–31 Dec. 1811	Jan.–Mar. 1 1811	Total
2nd	1st Brigade	22nd Chasseurs	114	62	176
		Hanover Chasseurs	289	73	362
	2nd Brigade	1st Hussars	142	63	205
		8th Dragoons	55	26	81
Total			*600*	*224*	*824*
6th	Light Cavalry	3rd Hussars	86	25	111
		15th Chasseurs	182	30	212
Total			*268*	*55*	*323*
8th	Dragoon Brigade	1st Prov. Dragoons	68	67	135
		2nd Prov. Dragoons	151	87	238
		3rd Prov. Dragoons	185	54	239
Total			*404*	*208*	*612*
Reserve	1st Brigade	3rd Dragoons	72	86	158
		6th Dragoons	35	16	51
Total			*107*	*102*	*209*
	2nd Brigade	11th Dragoons	65	12	77
Total			*65*	*12*	*77*
	3rd Brigade	15th Dragoons	76	20	96
		25th Dragoons	48	29	77
Total			*124*	*49*	*173*
Total losses in the Dragoon Division			*296*	*163*	*459*
Total losses			**1,568**	**650**	**2,218**

By 1 April the Army of Portugal had retreated to a defensive line along the Coa River. The army had about 5,200 cavalry, of which less than 4,800 men were fit for duty. Horses were at a premium, with less than 4,700 mounts available. The 8th Corps's Provisional Dragoon Brigade reported 1,041 men fit for duty, but had mounts for 768. The army was also short of brigade commanders. General Gardanne was relieved by Napoleon on

7 March for his failure to bring supplies to the Army of Portugal. The commander of the 6th Corps's Light Cavalry Brigade, General Lamotte, had been relieved by Marshal Ney on 15 March and was replaced by Colonel Mourier, of the 15th Chasseurs.

Table 3.12   Location and strength of the cavalry of the Army of Portugal, 1 April 1811

Brigade	Regiment	Location	Sqdns	Men	Horses
2nd Corps					
Soult's Division 1st	HQ	Sabugal	2	25	
(*Desfossés*)	1st Hussars	Sabugal	4	336	247
	22nd Chasseurs	Sabugal	3	342	238
2nd (*d'Ermenon- ville*)	Hanover Chasseurs	Sabugal	4	171	99
	8th Dragoons	Sabugal	2	344	287
Total			*13*	*1,195*	*899*
6th Corps					
*Mourier**	HQ	Villar Mayor		4	28
	3rd Hussars†	Villar Mayor	3	201	201
	15th Chasseurs‡	Villar Mayor	3	299	296
Total			*6*	*504*	*525*
8th Corps					
	HQ	Alfayates		2	9
	1st Prov. Dragoons§	Malhada Sorda	4	328	295
	2nd Prov. Dragoons¶	Albergaria	4	393	256
	3rd Prov. Dragoons	Nave**	4	328	208
Total			*12*	*1,051*	*768*
Trelliard's Dragoons	HQ	Cazillas de Flores		15	74

---

* Colonel Pierre Mourier, commander of the 15th Chasseurs.
† The 1st Hussars reported 42 men sick or as non-combatants (musicians, etc.).
‡ The 15th Chasseurs reported 68 men sick or as non-combatants.
§ The 1st Provisional Dragoons reported 7 men sick or as non-combatants.
¶ The 2nd Provisional Dragoons reported 12 men sick or as non-combatants.
** Koch says the 3rd Provisional Dragoons were at Novas, but this was probably a misspelling and they were at Nave.

Brigade	Regiment	Location	Sqdns	Men	Horses
1st (Lorcet)	3rd Dragoons*	Fuente Guinaldo	4	179	185
	6th Dragoons†	Novas Frias	4	508	520
Total			8	687	705
2nd (Cavrois)	10th Dragoons	Cuidad Rodrigo	4	224	233
	11th Dragoons‡	Puebla de Azava	4	571	525
Total			8	795	758
3rd (*Ornano*)	15th Dragoons§	Fuente Guinaldo	4	489	470
	25th Dragoons¶	Sabugal	4	556	501
Total			8	1,045	971
Army of Portugal total*			**55**	**5,292**	**4,700**

Although the cavalry of the Army of Portugal could muster close to 5,300 men and 4,700 horses on 1 April, the number of horses fit for campaigning was significantly less. A month later, the Army of Portugal could only field 2,200 mounted troops from the regiments that had returned from Portugal in April. This was less than 50 per cent of those listed being available on 1 April.

In late April the British army was threatening Ciudad Rodrigo and Marshal Massena brought the Army of Portugal together to protect it. Despite the threat from the British, General Soult was transferred from the command of the 2nd Corps's Light Cavalry Division to the Army of the South on 1 May. The division could barely muster a regiment's worth of troops two days later at the battle of Fuentes de Oñoro on 3 May. It was commanded by Colonel d'Ermenonville, of the 8th Dragoons. The 8th Corps's Provisional Dragoon Brigade was not present, nor were the Hanoverian Chasseurs. Although Marshal Bessières, commander of the Army of the North, brought down two brigades of cavalry to support the Army of Portugal, he had to leave a significant portion of the two brigades behind to protect his supply lines. General Lepic's Imperial Guard Cavalry Brigade was present, but he left two squadrons of the Empress Dragoons in Burgos. Likewise General Watier only brought his 1st Provisional Light Cavalry Regiment and the 28th Chasseurs, leaving the 9th Hussars in Navarre.

At the battle of Fuentes de Oñoro, 3–5 May the two armies were able to field almost 4,800 troopers, a third of them from the Army of the North.

---

* The 3rd Dragoons reported 32 men sick or as non-combatants.
† The 6th Dragoons reported 93 men sick or as non-combatants.
‡ The 11th Dragoons reported 118 men sick or as non-combatants.
§ The 15th Dragoons reported 16 men sick or as non-combatants.
¶ The 25th Dragoons reported 36 men sick or as non-combatants.
** Of which 424 men were sick or non-combatants.

Table 3.13   French cavalry at Fuentes de Oñoro, 3–5 May 1811

Corps	Brigade	Regiment	Men
Army of Portugal			
2nd	*d'Ermenonville*	1st Hussars	103
		22nd Chasseurs	360
		8th Dragoons	216
Total			*679*
6th	Mourier	3rd Hussars	164
		15th Chasseurs	170
Total			*334*
Cavalry Reserve	Lorcet	3rd Dragoons	93
		6th Dragoons	326
Total			*419*
	Cavrois	10th Dragoons	138
		11th Dragoons	178
Total			*316*
	Ornano	15th Dragoons	230
		25th Dragoons	222
Total			*452*
	Fournier	7th Chasseurs	282
		13th Chasseurs	270
		20th Chasseurs	242
Total			*794*
Total in the Army of Portugal			***2,994***
Army of the North			
	Lepic	Chasseurs of the Guard	235
		Polish Lancers	370
		Mamelukes	79
		Horse Grenadiers	197
Total			*881*
	Watier	1st Prov. Light Cavalry	784
		28th Chasseurs	150
Total			*934*
Total cavalry of the Army of the North			***1,815***
Total French cavalry at Fuentes de Oñoro			***4,809***

The Army of the South also had major changes in its organisation in the first six months of 1811. The dragoon divisions were still attached to the 1st and 4th Corps. The 1st Dragoon Division, which had eight regiments in four brigades, but only two generals to command its brigades, was reorganised into three brigades. The 20th Dragoons was reassigned from the 3rd Dragoon Division to the 1st Brigade of the 1st Dragoon Division. The 1st Dragoon Regiment was attached to the 1st Corps. Marshal Mortier, the commander of the 5th Corps, departed for France at the beginning of May and General Tour-Maubourg was given temporary command of the corps.

The cavalry of the Army of the South spent much of the first six months of 1811 in the field. The 1st Dragoon Division was particularly busy in western Estremadura, where they fought numerous skirmishes and battles, in the vicinity of Badajoz (February–March), Gebora (19 February), Campo Mayor (25 March), Albuera (16 May), Usagre (25 May) and Elvas (22 June). Much of the time, Briche's Brigade from the 5th Corps was also with them. The 3rd Dragoon Division, as well as General Perreimond's Brigade, were deployed in south-east protecting Grenada and Malaga Provinces. General Beaumont's Brigade was part of the force covering Cadiz and its 1st Dragoons fought at Barrosa (5 March).

Table 3.14 Organisation of the French cavalry in the Army of the South, spring 1811

Corps	Division	Brigade	Regiment
1st	1st Dragoon (Tour-Maubourg)	1st (Bron)	4th Dragoons
			20th Dragoons
			26th Dragoons
		2nd (Bouvier des Eclaz)	14th Dragoons
			17th Dragoons
			27th Dragoons
		3rd (*Quenot*)	2nd Dragoons
			9th Dragoons
1st		Beaumont	1st Dragoons
			2nd Hussars
			5th Chasseurs
4th	3rd Dragoon (Milhaud)	1st (Noirot)	5th Dragoons
			12th Dragoons

Table 3.14 continued

Corps Division	Brigade	Regiment
	2nd (*Corbineau*)	16th Dragoons
		21st Dragoons
	Perreimond	10th Chasseurs
		27th Chasseurs
		1st Vistula Lancers
5th	Briche	10th Hussars
		21st Chasseurs

In early May Marshal Soult, the commander of the Army of the South organised a force to go to the relief of Badajoz. The city had been captured by the French in March, but was being besieged by British and Portuguese forces under Marshal Beresford since April. Much of the infantry of the Army of the South was involved in operations at Cadiz or holding key cities, so only the 1st and 5th Corps would march. Marshal Soult relieved General Tour-Maubourg of his duties as the 5th Corps commander and appointed him commander of all of the cavalry in the relief expedition. The cavalry consisted of the 1st and 2nd Brigades of the 1st Dragoon Division, the 4th Corps's Light Cavalry Brigade with only two of its regiments and the 5th Corps's Light Cavalry Brigade which was reinforced with the 2nd Hussars from the 1st Corps. Total cavalry was a little over 4,000 men in 12 regiments.

Command and control of the cavalry rested with General Tour-Maubourg. For all practical purposes, he commanded a cavalry corps. He had only his normal division staff to do the functions of a corps staff. All three of the brigades were commanded by experienced generals; however, of the eleven French regiments that were under him, five were commanded by the senior chief of squadrons in the regiment. The twelfth regiment, the 4th Spanish Chasseurs, was commanded by a major.* Interestingly, Marshal Soult did not bring General Perreimond, the commander of the 4th Corps's Light Cavalry Brigade, despite the fact the brigade provided two of its three regiments to the force. Yet even with these problems, the cavalry performed superbly during the campaign.

---

* Dempsey, *Albuera*, pp. 270–1; the figures in table 3.15 are also taken from this book.

Table 3.15 Organisation of the French cavalry in the Albuera campaign, May 1811

Brigade	Regiment	Strength
1st (Bron)	4th Dragoons	406
	20th Dragoons	266
	26th Dragoons	421
Total		1,093
2nd (Bouvier des Eclaz)	14th Dragoons	316
	17th Dragoons	314
	27th Dragoons	249
Total		879
Briche	2nd Hussars	305
	10th Hussars	262
	21st Chasseurs	256
Total		823
Unattached	27th Chasseurs	431
	1st Vistula Lancers	591
	4th Spanish Chasseurs	195
Total		1,217
Total French cavalry in the Albuera campaign		*4,012*

June–December 1811

The latter half of 1811, saw operations along the Spanish–Portuguese border slow down considerably and by September most regiments were in cantonments. The cavalry continued to conduct counter-insurgency operations, but campaigning against the British was over for the year.

The Reorganisation of the Army of Portugal June–July 1811

On 26 May 1811 Napoleon wrote to Marshal Berthier telling him to 'Let General Marmont know that he has full powers to reorganise his army, to form it into six or seven divisions and to send back the generals who do not suit him . . .'* Marshal Marmont took the emperor at his word and by the end of June had disbanded the three corps and began cleaning house. General Lamotte, who had been relieved by Marshal Ney in April, was sent back to France. General Watier, the other light cavalry commander,

---

* Bonaparte, Napoleon. *The Confidential Correspondence.* vol. pp. 181–2.

would last only another month. At the end of July, he was promoted to general of division and he returned to the Army of the North in early September. General Lorcet, who commanded the 4th Dragoon Division's 1st Brigade, was seriously wounded at Fuentes de Oñoro and was sent back to France to recover. Only Generals Montbrun, Trelliard, Fournier-Sarlovèse and Cavrois were retained. Colonel Ornano, who commanded the 2nd Dragoon Brigade since March, was promoted to general of brigade in June and was also kept in command of his brigade. Yet even they did not last long. By the end of January all of these generals would be gone from the Army of Portugal.

Marshal Marmont also restructured the cavalry. All provisional dragoon regiments were disbanded and the cadres of the 3rd and 4th Squadrons were returned to France. The troopers were sent to their regiments to be incorporated into the other squadrons. The provisional dragoon regiments assigned to the 6th and 7th Governments were also dissolved by the end of the year. Additionally, the Hannover Chasseurs were disbanded, the cadres returning to the Regimental depot and the men being reassigned to the 1st Hussars.

General Montbrun stayed in overall command of the cavalry, while General Trelliard commanded the dragoons. The two light cavalry brigades were not formed into a division at this time.

Table 3.16   Cavalry in the Army of Portugal, August 1811

Brigade	Commander	Composition	Squadrons
1st Light Cavalry	Fournier	7th Chasseurs	3rd and 4th
		13th Chasseurs	3rd, 4th and 5th
		20th Chasseurs	3rd and 4th
2nd Light Cavalry	*Desfossés*	3rd Hussars	1st and 2nd
		22nd Chasseurs	1st, 2nd and 3rd
3rd Dragoon	Cavrois	3rd Dragoons	1st and 2nd
		8th Dragoons	1st and 2nd
		10th Dragoons	1st and 2nd
		15th Dragoons	1st, 2nd, 3rd 4th
4th Dragoon	Ornano	6th Dragoons	1st, 2nd and 3rd
		11th Dragoons	1st and 2nd
		25th Dragoons	1st, 2nd and 3rd

On 18 June 1811 Napoleon ordered the formation of lancer regiments. Instead of creating new regiments, six of the lancer regiments were formed by redesignating dragoon regiments as lancers. Five of those dragoon regiments were stationed in Spain, three of which were assigned to the

Army of Portugal. Only the cadres were sent back to France. The troopers and their horses were reassigned to other dragoon regiments. Sources vary on when the cadres departed for France, but all were in France by the end of the year.

Table 3.17   Regiments withdrawn from Spain to create the new lancer regiments, 1811

Regiment	Army assigned	New designation	Regiment troopers sent to
1st Dragoons	Army of the South	1st Lancers	?
3rd Dragoons	Army of Portugal	2nd Lancers	6th and 11th Dragoons
8th Dragoons	Army of Portugal	3rd Lancers	?
9th Dragoons	Army of the South	4th Lancers	?
10th Dragoons	Army of Portugal	5th Lancers	17th and 27th Dragoons
1st Vistula Lancers	Army of the South	7th Lancers*	Stayed with the regiment

In the Army of Portugal Marshal Marmont continued to shake up the cavalry chain of command. General Montbrun would remain in overall command of the cavalry. In October General Trelliard was released from his command and sent to the Army of the Centre, where he took command of the 3rd Dragoon Division. General Ornano was recalled to France and given a command of a light brigade in General Watier's Division in 1812. To replace these generals General Boyer, an infantry general, assumed command of the 4th Dragoon Brigade. When necessary General Cavrois would serve as the acting commander of the Dragoon Division. General Fournier-Sarlovèse was also deprived of his command when General Curto arrived from France and took command of the brigade. General Fournier-Sarlovèse was sent to the Army of Aragon for a new command.

In November several events caused the reorganisation of all the cavalry brigades. In the 1st Light Cavalry Brigade, the 7th and 20th Chasseurs were ordered to turn their squadrons over to the 13th Chasseurs. The 3rd and 4th Squadrons of the 7th Chasseurs were designated the 5th and 6th Squadrons of the 13th Chasseurs, while the 3rd and 4th Squadrons of the 20th Chasseurs became the 7th and 8th Squadrons of the 13th Chasseurs. The newly designated 5th Squadron was dissolved and the men incorporated into the 4th Squadron. The 2nd Light Cavalry Brigade was

---

* Unlike the other regiments, the 7th Lancers would stay in Spain until January 1813.

disbanded and the 3rd Hussars and the 22nd Chasseurs were transferred to the 1st Light Cavalry Brigade. Also in November, the cadres of the 3rd, 8th and 10th Dragoons departed for France to form the new lancer regiments. All three of the departing regiments came from the 1st Dragoon Brigade, so this caused a reorganisation of the dragoon brigades.

Most of the dragoon regiments had received replacements for the men lost in Portugal and averaged over 160 men per squadron. The 3rd Hussars had an average squadron strength of 260 men, while the 22nd Chasseurs had about 125 men per squadron. Due to the drafting of the men from the 7th and 20th Chasseurs into their ranks, the 13th Chasseurs could muster 830 men in five squadrons, for an average strength of 166 men for each squadron. The regiment received few replacements otherwise. By the end of 1811 the Army of Portugal had just over 4,000 men in its cavalry regiments.

Table 3.18   Cavalry of the Army of Portugal, November 1811

Brigade	Commander	Composition	No. Sqdns	Strength
1st Light Cavalry Brigade	Curto	3rd Hussars	2	523
		13th Chasseurs	5	830
		22nd Chasseurs	3	379
Total			*10*	*1,732*
1st Dragoon Brigade	Cavrois	6th Dragoons	4	622
		11th Dragoons	4	616
Total			*8*	*1,238*
2nd Dragoon Brigade	Boyer	15th Dragoons	4	659
		25th Dragoons	2	394
Total			*6*	*1,053*
Grand total			**24**	**4,023**

Cavalry in the Armies of the Aragon, Catalonia, the Centre and the North

On 10 March 1811 Napoleon authorised the transfer of all the troops in the Army of Catalonia that were in the field and not part of the garrisons in Catalonia to the Army of Aragon, which was commanded by General Suchet. This transfer included both the Italian and Neapolitan Divisions that had belonged to the 7th Corps. This meant that all cavalry regiments in the Army of Catalonia were transferred to the Army of Aragon, except for the 29th Chasseurs. The 3rd Provisional Cuirassiers were scheduled to be disbanded, so they returned to France. The expanded Army of Aragon received two new cavalry generals during the summer of 1811. Colonel

Jacques Delort, the commander of the 24th Dragoons, was promoted to general of brigade in July and would take command of the Light Cavalry Brigade. General Louis Maupoint, who was promoted on 6 August, arrived from France and assumed command of General Boussart's Brigade in December when General Boussart was seriously wounded in late December. In November the 9th Hussars were transferred to the Army of Aragon. The Army of Catalonia had a single chasseur regiment, whose squadrons were often operating separately in support of the infantry.

The Army of the Centre also underwent major changes. General Houssaye was recalled to France in July to take command of the 6th Dragoon Division in Germany. General Trelliard was transferred from the Army of Portugal to command the 4th Dragoon Division in October. Neither of its brigades had a general officer commanding it, since the 1st Brigade's commander, General Marizy, was killed the previous February. General Trelliard would also assume command of the German Division in October. For all practical purposes, he was commanding a combined arms corps. Fortunately for the Army of the Centre, the only threat to the security of central Spain was from guerrillas, so the fight was at the brigade and regimental level. General Trelliard could afford to divide his attention between the various commands.

In July General Poinsot, commander of the 3rd Provisional Dragoon Brigade was allowed to return to France and retire. In early August the Army of the North had three strong cavalry brigades, commanded by Generals Lepic, Watier and Laferrière. General Watier had been promoted to general of division the previous month and would command all the cavalry in the Army of the North. But like the Army of the Centre, the operations in northern Spain were mostly at the regimental level and there were few opportunities to exercise division command in the field. General Lepic, the commander of the Imperial Guard Cavalry Brigade, returned to France at the end of August and no replacement was named. Operational control of the brigade was kept by General Watier. The 1st Provisional Light Cavalry Regiment was also dissolved. The 4th Squadron of the 11th Chasseurs was assigned to the 6th Military Government in Valladolid. The 4th Squadron of the 12th Chasseurs was sent back to France, as was the 3rd Squadron of the 24th Chasseurs. The 4th Squadrons of the 24th Chasseurs and the 5th Hussars were assigned to the 7th Military Government in Salamanca. In September the 4th Squadrons of the 11th and 12th Chasseurs, as well as the 4th Squadron of the 5th Hussars became the nucleus of the new 31st Chasseur Regiment. The regiment would be part of General Laferrière's Brigade, which also included the veteran 15th Chasseurs and the 1st Squadron of the 1st Hussars.

Table 3.19   Organisation of the cavalry in the Armies of the Aragon, Catalonia, the Centre and the North, autumn 1811

Army	Division	Brigade	Regiment
Aragon		Boussart	13th Cuirassiers
			4th Hussars
		Delort	24th Dragoons
			1st Neapolitan Chasseurs
		Unattached	9th Hussars[*]
			Napoleon Dragoons
			1st Italian Chasseurs
			2nd Neapolitan Chasseurs
Catalonia			29th Chasseurs
			20th Chasseurs[†]
Centre	4th Dragoon (Trelliard)	1st (*Reiset*)[‡]	13th Dragoons
			22nd Dragoons
		2nd (*Mermet*)[§]	18th Dragoons
			19th Dragoons
		Unattached	26th Chasseurs
	German Division		Westphalian Lancers
			Nassau Light Horse
North		Laferrière	15th Chasseurs
			31st Chasseurs
			1st Hussars
		Watier	28th Chasseurs
			Lancers of Berg
		Imperial Guard	Heavy Cavalry Regiment
			Light Cavalry Regiment

Cavalry in the Army of the South July–December 1811

By July the Army of the South was in its cantonments and its mission reverted back to one of counter-insurgency. The cavalry was reorganised after Albuera and the two dragoon divisions were assigned to the 1st and 4th Corps. The squadrons and regiments would operate as part of combined

---

[*] The 9th Hussars were attached to General Reille's Division.
[†] The 2nd Squadron only.
[‡] Colonel Marie Reiset, commander of the 13th Dragoons.
[§] Colonel Joseph Merme, commander of the 18th Dragoons.

infantry and cavalry task forces in an effort to defeat the guerrillas and control the countryside. All of the brigades and divisions were commanded by general officers, except for the 2nd Brigade of the 3rd Dragoon Division. Additionally, the organisation of the cavalry had changed with several regiments being transferred between the corps, while four regiments were acting independently and were not assigned to any brigade.

Table 3.20 Cavalry in the Army of the South, July 1811

Corps	Division	Brigade	Regiments
1st	1st Dragoon (Tour-Maubourg)	1st (Bron)	1st Dragoons
			2nd Dragoons
			4th Dragoons
		2nd (Bouvier des Eclaz)	9th Dragoons
			14th Dragoons
			26th Dragoons
		Light Cavalry (Beaumont)	2nd Hussars
			5th Chasseurs
4th	3rd Dragoon (Milhaud)	1st (Noirot)	5th Dragoons
			12th Dragoons
			16th Dragoons
		2nd (*Corbineau*)	20th Dragoons
			21st Dragoons
		Light Cavalry (Perreimond)	10th Chasseurs
			7th Lancers
5th		Light Cavalry (Briche)	10th Hussars
			21st Chasseurs
Reserve		Unattached	17th Dragoons
			27th Dragoons
			27th Chasseurs
			4th Spanish Chasseurs

This organisation would soon change. On 12 July General Milhaud received permission from Marshal Soult to return to France. General Pierre Soult, the younger brother of the Army of the South's commander, was named provisional commander of the 3rd Dragoon Division. Colonel Jean Corbineau was promoted to general of brigade on 6 August 1811 and was recalled to France. General Tour-Maubourg was appointed the commander of the army's cavalry reserve and took three squadrons of the 4th Dragoons from the 1st Dragoon Brigade and the 2nd Dragoon Brigade with him, as well as the 1st Corps's Light Cavalry Brigade. They would be joined by the 17th and 27th Dragoons. General Perreimond was transferred from command of the 4th Corps's Light Cavalry Brigade to command of the 1st Dragoon Brigade of the 1st Dragoon Division. His brigade would be sorely depleted, for not only did he lose most of the 4th Dragoons to the army reserve, but dispatches had arrived ordering the 1st and 9th Dragoon Regiments back to France. The seven dragoon and one lancer regiments were formed into two brigades, commanded by Generals Bron and Bouvier des Eclaz. General Ormancey became the commander of the 4th Corps's Light Cavalry Brigade, when General Perreimond was transferred.

Table 3.21   Location of cavalry in the Army of the South, September 1811

Brigade	Regiment	Squadrons	September
1st Dragoon division, 1st Corps			
1st (Perreimond)	2nd Dragoons	3	Conil
	4th Dragoons	1	Xeres
3rd Dragoon Division (Soult), 4th Corps			
	HQ		Lumbreras
1st (Noirot)	5th Dragoons	4	Lumbreras
	12th Dragoons	2	Grenade
	16th Dragoons	4	Velez Blanco
2nd (?)	21st Dragoons	2	Malaga
Light Cavalry (Ormancey)	HQ		Lumbreras
	10th Chasseurs	4	Lumbreras
5th Corps			
Light Cavalry (Briche)	10th Hussars	4	Almendralejo
	21st Chasseurs	3	Iregenal
	27th Chasseurs	3	Almendralejo
Reserve Cavalry (Tour-Maubourg)			
	HQ		Seville
1st (Bron)	17th Dragoons	4	Cordoba
	20th Dragoons	4	Almendralejo
	27th Dragoons	4	Jaen
	7th Lancers	4	Seville
2nd (Bouvier des Eclaz)	4th Dragoons	3	Niebla
	14th Dragoons	3	Ecija
	26th Dragoons	3	Almendralejo
Light Cavalry (Beaumont)	2nd Hussars,	3	Almendralejo
	5th Chasseurs	3	Arcos

By October, the cavalry had undergone additional changes. The previous month General Noirot gave up command of the 1st Brigade of the 3rd Dragoon Division and returned to France. He was not replaced. The 2nd Brigade of the 3rd Dragoon Division cease to exist for all practical purposes in October, when its sole remaining regiment, the 21st Dragoons, were attached to the General Barrois's 2nd Infantry of the Reserve. The 2nd Hussars were reassigned from the reserves back to the 5th Corps.

Table 3.22   Cavalry in the Army of the South, October 1811

Brigade	Regiment	Squadrons	September
1st Dragoon Division, 1st Corps			
1st (Perreimond)	2nd Dragoons	3	Conil
	4th Dragoons	1	Xeres
3rd Dragoon Division (Soult), 4th Corps			
	HQ		Huescar
1st (*Ruat*)*	5th Dragoons	4	Huescar
	12th Dragoons	2	Grenade
	16th Dragoons	4	Velez Rubio
Light Cavalry (Ormancey)	HQ		Huescar
	10th Chasseurs	4	Huescar
5th Corps			
Light Cavalry (Briche)	2nd Hussars	3	Merida
	10th Hussars	1st, 2nd, 3rd	Merida
	10th Hussars	4th	Almendralejo
	21st Chasseurs	3	Fregenal
	27th Chasseurs	1st, 2nd, 4th	Almendralejo
	27th Chasseurs	3rd	Fregonal
Reserve Cavalry (Tour-Maubourg)			
	HQ		Seville
1st (Bron)	17th Dragoons	4	Cordoba
	20th Dragoons	4	Almendralejo
	27th Dragoons	4	Jaen
	7th Lancers	4	Utrera
2nd (Bouvier des Eclaz)	4th Dragoons	3	Niebla
	14th Dragoons	3	Ecija
	26th Dragoons	3	Almendralejo
	5th Chasseurs	3	Arcos
Barrois's Division	21st Dragoons	4	Malaga

---

* Colonel Jean Ruat, commander of the 21st Dragoons.

Although these were the administrative groupings of the cavalry, in reality the regiments and brigades were allocated to various commands as the situation or mission required. A good example of this was in October, when General Girard took an expedition deep into Estremadura. It consisted of his own division from the 5th Corps and parts of two cavalry brigades General Briche's Brigade, with the 10th and 27th Chasseurs and General Bron's Brigade, consisting of the 20th Dragoons, from the Army of the South's Cavalry Reserve. This force was surprised on 28 October at Arroyo dos Molinos by a British and Portuguese force commanded by General Hill. It was badly mauled and General Bron was captured.

By late October word had reached the Army of the South with news of promotions. Colonels Bonnemains (5th Chasseurs), Konopka (7th Lancers) and Lallemand (27th Dragoons) were promoted to general of brigade and given commands. About the same time General Bouvier des Eclaz was recalled to France, for duty with the Grande Armée. General Perreimond took command of the 2nd Dragoon Brigade in the Cavalry Reserve, while General Bonnemains took over General Perreimond's brigade. The 5th Dragoons were transferred to the control of General Ormancey, while the 2nd Hussars assigned to the 5th Corps. Additionally, General Beaumont, the commander of the 1st Corps Light Cavalry Brigade was recalled to France for service in Russia. His brigade was dissolved on his departure.

Table 3.23   Cavalry in the Army of the South, 16 November 1811

Brigade	Regiment	Squadrons	Location
1st Corps			
(Bonnemains)	2nd Dragoons	1st	Conil
	2nd Dragoons	2nd	Medina
	2nd Dragoons	3rd	Conil
	5th Chasseurs	3	Santa Maria
3rd Dragoon Division (Soult), 4th Corps			
	HQ		Baza
Dragoon (*Ruat*)	12th Dragoons	1st	Grenada
	12th Dragoons	2nd, 3rd, 4th	Mobile Column
	16th Dragoons	1st	Armilla
	16th Dragoons	2nd, 3rd, 4th	Garcia and Grenada
	21st Dragoons	4	Malaga
Light Cavalry	HQ		Baeza
(Ormancey)	10th Chasseurs	4	Huescar
	5th Dragoons	4	Baeza

Brigade	Regiment	Squadrons	Location
5th Corps			
Light Cavalry	2nd Hussars	3	Seville
(Briche)	10th Hussars	3	Merida
	21st Chasseurs	3	Santa Martha
	27th Chasseurs	3	Merida
	27th Chasseurs	3rd	Fregonal
Reserve Cavalry (Tour-Maubourg)			
	HQ		Seville
1st (Lallemand)	17th Dragoons	4	Cordoba
	20th Dragoons	4	Marchena
	27th Dragoons	2	Jaen
	27th Dragoons	2	Seville
2nd	4th Dragoons	3	Niebla
(Perreimond)	14th Dragoons	3	Ecija
	26th Dragoons	3	Seville
Light Cavalry			
(Konopka)	7th Lancers	4	Utrera

In December the Imperial Guard Cavalry Brigade was ordered to return to France in preparation for the imminent war with Russia. General Watier, who commanded the cavalry of the Army of the North, was also recalled to France for duty with the Grande Armée in Eastern Europe.

1812

In late December 1811 Marshal Soult received orders from Napoleon to reorganise the Army of the South. The 1st, 4th and 5th Corps were to be disbanded. The army's headquarters would have direct control over the infantry divisions. The cavalry were officially reorganised into three divisions and redesignated the 1st, 2nd and 3rd Cavalry Divisions. In January General Konopka was recalled to France for service with the Grande Armée. On 7 February the new organisation went into effect.

Table 3.24   The new cavalry divisions of the Army of the South, 7 February 1812

Division	Brigade	Regiment
1st (Perreimond)	1st (Lallemand)	2nd Hussars
		10th Hussars
		21st Chasseurs
		26th Dragoons
	2nd (Bonnemains)	2nd Dragoons
		5th Chasseurs

Table 3.24 continued

Division	Brigade	Regiment
2nd (Tour-Maubourg)	1st (Digeon)	14th Dragoons
		17th Dragoons
		27th Dragoons
		7th Lancers
	2nd (Briche)	4th Dragoons
		5th Dragoons
	Unattached	20th Dragoons
3rd (Soult)	1st (Bouillé)	12th Dragoons
		16th Dragoons
		21st Dragoons
	2nd (Ormancey)	10th Chasseurs
		21st Chasseurs
		27th Chasseurs

On 22 February Marshal Soult was ordered to send the 10th Hussars, the 20th Dragoons and the cadres of the 4th Squadrons of the 2nd, 5th, 12th and 17th Dragoons back to France. The 10th Hussars and the cadres of the 4th Squadrons were in Bayonne by 22 March, but the 20th Dragoons were diverted and assigned to the Army of the North.

In addition to their military duties, many of the generals in the Army of the South were also governors and commandants of provinces and cities. They were responsible for overseeing the civil government while maintaining order and security.

Table 3.25   Cavalry generals in the Army of the South who served as provincial governors or commandants of cities, February 1812

Name	Province or City
Jean Berton*	Osuna
Alexandre Digeon	Cordova
François Lallemand	Jaen
Jean Maransin	Malaga
François Ormancey	Antequera
Jacques Tilly	Xeres

* Jean Berton was an adjutant commandant and would be promoted to general of brigade on 30 May 1813.

In March the cavalry of the Army of the South went through another reorganisation. In the 2nd Division General Tour-Maubourg was recalled to France to take command of the 4th Cavalry Corps in Eastern Europe. Orders also came in February relieving General Briche of his command for his part in the disaster at Arroyo dos Molinos the previous October. He was sent back to France. General Digeon took command of the 2nd Division, but would not be officially appointed its commander until October! General Lallemand would transfer from the command of the 2nd Brigade of the 1st Cavalry Division to command the 1st Brigade of the 2nd Cavalry Division, while Colonel Sparre of the 5th Dragoons became the acting commander of the 2nd Brigade.

There was also a shortage of experienced leadership at the brigade and division level in the other armies in Spain. In the Army of Aragon General Boussart was seriously wounded the previous December and had to relinquish command of his brigade. The situation in the Army of the Centre was similar to that in the Army of Aragon. Neither of the brigades in General Trelliard's Dragoon Division were commanded by generals and the two colonels who served as the acting brigade commanders had limited experience at regimental command. Colonel Reiset had commanded for 18 months, while Colonel Rozat had been in command 21 months. This lack of general officers had caused a reorganisation of the brigades in the division. For the first time since the 1805 Austerlitz campaign, the 13th and 22nd Dragoons would no longer be in the same brigade, nor would the 18th and 19th Dragoons which had had also been together since 1805. Both of the colonels in the 18th and 19th Dragoons had less experience at command than Colonels Reiset and Rozat, having only assumed command of their regiments in October 1811. General Trelliard had to move the 18th Regiment to his 1st Brigade and the 22nd Regiment to his 2nd Brigade, to have his most experienced officers at the head of his brigades. In addition to commanding the cavalry of the Army of the Centre, General Trelliard was also the commander of the German Division, which was composed of the infantry regiments from the Confederation of the Rhine.

The cavalry divisions and brigades of the Army of Portugal were even in worst shape. General Montbrun had been recalled to France in January, while General Cavrois was relieved for insubordination. With their departure all the old generals in the Army of Portugal were gone. No one was sent out to replace them, so General Boyer, an infantry officer, who commanded the 2nd Dragoon Brigade, became its acting commander. February also saw General Carrié being appointed as the 2nd Brigade commander. He was an experienced commander who had led a cavalry brigade in 1808, but in late February 1810 he became governor of Palencia. That month the Light Cavalry Division was formed with General Curto as the acting commander. He had little experience as a brigade commander, having only been promoted to general the previous August. Neither of the brigades in the Light Cavalry Division had a general commanding them. The 2nd Brigade was formed with the 26th Chasseurs, from the Army of the Centre and the 3rd and 4th Squadrons of the 14th Chasseurs, which had first entered Spain in December 1811. In the Army of the North the two Imperial Guard Regiments had been recalled to France and would be gone from the Peninsula by April.

Table 3.26   Cavalry divisions and brigades in Spain, March 1812

Army	*Commander*	*Brigade*	*Regiment*
Aragon		Delort	4th Hussars
			24th Dragoons
		Maupoint	13th Cuirassiers
			Neapolitan Chasseurs[*]
			1st Italian Chasseurs
		Unattached	Napoleon Dragoons
		Unattached	9th Hussars (bis)[†]
Catalonia			29th Chasseurs
			20th Chasseurs
Centre	Trelliard	1st (*Reiset*)[‡]	13th Dragoons
			18th Dragoons
		2nd (*Rozat*)[§]	19th Dragoons
			22nd Dragoons
	German Division		Westphalian Lancers
			Nassau Light Horse
North		Laferrière	15th Chasseurs
			31st Chasseurs
			1st Hussars
			Lancers of Berg
	Bonet's		28th Chasseurs
		Unattached	20th Dragoons

---

[*] Was a combined force of two weak squadrons from the 1st and 2nd Neapolitan Chasseurs.

[†] The 9th Hussars were redesignated as the 9th Hussars (bis) on 9 January 1812. For all practical purposes, the three squadrons in Spain became a separate regiment from the 9th Hussars, which were located in Alsace. The regiment's 2nd Squadron was serving with the Army of Aragon, while the 3rd and 4th Squadrons were assigned to the 3rd Military Government.

[‡] Colonel Marie Reiset, commander of the 13th Dragoons.

[§] Colonel Nicolas Rozat, commander of the 22nd Dragoons.

Army	Commander	Brigade	Regiment
Portugal	Curto	1st (*Desfossés*)	3rd Hussars
			13th Chasseurs
			22nd Chasseurs
		2nd (*Vial*)*	14th Chasseurs
			26th Chasseurs
	Boyer[†]	1st (*Picquet*)[‡]	6th Dragoons
			11th Dragoons
		2nd (Carrié)[§]	15th Dragoons
			25th Dragoons
South	1st (Perreimond)	1st (*Vinot*)[¶]	2nd Hussars
			21st Chasseurs
			26th Dragoons
		2nd (Bonnemains)	2nd Dragoons
			5th Chasseurs
	2nd (Digeon)	1st (Lallemand)	14th Dragoons
			17th Dragoons
			27th Dragoons
			7th Lancers
		2nd (*Sparre*)**	4th Dragoons
			5th Dragoons
	3rd (Soult)	1st (Bouillé)	12th Dragoons
			16th Dragoons
			21st Dragoons
		2nd (Ormancey)	10th Chasseurs
			27th Chasseurs

In April Colonel Sparre was promoted to general of brigade and given command of the 1st Brigade in the 3rd Cavalry Division. The former commander, General Bouillé, was having health problems and relinquished command. Colonel Bouquerot des Essarts, commander of the 4th Dragoons, became the acting commander of the 2nd Brigade of the 2nd Cavalry Division. The 7th Lancers were transferred to the 1st Brigade

* Colonel Jacques Vial, commander of the 26th Chasseurs.
[†] As the senior general in the division, General Boyer was the acting commander of the division and took command in February 1812. He was the permanent commander of the 1st Brigade.
[‡] Colonel Cyrille Picquet, commander of the 6th Dragoons.
[§] Took command in early February 1812.
[¶] Colonel Gilbert Vinot, commander of the 2nd Hussars.
** Colonel Louis Sparre, commander of the 5th Dragoons.

of the 3rd Cavalry Division. The 28th Chasseurs were transferred from the Army of the North to the Army of Portugal in June.

The French armies in Spain in early July could muster almost 20,000 men in 134 squadrons.

Table 3.27 Number of squadrons and soldiers in the cavalry of the French Armies in Spain, 1 July 1812

Army	No. sqdns	Strength	Av. strength of sqdns
Aragon	22	3071	140
Catalonia	3	597	199
Centre	22	2,680	122
North	17	1,990	117
Portugal	22	3,773	171
South	50	7,773	152
Total	*136*	*19,884*	*146*

Of 20,000 cavalry of all ranks serving in the French armies, 17,700 men and 116 squadrons were French. A French cavalry squadron was authorised around 250 officers and men, depending on the type of regiment. (Beginning in 1811 a dragoon squadron's organisation changed, being authorised only 218 men compared with276 previously.) The average French cavalry squadron in Spain had 153 men or 63 per cent of its authorised strength. The dragoon squadrons of the Army of the Centre were particularly weak, averaging only 127 men or 58 per cent of their authorised strength. The dragoon squadrons of the 2nd Brigade of the 2nd Cavalry Division were at 94 per cent of authorised strength. Both of these brigades were in the Army of the South. The dragoon squadrons of the 1st Brigade of General Boyer's Division in the Army of Portugal were at 89 per cent strength. This was offset by the fact that the two regiments were only two squadron regiments and the brigade itself was one of the weaker ones in the army, mustering only 865 men. The division's 2nd Brigade had only 631 men and was the weakest cavalry brigade in Spain.

Table 3.28 Cavalry regimental strength in the French armies in Spain, 1 July 1812

Army	Division	Brigade	Regiment	Sqdns	Strength
Aragon		Delort	4th Hussars	4	521
			24th Dragoons	3	417
Total				*7*	*938*

Army	Division	Brigade	Regiment	Sqdns	Strength
		Maupoint	13th Cuirassiers	4	655
			Neapolitan Chasseurs	2	150
			1st Italian Chasseurs	3	300
Total				9	*1,105*
			9th Hussars (bis)*	3	578
			Napoleon Dragoons	3	450
Catalonia			29th Chasseurs	3	597
Centre	Trelliard	1st (*Reiset*)	13th Dragoons	3	350
			18th Dragoons	3	425
Total				6	*775*
		2nd (*Rozat*)	19th Dragoons	3	300
			22nd Dragoons	3	450
Total				6	*750*
Centre	Merlin		Nassau Light Horse	1	155
			Westphalian Lancers	3	250
			Spanish Guard Light Horse	3	450
Total				5	*855*
Centre			Miscellaneous Spanish Cavalry	3	300
North		Laferrière	15th Chasseurs	4	480
			31st Chasseurs	3	336
			1st Hussars	3	410
			Lancers of Berg	2	254
				12	*1,480*
Total			20th Dragoons	3	260
			15th Dragoons†	2	250
Portugal	Curto	1st (*Desfossés*)	13th Chasseurs	5	996
			22nd Chasseurs	2	203
			3rd Hussars	2	392
Total				9	*1,591*
		2nd (*Vial*)	14th Chasseurs	2	322
			26th Chasseurs	2	230
			28th Chasseurs	1	134
Total				5	*686*
Portugal	Boyer	1st (*Picquet*)	6th Dragoons	2	435

---

* Strength report of 1 October 1812.
† 3rd and 4th Squadrons, estimated strength of 250 men.

Table 3.28   continued

Army	Division	Brigade	Regiment	Sqdns	Strength
			11th Dragoons	2	430
Total				4	*865*
		2nd (Carrié)	15th Dragoons	2	288
			25th Dragoons	2	350
Total				4	*631*
South	1st (Perreimond)	1st (*Vinot*)	21st Chasseurs	3	239
			26th Dragoons	3	554
			2nd Hussars	3	308
Total				9	*1,101*
		2nd (Bonnemains)	2nd Dragoons	3	466
			5th Chasseurs	3	625
Total				6	*1,091*
South	2nd (Digeon)	1st (Lallemand)	14th Dragoons	3	591
			17th Dragoons	3	373
			27th Dragoons	2	271
			7th Lancers	4	652
Total				12	*1,887*
		2nd (*Bouquerot des Essarts*)	4th Dragoons	3	667
			5th Dragoons	3	568
Total				6	*1,235*
South	3rd (Soult)	1st (Sparre)	12th Dragoons	3	533
			16th Dragoons	4	610
			21st Dragoons	3	462
Total				10	*1,605*
		2nd (Ormancey)	10th Chasseurs	4	617
			27th Chasseurs	3	237
Total				7	*854*
Grand total				*136*	*19,884*

The cavalry of the Army of Portugal would be plagued by leadership problems throughout the Salamanca campaign during the summer of 1812. On 18 July General Carrié, the commander of the 2nd Dragoon Brigade in General Boyer's Division, was seriously wounded and captured by the British. He was replaced by Colonel Boudinhon-Valdec, of the 15th Dragoons. At the battle of Salamanca on 22 July, the acting brigade commander of the 1st Brigade of General Curto's Division, Colonel Desfossés, was seriously wounded, as well as the commander of the 3rd Hussars, Colonel Rousseau. Colonel Shée, the commander of the 13th Chasseurs assumed command. In General Boyer's Division, the 1st Brigade's commander, Colonel Picquet, and the 25th Dragoon's commander, Colonel Leclerc, were both seriously wounded. Colonel Thévenez d'Aoust would become acting commander of the 1st Brigade.

Compounding these problems was the number of chiefs of squadrons that became casualties. In the 2nd Brigade of General Boyer's Division, one of the two chiefs of squadrons in the 26th Chasseurs was wounded, which meant since the regimental commander was also the brigade commander, the regiment was down to one senior officer. In the single squadron of the 28th Chasseurs, its commanding officer, Chief of Squadrons Vallière, was wounded. In the 1st Brigade of General Boyer's Division, the senior unscathed officer in the 6th Dragoons was a lieutenant. Colonel Picquet, who was also the brigade commander, was wounded, as well as the two Chiefs of Squadron, Davout and Lecomte and all four captains. In the 2nd Brigade of the division, the 25th Dragoons had two of its captains wounded.

Although the Army of the South did not fight in the Salamanca campaign, it too lost one of its regimental commanders during the summer. Colonel Larcher of the 17th Dragoons was killed in a duel on 18 July. In the Army of the Centre, General Trelliard lost his 1st Brigade commander at Majalahona on 11 August, when Colonel Reiset of the 13th Dragoons was so badly wounded that he had to return to France to recover.

Chapter Four

The Long Retreat
(August 1812–April 1814)

The British offensive of 1812 had devastated the French Armies of the Centre and of Portugal. After their crushing defeat at Salamanca the French were forced to evacuate and retreat north towards France and by mid-September the great French supply depot at Burgos was under siege. The Army of the Centre had retreated eastward towards Valencia, while the Army of Portugal was deployed along the Ebro River. Marshal Soult had evacuated Andalusia but on 16 September was still in Granada. The destruction of the pontoon bridge across the Duero River at Almaraz by the British under General Hill on 19 May forced the Army of the South to march towards the east and they linked up with King Joseph and the Army of the Centre at Almanza on 2 October. The 1st Cavalry Division was in the vicinity of Tobarra, the 2nd Cavalry Division was near Alpera and the 3rd Cavalry Division had its headquarters at Yecla. By late October the French were in position to begin offensive operations. For the first time since 1809 the French armies were operating in unison. The Duke of Wellington realised that his forces, which stretched from Madrid to Burgos, could not beat the unified French force and ordered General Hill to evacuated Madrid while he lifted the siege of Burgos. Over the next month the British would retreat to the Portuguese border, vigorously pursued by the French cavalry all the way.

Considering the setbacks of the year, on paper the French positions at the end of 1812 did not look too bad. The Army of Portugal was back in its former area of operations centered on Salamanca and the Army of the Centre occupied Madrid, Segovia and Guadalajara. Marshal Suchet and his forces were still holding Aragon, while General Decaen held Catalonia. Strategically, however, the French position was weakened considerably. In the west the border fortresses of Badajoz and Cuidad Rodrigo had fallen and the French no longer controlled southern Spain. The two-year siege of Cadiz had been lifted and Seville, abandoned. Marshal Soult and his

Army of the South would finish the year in the vicinity of Toledo.

The French cavalry in the autumn of 1812 consisted of 16 brigades, which were organised into six divisions. The Army of the North had two brigades, one of which had been sent to support the Army of Portugal. On 8 September General Mermet, who had been seriously wounded the year before, returned to Spain and took command of the Army of Portugal's Light Cavalry Division. On 10 October General Perreimond, commander of the Army of the South's 1st Light Cavalry Division, received permission to retire and left for France later in the month. This was not the only change of command in the Army of the South. The same day that General Perreimond was given permission to retire General Digeon was confirmed as the commander of the 1st Dragoon Division and General Soult as commander of the 2nd Dragoon Division. Only General Soult's 2nd Dragoon Division had its full complement of general officers. Eight of the 16 cavalry brigades were commanded by the senior regimental commander. Both brigades in General Trelliard's Division were commanded by colonels. Some histories have the cavalry in the Army of Aragon organised into a division, with General Boussart as the commander. However, he had been seriously wounded the previous December and never took a field command again. Most operations in eastern Spain were at brigade level and there would have been no need to form a division.

Table 4.1   Cavalry divisions and brigades in Spain, 15 October 1812

Division	Brigade	Regiment
Army of Aragon		
	Delort	4th Hussars
		24th Dragoons
	Maupoint	13th Cuirassiers
		Neapolitan Chasseurs
	Unattached	9th Hussars (bis)*
		1st Italian Chasseurs
Army of Catalonia		
		29th Chasseurs
Army of the Centre		
Trelliard	1st (*Dard*)†	13th Dragoons
		18th Dragoons
	2nd (*Rozat*)	19th Dragoons
		22nd Dragoons

* The 9th Hussars were attached to General Reille's Division.
† Colonel François Dard, commander of the 18th Dragoons.

Table 4.1   continued

Division	Brigade	Regiment
	Unattached	Napoleon Dragoons
	Unattached	Westphalian Lancers
	Unattached	Nassau Light Horse
Army of the North		
	Laferrière	15th Chasseurs
		Lancers of Berg
	Unattached	20th Dragoons*
Army of Portugal		
Mermet†	1st (Curto)	3rd Hussars
		22nd Chasseurs
		26th Chasseurs
		28th Chasseurs‡
	2nd (*Shée*)	13th Chasseurs
		14th Chasseurs
	(*Merlin*)§	1st Hussars
		31st Chasseurs
Boyer	1st (*Thévenez d'Aoust*)¶	6th Dragoons
		11th Dragoons
	2nd (*Boudinhon-Valdec*)**	15th Dragoons
		25th Dragoons
Army of the South		
1st Dragoon Division (Digeon)††	1st (Lallemand)	2nd Dragoons
		4th Dragoons
		26th Dragoons
	2nd (*Ludot*)‡‡	14th Dragoons
		17th Dragoons
		27th Dragoons
2nd Dragoon Division (Soult)§§	1st (Sparre)	5th Dragoons

---

* Attached to Abbé's Division.
† Took command 8 September 1812.
‡ The 28th Chasseurs was down to 3 officers and 18 men.
§ The brigade was attached from the Army of the North and was commanded by Colonel Antoine Merlin, commander of the 1st Hussars.
¶ Colonel François Thévenez d'Aoust, commander of the 11th Dragoons.
** Colonel Jean Boudinhon-Valdec, commander of the 15th Dragoons.
†† Took command 10 October 1812.
‡‡ Colonel Denis Ludot, commander of the 14th Dragoons.
§§ Took command 10 October 1812.

Division	Brigade	Regiment
		12th Dragoons
		7th Lancers
	2nd (Ormancey)	16th Dragoons
		21st Dragoons
1st Light Cavalry Division (Tilly)*	1st (*Vinot*)	2nd Hussars
		10th Chasseurs
		21st Chasseurs
	2nd (Bonnemains)	5th Chasseurs
		27th Chasseurs

In November General Ormancey was transferred from command of the 2nd Brigade of the 2nd Dragoon Division and given command of the 2nd Brigade of the 1st Dragoon Division. Colonel Ruat, commander of the 21st Dragoons, took command of the 2nd Brigade of the 2nd Dragoon Division. In December General Mermet was appointed commander of all cavalry in the Army of Portugal.

1813

By January 1813 the cavalry of the French armies were deployed in a broad arc from Bilbao in the north to south-west towards Zamora and Salamanca and then sweeping east towards Madrid and Toledo. General Trelliard's Division in the Army of the Centre had the senior regimental commanders serving as brigade commanders. Two of the three Westphalian Lancers' squadrons returned to Germany in February. In the Army of Portugal General Mermet was appointed commander of all the Army's cavalry, but retained command of the light cavalry division. General Boyer's dragoon division had no generals to command its brigades, so it too had the senior regimental commanders as the commanders. The 1st Dragoon Division and 3rd Light Cavalry Division of the Army of the South, had acting commanders, while the 2nd Dragoon Division had only one brigade commanded by a general. The Army of Aragon's three cavalry brigades were commanded by generals. In an unusual move the 9th Hussars (bis) were redesignated as the 12th Hussars on 17 February 1813. In the Army of Catalonia the 29th Chasseurs were parcelled out in company and squadron size formations and attached to the infantry. The Army of North had five cavalry regiments, but in February General Laferrière was recalled to France and the brigade was commanded by Colonel Merlin.

---

* General Perreimond retired on 10 October; General Tilly took temporary command.

By April 1813, the cavalry of the Army of the South had gone through a major shuffling of its commanders, as well as a renaming of its divisions. The 1st and 2nd Cavalry Divisions were renamed the 1st and 2nd Dragoon Divisions, while the 3rd Cavalry Division was renamed the 1st Light Cavalry Division. In April General Bonnemains was recalled to France and replaced by the newly promoted General Vinot. On 7 April General Soult was confirmed in command of the 1st Light Cavalry Division, while General Digeon was transferred from the 1st Dragoon Division to become the commander of the 2nd Dragoon Division. General Tilly, who had been the provisional commander of the 1st Light Cavalry Division, took over the 1st Dragoon Division. He would be confirmed in command on 1 May. In General Tilly's 1st Dragoon Division, Colonel Ismert had been promoted in February to general of brigade.

Table 4.2 Cavalry divisions and independent brigades in Spain, spring 1813

Division	Brigade	Regiment
Army of Aragon		
	1st (Delort)	4th Hussars
		24th Dragoons
	2nd (Maupoint)	13th Cuirassiers
	Unattached	12th Hussars
		1st Italian Chasseurs
Army of Catalonia		
		29th Chasseurs
Army of Centre		
Trelliard	1st (*Dard*)	13th Dragoons
		18th Dragoons
	2nd (*Rozat*)	19th Dragoons
		22nd Dragoons
	Avy[*]	Nassau Light Horse
		Westphalian Lancers[†]
Army of North		
		20th Dragoons[‡]
	Merlin	1st Hussars
		15th Chasseurs
		31st Chasseurs

---

[*] Took command March 1813

[†] One squadron only, the other two returned to Germany in February.

[‡] Assigned to General Abbé's Infantry Division.

Division	Brigade	Regiment
	Unattached	Napoleon Dragoons*
Army of Portugal		
Boyer	1st (*Thévenez d'Aoust*)	6th Dragoons
		11th Dragoons
	2nd (*Boudinhon-Valdec*)	15th Dragoons
		25th Dragoons
Mermet	1st (Curto)	3rd Hussars
		22nd Chasseurs
		26th Chasseurs
	2nd (*Shée*)	13th Chasseurs
		14th Chasseurs
Army of South		
1st Dragoon (Tilly)†	1st (Ismert)‡	2nd Dragoons
		4th Dragoons
		26th Dragoons
	2nd (Ormancey)	14th Dragoons
		17th Dragoons
		27th Dragoons
2nd Dragoon (Digeon)§	1st (Sparre)	5th Dragoons
		12th Dragoons
		16th Dragoons
	2nd (*Ruat*)	21st Dragoons
1st Light Cavalry (Soult)**	1st (Vinot)¶	2nd Hussars
		21st Chasseurs
	2nd (*Houssin de Sainte-Laurent*)††	5th Chasseurs
		10th Chasseurs
		27th Chasseurs

---

* The 1st Squadron was attached to General Palombini's Divison.

† Was provisional commander until he took command on 1 May 1813.

‡ General Ismert was promoted to general of brigade on 8 February 1813.

§ Took command on 7 April 1813.

¶ General Vinot was the former commander of the 3rd Hussars and had been promoted on 3 March 1813.

** General Soult was commander of the 1st Brigade, but served as acting division commander until he assumed command on 7 April 1813.

†† Colonel Auguste Houssin de Saint-Laurent, commander of the 10th Chasseurs.

During the winter and spring of 1813 many cavalry regiments received orders to send the cadres of their 3rd and 4th Squadrons back to their depots. The troopers stayed in Spain and were incorporated into the 1st and 2nd Squadrons. Additionally, the 7th Lancers were ordered back to France on 7 January 1813

Table 4.3   Reduction of the cavalry regiments, winter and spring 1813

Regiment	What Left	When Left
5th Chasseurs	2nd Company, 2nd Squadron	1 Jun. 1813
10th Chasseurs	3rd Squadron	Mar. 1813
10th Chasseurs	4th Squadron	Jan. 1813
13th Chasseurs	3rd and 4th Squadrons	Mar. 1813
15th Chasseurs	3rd Squadron	Apr. 1813
24th Chasseurs	4th Squadron	Spring 1813
28th Chasseurs	1st Squadron	Winter 1813
2nd Dragoons	3rd Squadron	Spring 1813
5th Dragoons	3rd Squadron	Jan. 1813
12th Dragoons	3rd Squadron	Jan. 1813
14th Dragoons	3rd Squadron	Mar. 1813
15th Dragoons	3rd and 4th Squadrons	May 1813
16th Dragoons	3rd Squadron	15 Apr. 1813
17th Dragoons	3rd Squadron	Winter 1813
18th Dragoons	3rd Squadron	Jan. 1813
18th Dragoons	2nd Squadron	Apr. 1813
19th Dragoons	2nd Squadron	Apr. 1813
20th Dragoons	2nd Squadron	Feb. 1813
20th Dragoons	3rd Squadron	Mar. 1813
21st Dragoons	3rd Squadron	Winter 1813
22nd Dragoons	3rd Squadron	Jan. 1813
27th Dragoons	3rd Squadron	Jan. 1813
1st Hussars	3rd Squadron	Apr. 1813
2nd Hussars	3rd Squadron	Feb. 1813
7th Lancers	All	7 Jan. 1813
Napoleon Dragoons	HQ, 2nd and 3rd Squadrons	Feb. 1813
Neapolitan Chasseurs	All	May 1813
Westphalian Lancers	HQ, 2nd and 3rd Squadrons	Feb. 1813
Lancers of Berg	All	5 March 1813

On 6 April General Maransin assumed command of the 2nd Brigade of General Soult's Division. On 30 May Colonel François Grouvel, commander of the 16th Dragoons, was promoted to general of brigade

and took command of the 2nd Brigade of General Digeon's Division. In early May the French had over 15,800 cavalry troopers still in Spain. In the armies that would oppose the British in the upcoming offensive, the French cavalry would muster almost 12,600 men.

Table 4.4 Cavalry divisions and independent brigades in Spain, May 1813

Division	Brigade	Regiment	Strength
Army of Aragon			
	1st (Delort)	4th Hussars	680
		24th Dragoons	589
Total			*1,269*
	2nd (Maupoint)	13th Cuirassiers	508
		Westphalian Lancers*	178
Total			*686*
	Unattached	12th Hussars	574
	Unattached	1st Italian Chasseurs	146[†]
Army of Catalonia			
		29th Chasseurs	594
Army of the Centre			
Trelliard	1st (*Dard*)	13th Dragoons	192
		18th Dragoons	282
Total			*474*
	2nd (*Rozat*)	19th Dragoons	193
		22nd Dragoons	380
Total			*573*
	Avy	27th Chasseurs	329
		Nassau Light Horse	131
Total			*460*
Army of the North			
		20th Dragoons	172[‡]
		Napoleon Dragoons	71
	Merlin	15th Chasseurs	463
		31st Chasseurs	295
		1st Hussars	525
Total			*1,283*

* One squadron.
† Strength return of 15 April.
‡ Strength return of 1 April.

Table 4.4   continued

Division	Brigade	Regiment	Strength
Army of Portugal			
Boyer	1st (*Thévenez d'Aoust*)	6th Dragoons	418[*]
		11th Dragoons	373[†]
Total			791
	2nd (*Boudinhon-Valdec*)	15th Dragoons	363[‡]
		25th Dragoons	347[§]
Total			710
Mermet	1st (Curto)	22nd Chasseurs	347
		26th Chasseurs	294
		3rd Hussars	339
Total			980
	2nd (*Shée*)	13th Chasseurs	567
		14th Chasseurs	266
Total			833
Army of the South			
1st Dragoon (Tilly)	1st (Ismert)	2nd Dragoons	384[¶]
		4th Dragoons	544
		26th Dragoons	610
Total			1,538
	2nd (Ormancey)	14th Dragoons	245[**]
		17th Dragoons	359
		27th Dragoons	279
Total			883
2nd Dragoon (Digeon)	1st (Sparre)	5th Dragoons	476
		21st Dragoons	435
Total			911
	2nd (Grouvel)[††]	12th Dragoons	461
		16th Dragoons	528
Total			989
3rd Light Cavalry (Soult)	1st (Vinot)	21st Chasseurs	353

---

[*] Strength return of 31 March.
[†] Strength return of 31 March.
[‡] Strength return of 31 March.
[§] Strength return of 31 March.
[¶] Strength return of 16 February.
[**] Strength return of 16 February.
[††] Took command on 30 May.

Division	Brigade	Regiment	Strength
		2nd Hussars	366
Total			719
	2nd (Maransin)	5th Chasseurs	401
		10th Chasseurs	495
		27th Chasseurs	329
Total			1,225
Total cavalry in Spain			**15,881**

In June 1813 Napoleon, in a move to bolster his army in Germany, ordered the commanders of the different armies in Spain to send 17 cavalry regiments back to France. Most of these regiments only had their headquarters and two squadrons serving in Spain, with their other two squadrons already in Germany. The withdrawal of these regiments gutted both General Boyer's and General Trelliard's Divisions by sending back to France their 1st and 2nd Brigades, as well as the 2nd Brigade of General Mermet's Division. None of these five brigades had a general officer commanding them and they were disbanded when the regiments departed.

Table 4.5 Cavalry withdrawn from the French Armies in Spain and sent to the Grande Armée, June 1813

Army	Regiment	No. sqdns	Strength
Portugal	14th Chasseurs	2	256
Portugal	26th Chasseurs	2	294
South	27th Chasseurs	2	329
North	31st Chasseurs	3	295
South	2nd Dragoons	2	391
Portugal	6th Dragoons	2	403
Portugal	11th Dragoons	2	473
Centre	13th Dragoons	2	192
Portugal	15th Dragoons	2	352
Centre	18th Dragoons	1	282
Centre	19th Dragoons	1	193
North	20th Dragoons	1	116
Centre	22nd Dragoons	2	380
Portugal	25th Dragoons	2	343
North and Catalonia	1st Hussars	2	511
Portugal	3rd Hussars	2	339
North	Napoleon Dragoons	1	72
Total		31	5,221

After the defeat at Vitoria on 21 June the French were pushed out of most of Spain. On 12 July 1813 Marshal Soult, who had been recalled to France to serve in Germany in early January, returned to the Peninsula to take command of the new Army of Spain. The Armies of the Centre, North, Portugal and the South were disbanded and its units became part of the Army of Spain. On 16 July the cavalry was formed into two divisions commanded by Generals Soult and Trelliard. General Boyer was not given another cavalry division, but instead took command of the 9th Infantry Division. General Mermet returned to France and would serve with the Army of Italy.

Table 4.6   Cavalry Divisions in the Army of Spain, 16 July 1813

Division	Commander	Brigade	Regiment
1st	Soult	1st (Vinot)	5th Chasseurs
			10th Chasseurs
			22nd Chasseurs
			Nassau Light Horse
		2nd (Berton)	2nd Hussars
			13th Chasseurs
			15th Chasseurs
			21st Chasseurs
		3rd (Sparre)	5th Dragoons
			12th Dragoons
			27th Dragoons
2nd	Trelliard	1st (Ismert)	21st Dragoons
			26th Dragoons
		2nd Ormancey	14th Dragoons
			16th Dragoons
		3rd (Avy)	4th Dragoons
			17th Dragoons

On 1 September General Avy was recalled to France for service in Germany. His brigade was dissolved and its regiments were incorporated into the other brigades. Additionally, the 15th Chasseurs were transferred from General Berton's Brigade to General Vinot's Brigade. The 29th Chasseurs were stilled operating in company and squadron size forces and attached to the different brigades of the Army of Catalonia. General Digeon was transferred to the Army of Aragon and took command of the newly formed cavalry division there.

Table 4.7   French cavalry in Spain, September 1813

Division	Commander	Brigade	Regiment
Army of Spain			
1st	Soult	1st (Vinot)	5th Chasseurs
			10th Chasseurs
			15th Chasseurs
			22nd Chasseurs
			Nassau Light Horse*
		2nd (Berton)	2nd Hussars
			13th Chasseurs
			21st Chasseurs
		3rd (Sparre)	5th Dragoons
			12th Dragoons
			27th Dragoons
2nd	Trelliard	1st (Ismert)	4th Dragoons
			21st Dragoons
			26th Dragoons
		2nd Ormancey	14th Dragoons
			16th Dragoons
			17th Dragoons
Armies of Aragon and Catalonia			
	Digeon	1st (Delort)	4th Hussars
			13th Cuirassiers
		2nd (Meyer)	12th Hussars
			24th Dragoons
			Westphalian Lancers†
		Unattached	29th Chasseurs
			1st Italian Chasseurs

1814

On 1 January 1814 the cavalry of the Army of Spain consisted of the two divisions of Generals Soult and Trelliard, while the Army of Aragon had a one division under General Digeon.

---

* The two squadrons of the Nassau Light Horse were disbanded on 22 December 1813.
† The remaining squadron of the Westphalian Lancers were disbanded in December 1813.

Table 4.8 French cavalry in the Peninsula, 1 January 1814

Division	*Brigade*	*Regiment*
Army of Spain		
1st (Soult)	1st (Vinot)	5th Chasseurs
		10th Chasseurs
		15th Chasseurs
		22nd Chasseurs
	2nd (Berton)	2nd Hussars
		13th Chasseurs
		21st Chasseurs
	3rd (Sparre)	5th Dragoons
		12th Dragoons
2nd (Trelliard)	1st (Ismert)	4th Dragoons
		21st Dragoons
		26th Dragoons
	2nd Ormancey	14th Dragoons
		16th Dragoons
		17th Dragoons
		27th Dragoons
Armies of Aragon and Catalonia		
Digeon	1st (Delort)	4th Hussars
		13th Cuirassiers
	2nd (Meyer)	12th Hussars
		24th Dragoons
	Unattached	29th Chasseurs
		1st Italian Chasseurs

On 14 January Marshal Soult was ordered to send General Trelliard and his division, along with General Sparre's Brigade to the Grande Armée in eastern France. Marshal Suchet also received orders directing him to send General Digeon and General Delort's Brigade, plus the 12th Hussars to Lyon. The 1st Italian Chasseurs were sent back to Italy.

Table 4.9 Cavalry withdrawn from the Army of Spain and sent to the Grande Armée, January 1814

Division	*Brigade commander*	*Regiment*	*Strength*
1st	Sparre	5th Dragoons	265
1st	Sparre	12th Dragoons	289
2nd	Ismert	4th Dragoons	532

Division	Brigade commander	Regiment	Strength
2nd	Ismert	21st Dragoons	460
2nd	Ismert	26th Dragoons	627
2nd	Ormancey	14th Dragoons	341
2nd	Ormancey	16th Dragoons	182
2nd	Ormancey	17th Dragoons	325
2nd	Ormancey	27th Dragoons	399
Digeon	Delort	13th Cuirassiers	662
Digeon	Delort	4th Hussars	650
Digeon	Delort	12th Hussars	575
Total			5,307

In February General Vinot was sent to Versailles to command the cavalry depot. He was replaced by General Vial. Until peace was declared in April 1814, the French cavalry in the Peninsular Armies would consisted of three brigades, totalling less than 4,000 sabres — a far cry from the 23 brigades that entered Spain five and half years earlier.

Table 4.10 French cavalry in the Peninsula, April 1814

Division	Brigade	Regiment	Strength
Army of Spain			
Soult	1st (Vial)	5th Chasseurs	302
		10th Chasseurs	433
		15th Chasseurs	341
		22nd Chasseurs	285
Total			1,361
	2nd (Berton)	2nd Hussars	427
		13th Chasseurs	497
		21st Chasseurs	415
Total			1,339
Army of Aragon			
	Meyer	24th Dragoons	699
		29th Chasseurs	559
Total			1,258

Part II

The Peninsular Cavalry Generals

Chapter Five

The Cavalry Generals

Despite having tens of thousands of troops in the Peninsula, except for a six-month period in 1808 and 1809, the Peninsula was a secondary theatre of war for Napoleon. His focus was elsewhere and it affected the quality and numbers of general officers assigned there. After 1809 only two generals who had not previously served in the Peninsula were assigned to the cavalry in Spain. Furthermore, in 1811 Napoleon began to withdraw the better generals from the armies in Spain to provide him with seasoned commanders for the impending war with Russia. By 1812 it was not uncommon to find generals of brigade commanding cavalry divisions and colonels commanding brigades.

In the early days of the war, prior to massive build up of French troops in the autumn of 1808, the cavalry was led by such notables as Generals Grouchy, Kellermann and Lasalle, but their subordinates were not the leaders who made their reputations during the campaigns of 1805–7. They were not hard charging, young leaders. They tended to be older, with an average age of 44. General Dupont's Corps was almost geriatric for the French army. The four generals (Duprés, Fresia, Pryvé and Rigau) had an averaged 52 years of age. General Fresia, who commanded all of Dupont's cavalry, was 61!

November 1808 saw an influx of new leadership – mostly of dragoon and light cavalry generals who had seen much action in the previous three years. They were some of the best cavalry commanders in the French army, including Generals Caulaincourt, Colbert, Lefebvre-Desnouettes Montbrun, Milhaud and Tour-Maubourg. But in early 1809 war with Austria was on the horizon and Napoleon began to recall his favourites to France. By April Generals Arrighi, Bordessoulle, Bron, Lamotte, Lasalle, Lepic, Montbrun, Rioult-Davenay, Trelliard and Watier were gone. They were not initially replaced and coupled with the loss in combat of Generals Colbert, Charles Lefebvre-Desnouettes and Jean Franceschi, the command structure of the cavalry had thinned. General Beaurgard arrived in June to take command of the 5th Corps's Light Cavalry Brigade. Not until after the defeat of Austria in July did Napoleon slowly begin to send cavalry generals back to Spain. By the end of 1809 Generals Bron and Lamotte had returned, while General Poinsot, who had been part of General Dupont's Corps and surrendered at Bailen, was also sent back.* Napoleon also sent his 27-year-old protégé, General Escorches de Sainte-Croix, to command a dragoon brigade. General Fouler came too, but he would only last a few months before returning to France in January 1810.

By the late summer of 1810, much of Spain had been conquered and Generals Lepic, Montbrun, Trelliard and Watier had returned to Spain. The various commands were organised into different armies, based on geographical location. With this reorganisation came a change of mission. It was time for the French to hold what they had taken. The French army had changed from an army of conquest to an army of occupation. Except for the newly created Army of Portugal, the large French armies were dispersed throughout Spain consolidating the new Napoleonic kingdom of Spain. The Army of Portugal, located in the vicinity of Ciudad Rodrigo, would soon enter Portugal intent on evicting the British. The cavalry generals' jobs also changed. In addition to their traditional duties as brigade and division commanders, they were thrust into a political role and many became provincial governors and commandants of large cities and charged with keeping them pacified.

The year 1810 also saw the beginning of attrition among the cavalry generals. Three were killed in action or died of their wounds, one was captured, one was relieved from his duties due to corruption, one retired and one returned to France due to poor health. Balancing this leadership loss was the return of Generals Fournier-Sarlovèse and Lallemand who had left for France the previous autumn; while Colonels Bouillé, Bouvier des Eclaz and Ormancey were promoted to generals of brigade and kept in Spain. The following year attrition among general officers worsened. Three cavalry generals were killed and two were so badly wounded and another so worn out from campaigning that they all returned to France; two more were captured and four were relieved from command due to corruption, incompetence, or insubordination. Although Generals Maupoint and Curto came to Spain in August and October 1811, they were among the last cavalry generals to be assigned to Spain. Napoleon began to withdraw some of the more experienced commanders from Spain to serve in the upcoming war with Russia, compounding the loss among the army's leadership in Spain. Departures included four generals

---

* General Poinsot was one of the generals who were allowed to return to France after the surrender.

of division – Generals Houssaye, Lorge, Montbrun and Tour-Maubourg; plus Generals Beaumont, Bessières, Bouvier des Eclaz, Fournier-Sarlovèse, Lepic, Poinsott and Watier.

To counter the loss of these generals, Napoleon promoted 15 cavalry colonels serving in Spain.

Table 5.1   Cavalry colonels promoted to general of brigade, 1811

Name	Regiment	Date of Rank	Months in regimental command
Vital Chamorin	26th Dragoons	5 Mar. 1811	49
Louis Laferrière	3rd Hussars	13 May 1811	50
Philippe Ornano	25th Dragoons	16 Jun. 1811	52
A. d'Ermenonville	8th Dragoons	22 Jun. 1811	54
Jacques Delort	24th Dragoons	21 Jul. 1811	62
Frédéric Beurmann	17th Dragoons	6 Aug. 1811	69
Pierre Bonnemains	5th Chasseurs	6 Aug. 1811	59
Jean Corbineau	20th Dragoons	6 Aug. 1811	55
Pierre Dejean	11th Dragoons	6 Aug. 1811	55
Jean Dommanget	10th Dragoons	6 Aug. 1811	59
Jon Konopka	1st Vistula Lancers	6 Aug. 1811	49
François Lallemand	27th Dragoons	6 Aug. 1811	57
Pierre Mourier	15th Chasseurs	6 Aug. 1811	72
Mathieu Queunot	9th Dragoons	6 Aug. 1811	58
Jean Saint-Genies	19th Dragoons	6 Aug. 1811	59
Jacques Subervie	13th Chasseurs	6 Aug. 1811	57

But even this was not all it that it seemed. Of these 15 newly promoted officers, Generals Beurmann, Corbineau, Dejean, d'Ermenonville, Dommanget, Konopka, Laferrière, Mourier, Ornano, Queunot, Saint-Genies and Subervie were recalled to France, most to serve with the Grande Armée in Russia, while General Chamorin was killed in action before he was ever informed of his promotion. On the plus side, the three generals who stayed in the Peninsula were young, with an average age of 35 and very experienced at command – with an average of five years of regimental command. More importantly, all had been in the Peninsula for at least 30 months. They would have been the future of the French cavalry if Napoleon had not lost his throne.

The haemorrhaging in the command structure continued into 1812. Although no cavalry generals were killed, one was captured, one was relieved for insubordination and two left for health reasons, while two were permitted to retire. Colonel Sparre of the 5th Dragoons was promoted in April to command a brigade in General Soult's Division. Like his contemporaries, who were promoted the previous year, General Sparre was young – 32 years old, with 59 months of regimental command experience and had served 43 months in the Peninsula. He would stay with them until January 1814, when he and his brigade were ordered to eastern France. In September 1812 General Mermet, who had been shot in the stomach the previous year, returned. He was the last general officer to go to the Peninsula.

In early 1813 Colonels Berton, Ismert and Vinot were promoted from units in Spain, to fill some of the vacant brigade commander positions. In July 1813, after their defeat at Vitoria on 21 June, the French armies in Spain were reorganised under Marshal Soult. The Armies of the Centre, the North, of Portugal and of the South, were consolidated into the Army of Spain. About the same time, 17 cavalry regiments – the equivalent of 8 brigades were withdrawn from the theatre of operations and sent to the Grande Armée in Germany. This trimmed the cavalry from six divisions to two, suddenly presenting, Marshal Soult with an excess of general officers. Generals Soult and Trelliard were given command of the new cavalry divisions. By the end of the summer, General Tilly, who was 64 years old at the time and had 52 years of military service, was sent to Paris. General Digeon went to the Army of Aragon, while General Mermet was assigned to the Army of Italy. Generals Boyer and Maransin, who were infantry generals, were given command of the newly formed 9th and 5th Infantry Divisions respectively. Generals Curto and Avy were sent to Germany.

Marshal Soult's organisation for the Army of Spain would last through January 1814, when General Trelliard's Division, with Generals Ismert's, Ormancy's and Sparre's Brigades, were ordered to eastern France. This left the Army of Spain with General Soult's Division of two brigades of about 2,500 men – a mere shadow of the 25,000 cavalry troopers that entered Spain in November 1808.

The price of glory

'This war in Spain means death for the men; ruin for the officers; a fortune for the generals!'* read the sentiment that Charles Parquin saw scrawled upon a wall in Spain in 1811. Although the life of a general was much better than that of the cavalry trooper, they often paid for their privileges with their own blood. Of the 80 generals who commanded cavalry between 1808 and 1813, 34 of them were killed, wounded, or taken prisoner – a casualty rate of 43 per cent! Ten (13 per cent of all cavalry generals who

---

* Parquin, *Napoleon's Army*, p. 126.

served in the Peninsula) were either killed or died of their wounds or of disease, while 15 (19 per cent) were wounded. Of these 15, ten were wounded at least twice. General Ismert was wounded five separate times while commanding troops in the Peninsula! General Boussart, who eventually died from his wounds, had been wounded 21 times prior to arriving in the Peninsula and twice seriously while in the Peninsula! He also had the misfortune of also being captured in 1811. Additionally, campaigning took a physical toll on a soldier's body. One general was so worn out that he had to be returned to France and never had an active command again, while another went blind.

Table 5.2   French cavalry generals killed or died in the Peninsula

Date	Name	Circumstances
19 Jul. 1808	Claude-François Duprés	Shot in the final cavalry charge at Bailen
3 Jan. 1809	Auguste Colbert	In combat at Cacabellos, Spain
18 Nov. 1809	Antoine Paris d'Illins	In combat at Ocaña, Spain
19 Feb. 1810	Charles-Victor Beaurgard	In combat at Valverde de Leganés, Spain
11 Oct. 1810	Charles Sainte-Croix	Killed by a cannonball near Villafranca, Portugal
23 Oct. 1810	Jean Franceschi	Died of yellow fever while in captivity
11 Feb. 1811	Frédéric Marizy	Died of gangrene after being shot in the thigh
25 Mar. 1811	Vital-Joachim Chamorin	In combat at Campo-Mayor, Spain
13 Dec. 1811	Pierre Maupetit	From multiple wounds received over the years
10 August 1813	André-Joseph Boussart	From multiple wounds received over the years

Table 5.3   French cavalry generals wounded in the Peninsula

Name	Number of times wounded
Antoine-Sylvain Avy	1
Louis-Chrétien de Carrière Beaumont	1
André-Joseph Boussart	2
André Bron de Bailly	1
Carrié de Boissy	6 (5 times in one battle)

Name	Number of times wounded
Jacques-Antoine-Adrien Delort	2 (but multiple times in one battle)
Alexandre-Elisabeth-Michel Digeon	1
Pierre Ismert	5
Jan Konopka	1
Charles Lefebvre-Desnouettes	2
Jean-Baptiste Lorcet	2
Jean Maransin	3
Frédéric Marizy	2 (Died of from wounds the second time)
Julien-Augustin-Joseph Mermet	2
Gilbert-Julien Vinot	2

Besides running the risk of being killed or wounded, 12 cavalry generals (15 per cent of the total) were also captured by the enemy.

Table 5.4   French cavalry generals captured in the Peninsula

Date	Name	Circumstances
Jun. 1808	Antoine Maurin	Captured by insurgents at Faro, Portugal
22 Jul. 1808	Maurice Ignace Fresia	Surrender at Bailen
22 Jul. 1808	Pierre Poinsot	Surrender at Bailen
22 Jul. 1808	Ythier-Silvain Pryvé	Surrender at Bailen
Sep. 1808	François Kellermann	Capitulation in Portugal
Sep. 1808	Jean Maransin	Capitulation in Portugal
29 Dec. 1808	Charles Lefebvre-Desnouettes	Combat of Benavente
Jun. 1809	Jean Franceschi	Captured by guerrillas, died in captivity 23 Oct. 1810
5 Sep. 1810	François Schwarz	Surrendered to Spanish when surrounded at La Bispal
28 Oct. 1811	André Bron de Bailly	Combat of Arroyo dos Molinos
26 Dec. 1811	André-Joseph Boussart	Captured at Torrante but rescued the same day
18 July 1812	Jean Carrié de Boissy	After being wounded five times at the combat of Guarena

Becoming a casualty was not the only way for a general to come to grief. Nine cavalry generals were relieved for incompetence, insubordination, corruption, or for other reasons while they were in the Peninsula. Two of them were among the best-known of all French generals – Louis Montbrun and François Kellermann. Both were able to revive their careers, while six had their reputations permanently ruined.

Table 5.5   French cavalry generals relieved for cause in the Peninsula

Date	*Name*	*Circumstances*
7 Sep. 1808	Louis Montbrun	Missing movement*
21 Dec. 1808	Archange Rioult-Davenay	Insubordination to General Houssaye
2 Aug. 1809	César Debelle	Losses to his brigade at Sahagun 21 Dec. 1808
17 Sep. 1810	Nicolas Barthélemi	Accused of extorting funds from the Spanish
5 Jan. 1811	Charles Gardanne	Incompetence in relieving the Army of Portugal
15 Mar. 1811	Auguste Lamotte	Accused of negligence at Foz do Arouce
20 May 1811	François Kellermann	Corruption and insubordination
31 Dec. 1811	André Briche	Disaster at Arroyo dos Molinos 28 Oct. 1811
January 1812	Louis Cavrois	For insubordination to General Montbrun

So were the words of that unknown graffiti artist accurate? Was Spain a place where the French generals made their fortunes? Possibly, but at a price. Of the 80 Peninsular cavalry generals, 44 (55 per cent) were either killed, wounded, had their health permanently impaired, made prisoner, or relieved from command. If any of them had, indeed, significantly enriched himself there, the price had been very high!

An assessment of the Peninsular cavalry generals
It would not be fair to the generals who served in the Peninsula to compare their performance to generals who did not fight there, for the Peninsular War was unlike any war or campaign that Napoleon's army ever fought.

---

* Missing movement is when a soldier is not present when a unit is ordered to go somewhere. In General Montbrun's case, he was on leave when his brigade was ordered into Spain.

Until 1813 it was the only war on the Continent that did not end within six months from the onset of hostilities. The Peninsular War stretched from the autumn of 1807 to the spring of 1814 – almost six and a half years. In other wars and campaigns, excepting Haiti, the French and their allies would fight organised armies, while the civilian populace stood passively aside, refusing to take an active part in the conflict. This was in stark contrast to the attitude of the people of Spain and Portugal. From almost the very beginning, they rose up against the French invaders and fought them at every opportunity. Unlike with other campaigns, the French could not just focus on defeating the armies of their enemies. For the first time they had to expend vast resources against the guerrilla bands in order to keep the countryside pacified and their lines of communications secured. To do this required a different set of skills than those that were useful in the rest of Europe. Some of the generals were able to develop these skills, while others did not.

A typical year in the Peninsula would see the French spending about half their time fighting the British and Spanish armies and the rest of the time battling the guerrillas. So a cavalry general would not only have to know how to manoeuvre a large body of mounted troops on the battlefield and perform the traditional cavalry missions of reconnaissance and screening, but he would also have to know how to secure lines of communication and guard convoys. Plus he had to be an able administrator, for many of them would have additional duties such as governor of a province or city – exercising responsibility for administering justice, collecting imperial taxes, providing services and ensuring that the local economy did not collapse. This was as important as being able to fight, because Napoleon expected the French army to subsist on supplies drawn from the local area. If the situation was too unsecure for the farmers and herders to raise food, it would have devastating consequences for both the army and the civilians.[*]

By the time an individual became a general officer, he should have had the basic skills that would allow him to manoeuvre and administer his brigade. Logically, a general would have commanded a regiment, yet 17 of the 80 cavalry generals (21 per cent) were drawn from the staff and had no previous regimental command experience, while two others commanded infantry regiments. Even prior command was no indicator of overall success. While campaigning against the organised armies of the Spain, Portugal and Britain, these generals usually only commanded cavalry; but when fighting the guerrillas, a cavalry general often would have a command that included infantry and artillery. A typical force for a counter-guerrilla sweep would consist of a battalion of infantry, a squadron of cavalry and a section of

---

[*] By 1812 the economy of southern Spain was so disrupted by four years of war that the people were in danger of starving.

artillery. He needed to know how to command all three effectively.

Most generals performed their duties adequately. Some excelled at the job, while a handful were inept.

Part of the problem with evaluating them is that in November 1808, Napoleon went into Spain with some very good cavalry generals, but within a year they were no longer in Spain, having become casualties or been withdrawn. Their time in the Peninsula was so short that they had no long-term impact on operations there. These included Generals Colbert and Paris who were killed, Generals Franceschi and Lefebvre-Desnouettes who were captured and General Lasalle who was recalled to France to fight in the 1809 campaign against Austria and killed at Wagram.

The following assessment is based on these criteria:

1 Performance on campaign
2 Performance on the battlefield
3 Performance leading a joint cavalry, infantry and artillery force in counter-guerrilla operations
4 Ability as an administrator

The top cavalry division commanders in the Peninsular War
Eighteen generals commanded cavalry divisions in Spain from 1807–14. The best were:

1 *Louis-Pierre Montbrun* was a charismatic leader who always able to get the most out of his subordinates. During the invasion of Portugal he led the equivalent of a cavalry corps in one of the most hostile campaigning environments in Europe. Despite staggering losses due to attrition, he was still able to keep them as an effective force. He was one of the few French generals who could claim to have beaten the Duke of Wellington, winning the field at El Bodon in 1811.

2 *Edouard-Jean-Baptiste Milhaud* commanded the 3rd Dragoon Division for three years in Spain. It was his dragoons that played a pivotal role in capturing 26,000 Spanish infantry in less than an hour at Ocaña in November 1809. He would spend the next two years helping pacify southern Spain.

3 *Marie-Victor-Nicolas de Fay Marquis de La Tour-Maubourg* was a cold, professional leader, who commanded the 1st Dragoon Division for three years before being recalled to France in 1812. He distinguished himself on many battlefields in the Peninsula, including Medellin and Ocaña against the Spanish and at Albuera against the British. His most notable achievement in the Peninsula was his screening operations in the vicinity of Badajoz in early 1811.

4 *Anne-François-Charles Trelliard* was not one of Napoleon's favourites. However, he put in consistently solid performances during the four years he commanded divisions in the Peninsula. His division bloodied Wellington's advance guard at Majahalonda in 1812.

The five best cavalry brigade commanders in the Peninsular War
The French army was blessed with a large pool of talented cavalry generals at brigade level. Many had honed their skills on the battlefields of Spain as regimental commanders prior to being promoted to general. Owing to the nature of the Peninsular War, they were equally capable of commanding both a cavalry brigade as well as an independent force of infantry, cavalry and artillery, in counter-insurgency operations. The following generals stood out from their contemporaries for their superb leadership over many months and even years in the Iberian Peninsula.

1 *Jacques-Antoine-Adrien Delort* was an aggressive, charismatic commander who fought in the Army of Aragon. He led from the front, being wounded multiple times.
2 *Pierre Watier de Saint-Alphonse* was an outstanding brigade commander, who on occasion would command an ad hoc cavalry division. He was aggressive, when needed, but not reckless with the lives of his troops. General Watier was recalled to France in late 1811, after being promoted to general of division.
3 *Louis-Ernest-Joseph Sparre* was a superb regimental commander who was promoted to general of brigade at the age of 31. He commanded a dragoon brigade in General Soult's Division for two years before being transferred to eastern France in 1814.
4 *André Boussart* commanded the cavalry of the Army of Aragon for almost four years. Aggressive and brave, he never asked his men to do anything that he would not do himself. He had to give up active field command after being seriously wounded at Torrente in December 1811.
5 *Jean-Baptiste Lorcet* took command of the 6th Corps's Light Cavalry Brigade after General Colbert was killed in early 1809. During the invasion of Portugal in 1810 he commanded a dragoon brigade. He led by example and was always found where the fighting was the thickest. He was wounded 11 times in 17 years. He last wound, at Fuentes de Oñoro, was so serious, he was sent back to France to recover.

The five worst cavalry generals in the Peninsular War
The counter-balance to the outstanding commanders listed previously, were five individuals whose performance was consistently dismal.

1   *François Schwarz* commanded in eastern Spain and was out-manoeuvred and out-fought by guerrillas on several occasions. Twice he was surrounded and routed by a smaller, poorly armed Spanish force. In 1810 he was surrounded a third time and surrendered his command.

2   *Charles-Victor Woirgard dit de Beaurgard.* It is questionable why he was ever given command. He was relieved from command in 1802 and had no job for seven years until appointed to command the light cavalry of Marshal Mortier's Corps in 1809. His failure to take basic security precautions while bivouacking on campaign allowed his brigade to be surprised and routed at Valverde in 1810. He paid for it with his life.

3   *André-François Bron de Bailly* was outmanoeuvreed and barely escaped with his life at Villa Garcia in May 1811. Later that year at Arroyo dos Molino he failed to ensure picquets were set while his brigade was bivouacking in an area that was not secure. His brigade and the infantry division they were with were surprised at night by the British and mauled. Bron was captured and spent the rest of the war as a prisoner in England.

4   *Charles-Mathieu Gardanne* commanded the rear detachment of the Army of Portugal in 1810. In November he went forward with much needed supplies and replacements for the weakened Army of Portugal. While on the way he was opposed by Portuguese militia who bluffed him into turning back less than a day's march from the force he was trying to relieve. Napoleon called him an idiot and an arch imbecile! [*]

5   *François-Etienne Kellermann* excelled on the battlefield and at negotiating the Convention of Cintra, which allowed the French to withdraw from Portugal under favourable terms, but he failed miserably as the governor of the 6th Military Government, which comprised Palencia, Toro and Valladolid. He neglected his mission to support Marshal Masséna's Army of Portugal. Instead he spent much time consolidating his own power base and undermined the ability of the army to sustain operations by withholding much needed supplies. His administration was marked by rampant corruption and greed, for which he was eventually relieved of command.

---

[*] Pelet, *The French Campaign in Portugal*, p. 306.

Chapter Six

The Peninsular Cavalry Generals
Arrighi to Curto

The following are biographies of 80 generals who commanded cavalry brigades or divisions in the Peninsula. Not every cavalry general who served in the Peninsula is listed. For example, Generals Guillemet and Maucomble are not included, even though they were cavalry generals, because they commanded infantry and never commanded cavalry in the Peninsula. Additionally, at least two infantry generals, Pierre Boyer and Jean Maransin, are included because they commanded a cavalry division and a cavalry brigade respectively.

Some of the tables will have more information than others. For example some will have a line for regiments commanded or wounds in the Peninsula, while others will not. If the table is missing those categories, it is because the general did not command a regiment prior to being promoted to general or was not wounded in the Peninsula. In all cases, if no cause of death is listed, then the general died of natural causes.

Table 6.1   Arrighi de Casanova, Jean Toussaint

Awards and honours	Duke of Padua 20 Mar. 1808
Date and place of birth	8 Mar. 1778 in Corte
Regiments commanded	1st Dragoons 31 Aug. 1803–19 May 1806
Date of rank as general	General of brigade 25 Jun. 1807, General of division 25 May 1809
Time in the Peninsula	4 Nov. 1808–Mar. 1809
Command or post in the Peninsula	Empress Dragoons 19 May 1806– 12 Mar. 1809
Date and place of death	22 Mar. 1853 in Paris
Place of burial	Crypt, Chapel of the Hôtel des Invalides, Paris

---

Jean Arrighi was a cousin by marriage to Napoleon. He was promoted to general of brigade in 1807 at the age of 29 and would command the Empress Dragoons in the Peninsula from November 1808 until they were withdrawn in 1809. General Arrighi and his regiment spent most of their time in the Peninsula, escorting Napoleon. They saw little combat.

After leaving Spain in the spring of 1809 General Arrighi went to Germany where he would fight in the 1809 campaign against Austria. He was promoted to general of division within two months of leaving Spain and took command of General Espagne's Cuirassier Division, upon his death. He was in a series of administrative posts from 1810 until early 1813, when he commanded the 3rd Cavalry Corps during the campaign in Germany. General Arrighi commanded an infantry division during the 1814 campaign in France and did not receive another command after Napoleon abdicated. On Napoleon's return to France in 1815 he was appointed governor of Corsica. He refused to surrender to Royalist authority, declaring instead independence for Corsica. He was ordered arrested in July 1815 and went into exile in Lombardy. He was allowed to retire in 1819. He died in 1853 at the age of 75.

Table 6.2   Avy, Antoine-Sylvain

Awards and honours	Baron of the Empire 9 Jan. 1809
Date and place of birth	25 May 1776 at Cressier
Date of rank as general	General of brigade 19 May 1811
Time in the Peninsula	Jul. 1808–Sep. 1808, 1 Jun. 1810–8 May 1811 7 Jun. 1811–11 Sep. 1813
Command or post in the Peninsula	Chief-of-Staff, Reille's Division Jul.–Sep. 1808; HQ, Army of the South Jun. 1810–May 1811, Sep.–Oct. 1811; 2nd Brigade, Godinot's Division 1 Nov. 1811–12 Feb. 1812; 2nd Brigade, Semellé's Division Nov. 1812–Mar. 1813; Soult's Light Cavalry Division Mar. 1813–Jul. 1813; Light Cavalry Brigade, Army of the Centre Jul. 1813–31 Aug. 1813 3rd Brigade, Trelliard's Division, Army of Spain
Wounds in Peninsula	Figuières 1808
Date and place of death	13 Jan. 1814 at Merxem
Cause of death	Died of wounds sustained during the siege of Anvers.

General Avy was one of several French infantry generals who commanded cavalry brigades and even cavalry divisions during the Peninsular War. He was also unusual in that he never commanded a regiment. Before the Empire he was an aide-de-camp to several senior officers and during the Empire he served mostly in staff positions. During the summer of 1808 he was the chief-of-staff to General Reille and was wounded at Figuières. His wound was serious enough for him to return to France to recover. He came back to Spain in June 1810 and was assigned to the headquarters of the Army of the South. In May 1811 he was recalled to France and was promoted to general of brigade. In July he was ordered back to Spain and given command of an escort of 1,500 infantry and 500 cavalry that would protect a convoy of military chests for the French armies in Spain, with over 8,350,000 francs.[*]

When General Avy returned to the Army of the South in September 1811, he was assigned command of the 2nd Brigade of General Godinot's Infantry Division, of which General Semellé took command of after General Godinot died. He would command the brigade until February 1812. Later in 1812 he took command of the 3rd Light Cavalry Brigade in General Soult's Light Cavalry Division. In March 1813 he was transferred to the Army of the Centre and given command of a light cavalry brigade in General Trelliard's Division. During the summer of 1813 he stayed with General Trelliard, commanding the 3rd Brigade of General Trelliard's 2nd Division, Army of Spain. In September he went on leave and was reassigned to the defence of eastern France. He was mortally wounded defending Merxem on 13 January 1814.

General Avy was an able staff officer, but did not excel as a brigade commander. His inability to hold a command for very long is indicative that his superiors did not think very highly of him.

Table 6.3 Barthélemi, Nicolas-Martin

Awards and honours	Baron of the Empire 5 Oct. 1808
Date and place of birth	7 Feb. 1765 at Gray
Regiments commanded	15th Dragoons 21 Jun. 1799–3 Apr. 1807
Date of rank as general	General of brigade 4 Apr. 1807
Time in the Peninsula	Nov. 1808–Sep. 1810
Units commanded in the Peninsula	2nd Brigade, Milhaud's Division 4 Apr. 1807–11 Jul. 1809; 1st Brigade, Milhaud's Division 12 Jul.– Sep. 1809; Governor, Santander Province Sep. 1809–Sep. 1810
Date and place of death	23 Apr. 1835 at Gray

---

[*] Napoleon to Berthier, 7 July 1811.

The name is sometimes spelled Barthélemy. General Barthélemi was a cavalry general who came up through the ranks, after enlisting in the Royal Army in 1785. He first entered Spain as a brigade commander in General Milhaud's Dragoon Division, initially commanding the 2nd Brigade and then the 1st Brigade. In September 1809 he was appointed governor of Santander. He was recalled to France on 17 September 1810, accused of embezzlement. He would not have a position in the French military again until July 1811, when he was assigned to the 9th Military Division. He would serve in a variety of staff positions for the rest of his career.

General Barthélemi sided with Napoleon when he returned from Elba in 1815, but was not given an active command. Instead he became the director of the remount depot at Amiens in May. After the fall of Napoleon he took temporary command of the 2nd Brigade of the 4th Cavalry Division. He served briefly as the inspector general of the Army of the Loire, retired in September 1815 and died in 1835.

Table 6.4   Beaumont, Louis-Chrétien de Carrière

Awards and honours	Baron of the Empire 26 Oct. 1808
Date and place of birth	14 Apr. 1771 at Malplacey
Regiments commanded	10th Hussars 1 Feb. 1805–24 Dec. 1805
Date of rank as general	General of brigade 24 Dec. 1805; General of division 4 Dec. 1812
Time in the Peninsula	Nov. 1808–25 Dec. 1811
Command or post in the Peninsula	Light Cavalry Brigade, Victor's Corps Nov. 1808–Nov. 1811
Wounds in Peninsula	Talavera 28 Jul. 1809
Date and place of death	16 Dec. 1813 at Metz
Cause of death	Exhaustion

An early biography stated that Louis Beaumont was 'born for war',[*] which was an accurate assessment of his character. He enlisted in the Dragoons de la Reine at the age of 17. He would fight in Ireland, Egypt and Syria and led the 10th Hussars during the Austerlitz campaign. His performance during the campaign earned him promotion to general of brigade at the age of 34. With his promotion came an elevation to the first aide-de-camp of Marshal Murat, in which capacity he served during the 1806 campaign against Prussia. After the battle of Jena on 14 October 1806 he was given command of General Milhaud's light cavalry brigade, but also remained as Marshal Murat's aide. He would lead the brigade at Eylau and Friedland in 1807.

---

[*] Devimes, *Manuel historique du département de l'Aisne*, p. 184.

In September 1808 he was assigned initially as the light cavalry brigade's commander in Marshal Victor's 1st Corps, but then temporarily reassigned to Marshal Bessières 2nd Corps. He served under him until 15 December 1808, when he and his brigade were transferred back to Marshal Victor's 1st Corps. He would lead the brigade for the next three years, commanding them at Ucles, Medellin, Alcabon, Talavera, Ocaña and at the siege of Cadiz. Although in command of the cavalry during the siege, he also had infantry forces under his control. During a Spanish sortie on 5 March 1811 he led the French force that defeated it.

In December 1811 General Beaumont was recalled to France and given a command of a brigade of cuirassiers under Saint-Sulpice. He fought in Russia in 1812. Promoted to general of division in late 1812, he commanded the light cavalry divisions of the 3rd, 6th and 12th Corps during the 1813 campaign in Germany. In early December 1813 he received command of the 5th Heavy Cavalry Division. He did not command it for long, dying of exhaustion at Metz on 16 December 1813 at the age of 42.

Table 6.5   Beaurgard, Charles-Victor Woirgard dit de

Date and place of birth	16 Oct. 1764 at Metz
Date of rank as general	General of brigade 18 Apr. 1793
Time in the Peninsula	19 Jun. 1809–19 Feb. 1810
Command or post in the Peninsula	Light Cavalry Brigade, 5th Corps 19 Jun.–Oct. 1809; 1st Brigade, 5th Dragoon Division Oct. 1809–19 Feb. 1810
Date and place of death	19 Feb. 1810 at Valverde de Leganés, Spain
Cause of death	Killed in combat

His name was sometimes spelled Beauregard. His nom-de-guerre was Woirgard, which was occasionally spelled Woiregard. Some historians refer to him by his nom-de-guerre.

Charles-Victor Beaurgard was promoted to general of brigade in 1793, at the age of 29. In June 1809 he was given command of the light cavalry brigade in Marshal Mortier' 5th Corps and would command it until October 1809, when he was transferred to take command of the 1st Brigade of the 5th Dragoon Division. He performed well at Ocaña in November 1809. In February 1810 he and his brigade were screening the corps while it was conducting operations in the vicinity of Badajoz. Beaurgard occupied Valverde de Leganés for the night and was in bed when his brigade was hit by Spanish infantry and cavalry around 2:00 a.m. The surprise was total and the Spaniards were in the village before the alarm was raised. He rallied a small group of men and counter-attacked through the streets. He was killed in the desperate fighting.[*]

It is difficult to determine why Napoleon gave General Beaurgard command of a cavalry brigade. He had no experience commanding cavalry, no active field experience since 1800 and served mostly in staff positions. Ten years prior to receiving his command, one of his superiors noted that he was 'brave, a very good officer, knowledgeable in tactics and fortifications',[†] yet in 1802 he was relieved by General Barbou for his 'his erratic behaviour, including indiscreet and troublesome conduct and for a tendency to forget things.'[‡] This may have been the reason why he was surprised by General Ballasteros at Valverde de Leganés in 1810 and paid for it with his life. Other than General Schwarz, there were fewer generals commanding French troops in the Peninsula as inept as General Beaurgard.

Table 6.6   Berton, Jean-Baptiste Breton dit

Awards and honours	Baron of the Empire 22 Nov. 1808
Date and place of birth	15 Jul. 1767 at Euilly
Date of rank as general	General of brigade 30 May 1813
Time in the Peninsula	Nov. 1808–Apr. 1814
Command or post in the Peninsula	HQ, Polish Division, 4th Corps Nov. 1808–Aug. 1811; Governor, Malaga Aug. 1811; Commandant, Antequera 5 Nov. 1811–7 Feb. 1812; Commandant, Osuna 7 Feb.–Aug. 1812; 2nd Light Cavalry Brigade, Soult's Division 16 Jul. 1813–13 Aug. 1814
Date and place of death	5 Oct. 1822 at Poitiers
Cause of death	Executed for conspiracy against the state
Place of burial	Poitiers

Jean-Baptiste Breton dit Berton's real name was Jean-Baptiste Breton. Breton was his nom-de-guerre. Unlike General Beaurgard, who also had a nom-de-guerre but was usually referred to by his family name, General Jean-Baptiste Breton is best known by his nom-de-guerre, Berton.

General Berton never commanded a regiment of cavalry. He first went to the Peninsula in November 1808, assigned to the headquarters of the 1st Corps and would be the adjutant commandant chief of staff of the headquarters of General Valence's Polish Division. He would serve with them at Talavera, Almonacid and Ocaña in 1809. In 1810 he was at the

---

[*] Lapène, *Conquête de l'Andalousie*, p. 39; Warre, *Letters from the Peninsula*, p. 117.
[†] Six, *Dictionnaire Biographique*, vol. 1, p. 70.
[‡] Ibid.

capture of Malaga and Ronda and became the governor of Malaga for a short period in 1811. When General Maransin was appointed governor of Malaga in October, General Berton initially served as the Chief-of-Staff for him and then as commandant of Antequera and Ossuna, small cities in Malaga Province. In May 1813 he was promoted to general of brigade. After the disaster at Vitoria he commanded an infantry brigade for a few weeks before taking command of a light cavalry brigade in the reorganised Army of Spain in July 1813.

General Berton commanded a brigade of dragoons in the Waterloo campaign and fought at Wavre. He was dismissed from the army in 1815. Over the next seven years he was involved in a conspiracy to overthrow the Bourbons. He was tried on 11 September 1822 and executed 24 days later.

Table 6.7 Bessières, Bertrand

Awards and honours	Baron of the Empire 16 Dec. 1810
Date and place of birth	6 Jan. 1773 at Prayssac
Regiments commanded	11th Chasseurs 11 Jan. 1800–24 Dec. 1805
Date of rank as general	General of brigade 24 Dec. 1805
Time in the Peninsula	Feb. 1808–Dec. 1811
Command or post in the Peninsula	Cavalry Brigade, Corps of Observation of the Eastern Pyrenees Feb.–7 Sep. 1808; Cavalry Brigade, 5th Corps 7 Sep.–Oct. 1808; Cavalry Brigade, 7th Corps Oct. 1808–Jan. 1809; 1st Infantry Brigade, Souham's Division Jan.–7 Dec. 1809; Prov. Dragoon Brigade, Caulaincourt's Division 7 Dec. 1809–28; Feb. 1810; Prov. Dragoon Brigade, Kellermann's Division 4 Mar.–17 Apr. 1810; Prov. Dragoon Brigade, Trelliard's Division 26 Apr.–26 Jun. 1810; Prov. Dragoon Brigade, Seras's Division, 6th Military Government 26 Jun.– Sep. 1810; Staff, 6th Military Government Sep. 1810–May 1811; 6th Military Government May–Dec. 1811
Date and place of death	15 Nov. 1854 at Chantilly
Place of burial	Père Lachaise Cemetery

Bertrand Bessières was the younger brother of Marshal Jean Bessières.

General Bessières arrived in the Peninsula in February 1808 as commander of the cavalry brigade assigned to General Duhesme's Corps of Observation of the Eastern Pyrenees. General Bessières's brigade had two provisional regiments the 3rd Provisional Cuirassiers and the 3rd Provisional Chasseurs. He would command them for ten months, during which time they were involved in the pacification of Barcelona. In September 1808 the corps was renamed the 5th Corps and its command was given to Marshal Saint-Cyr. In October the 5th Corps was redesignated the 7th Corps. General Bessières's brigade was disbanded in January 1809 and he was given command of the 1st Infantry Brigade of General Souham's Division. His new brigade was actually a combined arms brigade, comprising the 1st and 3rd Légère Régiments and the 24th Dragoons. He would command it throughout 1809 and was part of the force that besieged Gerona. In December 1809 General Bessières was transferred to western Spain and was given command of a provisional dragoon brigade in General Caulaincourt's Dragoon Division. His brigade consisted of the 6th and 7th Provisional Dragoon Regiments. In March he and his brigade were transferred to General Kellermann's Dragoon Division, which would be taken over by General Trelliard in April. In June General Bessières and his brigade were transferred to the 6th Military Government, where he would remain until he left the Peninsula in late 1811. His new mission was to help protect the Army of Portugal's lines of communication. In September 1810 he gave up command and was assigned to the headquarters of the 6th Military Government in Valladolid. He replaced General Kellermann as governor of the 6th Military Government in May 1811.

On 31 July 1811 General Bessières was selected for promotion to general of division, but he refused the promotion. It was officially annulled by a decree of 30 November 1811. He left the Peninsula in December and was assigned as a commander of a cuirassier brigade in Germany. He fought in Russia in 1812, where he was wounded at Borodino. In the 1813 campaign in Germany he commanded the 2nd Cuirassier Brigade in General Bordessoulle's Division and was wounded at Leipzig in 1813. He would never command in the field again. During the 1815 campaign he commanded a cavalry depot. He retired in 1824 and died 30 years later.

General Bessières was overshadowed by his older brother and had a prickly personality. His early years in the Peninsula were marked by tension between him and General Duhesme. It had reached a point that Bessières threatened to resign. Instead he was reassigned. What caused the rift between the two is not known, but General Duhesme was eventually relieved from command for abuses of power in Barcelona. General Bessières's refusal of his promotion to general of division was also unheard of. Why he refused it remains a mystery, but he was never promoted again.

Table 6.8   Bonnemains, Pierre

Awards and honours	Baron of the Empire 19 Mar. 1808
Date and place of birth	13 Sep. 1773 at Tréauville
Regiments commanded	5th Chasseurs 20 Sep. 1806–6 Aug. 1811
Date of rank as general	General of brigade 6 Aug. 1811
Time in the Peninsula	16 Nov. 1808–13 Apr. 1813
Command or post in the Peninsula	5th Chasseurs 15 Nov. 1808–6 Aug. 1811; Light Cavalry Brigade, Victor's Corps 16 Nov. 1811–7 Feb. 1812; 2nd Brigade, Perreimond's Division, Army of the South Feb. 1812–Oct. 1812; 2nd Brigade, 1st Light Cavalry Division, Army of the South Oct. 1812–13 Apr. 1813
Date and place of death	9 Nov. 1850 at Mesnil-Garnier
Place of burial	In the church cemetery at Mesnil-Garnier

Pierre Bonnemains led the 5th Chasseurs at Burgos in 1808; at Almaraz, Truxille, Villamerique, Medellin and Talavera in 1809; and Montellano in April, 1810. During the rest of 1810 and for much of 1811 he and the regiment conducted counter-guerrilla operations in Andalusia. In August 1811 he was promoted to general of brigade and assumed command of General Beaumont's Light Cavalry Brigade in the 1st Corps. After the reorganisation if the Army of the South in late 1811, which did away with its corps structure, Bonnemains and his brigade were assigned to the newly formed 1st Cavalry Division, commanded by General Perreimond. In the autumn of 1812 the brigade formed the rearguard of the Army of the South as it withdrew northward to the Ebro River. He returned to France in the spring of 1813 and was sent to Italy, where he commanded a light cavalry brigade.

During the Waterloo campaign General Bonnemains commanded a dragoon brigade under General Exelmans. After Waterloo he was dismissed from the army, but was reinstated in 1816. He appeared to lead a charmed life. He was an ardent Bonapartist, yet after a brief exile in 1815, he was allowed to serve in the army another 26 years. General Bonnemains became a viscount in 1826 and a peer of France in 1845.

Table 6.9   Bordessoulle, Etienne Tardif de Pommeroux

Awards and honours	Baron of the Empire 17 May 1810
Date and place of birth	4 Apr. 1771 at Luzeret, India
Regiments commanded	22nd Chasseurs 27 Dec. 1805–25 Jun. 1807

Table 6.9 continued

Date of rank as general	General of brigade 25 Jun. 1807; General of division 4 Dec. 1812
Time in the Peninsula	15 Nov. 1808–Apr. 1809
Command or post in the Peninsula	2nd Chasseur Brigade, Lasalle's Light Cavalry Division 15 Nov. 1808–Apr. 1809
Date and place of death	3 Oct. 1837 at Fontaine
Place of burial	Cemetery of Fontaine-Bonnelau

General Bordessoulle entered Spain at the head of the 2nd Brigade of General Lasalle's Light Cavalry Division in November 1808. His command had two regiments, the 10th Chasseurs and his old regiment, the 22nd Chasseurs. He was recalled to France in January 1809, but avoided going for several months, refusing to abandon his brigade while on campaign. He led them at Medellin on 28 March, but afterwards gave up command and returned to France. He arrived in Germany in May and took command of a cuirassier brigade and was wounded at Wagram. Bordessoulle would command light cavalry brigades in 1810 and 1811 and would lead one in Russia in 1812. He was wounded at Borodino and promoted to general of division in December. He commanded a cuirassier division in the 1813 and 1814 campaigns.

By late March 1814 General Bordessoulle had had enough. After 22 years of campaigning and 8 wounds, he was tired. He had even reached a point where he was discouraging his own soldiers.[*] When Marshal Marmont defected with his troops to the Allies in early April, Bordessoulle did not oppose him. When Napoleon returned in 1815, he fled to Ghent with King Louis XVIII. At the Second Restoration he was rewarded for his loyalty by the king and was given a series of active commands until he retired in 1832. He died five years later.

Table 6.10 Bouillé du Chariol, Louis-Joseph Amour Marquis de

Awards and honours	Count of the Empire 2 Sep. 1810
Date and place of birth	1 May 1769 in Martinique
Date of rank as general	General of brigade 23 Jun. 1810
Time in the Peninsula	17 Oct. 1808–9 Nov. 1812
Command or post in the Peninsula	Chief-of-Staff, Sebastini's Division, 4th Corps 10 Sep. 1808–14 Sep. 1809; Chief-of-Staff, Sebastini's 4th Corps 14 Sep. 1809–11 Apr. 1811; Chief-of-Staff, Leval's 4th Corps

---

[*] Elting, *Swords around the Throne*, p. 173.

11 Apr. 1811–21 Feb. 1812; 1st Dragoon
Brigade, 3rd Cavalry Division, Army of the
South 21 Feb.–14 Apr. 1812; Commandant of
Antequera Mar.–Oct. 1812
Date and place of death 20 Nov. 1850 in Paris

General Bouillé never commanded a regiment in French service and actually led troops against France. In 1794 he commanded the French émigré regiment of Uhlans Britanniques in the Flanders campaign. This regiment was one of the British army's foreign regiments and it was quite unusual for an officer to have served successfully in two enemy armies in his career. Bouillé came back to France in 1800 and served in the Army of Naples. On 10 September 1808 Louis Bouillé was appointed chief-of-staff of General Sebastini's Division and would serve in Spain with him for the next three years. In 1809, when General Sebastini was given command of the 4th Corps, Bouillé became his chief-of-staff. In June 1810 he was promoted to general of brigade, a rank more appropriate for his responsibilities as a Corps's chief-of-staff. He would serve in that position until Marshal Soult reorganised the Army of the South and did away with the corps structure. In February 1812 General Bouillé was given command of the 1st Dragoon Brigade (16th and 21st Dragoons) of General Soult's 3rd Cavalry Division. He had no illusions about what his new command would entail. His brigade headquarters was located in Antequera, but the two regiments were scattered throughout Malaga and Grenada Provinces. Furthermore the regiments had taken so many losses among its horses they could only muster 250 mounts.[*]

In addition to being a brigade commander, General Bouillé was the commandant of Antquera and was responsible for pacifying the area. Much of his time was spent with a mobile column of infantry and cavalry chasing guerrillas. He began to have trouble with his vision, which he described in a letter to his wife, saying that the hot weather was affecting his 'eyesight in frightful manner'.[†] In April 1812 he gave up command of the 1st Brigade on account of his failing health and in October he received permission to return to France owing to a severe case of ophthalmia. He travelled to France with General Perreimond, the commander of the Army of the South's 1st Cavalry Division. He left Almansa, where the Army of the South's headquarters was located, on 8 October and arrived in France on 9 September. General Bouillé retired in December 1812. He went blind shortly after he retired but survived until 1850.

---

[*] Bouillé, *Souvenirs et Fragments*, vol. III, p. 500.
[†] Ibid, p. 508.

Table 6.11   Boussart André-Joseph

Awards and honours	Baron of the Empire 10 Feb. 1809
Date and place of birth	13 Nov. 1758 at Binche
Regiments commanded	20th Dragoons 7 Jan. 1797–23 Sep. 1800
Date of rank as general	General of brigade 14 Dec. 1801; General of division 16 Mar. 1812
Time in the Peninsula	Jan. 1808–12 Nov. 1808; 28 Nov. 1808–Jun. 1813
Command or post in the Peninsula	1st Brigade, Fresia's Division, Dupont's Corps Jan. 1808–12 Nov. 1808; Light Cavalry Brigade, 5th Corps 28 Nov. 1808–Jun. 1809; Cavalry Brigade, 3rd Corps Jun. 1809–Sep. 1811; Governor of Valencia Mar. 1812–Jun. 1813
Wounds in Peninsula	Lerida shot in the stomach on 23 Apr. 1810; Torrente 26 Dec. 1811
Date and place of death	10 Aug. 1813 at Bagnères-de-Bigorre
Cause of death	Multiple wounds
Place of burial	Bagnères-de-Bigorre

In some histories Boussart is spelled Boussard. André-Joseph Boussart served in the Austrian Army for seven years, but joined the insurrection in Belgium in 1789. He commanded the 20th Dragoons in Egypt. He was captured twice as a general officer. The first time was on 19 July 1808, when General Dupont surrendered at Bailen. Part of the surrender terms was the repatriation of general officers to France. Boussart was one of those allowed to return to France instead of going into captivity.

Most of the five years General Boussart spent in the Peninsula were in eastern Spain, where he commanded the cavalry brigade assigned to Marshal Suchet. This brigade fought in most of the campaigns there, including Lerida on 23 April 1810, where he was shot in the stomach, Vinaros on 26 November 1810 and the sieges of Saguntum and Valencia in 1811. In addition to having to surrender at Bailen, Boussart was also briefly captured at Torrente on 26 December 1811. He was riding with the 4th Hussars, when they were charged by Spanish cavalry. He was seriously wounded and thrown from his horse. He was rescued by a timely charge of the 13th Cuirassiers. Among those killed was Captain Robert, his second aide-de-camp, and the commander of his escort, Adolphe de Villeneuve, who was the cousin of Marshal Suchet.* This was the fifth time that General Boussart had been badly wounded.

---

* de Gonneville, *Recollections of Colonel de Gonneville*, vol. 2, p. 50; Suchet, *Memoirs of the War in Spain*, vol. 2, p. 226.

The wounds from Torrente were too serious for him to remain in a field command. He became governor of Valencia in March 1812; he governed the city fairly and its inhabitants nicknamed him 'The Brave Walloon'. In June 1813 his health began to deteriorate to a point where he could not continue in command. He was sent back to southern France to aid recovery but on 10 August he died from complications caused by his many wounds over the years. After his death he became a national hero to Belgian nationalists. At the park next to the church, in his hometown of Binche, Belgium, there is a memorial to him.[*]

Without a doubt General Boussart was the bravest French general in the Peninsula. His numerous wounds attest to this. However, at least one of his officers felt that his bravery caused him to expose his troops unnecessarily to enemy fire at times. For example, during the siege of Saguntum in the autumn of 1811, his brigade was part of the covering force. Captain de Gonneville, who was an officer in the 13th Cuirassiers, wrote:

> Every morning at day-break we mounted our horses and went to take up a position on the right front of the fort, having to pass under its cannon. We marched in column by twos and as soon as the head of the regiment came within range, fire upon us began. Shot and shell were poured upon us without interruption all the time we were marching past and this took nearly a quarter of an hour at a walk, through the folly of Boussard, the General of the Division; for he imagined that if we had passed at a trot the enemy would have thought us afraid.[†]

It is obvious that Captain de Gonneville did not like Boussart and left a damning description of his character. 'This General was the most stupid being that I ever met; he could hardly read or write, was incapable of giving an order, or even understanding those he received.'[‡] Furthermore, he felt the general was a bully, who used his position to further his own means. In one case Captain de Gonneville requested to return to France on personal leave, but permission was withheld by General Boussart until de Gonneville agreed to give him one of his horses.[§]

De Gonneville's critical opinion notwithstanding, General Boussart was an effective brigade commander who led by example. He may have exposed his men needlessly, but in most cases he shared the danger with

---

[*] Chappet, *Guide Napoléonien*, p. 189.
[*] de Gonneville, *Recollections of Colonel de Gonneville*, vol. 2, p. 13.
[†] Ibid.
[‡] Ibid, vol. 2, pp. 73–5

them. He had much experience at commanding both cavalry and combined units of cavalry, infantry and artillery. His promotion to general of division was earned the hard way – on multiple battlefields, far from the eyes of Napoleon. It was something that few generals in the Peninsula achieved.

Table 6.12   Bouvier des Eclaz, Joseph

Awards and honours	Baron of the Empire 22 Nov. 1808
Date and place of birth	3 Dec. 1757 at Belley
Regiments commanded	14th Dragoons 20 Sep. 1806–8 Oct. 1810
Date of rank as general	General of brigade 8 Oct. 1810
Time in the Peninsula	Nov. 1808–18 Dec. 1811
Command or post in the Peninsula	14th Dragoons 20 Sep. 1808–8 Oct. 1810; 3rd Brigade, Tour-Maubourg's Division, Army of the South 7 Nov. 1809–18 Dec. 1811
Date and place of death	13 Jan. 1830 at Belley

Joseph Bouvier des Eclaz's name is often misspelled as Bouvier des Eclats.

Joseph Bouvier des Eclaz entered Spain with his regiment in November 1808 and commanded them for two years until he was promoted to general of brigade in October 1810. He took command of the 2nd Dragoon Brigade of General Tour-Maubourg's Dragoon Division and led them until December 1811. He distinguished himself at the head of his former regiment, the 14th Dragoons, on 19 February 1811 at the battle of Gebora. They were mentioned in the Marshal Mortier's dispatch:

> The 14th Dragoons have gained much honour by forcing, under fire from the enemy, the portion of the Gebora Bridge. General Bouvier Eclaz stood out. This bold action deserves to be mentioned.[*]

Marshal Soult, the commander of the Army of the South, echoed these sentiments, in his order of the day

> It is impossible to praise the troops of all arms who have contributed. Their value is beyond praise, but we must mention the corps that have been fortunate enough to participate . . . the 14th Dragoons, commanded by Chief of squadrons Hardy and General Bouvier Eclaz are worth mentioning.[†]

He also distinguished himself at the battle of Albuera on 16 May 1811,

---

[*] Menuau, *Historique du 14e Régiment de Dragons*, pp. 245–6.
[†] Ibid, p. 246.

but Marshal Soult misspelled his name in the official dispatch!

In December 1811 General Bouvier des Eclaz returned to France and was given command of the Carabinier Brigade. He would lead them in Russia in 1812. In March 1813 he returned to France in poor health. By July, he was well enough to return to duty and he was appointed the commandant of the Department of Frise. On 7 December 1813 he was arrested and subjected to a court of inquiry for surrendering the Chateau de Binenhof to insurgents on 17 November 1813. General Bouvier des Eclaz retired in January 1814 but was called to active duty when Napoleon returned to France in 1815. He was responsible for oranising the national guard in the 6th Military Division during the Hundred Days. He retired in November 1815.

Table 6.13   Boyer, Pierre-François-Joseph

Awards and honours	Baron of the Empire 1 May 1812
Date and place of birth	7 Sep. 1772 at Befort
Regiments commanded	4th Line Infantry Regiment 20 Dec. 1796–18 Jan. 1797
Date of rank as general	General of brigade 29 Mar. 1801 General of division 16 Feb. 1814
Time in the Peninsula	Apr. 1809–Jan. 1814
Command or post in the Peninsula	Chief-of-Staff, 8th Corps 11 Aug. 1809–Jun. 1811; 1st Brigade, Foy's Division, Army of Portugal Jun. 1811–Jul. 1811; 2nd Dragoon Brigade, Montbrun's Division Oct. 1811–Feb. 1812; Dragoon Division, Army of Portugal Feb. 1812–May 1813; Chief-of-Staff, Army of Portugal 8 May 1813–16 Jul. 1813; 9th Division, Army of Spain 16 Jul. 1813–Jan. 1814
Date and place of death	11 Jul. 1851 at Lardy

Pierre Boyer was another infantry officer who commanded cavalry in the Peninsula. He had little experience commanding at the regimental level and spent most of his time as a staff officer. He served in Egypt and was part of the expedition to Santo Domingo. In early 1803 he was sent home to France to meet Napoleon. The frigate transporting him was captured by the British. Boyer was paroled and returned to France. He would not be employed again until the summer of 1806. He was the Chief-of-Staff to Marshal Kellermann until June 1809, when he was assigned to Junot's Corps in Spain. As the commander of the Army of Portugal's Dragoon Division, Boyer received the nickname of 'Pierre le Cruel', for the reprisals he took against captured guerrillas. These reprisals were supposedly undertaken as vengeance for atrocities the guerrillas committed against captured French soldiers.[*]

General Boyer's Division had some success at Salamanca, charging the fleeing men of the British 4th Division and hitting the eastern flank of the British 6th Division, inflicting heavy casualties on the 53rd Foot. Rory Muir wrote that, when compared to the British Dragoon Brigade under General Le Marchant,

> The contrast between the results achieved by Le Marchant and Boyer is striking, yet both charged when the infantry facing them were already disordered and broken. The good discipline of the allied infantry and the advance of the Sixth Division no doubt helped limit Boyer's success and he might have done better if he had charged rather later, after Clinton's line had been weakened and disrupted by fighting Bonnet's infantry, but the crucial difference lay in the quality of the two brigades of cavalry. One was well mounted, full of confidence and eager for action; the other was intimidated by the knowledge that for once the allied cavalry were clearly superior.[†]

General Boyer would continue to command the Dragoon Division until May 1813, when he became the chief-of-staff of the Army of Portugal. After the reorganisation of the French armies in Spain in July 1813, he was given command of the 9th Infantry Division. In January 1814 He and his division were sent to eastern France. During the Hundred Days he rallied to Napoleon but did not have an active command. He was proscribed in July 1815 and was in allowed to retire in 1826. He was recalled to active duty in 1830 and died in 1851.

Table 6.14   Briche André-Louis-Elisabeth-Marie

Awards and honours	Baron of the Empire 15 Oct. 1809
Date and place of birth	12 Aug. 1772 at Neuilly-sous-Clermont
Regiments commanded	10th Hussars 13 Jan. 1806–17 Dec. 1809
Date of rank as general	General of brigade 17 Dec. 1809; General of division 19 Nov. 1813
Time in the Peninsula	2 Oct. 1808–10 Feb. 1812
Command or post in the Peninsula	10th Hussars 13 Jan. 1806–17 Dec. 1809 Light Cavalry Brigade, 5th Corps 19 Feb.– May 1810; Light Cavalry Brigade, Marizy's

---

[*] Corret, *Histoire Pittoresque*, pp. 154–5.

[†] Muir, *Salamanca 1812*, p. 153.

Division May–Autumn 1810; Light Cavalry
Brigade, 5th Corps Feb. 1811–7 Feb. 1812;
2nd Brigade, Tour-Maubourg's Division 7–10
Feb. 1812;

Date and place of death 21 May 1825 at Marseille

During his 40 months in the Peninsula General Briche saw much
combat, including Ocaña on 18 November 1809, Fuente de Cantos on 14
September 1810, Merida on 6 January 1811, Botoa on 20 January 1811,
Gebora on 19 February 1811, Albuera on 16 May 1811 and at Arroyo dos
Molinos 28 October 1811. He was relieved of his command because of
the disaster at Arroyo dos Molinos and recalled to Paris on 31 December
1811. On 2 January 1812 Napoleon wrote to Marshal Berthier giving the
reasons why he was relieving General Briche for the role he played at
Arroyo dos Molinos:

> I wish you to write to me a report, which will be printed, on the
> correspondence respecting General Girard's affair. It seems that
> General Britche [sic] was posted on the side by which the enemy
> attacked; that he was completely surprised, not in his bivouac, but
> in bed in a comfortable house, while the horses of his hussars were
> unsaddled. I will dictate this report to you. My object is to impress
> on the colonels and generals of light troops the general principle
> that a colonel of chasseurs or hussars who goest to bed, instead
> of spending the nights in bivouac and in constant communication
> with his main-guard, deserves death. I think that Marshal Mortier
> has some information on the subject. As my object is not merely to
> punish General Britche [*sic*], but to excite the zeal of the whole light
> cavalry, this report must be vigorously drawn up.[*]

Before General Briche received word that he had been relieved, he was
appointed to command the 2nd Brigade in Tour-Maubourg's Division
in February 1812. He would command for only three days before being
ordered to France. In 1813 he commanded a Wurttemberg Light Cavalry
Brigade in the 4th Corps. He was promoted to general of division on 19
November 1813 and commanded the 5th Heavy Cavalry Division during
the 1814 campaign in France. He did not side with Napoleon during the
Hundred Days.

General Briche's performance as a cavalry commander in the Peninsula
was mixed. At least one of his regiments, the 2nd Hussars, performed

---

[*] Bonaparte, Napoleon, *The Confidential Correspondence*, vol. 2, pp. 203–4.

spectacularly at Albuera, taking part in the charge that destroyed Colborne's brigade. Yet Briche's reputation was tarnished by the disaster at Arroyo dos Molinos. Two months later he was relieved from his command. He would not have another active command until the spring of 1813, when he commanded a Wurttemberg Light Cavalry Brigade. During the 1813 campaign in Germany his performance was considered good enough for him to be promoted to general of division.

Table 6.15   Bron de Bailly, André-François

Awards and honours	Baron of the Empire 1 Jan. 1813
Date and place of birth	30 Nov. 1758 at Vienne
Regiments commanded	3rd Dragoons 26 Sep. 1797–22 Sep. 1800
Date of rank as general	General of brigade 30 Nov. 1801
Time in the Peninsula	17 Oct. 1808–6 Mar. 1809; Jan. 1810–Nov. 1811
Command or post in the Peninsula	Staff Officer in the Army of Spain 17 Oct. 1808–15 Jan. 1809; Prov. Dragoon Brigade, Caulaincourt's Division 7 Dec. 1809–28 Feb. 1810; Prov. Dragoon Brigade, Kellermann's Division 4 Mar.–17 Apr. 1810; Prov. Dragoon Brigade, Trelliard's Division 26 Apr.–26 Jun. 1810; Prov. Dragoon Brigade, 6th Military Government 29 May 1810–Oct. 1810; 1st Dragoon Brigade, Tour-Maubourg's Division, Army of the South May 1811–28 Oct. 1811
Wounds in Peninsula	Arroyo dos Molinos 28 Oct. 1811
Date and place of death	18 May 1847 at Batignolles-Monceau
Place of burial	Cimetière du Nord, Montmartre, Paris

His name is sometimes spelled as Brun, Le Bron, or Le Brun. General Bron served on the staff in the HQ of the Army of Spain in 1808 until he was recalled to France in January 1809. He commanded a light cavalry brigade in Marulaz's Division in the 1809 campaign against Austria. General Bron returned to Spain in January 1810 and commanded a provisional dragoon brigade protecting the lines of communication for the Army of Portugal. His brigade was disbanded in the autumn of 1810 and he worked in the Headquarters of the 6th Military Government. In May 1811 he was reassigned to the Army of the South and commanded the 1st Dragoon Brigade in Tour-Maubourg's Division. At Usagre on 25 May 1811, after chasing Spanish cavalry out of Villa Garcia, General Bron's brigade was ordered to continue its pursuit across a steep ravine. This was an unfortunate move, for hidden behind a ridge on the far side of the ravine were three British and eight Portuguese cavalry regiments. His brigade had just begun to reform after crossing the narrow bridge, with the 4th and 20th Dragoons in front and the 26th Dragoons still crossing the bridge, when the British and Portuguese cavalry charged. His regiments were shattered and fled in every direction. His brigade lost about 300 casualties, including 78 men captured. Bron himself barely avoided capture, because 'being well mounted, he was able to leap a wall and got away. . .'* Five months later, his luck ran out. He was captured by the British at Arroyo dos Molinos on 28 October 1811. He was a surly prisoner, with a 'haughty and overbearing manner'† and initially refused to sign his parole, stating his word as a French officer should be sufficient. Only after being threatened with being treated like the rest of the prisoners did he consent.‡ He returned to France in June 1814. General Bron was the commandant at Dôle in December 1814 and would be at the cavalry depot at Troyes during the Hundred Days. He retired on 4 September 1815.

Table 6.16 Cambacérès, Jean-Pierre-Hubert

Awards and honours	Baron of the Empire 1 Jun. 1808
Date and place of birth	13 Nov. 1778 at Montpellier
Date of rank as general	General of brigade 10 Jul. 1806
Time in the Peninsula	7 Sep. 1808–25 Sep. 1810
Command or post in the Peninsula	Headquarters, Army of Spain Sep. 1808–Jan. 1809; Cavalry Depot at Palencia Jan.–29 Jun. 1809; 1st Dragoon Brigade, 5th Dragoon Division 29 Jun.–Oct. 1809; Headquarters, 2nd Corps Nov. 1809–25 Sep. 1810
Date and place of death	5 Sep. 1826 in Paris
Place of burial	Père Lachaise Cemetery

Jean Cambacérès was a member of one of the most powerful families in France. One brother, Jean Jacques Cambacérès, was the Arch-Chancellor of the Empire, a Prince of the Empire and President of the House of Peers in 1815. Etienne, his other brother, was a cardinal. When Jean Cambacérès was promoted to general of brigade in 1806, he was only 27 years old and would be the second-youngest cavalry general to serve in Spain. He commanded a brigade under General Tilly in the 1807 campaign in

---

* Long, *Peninsular Cavalry General*, p. 142.
† Blakeney, *A Boy in the Peninsular War*, p. 248.
‡ Ibid, pp. 248–9.

Eastern Europe. In September 1808 he was sent to Spain and served with the army's headquarters. In January 1809 he was given command of the cavalry depot at Palencia. He commanded it until October, when he was assigned to the Headquarters of the 2nd Corps.

Despite his political connections General Cambacérès ran afoul of Napoleon. In early May 1809 the Minister of War proposed to Napoleon that Cambacérès be sent from Spain to join the army in Germany. Napoleon refused stating 'No, he is good for nothing.'* General Cambacérès remained in Spain until September 1810, when he was recalled to France and appointed the commandant of the Department of Mont-Tonnerre. He was given command of a cavalry brigade in the Grande Armée during the 1813 campaign in Germany. He did not have an active command from 1814 until he retired in 1824.

Table 6.17   Carrié de Boissy, Jean-Augustin

Awards and honours	Baron of the Empire 20 Apr. 1810
Date and place of birth	7 Jul. 1764 at Entraygues
Regiments commanded	1st Chasseurs 5 May–4 Dec. 1800; 22nd Dragoons 4 Dec. 1800–4 Apr. 1807
Date of rank as general	General of brigade 4 Apr. 1807
Time in the Peninsula	Nov. 1808–Aug. 1812
Command or post in the Peninsula	2nd Dragoon Brigade, Kellerman's Divison Nov. 1808–28 Feb. 1810; Governor of Palencia 28 Feb.–20 Jun. 1810–Feb. 1812 Infantry Brigade, Seras's Division 20 Jun. 1810–15 Sep. 1810; Dragoon Brigade, Boyer's Division Feb.–18 Jul. 1812
Wounds in Peninsula	Alba des Tormes wounded in the chest on 28 Nov. 1809; Guarena on 18 Jul. 1812 wounded twice in the head, once in the right hand, once in the left arm and once between the shoulders; he was also taken prisoner.
Date and place of death	9 Jul. 1848 at Entraygues

Jean-Augustin Carrié de Boissy led from the front and paid the price. He was wounded 11 times in his career, seven times leading his brigade. He was captured twice, the first time as a chief of squadron on 8 August 1796. The second time was at the head of his brigade on 18 July 1812, after crossing the Guarena River. His brigade, consisting of the 15th and

---

* Bonaparte, Napoleon, *The Confidential Correspondence*, vol. III, p. 42.

25th Dragoons, charged General Alten's Light Cavalry Brigade (1st King's German Legion Hussars and the 14th Light Dragoons). The initial charge was successful and the British were forced back, but then the British 3rd Dragoons came to the rescue. Carrié became separated from his escort of a company from the 15th Dragoons and was surrounded by German Hussars. After being wounded five times he was forced to surrender.[*] He was imprisoned in Great Britain and did not return to France until June 1814. Although he supported Napoleon upon his return in 1815, he did not have an active command. He retired shortly after the Second Restoration.

Table 6.18 Caulaincourt, August-Jean-Gabriel de

Awards and honours	Baron of the Empire 19 Mar. 1808
Date and place of birth	16 Sep. 1777 at Caulaincourt
Regiments commanded	19th Dragoons 24 Aug. 1801–5 Jun. 1806
Date of rank as general	General of brigade 11 Feb. 1808; General of division 7 Sep. 1809
Time in the Peninsula	19 Mar. 1808–15 Sep. 1809; Dec.? 1809–28 Feb. 1810
Command or post in the Peninsula	Staff officer, HQ of the Army of Spain 19 Mar.–28 Dec. 1808; 2nd Dragoon Brigade, Houssaye's Division 24 Dec. 1808–7 Sep. 1809; Commander of 5 brigades of Prov. dragoons assigned to the 8th Corps 29 Nov. 1809–28 Feb. 1810
Date and place of death	7 Sep. 1812 at Borodino, Russia
Cause of death	Shot in the breast while leading the 5th Cuirassiers in a charge against the Grand Redoubt at Borodino
Place of burial	The Grand Redoubt at Borodino

August-Jean-Gabriel de Caulaincourt was the younger brother of General Armand de Caulaincourt. He became the commander of the 19th Dragoons in 1801 at the age of 21. He transferred into Dutch service in 1806 but returned to French service in February 1808. He commanded a March Brigade in the Corps of the Western Pyrenees in 1808, but once the men were delivered to their units, the brigade was disbanded. He would serve on the staff until he was given command of the 2nd Dragoon Brigade in General Houssaye's Division. He replaced General Davenay, who had

---

[*] Muir, *Salamanca 1812*, pp. 13–14.

been relieved by General Houssaye. While in the Peninsula, he and his brigade were part of Marshal Soult's invasion of northern Portugal and fought at Oporto on 29 March 1809 and at Arzobispo on 8 August 1809. Three months after assuming command of the cavalry of the 8th Corps, General Caulaincourt received permission to return France due to poor health. During the 1812 Russian campaign he served as the commandant of the Imperial Headquarters, but replaced General Montbrun as commander of the 2nd Cavalry Corps, after he was killed in the battle of Borodino. Caulaincourt would not live for long. He was killed a few hours later in a charge against the Grand Redoubt.

General Philippe de Ségur, one of Napoleon's Imperial aides-de-camp, wrote:

> Caulaincourt went to replace him and found the aides-de-camp of the unfortunate Montbrun weeping over their loss. 'Follow me!' he shouted. 'Don't weep, but come and take your revenge!'
>
> The King [Murat] pointed out to Caulaincourt the enemy's new flank which he must break through till he was abreast of the defile where the principal battery was stationed. While the light cavalry was carrying the charge to a successful issue he, Caulaincourt, would suddenly swing to the left with his cuirassiers and take the rear of the terrible redoubt which was still raining death on Prince Eugèné's troops.
>
> Caulaincourt replied, 'You'll see me up there very soon – dead or alive!' With that he dashed off and mowed down everything that stood in his way. Then having led his cuirassiers around to the left, he was the first to enter this gory redoubt, but a bullet struck and killed him. His conquest became his grave![*]

Colonel Louis Lejeune, another Imperial aide-de-camp, described his burial:

> We too spent a short time over the sacred duty of interring our dead and when I climbed up into the Grand Redoubt to examine the condition of fortification which had given us so much trouble the day before, I found our men digging graves for their many comrades and officers who had fallen. Caulaincourt was placed in the centre of the entrenchment... As in the case of General Gudin, I made the men cover over these two bodies with quantities of broken armour and weapons.[†]

---

[*] de Ségur, *Napoleon's Russian Campaign*, p. 75.
[†] Lejeune, vol. 2, *Memoirs of Baron Lejeune*, p. 189.

On hearing of Auguste de Caulaincourt's death, Napoleon told his brother 'He has died as a brave man should and that is in deciding the battle. France loses one of her best officers.'[‡]

Table 6.19   Cavrois, Louis-Joseph

Date and place of birth	27 Jun. 1756 at Gaudeimpré
Regiments commanded	14th Chasseurs 29 Sep. 1793–27 Oct. 1793
Date of rank as general	General of brigade 16 Nov. 1793
Time in the Peninsula	19 May 1808–24 Oct. 1808; 7 Feb. 1809–16 Jan. 1812
Command or post in the Peninsula	Staff Officer, Gobert's Division 14 Dec. 1807–24 Oct. 1808; Staff Officer, 2nd Corps 7 Feb. 1809–12 Jul. 1809; 2nd Dragoon Brigade, Tour-Maubourg's Division 12 Jul. 1809–Apr. 1810; 2nd Dragoon Brigade, Trelliard's Division Apr. 1810–Oct. 1811; 2nd Dragoon Divison, Army of Portugal Oct. 1811–16 Jan. 1812
Date and place of death	26 Mar. 1833 at Pas-en-Artois

General of brigade Louis-Joseph Cavrois was a staff officer assigned to Gobert's Division, part of Dupont's army that surrendered at Bailen on 21 July 1808. He was sent to Cadiz and was one of the fortunate few, who were returned to France three months later. (This was the second time he had been captured. The first was on 25 November 1795 at the surrender of Mannheim to the Austrians.) General Cavrois would be in the Peninsula for over 18 months before he was given command of a brigade. In April 1810 he assumed command of the 3rd Dragoon Brigade (10th and 11th Dragoons). During the invasion of Portugal from August 1810 to April 1811 the 10th Dragoons were detached, essentially reducing his brigade to a single regiment under his command. In July 1811, with the reorganisation of the Army of Portugal, he was given command of the 2nd Dragoon Brigade of General Trelliard's Division. In October he assumed temporary command of the division, when General Trelliard was transferred to the Army of the Centre. He would remain in command until January 1812, when he was relieved for insubordination to General Montbrun, the commander of the French cavalry in the Army of Portugal. General Cavrois returned to France and retired on 9 October 1813.

---

‡ de Caulaincourt, *With Napoleon in Russia*, p. 100.

Table 6.20   Chamorin, Vital-Joachim

Awards and honours	Baron of the Empire 10 Feb. 1809
Date and place of birth	16 Aug. 1773 at Bonnelles
Regiments commanded	26th Dragoons 16 Feb. 1807–25 Mar. 1811
Date of rank as general	General of brigade 5 Mar. 1811
Time in the Peninsula	4 Nov. 1808–5 Mar. 1811
Command or post in the Peninsula	26th Dragoons 4 Nov. 1808–5 Mar. 1811
Date and place of death	25 Mar. 1811 at Campo Mayor, Spain
Cause of death	Killed in combat by Corporal Logan of the 13th Light Dragoons

Vital-Joachim Chamorin led the 26th Dragoons the entire 29 months he was in the Peninsula. He never commanded a cavalry brigade. His leadership at the battle of Medellin on 28 March 1809 was superb and his division commander, General Tour-Maubourg requested that he be given a battlefield promotion to general of brigade. Marshal Victor however did not forward the request. Colonel Chamorin distinguished himself at Gebora on 11 February 1811, where the French dragoons mauled General Mendizabal's Spanish army before the walls of Badajoz. He was cited in the Army's of the South Orders of the Day. Once again, General Tour-Maubourg put Colonel Chamorin in for promotion and this time Marshal Soult became involved.[*] Colonel Chamorin was so certain that he would be promoted, that he wrote to his wife that

> General Latour Maubourg wanted to be the first to share it with you and handed me a letter for you. . . I wanted to wait, fearing that it would not succeed any more than the first time. But the general believes in its success and he wants to let you know. I know that the order of the army mentioned it and if it comes, I think that you'll also be pleased for me because it will prove that your friend always and everywhere gained advancement by always doing his glorious duty.[†]

On the evening of 24 March 1811 Colonel Chamorin had a premonition of his own death. He told his adjutant, de Sainte Avoye 'I hate the English. I do not want to become their prisoner and if I ever fell into their hands, then I am dead.' The next morning he told Sainte Avoye, 'I dreamed we were struggling with the English. I did not want to be taken and I was killed.'[‡]

---

[*] Thoumas, *Les Grands Cavaliers*, vol. 2, pp. 334–5.

[†] Ibid, vol. 2, p. 334.

[‡] Ibid, vol. 2, p. 336.

Colonel Chamorin did not have long to live. He was killed in action around noon, leading his regiment at Campo Mayor, never knowing that he had been promoted to general of brigade 20 days before. An anonymous officer of the 13th Light Dragoons wrote an account in 20 April 1811 edition of the *The Courier* newspaper that Colonel Chamorin was killed by Corporal Logan:

> ... this corporal had killed one of his men and he was so enraged, that he sallied out himself and attacked the corporal – the corporal was well mounted and a good swordsman, as was also the Colonel – both defended for some time, the corporal cut him twice in the face, his helmet came off at the second, when the corporal slew him by a cut which nearly cleft his skull asunder, it cut in as deep as the nose through the brain.[*]

Within an hour of the battle, Lieutenant Moyle Sherer of the 34th Foot, passed the spot where Colonel Chamorin was killed:

> I remember well, among the events of this day, having remarked one fine manly corpse very particularly; it lay a few yards from the road-side, alone, naked, the face and breast downwards and on the back of the head a deep and frightful cleft, inflicted by the sabre; all around the spot where it lay the ground was deeply indented with the print of horses' feet, who appeared to have gone over it at a furious pace. The sky was cloudy and the wind high; the body was cold and pale, the fine-formed limbs stiff and motionless; the spirit, which had animated it, not an hour before, had indeed fled; yet, I know not how it was, the very corpse made a forcible appeal to the feelings and seemed to suffer, it looked so comfortless, so humbled, so deserted. An English dragoon, leading a wounded horse and conducting two prisoners, one of whom had sabre-cuts on the cheek and shoulder, passed me while I was contemplating the scene. 'Do you recollect,' said I, 'friend, what took place here?' 'Yes, sir; they shewed us a front here and we charged and drove them; but this man, who was an officer, tried to rally them and was cut down by our adjutant, as I think.' At this moment, one of the French horsemen, leaning down, exclaimed, '*C'est le colonel.*' '*Comment diable,*' said the other. '*C'est bien lui,*' said his comrade; '*il est mort. Ah! Qu'il etoit brave soldate, ce vilain champ de bataille n'est pas digne d'un tel victim.*' They passed on. What! This carcase, on which

---

§ Haythornthwaite, *British Cavalryman 1792–1815*, p. 28.

the flies were already settling, which lay, all spurned and blood-stained, on the rude and prickly heath, had been, but one short hour before, a man of rank, perhaps also of talent, fortune, courage, whose voice breathed command, whose eye glanced fire, whose arm shook defiance – even so, such is war![*]

According to the anonymous officer in the 13th Light Dragoons, the following day a wounded French dragoon officer came under a flag of truce to find Chamorin's body:

it was truly a bloody scene, being almost all sabre wounds, the slain were all naked, the peasants having stripped them in the night. . . he was lying on his face, his naked body weltering in blood and as soon as he was turned up, the Officer knew him, he have a sort of scream and sprung off his horse, dashed his helmet on the ground, knelt by the body, took the bloody hand and kissed it many times in an agony of grief; it was an effecting and awful scene[†]

The regimental paymaster of the 13th Light Dragoons, E. Gardiner, kept Colonel Chamorin's helmet as a souvenir. His sword was given to Lieutenant Colonel Michael Head, the 13th Light Dragoon's commander.[‡]

Vital Chamorin was one of those charismatic cavalry officers which the French army seemed to produce in abundant quantity. One of his subordinates wrote later that:

This man had friends in all his superiors. He never profited from his position and he inspired by example. He insisted that discipline be strictly observed. But he did it by persuading and not through constraint. This man, so brave, so intrepid, was the most devoted friend and he took every opportunity to help his officers. He especially liked to surprise them with official recognition before they knew it had been solicited.[§]

Table 6.21   Colbert de Chabanais, Auguste-François-Marie

Awards and honours	Baron of the Empire 2 Jul. 1808
Date and place of birth	18 Nov. 1777 at Paris

---

[*] Sherer, *Recollections of the Peninsula*, pp. 143–4.
[†] Haythornthwaite, *British Cavalryman 1792–1815*, p. 28.
[‡] Cannon, *Historical Record of the Thirteenth Regiment of Light Dragoons*, p. 45.
[§] Thoumas, *Les Grands Cavaliers*, vol. 2, pp. 337–8.

Regiments commanded	10th Chasseurs 18 Jul. 1800–24 Dec. 1805
Date of rank as general	General of brigade 24 Dec. 1805
Time in the Peninsula	Nov. 1808–3 Jan. 1809
Command or post in the Peninsula	Light Cavalry Brigade, Ney's Corps Nov. 1808–3 Jan. 1809
Date and place of death	3 Jan. 1809 at Cacabellos, Spain
Cause of death	Killed by Thomas Plunkett of the 95th Rifles

Auguste-François-Marie Colbert de Chabanais was one of the bright young officers, who made a name for themselves as light cavalry officers. At the age of 22 he took command of the 10th Chasseurs, a regiment noted for poor discipline and even poorer performance on the battlefield. Within a few years Colbert made them into one of the finest regiments in the French army. He was promoted to general of brigade at the age of 28 and took command of the 2nd Light Cavalry Brigade in Tilly's Division, 1st Corps on 11 July 1806. Eleven days later, he was transferred to command the light cavalry brigade of Marshal Ney's 6th Corps. General Colbert would command this brigade until his death in 1809. He would lead them at Jena on 14 October 1806 and Friedland on 14 June 1807.

Auguste Colbert was highly regarded and had many connections to senior officers. In 1798 he was aide-de-camp to the future marshal, Joachim Murat, while Marshal Ney considered him a friend. In 1803 he married the daughter of General Jean Canclaux, the Inspector of Cavalry, who was also a senator and the Secretary of the Senate. In Spain three of his aides-de-camp were sons of a senior officer or from one of the distinguished old families of France: Alfred and Rudolphe Tour-Maubourg and Adrien-Louis-Antoine-Jerome d'Astorg.

In Spain during late December 1808 and early January 1809 General Colbert and his brigade, consisting of the 15th Chasseurs and the 3rd Hussars, led the French army in the pursuit of the retreating British army under General Moore. On the afternoon of 3 January 1809 he caught up with the British rearguard, under the command of General Paget, near the town of Cacabellos. The British rearguard, which had five battalions of infantry, the 15th Hussars and a Royal Horse Artillery troop, were drawn up on the western bank of the Cua River. General Paget left one squadron of Hussars and four companies of the 95th Rifles on the eastern bank.

Around 1.00 p.m. Colbert's Brigade appeared and he immediately ordered them to charge the 15th Hussars. The hussars and riflemen, immediately fled across the bridge, but Colbert's men were able to capture about 50 of the riflemen. He halted his brigade when he saw the British infantry and guns on the slopes above the river on the far side. General

Colbert did not wait long, before ordering his regiments to form a column of fours and charge across the bridge. They were able to cross despite the heavy artillery fire, but were halted by fire of the infantry that were protected by walls. General Colbert was urging his men with shouts of 'Are you afraid to die today' when he was shot in the forehead above the left eyebrow. He was killed by Thomas Plunkett of the 95th Rifles, who shot him from a distance of over 200 metres, an amazing feat of marksmanship for the time. The brigade retreated across the river, with their mortally wounded general. Legend has it that he was still alive and that he ordered troopers to put him back on his horse so that he could see the British defeated. His finals words supposedly were 'I am very young to die, but at least my death is worthy of a soldier Grande Armée, since in dying I see fleeing the eternal enemies of my country.'*

Auguste Colbert was the consummate light cavalry officer – bold and aggressive and highly competent at performing the variety of duties the light cavalry were called on to do. He led from the front and was able to motivate his men to accomplish the near impossible. Marshal Ney summed up his skill as a light cavalry commander with 'I do not sleep easy until I learn Colbert commands the outposts.'†

Table 6.22 Curto, Jean-Baptiste-Théodore

Awards and honours	Baron of the Empire 9 Sep. 1810
Date and place of birth	25 May 1770 at Montpellier
Regiments commanded	8th Chasseurs 19 Oct. 1804–6 Aug. 1811
Date of rank as general	General of brigade 6 Aug. 1811
Time in the Peninsula	Oct. 1811–16 Jul. 1813
Command or post in the Peninsula	1st Light Cavalry Brigade, Army of Portugal 14 Oct. 1811–Winter 1812; Light Cavalry Division, Army of Portugal Winter 1812–Sep. 1812; 1st Light Cavalry Brigade, Mermet's Division Sep. 1812–Jul. 1813;
Date and place of death	14 Sep. 1835 in Paris
Place of burial	Cimetière du Nord, Montmartre, Paris

General of brigade Jean Curto arrived in the Peninsula to take command of the 1st Light Cavalry Brigade of the Army of Portugal in October 1811. He was the next-to-last cavalry general sent to the Peninsula. The brigade consisted of the 13th and 22nd Chasseurs and the 3rd Hussars. In the winter of 1812 he assumed command of the light cavalry division

---

* Thoumas, *Les Grands Cavaliers*, Series 1, pp. 374–5.
† Ibid., p. 377.

assigned to the Army of Portugal. This division consisted of two light cavalry brigades, his and the 2nd Brigade, which had the 14th, 26th and 28th Chasseurs assigned to it. On paper he still commanded the 1st Brigade. However, the actual brigade commander was the senior colonel in the brigade, Colonel Desfossés of the 22nd Chasseurs. The 2nd Brigade was missing its general also and was commanded by the senior regimental commander, Colonel Vial of the 26th Chasseurs.

At the battle of Salamanca on 22 June 1812, General Curto's division was on the left flank of the French Army and covered Maucune's Division as it advanced. It acquitted itself quite well against Alten's Brigade of the 1st KGL Hussars and the 14th Light Dragoons in the middle of the afternoon. Later it was screening the left flank of Thomières's Division when Pakenham's Division attacked. Curto's cavalry counter-attacked the right flank of the British line with some success. However, the lead squadrons were counter-charged by the KGL Hussars in Alten's Brigade and forced to fall back on their supports. The supporting French regiment charged the Hussars, who fell back on their supports – the 14th Light Dragoons, who charged them in turn and forced them to retreat. The impact of the French charge would have been greater, if Curto had committed both brigades, but instead he only sent in one. The division was still covering the French left flank, when the British heavy dragoons, commanded by General le Marchant, charged Thomières's Division. There was little Curto's cavalry could do to stop the charge and they withdrew, leaving the infantry to be destroyed by the British cavalry. Curto's Division helped screen the retreating French forces, but when attacked by Bock's KGL Dragoon Brigade at Garcia Hernandez, they fled, leaving the infantry to be crushed again by the British cavalry.

At Salamanca Curto's Division performed well initially, but as the day wore on, its effectiveness declined. This was probably due to the ad hoc command structure that was in place. General Curto was an inexperienced brigade commander with less than six months time in command, before being given command of the division. Colonel Desfossés took over as command of the 1st Brigade, leaving the command of the 22nd Chasseurs in the hands of its senior chief of squadron. Colonel Desfossés was wounded at Salamanca and command of the 1st Brigade was assumed by Colonel Shée of the 13th Chasseurs, which forced the 13th Chasseurs' senior chief of squadron to take command of the regiment. Compounding the problem was that the commander of the third regiment in the brigade, Colonel Paulin Louis Rousseau of the 3rd Hussars, was also wounded at Salamanca, while one of the chiefs of squadron of the 22nd Chasseurs was also wounded. In the 2nd Brigade the situation was better; however both the 26th and the 28th Chasseurs each had a chief of squadron wounded.

General Curto would stay in command of the Light Cavalry Division of the Army of Portugal until General Mermet assumed command in September 1812. General Curto would continue to command the 1st Brigade until July 1813, when Marshal Soult combined the French Armies of the Centre, the South and Portugal into the Army of the Pyrenées. He was not given another command and was sent to Germany, where he was assigned to the Grande Armée Headquarters. Curto opposed Napoleon's return in 1815 and was initially dismissed from the army, but allowed to retire in May 1815.

It is difficult to determine how effective a commander General Curto was. He had little experience as a brigade commander before being appointed as a division commander. His performance in the Salamanca campaign was mediocre at best.

Chapter Seven

The Peninsular Cavalry Generals
Davenay to Konopka

Table 7.1   Davenay, Archange-Louis Rioult

Awards and honours	Baron of the Empire 15 Jan. 1809
Date and place of birth	21 Nov. 1768 at Caen
Regiments commanded	6th Cuirassiers 24 Feb. 1805–25 Jun. 1807
Date of rank as general	General of brigade 25 Jun. 1807
Time in the Peninsula	7 Oct. 1808–Mar. 1809
Command or post in the Peninsula	2nd Dragoon Brigade, Houssaye's Division 7 Sep. 1808–21 Dec. 1808; Prov. Cavalry Brigade at Madrid 22 Dec. 1808–Mar. 1809
Date and place of death	29 May 1809 at Treviso, Italy
Cause of death	Died of wounds: hit in thigh by cannonball at the battle of Piave 8 May 1809
Place of burial	Treviso, Italy

Archange-Louis Rioult-Davenay is often referred to as Davenay. He commanded the 2nd Brigade (18th and 19th Dragoons) of Houssaye's Division in the autumn of 1808. General Davenay and his brigade was at Somosierra in a supporting role, but he ran into personality problems with his division commander and was relieved of his command shortly afterwards. He was sent to Madrid where he was given command of an independent brigade consisting of the 3rd Dutch Hussars and a provisional dragoon regiment on 22 December 1808. In January his brigade was augmented with 5,000 infantry, artillery and another five squadrons of dragoons. They were sent to Zamora where they were ordered to observe the Spanish army under General Romana. In March 1809 Davenay was ordered back to France, where he was transferred to the Army of Italy in May 1809. There he commanded a brigade, consisting of the 8th and 25th Chasseurs, in Sahuc's Light Cavalry Division. He died of wounds received

at the battle of Piave on 8 May 1809. Aymar de Gonneville, Davenay's
aide-de-camp, left a vivid description of his death.

> Just as we were turning to go back to our men, a sound that still
> rings in my ear, together with the whistle of a shot, informed me
> that either the General or his horse was hit; a hasty movement of
> the latter gave me hopes for a moment, that he was the only sufferer.
> To my anxious question the General replied as he let himself fall
> forward on his horse's neck 'My thigh is carried away.' I still hoped
> it was not the case. Seeing him totter, I took him by the arm and
> tried to keep him in the saddle; but our horses were at a gallop, he
> could not guide his own and in a few moments I could not prevent
> his falling to the ground . . . We made the General sit upon the
> sergeant's fusee. I supported him behind in my arms, the chasseurs
> raised him up upon the two ends of the fuse, the sergeant supported
> his leg, which only remained attached by the flesh on each side. The
> ball had shattered the knee, striking it from below and had made
> a diagonal furrow on the horse's neck . . . The horse of one of the
> chasseurs who was carrying an end of the fuse that supported the
> General was hit by a shot. The fall of the horse nearly caused that of
> the man as his arm was through the reins. This accident stopped us.
> And the General desired to be placed on the other orderly's horse.
> I had let my own go and he had run away without my troubling
> myself about him, as may be well supposed. With great difficulty
> we put the General on the horse; I walked by his sided holding up
> the poor wounded leg, while he begged me to cut it quite off with
> my knife. . . I was in difficulties how to get the General across this
> river a hundred yards wide, when I discovered a little boat at some
> distance; it was brought up to the spot where I had laid the General
> and I found him sound asleep. I thought him unconscious, as was
> quite likely from the quantity of blood he had lost and continued to
> lose. He awoke during the crossing and it caused him considerable
> suffering; the smallest wrong movement made the dreadful leg swing
> aside. At last we reached the other side, where an ambulance was
> established in an abandoned inn. An amputation was immediately
> performed, lasting five minutes and I supported the General in my
> arms all the time.[*]

Archange-Louis Rioult-Davenay died from complications of his wounds
on 29 May 1809.

---

[*] De Gonneville, *Recollections of Colonel de Gonneville*, vol. 1, pp. 267–77.

It is hard to determine how good a commander, General Davenay was. He was relieved by his division commander, but immediately given another command by Marshal Berthier. According to de Gonneville, Davenay was the victim of pettiness on the part of Houssaye.* This is supported by the contention that not only was he given an independent command in Spain for three months, but he was sent to Italy to take command of another brigade. De Gonneville felt that General Davenay was being groomed for a division command, probably to replace General Sahuc. De Gonneville summed him up with a few lines:

> I may say, without the least partiality, that in the important command entrusted to him, General Davenay had displayed great capacity, remarkable activity and in a word, every quality that marked him to all eyes as fit to perform the highest military services. His foresight extended to the smallest details and he could not be found at fault in anything.†

Table 7.2   Debelle, César-Alexandre

Awards and honours	Baron of the Empire 5 Nov. 1808
Date and place of birth	27 Nov. 1770 at Voreppe
Regiments commanded	11th Dragoons 21 Mar. 1797–1 Feb. 1805
Date of rank as general	General of brigade 1 Feb. 1805
Time in the Peninsula	10 Nov. 1808–2 Aug. 1809
Command or post in the Peninsula	1st Dragoon Brigade, Milhaud's Division 10 Nov. 1808–Dec. 1808; Cavalry Brigade, Soult's Corps Dec. 1808–31 Jan. 1809; Cavalry Brigade, Franceschi's Division 1 Feb.–2 Aug. 1809
Date and place of death	19 Jul. 1826 at Voreppe
Place of burial	In the funeral chapel of Voreppe

General Debelle went into Spain in on 10 November 1808, commanding the 1st Brigade (8th and 12th Dragoons) of Milhaud's Dragoon Division. Within a month, he and the 8th Dragoons were transferred to Soult's 2nd Corps. As a replacement for the 12th Dragoons, he was given the Auxiliary Chasseurs Regiment, commanded by Colonel Jean Pierre Tascher de la Pagerie, a cousin of Empress Josephine. Disaster struck Debelle and his brigade early on the morning of 21 December 1808. They were in advance

---

* For more on this incident, see the entry for General Houssaye.
† De Gonneville, *Recollections of Colonel de Gonneville*, vol. 1, p. 248.

of the 2nd Corps screening it from what they thought were General Romana's Spaniards. On the night of 20 December the brigade occupied the village of Sahagun in northern Spain. The men were ordered to keep their horses saddled. Yet Debelle was careless about ensuring there was no enemy in the vicinity. No outlying vedettes were set. Under the cover of darkness, Paget's Hussar Brigade (10th and 15th Hussars) was able to move into the area and surprise the guard, capturing all but one trooper. He was able to escape and alert his comrades. The French leapt to their horses and formed up in a field on the outskirts of the town. The Auxiliary Chasseurs Chasseurs were in the front line, while the 8th Dragoons were in support. General Paget ordered the 15th Hussars to charge. The French mistook the British hussars for Spanish and instead of counter-charging, the chasseurs fired their carbines. The hussars rode down the chasseurs, hacking their way through their lines. The chasseurs broke and fled towards the 8th Dragoons who were also broken. General Debelle was thrown from his horse but manage to escape. However, his brigade was shattered. Of the estimated 800 men Debelle's Brigade had in the affair, 17 officers and 150 troopers were captured and another 120 men killed; over a third of those present. And that did not include the wounded who escaped. General Debelle lost all of his baggage, horses and the brigade's papers. The Auxiliary Chasseurs lost so many men they were disbanded.

General Debelle was not relieved for the fiasco at Sahagun, though it must have shaken his superiors' confidence in him. On 1 February he and his brigade were placed under operational control of General of Brigade Franceschi, who was junior to Debelle. Debelle was recalled to France on 2 August 1809. He would not have an active command again until March 1815, when Napoleon returned to France and gave him command of the Department of Drôme. He was wounded on 29 March by a national guardsman who thought that he was committing treason against Napoleon. After the fall of Napoleon General Debelle was arrested and condemned to death on 24 March 1816. His sentence was commuted to 10 years in prison. In 1817 he was released from prison and allowed to retire.

General Debelle had appeared to be a competent general, trusted by his superiors. His command of 1808 was potentially a sensitive position, because of the connection with the empress's family, but it was his performance on 21 December 1808 that destroyed his reputation and he was eventually recalled to France. He was never given another command. At least one British officer accused him of cowardice at Sahagun, stating that hee '. . . was one of the first men that took to his heels'.*

---

* Edwin Griffith, ed. G. Glover, *From Corunna to Waterloo*, p. 80.

Table 7.3   Delort, Jacques-Antoine-Adrien

Awards and honours	Baron of the Empire 4 Jan. 1811
Date and place of birth	16 Nov. 1773 at Arbois
Regiments commanded	24th Dragoons 8 May 1806–21 Jul. 1811
Date of rank as general	General of brigade 21 Jul. 1811; General of division 26 Feb. 1814
Time in the Peninsula	16 Dec. 1808–Jan. 1814
Command or post in the Peninsula	24th Dragoons 8 May 1806–21 Jul. 1811 Cavalry Brigade, Army of Aragon 21 Jul. 1811–Jan. 1814
Wounds in Peninsula	Valls – shot in right thumb 25 Feb. 1809 and seriously wounded by many sabre blows on 15 Jan. 1811
Date and place of death	28 Mar. 1846 at Arbois
Place of burial	Chateau de Vadans

Jacques Delort served five continuous years in Spain from December 1808 to December 1813. During that time he led his regiment and his brigade in almost every battle and campaign that Marshal Suchet's Army of Aragon fought. He commanded the 24th Dragoons until July 1811, when he was promoted to general of brigade. General Delort's Brigade usually consisted of the 24th Dragoons and the 4th Hussars, but by 1813 it sometimes included the 13th Cuirassiers in place of one of the other regiments. Delort was recalled to France in January 1814 and given command of a light cavalry brigade in Pajol's Corps in eastern France.

At the battle of Montereau on 18 February 1814 General Delort's Brigade made numerous charges against the Austrian line that were instrumental in forcing the Austrian Army to retreat. During the battle he was wounded in the left thumb. Napoleon noticed his fine performance and had General Pajol, his corps commander, pass on to him that 'His majesty told me to tell you that he is extremely satisfied with what you have done.'* Delort was promoted to general of division 8 days later on 26 February 1814. He commanded a cuirassier division in Milhaud's Corps during the Waterloo campaign. At Waterloo he was wounded in the arm by a sabre cut and shot in a third time in the thumb! He retired to Arbois in August 1815, but was recalled to active duty in 1820; he retired again in 1825, and was recalled to duty yet again in 1830.

General Delort was an outstanding cavalry general who inspired his men by leading from the front. Marshal Suchet, who was Delort's superior

---

* Sarrut, *Biographie des hommes du jour*, vol. 1, p. 232.

during the five years he served in the Peninsula, stated that 'The 24th Dragoons, commanded by Colonel Delort, inspired confidence by its intrepidity and by the excellent spirit which its chief had the skill to keep up.'* He was also aggressive – Marshal Suchet described one of his actions as him charging with '. . . usual boldness and rapidity'.† He enjoyed the confidence of Marshal Suchet and was often called upon by him to lead combined cavalry and infantry task forces. He was also a bit of a showman. At the end of the successful siege of Tarragona, in June 1811, General Delort asked Marshal Suchet for permission for his regiment, which was part of the covering force, to ride through the breach in the wall. The marshal allowed him the honour.‡ Unfortunately for General Delort, he was not noticed by Napoleon until the 1814 campaign in France.

Table 7.4   Digeon, Alexandre-Elisabeth-Michel

Awards and honours	Baron of the Empire 23 May 1809
Date and place of birth	26 Jun. 1771 in Paris
Regiments commanded	26th Chasseurs 28 Feb. 1802–31 Mar. 1807
Date of rank as general	General of brigade 31 Mar. 1807
	General of division 3 Mar. 1813
Time in the Peninsula	Sep. 1808–24 Jan. 1814
Command or post in the Peninsula	3rd Dragoon Brigade, Tour-Maubourg's Division Sep. 1808–11 Jul. 1809; 2nd Dragoon Brigade, Milhaud's Division 12 Jul.–Nov. 1809; Nov. 1809–Mar. 1810 Commander of the Cavalry, Losion's Reserve Division; 1st Dragoon Brigade, Houssaye's Division May–Oct. 1810; Governor of Cordova 4 Oct. 1810–14 May 1811; Governor of Jaen 14 May 1811–7 Feb. 1812; 1st Dragoon Brigade, 2nd Cavalry Division 7 Feb.–Mar. 1812; Governor of Cordova 7 Feb.–Aug. 1812; 2nd Cavalry Division, Army of the South Mar. 1812–10 Oct. 1812; 1st Dragoon Division, Army of the South 10 Oct. 1812–7 Apr. 1813; 2nd Dragoon Division, Army of the South 7 Apr.–13 Jul. 1813; Commander of the Cavalry of the Armies of Aragon and Catalonia 25 Sep. 1813–24 Jan. 1814

---

* Suchet, *Memoirs of the War in Spain*, vol. 2, p. 6.
† Ibid, vol. 2, p. 344.
‡ Ibid, vol. 2, p. 102.

Wounds in Peninsula	Vitoria seriously wounded by a sabre cut to the right check on 21 Jun. 1813
Date and place of death	2 Aug. 1826 at Ronqueux
Place of burial	Bullion

Alexandre Digeon spent almost the whole Peninsular War serving in Spain. His first command was the 3rd Dragoon Brigade of Tour-Maubourg's Division, attached to the 4th Corps. They saw action at Tudela on 23 November 1808, but it was mostly in a supporting role. In July 1809 General Digeon was assigned to General Milhaud's Dragoon Division, where he commanded the 2nd Brigade, of the 16th, 20th and 21st Dragoons. He was reassigned in November 1809 to command the cavalry of General Loison's Reserve Division, which was forming in France. In May 1810 he was appointed as the commander of the 1st Brigade of General Houssaye's Dragoon Division. The 1st Brigade had the 18th and 19th Dragoons. The brigade saw little action during 1810 and in October, General Digeon was appointed governor of Cordova. He would rule there for seven months, until May 1811 when he was appointed governor of Jaen. In February 1812 he was reappointed the commander of the newly formed 1st Brigade of 2nd Cavalry Division, which was commanded by General Tour-Maubourg. A month later Tour Maubourg was recalled to France, to command a cavalry corps in the Grande Armée that was preparing to invade Russia. Digeon was appointed provisional commander of the 2nd Cavalry Division of the Army of the South in his place. In October 1812 this division was redesignated the 1st Dragoon Division. He commanded them in the pursuit of the British Army retreating from Burgos. On 3 March 1813 he was promoted to general of division and in April took command of the 2nd Dragoon Division. He commanded the division through the Vitoria campaign, where he was seriously wounded in the face by a sabre blow. He did not receive a command in July, when Marshal Soult reorganised the French forces in Spain. In September 1813 General Digeon was appointed commander of the cavalry of the Armies of Aragon and Catalonia. The following February he was sent to eastern France, where he commanded the cavalry of the Army of Lyon.

General Digeon did not rally to Napoleon in 1815. Instead he claimed poor health and retired. After Waterloo he was reinstated and became the Minister of War in 1823. In 1824 he returned to Spain with the French Army. He died in 1826.

Alexandre Digeon was a competent cavalry general, but one who was rarely in the right place at the right time. Although he spent almost 66 months in the Peninsula, he was only in one major battle during his first 42 months. The rest of the time was spent in doing the drudgery work of an army of occupation – counter-guerrilla operations, convoy escorts, etc. He was competent enough to be appointed a division commander a year before he was promoted to general of division, but he did nothing to stand out in the job. This appointment was most likely a reflection of his being available for the job rather than any indication of hidden abilities. His performance during the vigorous pursuit of the retreating British in 1812 was lacklustre and after Vitoria, when Marshal Soult reorganised the army, he was not given another command, although this was probably due to his severe wound.

General Digeon is remembered more for being an able administrator than an inspiring general. During his 17-month tenure as the governor of Cordoba and Jaen, he tried to alleviate the impact of the French occupation on the provinces. He convinced his fellow officers to contribute a part of their pay into a fund to ensure that the poor of the provinces would not starve. To ensure that the fund reached those in need and not line the pockets of local officials, he appointed the Abbot of Vienne, a French émigré priest, to administer it. (The abbot would one day become the canon of the Notre Dame Cathedral in Paris.) After to the ravaging of the countryside in 1811, General Digeon foresaw a rough winter, during which grain would be in short supply for the local population. He ordered large quantities of potatoes be planted and in March 1812 their harvesting prevented a famine among the poor. His actions saved thousands of lives and were in stark contrast to those of Soult, who was known for imposing huge contributions on the Spaniards, to not only help pay for the occupation, but for his own personal gain.

Table 7.5 Duprés, Claude-François

Awards and honours	Baron of the Empire 19 Mar. 1808
Date and place of birth	3 Oct. 1755 at Fort Vauban
Regiments commanded	21st Chasseurs 18 Nov. 1793–29 Aug. 1803
Date of rank as general	General of brigade 29 Aug. 1803
Time in the Peninsula	2 Nov. 1807–19 Jul. 1808
Command or post in the Peninsula	3rd Light Cavalry Brigade, Grouchy's Division 2 Nov.–6 Dec. 1807; 3rd Light Cavalry Brigade, Fresia's Division 6 Dec. 1807–19 Jul. 1808
Date and place of death	19 Jul. 1808 at Bailen, Spain
Cause of death	Shot while charging Spanish infantry

General Duprés was given command of the 3rd Light Cavalry Brigade in the Cavalry Division of the 2nd Corps of Observation of the Gironde in November 1807. His brigade consisted of two regiments: the 1st and 2nd Provisional Chasseurs. In January 1808 he and his brigade were in northern Spain, stationed in Vitoria. In early January the brigade had 31 officers, 919 chasseurs and 957 horses present for duty. The soldiers in his brigade were young conscripts and not the seasoned veterans of previous campaigns. The brigade rarely operated together during the 1808 campaign. The squadrons and companies were parcelled out in support of the infantry and by the battle of Bailen, the wear and tear of months of campaigning had taken its toll on it. With the added stresses of food and water shortages, the brigade was only a shadow of itself.

On the day of battle the brigade was on the army's left. The 1st Provisional Chasseurs charged early in the morning and dispersed the Spanish cavalry to its front, but were forced to retire by the infantry. The 2nd Provisional Chasseurs came up in support and the brigade held its ground until the Spanish infantry forced it to pull back. In the early afternoon the brigade charged the infantry to its front and forced the enemy back, but could not penetrate the second Spanish line. Maurice de Tascher, a chasseur officer in the 1st Provisional Chasseurs described the aftermath of the charge:

> The heat was terrible and there was not a drop of water. Men were dropping, some dead and some of exhaustion, even as they cried out for water. Our horses, short of food for a month and having endured a march of 6 leagues, as well as a battle lasting ten hours, fell beneath us. We remained under the enemy fire until two in the afternoon. Shot and shell continued to rain down on us; it was so heavy that most of the trees were shattered and over large areas of, the grass and bushes were burning, set alight by the shells.[*]

Around 2 p.m. General Dupont ordered Duprés to make one last attempt to break the Spanish line. His brigade was down to fewer than 250 men.

> He advanced at the head of the Marines of the Guard, much less in the hope of victory than in the certainty of dying honourably. In actual fact, no sooner had we shown ourselves on the hillside, than an infantry square, twelve or fifteen times stronger than we, began to rake this group of men with bullets, thinning the ranks with amazing speed. They spared us the trouble of marching up to the enemy for, before we could reach the valley, a large proportion of the officers

---

[*] de Tascher, *Campaigning for Napoleon*, p. 73.

and men were stretched upon the ground and the rest forced to retreat to the hillside.*

General Duprés did not survive the charge.

The gallant General Duprés, at the end of a 30-year-long career, in the course of which fortune had been as devoted to him as he himself was to honour, now saw himself betrayed by the first and dying faithful to the second. A musket ball passed through his body.†

Duprés was typical of the cavalry generals assigned to General Dupont's army — older than the average French light cavalry general of the era. The rigours of the campaign, caused by a combination of poor supply and inexperience of his troops, took a toll on his brigade and by Bailen it weakened to the point it where it was no longer effective. Although some of this was beyond his control, it was still his responsibility to keep his brigade as a potent force when it was needed most, but in this he failed.

Table 7.6   Escorches de Sainte-Croix, Charles-Marie-Robert

Awards and honours	Count of the Empire 15 Aug. 1809
Date and place of birth	20 Nov. 1782 at Versailles
Date of rank as general	General of brigade 21 Jul. 1809
Time in the Peninsula	15 Dec. 1809–11 Oct. 1810
Command or post	Prov. Dragoon Brigade, Caulaincourt's Division in the Peninsula 15 Dec. 1809–Feb. 1810 Prov. Dragoon Brigade, 8th Corps 1 Mar.–11 Oct. 1810
Date and place of death	11 Oct. 1810 near Villafranca, Portugal
Cause of death	Hit by a ricochet artillery round fired by a Portuguese gunboat on the Tagus

---

Charles Escorches de Sainte-Croix, usually referred to as Sainte-Croix, was 26 years old when he was promoted to general of brigade in 1809, one of the youngest in the army. He was still a civilian in 1805, working for the Ministry of Foreign Affairs, when he was assigned to examine foreign regiments that were part of the old royal army. The emperor liked his work so much that he commissioned him as a chief of battalion in the Tour d'Auvergne Regiment without ever meeting him. Legend has it that the regimental commander would demand bribes from future officers if

---

* Ibid., p. 74.
† Ibid.

they wanted a commission. If the commission fell through or was slow, the colonel would blame Sainte-Croix. One candidate was so outraged he challenged Sainte-Croix to a duel and was killed.*

Charles Sainte-Croix was a protégé of Marshal Masséna, serving as his aide-de-camp in 1807 and during the 1809 War with Austria. He fought at Landshut on 21 April, captured a flag at Neumarkt on 1 May and was wounded at Wagram on 6 July. He was promoted to colonel on 5 May 1809 and was given command of the 2,500 grenadiers that landed on the left bank of the Danube River on 5 July, to secure a bridgehead for the army's crossing. For his performance during the campaign, Colonel Sainte-Croix was promoted to general of brigade on 21 July 1809. General Sainte-Croix was given command of the 1st Provisional Dragoon Brigade assigned to General Junot's 8th Corps, on 15 December 1809. It consisted of the 1st, 2nd and 3rd Provisional Dragoon Regiments and had about 2,000 men. His would be one of the lead units in the 1810 French invasion of Portugal and it was he who found the route that allowed the French to by-pass the impregnable Anglo-Portuguese position at Bussaco. Baron Marbot, who accompanied him, said

> As we passed through the village we picked up the convent gardener, who, at sight of a piece of gold, consented to act as our guide, laughing when he was asked if there really existed a road to Boialva. While Sainte-Croix's brigade and a regiment of infantry, led the way in this new direction, the 8th corps and Montbrun's cavalry followed close behind and the rest of the army prepared to do the same. Urged by Sainte-Croix, Masséna had at last spoken with authority and imposed silence on his lieutenants when they persisted in denying the existence of a pass on the right.†

General Sainte-Croix's luck ran out on 11 October 1810, near the village of Villafranca, Portugal, overlooking the Tagus River. Major Jean Pelet, who replaced General Sainte-Croix as Marshal Masséna's primary aide-de-camp wrote

> I saw General Sainte-Croix at the window of the Duc's [sic] [residence]. He paid me a number of compliments and two hours later he was killed by a cannonball that cut him in half at the kidneys as he was coming out of Vilafranca. Accompanied by General Montbrun, he was going along a low road to examine the position of the enemy. A random shot from a boat on the Tagus fell at a spot where he

---

* Elting, *Swords around the Throne*, p. 358.
† Marbot, *The Memoirs of Barin de Marbot*, vol. 2, p. 119.

should have been safe. . . Until then Sainte-Croix had been singularly protected by fate. What a blow! What an example! At least we are left only with regrets. I was affected very much by this loss.'[*]

General Sainte-Croix was a rising star in the French army, when he was killed at the age of 28. Napoleon saw him as another Desaix or Lannes.[†] Marshal Masséna 'cried bitterly about this young man, whom he had liked very much'.[‡]

Table 7.7   Fouler, Albert-Louis-Emmanuel de

Awards and honours	Count of Relingue 16 Sep. 1808
Date and place of birth	9 Feb. 1769 at Lillers
Regiments commanded	24th Cavalry Regiment 26 Oct. 1800–20 Nov. 1801; 11th Cavalry Regiment 20 Nov. 1801–31 Dec. 1806
Date of rank as general	General of brigade 31 Dec. 1806
Time in the Peninsula	30 Oct. 1809–12 Feb. 1810
Command or post in the Peninsula	2nd Cavalry Reserve Division Dec. 1809–12 Feb. 1810
Date and place of death	17 Jun. 1831 at Lillers

Albert de Fouler saw very little time in the Peninsula. He was captured by Austrians at the battle of Essling on 22 May 1809 and was held prisoner for two months. In August 1809 General Fouler was appointed to command the cavalry of the General Junot's 8th Corps, which was being formed for service for in Spain. It consisted of three provisional dragoon brigades. He only commanded it for two months, when he was given the mission of organising the 2nd Cavalry Reserve Division. In late January 1810 Napoleon told Marshal Berthier to give him command of the 4th Dragoon Brigade, Milhaud's Division. However, General Fouler was recalled to France before he took command.

General Fouler was well connected politically to the emperor. He served as equerry to Empress Josephine in 1806 and to the emperor from February 1810–March 1814 and during the Waterloo campaign. He retired in September 1815. It is difficult to determine his ability as a cavalry commander in the Peninsula, since he served less than four months there and only in an administrative position.

---

[*] Pelet, *The French Campaign in Portugal*, pp. 220–1.
[†] Elting, *Swords around the Throne*, p. 710.
[‡] Pelet, *The French Campaign in Portugal*, p. 221.

Table 7.8   Fournier-Sarlovèse, François

Awards and honours	Baron of the Empire 17 Mar. 1808
Date and place of birth	6 Sep. 1773 at Sarlat
Date of rank as general	General of brigade 25 Jun. 1807; General of division 11 Nov. 1812
Time in the Peninsula	7 Sep. 1808–15 Dec. 1809 10 Sep. 1810–31 Dec. 1811
Command or post in the Peninsula	2nd Dragoon Brigade, Lorge's Division 7 Sep. 1808–15 Dec. 1809; 2nd Prov. Cavalry Brigade, Army of Portugal 10 Nov. 1810– Nov. 1811
Date and place of death	18 Jan. 1827 in Paris
Place of burial	Sarlat

François Fournier-Sarlovèse was the archetypal light cavalry officer – hard-fighting, hard-drinking, brusque, rude and at times insubordinate. He was a superb leader whose reputation on the battlefield was only outshone by his reputation as a duellist and one who used his position for bettering his personal finances. In the autumn of 1808 he went into Spain with his brigade (15th and 25th Dragoons) and was part of the pursuit of General Moore's army to Corunna. In May 1809 he was responsible for defending Lugo with three infantry battalions, the 15th Dragoons, two squadrons of hussars and four artillery pieces against the 15,000 man Spanish Army of General Mahy. Although outnumbered 10 to 1, General Fournier-Sarlovèse was able to hold out until relieved by Marshal Soult. He would continue to serve in Spain until December 1809, when he returned to France.

In November 1810 General Fournier-Sarlovèse returned to Spain, this time commanding a cavalry brigade in the Army of Portugal, consisting of the 3rd and 4th Squadrons of the 7th, 13th and 20th Chasseurs. This brigade was also referred to as the 2nd Provisional Light Cavalry Regiment. They would fight at Fuentes de Oñoro on 3–5 May. It was his brigade that was involved in the running battle with the Light Division on the right of the Anglo-Portuguese line and the destruction of the British Guards skirmishing force. He had a horse shot out from under him and claimed in his dispatch that his brigade broke two squares of the Light Division, capturing their commander, General Robert Craufurd, and 1,500 men. (This claim cannot be substantiated by any of the contemporary British memoirs and British casualty figures for the battle do not support it either. The only possibility is that in the confusion of the counter-attack by the British cavalry the prisoners were able to make their escape.) General

Fournier-Sarlovèse would command the brigade until November, but was not given another command when Marshal Marmont reorganised the Army of Portugal. He was ordered to the Army of Aragon, but returned to France in December 1811 to take convalescent leave.

General Fournier-Sarlovèse would fight in Russia and in the 1813 campaign in Germany. He was dismissed from command and arrested in November 1813 for making negative remarks about the Emperor's handling of the campaign. He was restored to active duty in May 1814, but did not take an active role in the Waterloo campaign.

Despite being an outstanding cavalry officer, General Fournier-Sarlovèse alienated his superiors with his brusque manner and rudeness. Although he was never formally relieved while in Spain, those above him took the first opportunity available to get him out of their command. Twice he was sent back to France (in December 1809 and November 1811), when his commanders dissolved his commands and thus had the excuse to get rid of him. In late 1813, when Napoleon needed every competent general officer he could find, General Fournier-Sarlovèse was dismissed from command and arrested for his injudicious remarks.

General Fournier-Sarlovèse had a reputation for being a duellist and a bully. Marshal Ney did not like him because he thought General Fournier-Sarlovèse deliberately went out of his way to provoke duels against weaker opponents. Legend has it that Joseph Conrad's story, *The Duellists*, is based on General Fournier-Sarlovèse life. In the spring of 1811 he provoked a duel with General Poinsot, by stealing 20 gold coins, worth 1,700 francs, from him. General Poinsot was sick at the time and could not challenge him until later. He did this by going to General Fournier-Sarlovèse's headquarters and walking in unannounced. He then said:

> General Fournier, I am aware that you are able to snuff out a candle at fifteen paces with a pistol-shot. My ability is with the sword and I could hit you exactly on the spot where the fourth button of your uniform would be. That is my way of snuffing out insolent fellows like you.[*]

Fournier-Sarlovèse's second, Major de Vérigny, was able to convince him that a duel at that point of the campaign would have been very bad for French morale.

General Fournier-Sarlovèse was also known for using his position to better his own financial position. He was not above taking prizes from his own troops or requisitioning money from local villages. Charles Parquin,

---

[*] Parquin, *Napoleon's Army*, pp. 129–30.

an officer in the 20th Chasseurs, was on an anti-guerrilla patrol, when he and his men came across a village *alcalde* (local magistrate) collecting money for Don Julian's guerrillas. Parquin confiscated the money (6,000 francs) and left. He distributed the money among his men, who had not been paid in over a year. The next day General Fournier-Sarlovèse came by the village and demanded the *alcalde* give him money. The *alcalde* explained that he had no money, because Parquin had taken it all the previous day. General Fournier-Sarlovèse summoned Parquin and ordered him to hand over the money. He was able to convince the General that his men needed it more. However, General Fournier-Sarlovèse warned him, '. . . the next time, do not attempt the same thing without informing me.'*

Table 7.9 Franceschi-Delonne, Jean-Baptiste Francesqui dit

Date and place of birth	4 Sep. 1767 at Lyon
Regiments commanded	8th Hussars 1 Feb.–24 Dec. 1805
Date of rank as general	General of brigade 24 Dec. 1805
Time in the Peninsula	15 Aug. 1808–23 Oct. 1810
Command or post in the Peninsula	Light Cavalry Brigade. Ney's Corps Sep. 1808–7 Nov. 1808; Light Cavalry Division, Soult's Corps 7 Nov. 1808–Jun. 1809
Date and place of death	23 Oct. 1810 at Carthagena, Spain
Cause of death	Yellow Fever

Jean Baptiste Francesqui dit Franceschi-Delonne is usually referred to in most histories and memoirs as Franceschi. He did not want to be a soldier at first. He was a sculptor, but was caught in the wave of patriotism that swept France in 1792 and he joined a company of artists from Paris. He was initially an infantryman, but joined the cavalry in 1797. He was promoted to colonel in 1802 and was given command of the 8th Hussars in February 1805. Ten months later he was promoted to general of brigade. He commanded a cavalry brigade in southern Italy in 1806 and was an aide-de-camp to King Joseph in 1807. He was allowed to continue in the position when Joseph accepted the crown of Spain. In September 1808 General Franceschi was appointed to command a light cavalry brigade in Marshal Ney's corps and fought with them at Lerin on 25 October 1808. In November 1808 he took command of the Light Cavalry Brigade in Marshal Soult's 2nd Corps. This brigade consisted of the 1st Hussars and the Hanoverian Chasseurs. His brigade vigorously pursued the retreating British Army under General Moore. In February 1809 General Franceschi

---

* Ibid., pp. 132–3.

was given operational control of General Debelle's Light Cavalry and was in command of both brigades during the invasion of northern Portugal from March to June 1809.

In early June 1809 General Franceschi was sent by Marshal Soult to Madrid with dispatches describing in detail the situation in Galicia. The Marshal felt that General Franceschi would provide additional information to what was in the dispatches. General Franceschi declined an escort and set off with only his aides-de-camp. In the vicinity of Tordesillas, in a village named San Pedro de Latarce, he was attacked by 'El Capucino' (the Monk) and eight guerrillas and made prisoner.* In late June El Capucino and his prisoner were crossing Spain, when they came upon the British Headquarters. General Franceschi was in a foul mood when he was interviewed by Wellington. He kept repeating, 'Oh! How pitable is it for hussar general to be taken by a monk!'† The monk refused to turn him over to the British and General Franceschi was taken to Seville, then to Grenada and eventually Carthagena. On 23 October 1810 General Franceschi died of yellow fever while a prisoner.‡

General Franceschi was the typical light cavalry officer – aggressive, cocky and well regarded by his superiors. He was a confidant of King Joseph both in Naples and in Spain. His performance as a brigade commander was competent enough that he was given operational control of another brigade – in effect giving him a light cavalry division to command.§ Marshal Soult trusted him to speak on his behalf to King Joseph. But, General Franceschi was also arrogant. He believed in the superiority of the light cavalry and that he did not need an escort, since the only opposition he might face would be guerrillas. This was a fatal mistake. If he had avoided capture, he might have gone far.

Table 7.10   Fresia d'Oglianico, Maurice Ignace

Awards and honours	Baron of the Empire 7 Jun. 1808
Date and place of birth	1 Aug. 1746 at Saluces, Italy
Date of rank as general	General of brigade 3 Apr. 1802; General of division 3 Jun. 1807
Time in the Peninsula	6 Dec. 1807–5 Sep. 1808

---

* 'El Capucino' was Juan Mendieta who, upon becoming a monk, changed his name to Julián de Delica.
† Vane, *Story of the Peninsular War*, p. 174.
‡ Marbot, *The Memoirs of Jean Marbot*, vol. 2, p. 102.
§ Interestingly, General Franceschi was junior to one of the brigade commanders (General Debelle) in this 'division'. This is very puzzling since the senior officer is normally in command. Perhaps the explanation is that Napoleon appointed him in command and General Debelle had no choice but to accept the situation.

Command or post in the Peninsula	Cavalry Division, Dupont's Corps 6 Dec. 1807– 5 Sep. 1808
Date and place of death	3 Nov. 1826 in Paris
Place of burial	Père Lachaise Cemetery

Maurice Fresia served in the Sardinian army against the French during the early days of the French Revolution. He transferred to the French Army on 14 December 1798. He never commanded a French regiment, but did command the Sardinian Chevaux-légers du Roi against the French in Italy. He was the commander of a dragoon brigade in Italy in 1805 and a cuirassier brigade in the 1806–7 campaign in Prussia and Poland. In December 1807 he assumed command of the Cavalry Division of Dupont's Corps. His division consisted of three brigades of five provisional regiments and a squadron of provisional cuirassiers. Unfortunately for him, his division was part of General Dupont's Corps and, despite fighting well at Bailen, they were forced to surrender on 22 July 1808. General Fresia went into captivity at Cadiz and returned to France on 21 September 1808.

General Fresia returned to Italy and would serve in a various commands there until February 1813, when he commanded the 4th Cavalry Corps in Saxony. In May 1813 he returned to Italy and served in a variety of positions there. He was an inspector General of cavalry during the Hundred Days and retired in August 1815, at the age of 70.

General Fresia was 61 years old when he assumed command of his division in Spain! His regiments were made up of raw conscripts with few experienced cadres. The combined effects of very harsh campaigning conditions – poor supply, a hostile environment and no sense of regimental unity – caused discipline to deteriorate. It was not surprising that crimes and violence against the local population escalated. Looting became commonplace and the division was involved in the sacking of Cordova, which inflamed the population even further. One cavalry officer, who was present at the court martial of two soldiers, possibly summed up the division best, when he noted in his diary that 'These wretches possess to a high degree the defects of our old soldiers without having a single one of their good qualities.'* Hs performance at Bailen was adequate, but it was far outweighed by his inability to meld his division into a disciplined, effective fighting force. This may have been due to his age.

Table 7.11 Gardanne, Charles-Mathieu

Awards and honours	Count of the Empire May 1808
Date and place of birth	11 Jul. 1766 at Marseille

---

* de Tascher, *Campaigning for Napoleon*, p. 51.

Table 7.11   continued

Regiments commanded	9th Chasseurs 2 Jun. 1796–19 Oct. 1799
Date of rank as general	General of brigade 19 Oct. 1799
Time in the Peninsula	7 Dec. 1809–5 Jan. 1811

Command or post
    in the Peninsula
	2nd Prov. Dragoon Brigade, Caulaincourt's
	    Division, 8th Corps 7 Dec. 1809–8 Feb. 1810
	    3rd Dragoon Brigade, Trelliard's Division
	    29 May 1810–7 Mar. 1811

Date and place of death	30 Jan. 1818 at the Chateau of Lincel

Prior to being assigned to the Peninsula, General Gardanne did not have an active command after 1801. In 1805 he was Governor of the Pages in the Imperial Household. During the campaigns of 1805 he served as a staff officer in the Imperial Headquarters, while in 1806 and 1807 he was assigned to Marshal Soult's Corps. In 1807 he was sent to Persia as the French ambassador and returned in the summer of 1808. In December 1809 he assumed command of the 2nd Provisional Dragoon Brigade, part of the 8th Corps. It consisted of the 4th and 5th Provisional Dragoon Regiments. His brigade was disbanded on 8 February 1810 and he served on the staff of the 6th Corps until 29 May 1810, when he was given command of the 3rd Dragoon Brigade, Trelliard's Division. The brigade consisted of the 15th and 25th Dragoons. When the French Army of Portugal invaded Portugal in the late summer of 1810, Gardanne was left behind with the 10th Dragoons and the 4th Battalions of the 14th and 86th Line Infantry Regiments at Cuidad Rodrigo to secure the army's lines of communication. To all intents and purposes Gardanne and his force were under a state of blockade by the guerrillas, cut off from the French army in Portugal.

On 8 November General Foy arrived with dispatches from Marshal Masséna. General Gardanne was to gather all the convalescents in the area, strip the garrisons of Ciudad Rodrigo and Almeida of their troops and march to the succour of the Army of Portugal with much-needed food and ammunition. General Gardanne and his relief force of 5,000 men marched on 20 November. He made little progress owing to the slow convoy, bad weather and the poor discipline of his troops. On 27 November General Gardanne and his column were within 25 kilometres of General Loison's Division at Punhete, when he decided to turn back. When Napoleon heard of this, he wrote to Marshal Berthier on 4 January 'the English mock General Gardanne greatly. That idiot was no more than three leagues from the French corps on the Zezere. You will find the entire dispatch. Send it to General Drouet, giving him orders to send this general, who appears to be an arch-imbecile, back to France.'*

General Thiébault in Salamanca received the orders to recall and to publish it in the orders of the day. He wrote:

> Grieved as I was at seeing so cruel an ending to so honourable a career, I went at once to impart to him the order that I had received and ask him to leave Salamanca before daylight, so that he might not be there when the severe treatment meted out to him became generally known. He yielded to my wish and I had a sad parting with him.†

General Gardanne left for France on 7 March 1811 and was dismissed from the army. In June 1814 he was reinstated in his grade after the fall of Napoleon. When Napoleon returned to France in 1815, Gardanne rallied to his cause. He retired in September 1815.

Table 7.12   Grouchy, Emmanuel

Awards and honours	Count of the Empire 28 Jan. 1809
Date and place of birth	23 Oct. 1766 in Paris
Regiments commanded	2nd Dragoons 1 Feb.–8 Jul. 1792; 6th Hussars 8 Jul. 1792–8 Oct. 1794
Date of rank as general	General of division 13 Jun. 1795; Marshal 15 Apr. 1815
Time in the Peninsula	8 Jan.–Nov. 1808
Command or post in the Peninsula	Cavalry of the Corps of Observation of the Coasts and the Ocean 5 Nov. 1807–Feb. 1808 Cavalry of the Army of Spain Feb.–Oct. 1808 Governor of Madrid 23 Mar.–1 Aug. 1808
Date and place of death	29 May 1847 at Saint-Etienne
Place of burial	Crypt, Chapel of the Hôtel des Invalides, Paris

---

Emmanuel Grouchy was a noble who sided with the revolutionaries during the French Revolution. By 1793 he had commanded both the 2nd Dragoons and the 6th Hussars, but because of his noble background he was suspended from command on 30 September 1793. He was not cleared for duty until 29 November 1794. This did not hinder his career, for seven months later he was directly promoted to general of division at the age of 29. He had skipped the rank of general of brigade. He would serve in a variety of command and staff positions over the next ten years, including

---

* Pelet, *The French Campaign in Portugal*, p. 306.
† Thiébault, *The Memoirs of Baron Thiébault*, vol. 2, p. 297.

the second-in-command of the French expedition to Ireland in late 1796.

In August 1805 General Grouchy took command of the 2nd Infantry Division of the 2nd Corps and served in the Austerlitz campaign of 1805. In September 1806 he was appointed commander of the 2nd Dragoon Division in Marshal Bessières's 2nd Cavalry Corps. He would lead them throughout the 1806 Prussian campaign and in the 1807 campaign in Poland. He was wounded at Eylau on 8 February and fought at Friedland on 14 June.

Peace would be fleeting for General Grouchy. In November 1807 he was appointed commander of the cavalry of Marshal Moncey's Corps of Observation of the Coasts and the Ocean. This command consisted of four provisional dragoon regiments. They would stay in the vicinity of Burgos until March, when orders came to occupy Madrid. General Grouchy led the advance guard and entered the city on 23 February. General Grouchy was named governor of the city and ruled it when the city rose in revolt on 2 May. After the surrender of General Dupont and his army at Bailen on 23 July, the French position in Madrid became untenable. King Joseph ordered the evacuation of the city and on 1 August, General Grouchy was in charge of overseeing the movement of King Joseph and the garrison to Miranda. The French forces would deploy along the Ebro River in the vicinity of Vitoria for the next three months. By September General Grouchy was tired of the situation in Spain and wrote to the Minister of War asking to be reassigned. He was offered the command of a dragoon division if he agreed to stay, but declined it.

General Grouchy left Spain in late November 1808, after Napoleon arrived with the rest of the French army. He was assigned to the Army of Italy in April 1809, where he commanded the 1st Dragoon Division during the 1809 Austrian campaign. He would command the 3rd Reserve Cavalry Corps during the 1812 campaign in Russia and commanded the Sacred Squadron, a bodyguard for Napoleon formed of officers who no longer had commands, during the retreat from Moscow. Grouchy declined several commands during the 1813 campaign in Germany, due to poor health. In December 1813 he was named commander of the cavalry of the Grande Armée and would lead it during the 1814 campaign in France.

General Grouchy rallied to Napoleon in 1815 and was promoted to Marshal on 15 April 1815. He would command the right wing of the army during the Waterloo campaign and distinguished himself organising and leading the remnants of the shattered French Army back to France. In July Marshal Grouchy was proscribed by the Second Restoration, but escaped to the United States, where he lived in Philadelphia. On 24 November 1819 he was given amnesty and reinstated into the French army with the rank of lieutenant general. He returned to France on 20 June 1820. He was reinstated as a Marshal of France on 19 November 1831 and made a peer on 11 October 1832.

Table 7.13   Grouvel, François

Awards and honours	Baron of the Empire 17 Jan. 1814
Date and place of birth	17 Oct. 1771 at Rouen
Regiments commanded	9th Prov. Dragoons 31 Dec. 1809–20 Jan. 1810
	16th Dragoons 20 Jan. 1810–30 May 1813
Date of rank as general	General of brigade 30 May 1813
Time in the Peninsula	Jan. 1810–Jul. 1813
Command or post	9th Prov. Dragoons 31 Dec. 1809–20 Jan. 1810
in the Peninsula	16th Dragoons 20 Jan. 1810–30 May 1813
	2nd Brigade, Digeon's Division, Army of the South 30 May–1 Jul. 1813
Date and place of death	26 Dec. 1836 at Strasbourg
Place of burial	Chateau of Osthoffen

François Grouvel entered Spain in January 1810 as the commander of the 9th Provisional Dragoon Regiment, but was given command of the 16th Dragoons within a week of arriving in there. He would command the regiment for the next three years, during which they were engaged in numerous counter-guerrilla operations in the Army of the South. In May 1813 he was promoted to general of brigade and took command of the 2nd Brigade in General Digeon's Division. He would command the brigade at Vitoria, but in July 1813, he was recalled to France for service with the Grande Armée. He would command a light cavalry brigade and was shot in the chest in March 1814. He joined Napoleon upon his return in 1815 and was assigned to the Army of the Rhine. He went into retirement in 1815, upon the disbanding of the army. In 1817 he bought the Chateau Osthoffen in Alsace and it remains in his family to this day. He was recalled to active duty in 1818. He would serve in a variety of staff positions, mostly as an inspector general of cavalry, until he retired on 1 December 1836. General Grouvel died 25 days after he retired.

Table 7.14   Houssaye, Armand Lebrun de la

Awards and honours	Baron of the Empire 22 Nov. 1808
Date and place of birth	20 Oct. 1768 in Paris
Regiments commanded	3rd Hussars 21 Mar. 1794–4 Oct. 1803
	16th Chasseurs 4 Oct. 1803–1 Feb. 1804
Date of rank as general	General of brigade 1 Feb. 1804
	General of division 14 Jun. 1807

Table 7.14 continued

Time in the Peninsula   5 Aug. 1808–16 Jul. 1811

Command or post   4th Dragoon Division 5 Aug. 1808–16 Jan. 1811;
  in the Peninsula   Governor of Toledo Aug. 1810–Apr. 1811
      Governor of the Province of Cuenca Apr.–
      Jul. 1811

Date and place of death   19 Jun. 1846

General Houssaye's name is also spelled La Houssaye in many sources. He entered Spain as the commander of the 4th Dragoon Division in August 1808. It consisted of two brigades and was initially part of the cavalry reserve of the Army of Spain. In early January 1809 it was attached to Marshal Soult's 2nd Corps and took part in the vigorous pursuit of General Moore's army, that ended at the battle of Corunna on 16 January 1809. He and his division remained with the 2nd Corps until August 1810, when they were assigned to the Army of the Centre. General Houssaye would be involved in many small actions during counter-guerrilla operations in the following year. He was recalled to France in July 1811 and given command of the 6th Dragoon Division in Germany in January 1812. He was seriously wounded at Borodino on 7 September 1812 and captured by the Russians on 10 December 1812. He returned to France in June 1814. During the Hundred Days in 1815 General Houssaye served as initially as the commander of the 2nd Cavalry Division and then as the commander of cavalry depots. He was not given another command until 1819, when he became commander of the 14th Military Division. He would serve in a variety of staff positions until he retired in 1833.

General Houssaye was a competent division commander and distinguished himself in counter-guerrilla operations in central Spain. He was noted for his success at Rocca on 21 April 1810, where he charged a Spanish force with two regiments – killing or capturing 1,400 Spaniards; at Tarancon, on 21 October 1810, where he dispersed a 1,000 man guerrilla force that was attacking a French convoy; and at Val de Olivar, on 10 July 1811, where he caught General Zayas in the open, his dragoons killing or capturing 1,600 men, as well as seizing a flag and all the Spanish army's baggage.

Although successful, General Houssaye was not well thought of by his subordinates. Aymar de Gonneville, the aide-de-camp to General Davenay — who commanded the 2nd Brigade in General Houssaye's division during the autumn of 1808 – left a very unflattering portrayal of his character. After the battle of Somosierra on 30 November General Davenay and his brigade were billeted in a Spanish village, when General Houssaye

. . . came up with his three aides-de-camp and the whole staff of
the division. General Davenay received them all with perfect grace,
had every possible addition made to the meal and the new comers
seemed delighted to have nothing to do but to sit down to table
on their arrival. After supper General Davenay offered a share of
his room to General Houssaye, while the aides-de camp settled
themselves in a neighbouring room. It was nothing but just lying
down on mattresses on the floor, as, holding the position of extreme
advanced guard, we could not even take off our boots. The chief of
the staff and his officers went to find other lodgings, for the house
we occupied was much too small to accommodate everyone. On
hearing General Davenay's proposal General Houssaye burst into
a rage and told him that he had been neglectful in not offering the
exclusive possession of the house as soon as he arrived, as was his
due, since it was the best in the place. General Davenay replied
that however unsuitable the claim might have seemed to him
before supper, he would however at that time have allowed it, but
that having performed the duties of hospitality in that house, he
considered himself at home in it and would not go.[*]

Things became very heated between the two generals and General Davenay
told General Houssaye '. . . that if he was not contented there was plenty
of moonlight for them to go down into the courtyard that moment and
settle their differences.'[†] Houssaye declined the offer of a duel, since it
would be in conflict with their duties. Later, one of Houssaye's aides pulled
Gonneville aside and told him 'Do not let your General trust him. He
makes semblance of wishing to forget this scene altogether, but he would
remember it a hundred years if were to live so long. He was afraid, like
a coward as he is. . . and he will never forgive your General.'[‡] The aide's
prediction was correct. Davenay was transferred from the division three
weeks later.

Interestingly, this was not the only charge of cowardice against General
Houssaye. During the 1812 campaign in Russia he was viewed by his
subordinates not only as incompetent but as a coward. Colonel Griois
left a very vivid account of him in action. In one case, when his force was
surprised by the enemy, General Houssaye

lost his feeble head and at the sight of these forces he hadn't expected
to run into, he turned tail as quickly as he'd come 'Retreat at the

---

[*] de Gonneville, *Recollections of Colonel de Gonneville*, vol. 1, pp. 180–1.
[†] Ibid, p. 181.
[‡] Ibid.

gallop!' he shouted giving the example; and ordered my artillery to do the same. In vain I pointed out to him it was the infallible way to lose it and that it would be much better to retire by echelons, successively taking up position. He wouldn't listen and went on yelling 'At the gallop'. I took care not to carry out his order and General of Brigade Watier, who was in command of the advance guard's light division, didn't do so either.*

During the retreat from Moscow Colonel Griois stated that '. . . inept, almost dazed, Lahoussaye is just riding along in his carriage, indifferent to everything'.† He was captured at Vilna on 10 December and would sit out the rest of the war as a Russian prisoner.

Table 7.15   Ismert, Pierre

Awards and honours	Baron of the Empire 26 Oct. 1806
Date and place of birth	30 May 1768 at Tetting
Regiments commanded	2nd Dragoons 14 May 1807–3 Dec. 1812
Date of rank as general	General of brigade 8 Feb. 1813
Time in the Peninsula	Nov. 1808–16 Jan. 1814
Command or post in the Peninsula	2nd Dragoons Nov. 1808–3 Dec. 1812 1st Dragoon Brigade, Perreimond's Division Autumn 1812; 1st Dragoon Brigade, Tilly's Division 8 Feb.–16 Jul. 1813; 1st Dragoon Brigade, Trelliard's Division 16 Jul. 1813–16 Jan. 1814
Wounds in Peninsula	wounded in chest at Medellin 28 Mar. 1809 shrapnel in right foot at Talavera 28 Jul. 1809 Villa-Martine on 21 Mar. 1811; Tarifa Jan. 1812; Monzarbès 14 Nov. 1812
Date and place of death	29 Sep. 1826 at Arengosse
Place of burial	Church in Mont-de-Marsan.

Colonel Ismert believed in leading from the front of his regiment and paid for it by being wounded five times in four years. As a regimental commander he was cited in numerous after-action reports for the way he handled his regiment in combat. During the pursuit of the retreating British army during the autumn of 1812 Colonel Ismert served as the acting brigade commander of the 1st Dragoon Brigade of General Perreimond's Division. He would serve as the temporary commander until 8 February

---

* Austin, *Napoleon's Invasion of Russia*, part 2, p. 77.
† Ibid., part 3, p. 103.

1813, when he was promoted to general of brigade and was officially given command of the brigade. By this time General Tilly had assume command of the division. His brigade consisted of the 2nd, 4th and 26th Dragoons. He and his brigade fought at Vitoria in June 1813 and when Marshal Soult reorganised the French Army of Spain, General Ismert was given the 1st Dragoon Brigade, of Trelliard's Division. About the same time, many dragoon regiments were withdrawn from the Peninsula and sent to Germany. His brigade was not, but it was reduced to the 21st and 26th Dragoons and had a strength of about 800 men. In October the 4th Dragoons were added to his brigade and the total strength of the brigade was over 1,500 men. Three months later Ismert and his brigade were ordered to eastern France. His outstanding performance in the battles of February and March of 1814, was mentioned several times in after-action-reports. General Ismert commanded the Department of Landes when Napoleon returned to France in 1815. He retired in October 1815.

General Ismert's service as a regimental commander in Spain was superb. He commanded a cavalry brigade for only 14 months and saw little action until the final months of the Empire in the winter of 1814. He commanded his brigade with distinction, but by then it was for a lost cause.

Table 7.16   Kellermann, François-Etienne

Awards and honours	Count of Valmy May 1808; Marquis of Valmy 31 Aug. 1817; 2nd Duke of Valmy 12 Sep. 1820
Date and place of birth	4 Aug. 1770 at Metz
Date of rank as general	General of brigade 28 May 1797; General of division 5 Jul. 1800
Time in the Peninsula	2 Aug. 1807 –30 Sep. 1808; Jan. 1809–20 May 1811
Command or post in the Peninsula	2nd Dragoon Division 9 Jan. 1809–4 Jun. 1810 6th Corps 6 Nov. 1809 –12 Feb. 1810; 6th Military Government 4 Jun. 1810 –20 May 1811; Army of the North Sep. 1810–20 May 1811
Date and place of death	2 Jun. 1835 in Paris
Place of burial	Père Lachaise Cemetery

François Kellermann was the son of Marshal François-Christophe Kellermann, the Duke of Valmy.

General Kellermann made his mark on history on 14 June 1800 at the battle of Marengo. He took the initiative to charge with his brigade, breaking the Austrian attack, thus securing the victory for Napoleon. Three weeks later, in recognition for his service, he was promoted to general of division. General Kellermann commanded the 1st Corps's Light Cavalry Division in the 1805 campaign and two years later was given command of the cavalry in General Junot's Corps of Observation of the Gironde. He would lead them in the expedition to Portugal that was the opening round of the Peninsular War.

After conquering Portugal with relative ease, General Junot was forced to contend with a British expeditionary force under the future Duke of Wellington. In August 1808 General Kellermann was part of the French army that fought at Roliça and Vimeiro, where he commanded several battalions of grenadiers of the reserve in a final attempt to break the British line. After his defeat at Vimeiro Junot entered negotiations with the British. Kellermann, being fluent in English, led the French negotiating team. The final agreement was known as the Convention of Cintra and the French army would be transported to France aboard British ships with all of its weapons, equipment, baggage and military chest. The French commanders took advantage of these and included their plunder of Portugal in their baggage.

General Kellermann sailed from Lisbon on 30 September and was in France by mid-October. He was supposed to command the 2nd Dragoon Division during the invasion of Spain, but arrived too late to take command. He would assume command of it on 9 January 1809 and would operate in northern Spain for the next two years. In November 1809 he became the provisional commander of the 6th Corps and led them to victory at what would be one of his most notable achievements – the mauling of the Spanish Army under General Del Parque at Alba de Tormes on 28 November. Kellermann was riding with 3,000 dragoons, chasseurs and hussars when he came across the Spanish army. The French 6th Corps was 15 kilometres away and if he waited for them to come up, the Spanish would escape. In a bold move he decided to attack the 18,000 Spaniards with just his cavalry in the hopes of pinning them in place until his infantry arrived. The attack was a cavalry trooper's dream. In a succession of charges, Kellermann and his cavalry broke three infantry divisions, capturing five flags, nine guns and 2,000 men, while killing another 1,000. Two and a half hours later, the infantry came up, but by then the Spaniards were broken and in flight.

In June 1810 General Kellermann became governor of the 6th Military Government and was in charge of the provinces of Palencia, Toro and Valladolid. His headquarters was in Valladolid, from where he was responsible for securing the lines of communication between the Army of Portugal and France. To accomplish this, he had two brigades

1   General Auguste de Colbert
    by Forestier

2   General August-Jean-Gabriel
    de Caulinourt by Forestier

3   The Death of Colonel Vital Chamorin, 26th Dragoons by Paul Jazet

4   *General François Fournier-Sarlovèse*
by Forestier

5   *General Jean Franceshi by Forestier*

6   *General François Kellermann by Forestier*

7 *General François-Antoine Lallemand*
by Forestier

8 *General Antoine-Charles-Louis*
Lasalle by Forestier

9 *General Charles Lefebvre-Desnouettes by Forestier*

10   *General Pierre Margaron by Forestier*

11   *General Louis Montbrun by Forestier*

12   *General Ythier-Silvain Pryvé by Forestier*

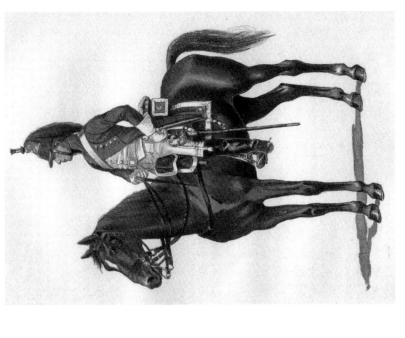

14   *6th Dragoon*

13   *Elite Company, 2nd Dragoons by E. Pendon and L. Gaudibert*

16   *16th Dragoon by Lieutenant Rozat de Mandres*

15   *Maréchal des Logis Damien of the 14th Dragoons capturing a Swiss colonel in Spanish service at Valselle on 24 September 1809*

18 *Trumpeter and Trooper, 25th Dragoons*

17 *17th Dragoon by Richard Knötel*

20 *3rd Hussars by Richard Knötel*

19 *Elite Company, 5th Chasseur*

of provisional dragoon regiments and an infantry division commanded by General Seras. He was also responsible for assisting in the supply of Marshal Masséna's Army of Portugal. Kellermann forgot that even though he was nominally an independent commander, his primary mission was to support the Army of Portugal. His relationship with Masséna deteriorated during the build-up to the invasion of Portugal in the summer of 1810. Instead of doing what he could to provide supplies to the army, he began undercutting the marshal in his efforts to prepare rations for the move into Portugal. Kellermann would not supply wagons or transport after the supplies were gathered or, if the wagons were available, permit them to bring the supplies all the way to the army's forward supply dumps. On 26 July he even went as far as order the civil authorities in Zamora and Leon not to provide any supplies unless the request went through him first. Masséna was furious about this and sent him a sharply worded letter, reminding him who was in charge:

> I am obliged to remind you of your assignment . . . As commander in chief of the Army of Portugal, I have supreme command of northern Spain and your government is included within it . . .
> I forbid you to touch the treasury . . . You will conform to the contents of my letter and be cautious in the future . . .*

The situation improved marginally; but in late August, Kellermann once again refused to send his wagons forward from Salamanca to Ciudad Rodrigo and told his commissary officer to dump the supplies along the road. Marshal Masséna had enough and wrote a letter to Napoleon denouncing him for gross insubordination.

General Kellermann also got into trouble over finances. In addition to being unable to raise funds through taxes, he was accused of letting Spanish officers buy their freedom. The going rate was between 3,000 and 4,000 gold reals. Marshal Ney reported that 40 prisoners in Ciudad Rodrigo had paid 24,000 reals each for their freedom.†

On 17 September 1810 Napoleon wrote to Marshal Berthier:

> My Cousin,
> Heavy charges are brought to me on all sides against General Kellermann. Send an officer to him with a letter, in which you will express to him my extreme displeasure at the abuses committed in his government; and ask him for a categorical statement of all the contributions which he has levied. In his government, at Valladolid,

---

* Horward, *Napoleon and Iberia*, p. 235.
† Ibid., p. 240.

for instance, even the liberation of the prisoners of war is sold. Tell him that I consider him responsible for abuses which are so opposed to the well-being and the interests of the army. Let him know that I have asked for a report on these complaints; that the officer whom you send is desired to bring back an answer in which I expect you to be told that he has arrested the individuals guilty of these crimes and tried them by a court-martial. Give him to understand that, if he does not deal severely with these horrible abuses and remedy them, I shall believe the general rumour that he connives at them. Tell him that, of all the governments in Spain, his is that in which most robbery is perpetrated.*

In April 1811 a Council of State investigated General Kellermann's conduct. He was relieved of his command and recalled to France in May.† He was not given another command until 1813. Supposedly, he was too sick to participate in the 1812 campaign in Russia. By 1813 Napoleon had forgiven him (probably because he needed experienced cavalry commanders) and General Kellermann became the commander of the 4th Cavalry Corps. He would command the corps throughout 1813, but in 1814 he took command of the newly formed 6th Cavalry Corps.

Kellermann joined Napoleon in 1815 and commanded the 3rd Cavalry Corps during the Waterloo campaign. It was his cuirassiers who rode down Maitland's Brigade at Quatre Bras and were part of the numerous cavalry attacks on the British line at Waterloo. After Waterloo Kellermann was part of the delegation that negotiated the fate of the French army with King Louis XVIII. On the death of his father in 1820 General Kellermann became the 2nd Duke of Valmy and a member of the Council of Peers. In 1830 he was the president of the commission that oversaw the reorganisation of the French cavalry.

Despite being one of the foremost cavalry generals of the Napoleonic era, General Kellermann's reputation was tarnished by his greed and his practice of extortion from the Spanish population that rivalled Marshal Soult's. Aymar de Gonneville, who visited him in Valladolid, left the following impression of him:

> He was a little man, of unhealthy and insignificant appearance, with a clever look, but false. During our short stay at Valladolid we heard some things about him that lowered him considerably in our estimation. He was a merciless peculator. Under political pretexts he would bury the most notable inhabitants of places under his control,

---

* Bonaparte, *The Confidential Correspondence*, vol II, p. 141.
† Ibid., p. 369.

extending over a fourth part of Spain, in the ancient dungeons of the Inquisition; he would then make a composition with their families and set the prisoners at liberty for a price that he pocketed. In later days, under the Restoration, he had a great reputation for piety. Without wishing to contest the sincerity of his religious feelings at this later period, I cannot help making the remark that, at the dedication of a church that was built at his expense near Paris, in a commune where he was owner of a house and lands, the Abbé Fraissinous, renowned for his piety and eloquence, preached a sermon in praise of the virtues of the founder. It is likely that both house and church were the result of exactions committed in Spain.[*]

Table 7.17   Konopka, Jan

Date and place of birth	27 Dec. 1777 in Skoldycze Castle, Lithuania
Regiments commanded	1st Vistula Legion Lancers 15 Jul. 1807–6 Aug. 1811
Date of rank as general	General of brigade 6 Aug. 1811
Time in the Peninsula	Jun. 1808–27 Jan. 1812
Command or post in the Peninsula	1st Lancers of the Vistula 15 Jul. 1807–6 Aug. 1811; Light Cavalry Brigade Nov. 1811–27 Jan. 1812
Wounds in Peninsula	At the siege of Saragosa (4 Aug. 1808)
Date and place of death	12 Dec. 1814 in Warsaw
Cause of death	Exhaustion and wounds received during 1812 campaign in Russia

Jan Konopka was a Polish noble who went into exile after the defeat of the Polish army at Maciejowice in 1794. He initially enlisted in the French 2nd Hussars, but transferred to the Polish Legion in Italy in 1797. In July 1807 Colonel Konopka took command of the 1st Regiment of Polish Lancers, which was also known as the Vistula Legion Lancers. He would lead them into Spain in June 1808 and command them there until they were officially incorporated into the French army as the 7th Lancers. Jan Konopka was best known for two things. The first was for convincing Napoleon to let his regiment keep their lancers, even though Napoleon thought the weapons were inefficient. Just prior to entering Spain in June 1808, the regiment was being reviewed by Napoleon. Napoleon said to Colonel Konopka:

---

[*] de Gonneville, *Recollections of Colonel de Gonneville*, vol. 1, pp. 250–1.

> Since your lances cannot, in a charge, parry a sabre blow and since
> the red and white pennons are merely childish playthings, I am
> going to re-arm your regiment with carbines.[*]

Colonel Konopka replied:

> Sire, because of its length alone the lance is a weapon that in the
> hands of a skilled user can create a powerful moral superiority over
> an enemy because the enemy can be killed or wounded without
> coming close enough to strike back with a sword. In addition, the
> pennons scare the horses of the enemy hussars and dragoons and
> give us a great advantage.[†]

Napoleon was sceptical about this, so Konopka '. . . offered a demon-
stration on the spot. He thereupon led his men in a mock charge against
the Emperor and his staff that caused Napoleon's own horse to bolt.' The
chastened emperor had the last word, however: 'You can keep your lances,
but I am going to give carbines to the men in your second rank.'[‡]

Colonel Konopka also led the regiment at Albuera on 16 May 1811.
There the regiment caught the British left flank in line and destroyed
Colborne's brigade. In less than 30 minutes the lancers rode down three
British regiments and an artillery brigade, capturing four flags, five
artillery pieces and came close to capturing the commander of the British
forces – Marshal William Beresford. The lancers inflicted 1,378 casualties
on the brigade – 68 per cent of its total effectives.

Jan Konopka was rewarded for his actions by being promoted to general
of brigade in August. He would command a light cavalry brigade in the
Army of the South until January 1812, when he was ordered to return to
France. He was assigned to the 1st Regiment of Lancers of the Imperial
Guard (the Polish Lancers) and in July 1812 was appointed commander
of the newly raised 3rd Regiment of Lancers of the Imperial Guard (the
Lithuanian Lancers). He commanded the regiment during the Russian
campaign and was severely wounded and captured by the Russians on 19
October 1812 at Slonim, his childhood home. General Konopka spent the
rest of the war in captivity, returning to Warsaw in July 1814. He died five
months later from the wounds he received in the Russian campaign.

General Konopka's service as a regimental commander was often
brilliant. He led the Vistula Legion Lancers in some spectacular charges
on the battlefield. While the destruction of the British brigade at Albuera

---

[*] Dempsey, *Napoleon's Mercenaries*. p. 124.
[†] Ibid.
[‡] Ibid., pp. 124–5.

was its finest hour, the regiment also distinguished itself at Ocaña where it charged the flank of the Spanish infantry and took thousands of prisoners. Yet while exercising independent command, he was occasionally arrogant and it cost him. On 24 March 1809, while on a route march, his regiment was surprised by a Spanish force and General Bouillé gave a damning indictment in his memoirs

> the regiment of Polish lancers, a brave unit, but one which, out of overconfidence and an unprofessional disdain for its enemies, committed the unpardonable military sin of letting itself be surprised . . . The baggage of the regiment plus three officers and 57 lancers fell into the hands of the Spanish cavalry.

In the wagons were the regiments' standards.[*]

In Russia in 1812 once again a regiment he commanded was operating independently and he was surprised by a Russian force that inflicted casualties on it. Although warned that there were Russians in the area, he failed to put out proper security and the regiment was attacked. General Konopka, 13 officers and 235 men were captured, along with the regimental treasury.[†]

---

[*] Ibid., pp. 125–6.
[†] Ibid., p. 77.

Chapter Eight

The Peninsular Cavalry Generals
Laferrière to Montbrun

Table 8.1   Laferrière, Louis-Marie Levesque

Awards and honours	Count of the Empire 28 Nov. 1813
Date and place of birth	9 Apr. 1776 at Redon
Regiments commanded	3rd Hussars 8 Mar. 1807–13 May 1811
Date of rank as general	General of brigade 13 May 1811; General of division 28 Nov. 1813
Time in the Peninsula	Nov. 1808–Jun. 1811; Oct. 1811–Feb. 1813
Command or post in the Peninsula	3rd Hussars 8 Mar. 1807–13 May 1811 Cavalry Brigade, Army of the North Oct. 1811–Feb. 1813
Wounds in Peninsula	Slightly wounded at Col de Banos 12 Aug. 1809; shot in left arm at Alba de Tormes, 28 Nov. 1809; shot in left hand and right arm at Miranda de Corvo, 12 Mar. 1811
Date and place of death	22 Nov. 1834 in Paris
Place of burial	Vallery

General Laferrière's full name was Louis-Maire Levesque, the Count Laferrière. He is more often referred to as Laferrière than Levesque.

Louis Laferrière led from the front and was rewarded by being wounded eight times in five years, four of those times leading the 3rd Hussars in Spain. He commanded the regiment for four years, of which 30 months were in combat operations in Spain. After being promoted to general of brigade in 1811, he was allowed to return to France in June, but four months later was sent back to Spain to take command of a cavalry brigade in the Army of the North. His new command was large, with four regiments and almost 1,500 men. His mission was to secure the lines of communications with France. He would command the brigade until

February 1813, when he was recalled to France and appointed as a major in the Horse Grenadiers of the Imperial Guard.

General Laferrière would fight throughout 1813 in Germany. He was promoted to general of division in November and in December 1813 took command of the 3rd Old Guard Cavalry Division. He led them in 1814 and was shot twice at Craone on 7 March 1814. He rallied to Napoleon in 1815 and was made a peer of France on 2 June 1815. He was allowed to retire in 1818.

Table 8.2   Lallemand, François-Antoine

Awards and honours	Baron of the Empire 29 Jun. 1808
Date and place of birth	23 Jun. 1774 at Metz
Regiments commanded	27th Dragoons 20 Nov. 1806–6 Aug. 1811
Date of rank as general	General of brigade 6 Aug. 1811; Lieutenant General 30 Mar. 1815
Time in the Peninsula	Sep. 1808–Sep. 1809; Jan. 1810–5 Feb. 1813
Command or post in the Peninsula	27th Dragoons 20 Nov. 1806–Sep. 1809; 27th Dragoons Jan. 1810–6 Aug. 1811; 1st Dragoon Brigade, Tour-Maubourg's Division 1 Nov.–Dec. 1811; Governor of Jaen Province Jan.–Feb. 1812; 1st Brigade, 1st Cavalry Division Feb.–Mar. 1812; 1st Dragoon Brigade, 2nd Cavalry Division Mar. 1812–5 Feb. 1813
Date and place of death	9 Mar. 1839 in Paris
Place of burial	Père Lachaise Cemetery

François Lallemand commanded the 27th Dragoons in Spain for almost a year before he returned to France because of his poor health. He had been in France for less than four months when he returned to his regiment in January 1810. While he commanded the regiment in the Peninsula, it was part of Marshal Soult's invasion of northern Portugal in 1809. However, beginning in 1810, the regiment spent most of its time performing counter-guerrilla operations in southern Spain. In 1811 Colonel Lallemand and the regiment fought at Albuera, on 16 May 1811 and the relief of Badajoz during June and July. On 6 August 1811 he was promoted to general of brigade and three months later, in November, he assumed command of the 1st Dragoon Brigade of General Tour-Maubourg's Division. The brigade had been commanded by General Bron, who had been captured a few weeks before at Arroyo dos Molinos. General Lallemand's new command consisted of the 17th, 20th and 26th Dragoons. He would only command it for two months before he was appointed governor of Jaen Province. His tenure as governor was short and in February 1812, he became the commander of 1st Brigade of Perreimond's Division. Two months later he was transferred again. This time to command the 1st Dragoon Brigade of the 2nd Cavalry Division. His new brigade consisted of the 14th, 17th and 27th Dragoons and the 7th Lancers. On 11 June 1812 he met General Slade's British Cavalry Brigade at Maguilla. It was one of the few cavalry combats during the Peninsular War where both sides had equal numbers of troops. During the battle Slade's regiments broke Lallemand's regiments and pursued them vigorously. Slade lost control of his command after a chase of several miles. At that point Lallemand sent in his reserve, which hit the British in the flank. The rest of the French turned around and joined in the fray. Within a few minutes, the British broke and ran away in complete disorder. Lallemand and his dragoons inflicted heavy casualties on Slade's command – 22 killed, 26 wounded and 118 captured. Lallemand would command the brigade until February 1813, when he was recalled to France. He would serve in various cavalry commands in Germany in the Grande Armée. His last command in 1814 was in the defence of Hamburg, where he commanded Danish troops.

In 1812 General Lallemand spent much of his time deployed against General Robert Long's Light Cavalry Brigade. They engaged in quite a bit of correspondence and Long had much respect for him. In one case Lallemand had two King's German Legion hussars his troops had captured returned to Long, because 'It gave him great pleasure to show his respect for the German Hussars.'* This relationship ended in September 1812, when Long's brigade occupied a village that Lallemand's men had held for three years. General Long wrote in a letter home that

> I little thought that whilst I was complimenting him on his
> humanity, he was in the act of directing the execution of two
> poor wretches at Hornaches, one on the suspicion (but without
> foundation) of being a spy in our pay, the other for robbing one
> of his men. He will receive no more billet doux from me – the
> Murderer!†

On Napoleon's return from Elba in 1815, General Lallemand led an uprising in support of him. He was arrested by the Royalists, but freed by Napoleon. In return for his loyalty, Lallemand was given command of the Mounted Chasseurs of the Imperial Guard during the Waterloo

---

* Long, *Peninsular Cavalry General*, p. 220.
† Ibid.

campaign. After the defeat of the French army, it was Lallemand who asked the captain of the *Bellerophon* for asylum for Napoleon. He sailed to Plymouth with Napoleon, but was not allowed to go to Saint Helena. In acknowledgment of his service, Napoleon left him 100,000 francs in his will. Lallemand was condemned to death in August 1816 for the part he played in Napoleon's return to France in 1815. In 1817 he went to Alabama and founded a colony composed of former French soldiers. After it failed he tried setting up another colony in Texas, but it too was unsuccessful. He returned to France in 1830 and was reinstated into the French army. He would serve in as the inspector general of cavalry several times and was promoted to lieutenant general in 1831. He stayed on active duty until his death in 1839.

Table 8.3 Lamotte, Auguste-Etienne-Marie Gourlez

Awards and honours	Baron of the Empire 26 Oct. 1808
Date and place of birth	5 Apr. 1772 in Paris
Regiments commanded	4th Dragoons 12 Jan. 1806–21 Mar. 1809
Date of rank as general	General of brigade 21 Mar. 1809
Time in the Peninsula	Nov. 1808–21 Mar. 1809; 7 Dec. 1809–Jun. 1811

Command or post in the Peninsula	4th Dragoons Nov. 1808–Apr. 1809
	    5th Prov. Dragoon Brigade, Caulaincourt's Division, 8th Corps 7 Dec. 1809–8 Feb. 1810
	    Light Cavalry Brigade, Ney's 6th Corps 24 Jul. 1810–15 Mar. 1811

Date and place of death	8 May 1836
Place of burial	Père Lachaise Cemetery

Auguste Lamotte had the all the makings of a rising star. After successfully commanding the 4th Dragoons during the 1806 and 1807 campaigns, he and his regiment were sent to the Peninsula in November 1808. After leading them at Ucles on 13 January 1809 and Medellin on 28 March 1809 he was promoted to general of brigade in March 1809 and sent to command a dragoon brigade in the Grande Armée in Germany. After the defeat of Austria General Lamotte was then assigned to Junot's 8th Corps which was going to Spain and he took command of the 5th Provisional Dragoon Brigade in December 1809. His brigade was dissolved in February 1810 and he was attached to the headquarters of the 6th Corps. In July 1810 he was given command of the Light Cavalry Brigade (3rd Hussars and the 15th Chasseurs) of Marshal Ney's 6th Corps. He led them at the combat on the River Coa on 24 July 1810 and into Portugal in September. It was during the retreat back to Spain during the winter of 1811 that disaster struck General Lamotte destroying his career and reputation.

Marshal Ney commanded the rearguard and Lamotte's brigade was in the thick of the fighting retreat. On 15 March the rearguard approached the village of Foz d'Arouce, along the rain swollen Ceira River. Ney thought the pursuing British were too far away to be a threat, so instead of sending all of his troops to cross the bridge, he permitted half his force (three infantry brigades and Lamotte's Cavalry Brigade) to stop on the west side of the river. Lamotte did not post picquets and sent a good part of his brigade to forage on the far side of the river. The British attack took the French by surprise – because the cavalry, which should have been manning outposts, was not there. The French barely had time to form when they were hit by the British 3rd and Light Divisions. The centre of the French line panicked and raced to the bridge. General Lamotte ordered his brigade across the bridge, trampling the fleeing French 39th Line. The infantry, finding their passage blocked fled down river to a ford, where many men drowned, including the regiment's eagle bearer, who dropped the eagle, which was swept away by the raging water. The regimental commander was captured. Marshal Ney was able to stabilise the situation after some desperate fighting and withdraw the rest of his force. Emmanuel Sprünglin, Marshal Ney's aide-de-camp, described the Marshal's mood after the battle:

> Never have I seen Marshal Ney in such bad humor as on this day. He was very angry with the 39th Line for the disorders of the previous night and the loss of its eagle and colonel. He was furious with General Lamotte, whose inconceivable conduct had caused the congestion on the bridge and the disaster that resulted. He refused a company of the 39th Line who came to form the guard for his quarters, he removed General Lamotte from command of the light cavalry, he sent him to the Prince d'Essling's headquarters . . . and he was carried to the point of seizing a pistol from his holster and threatening to blow his [Lamotte's] brains out if he did not retire at that instant.[*]

General Lamotte returned to France in disgrace and was allowed to retire on 3 March 1812. He was recalled to active duty two years later. He would command a brigade in Milhaud's Corps in Germany. General Lamotte did not join Napoleon in 1815. He was dismissed from the army in April 1815 when he was charged with promising to deliver Bayonne to the Spanish. He died in 1836.

---

[*] Pelet, *The French Campaign in Portugal*, pp. 476–7.

Table 8.4   Laplanche, Jean Baptiste

Awards and honours	Baron of the Empire 21 Sep. 1808
Date and place of birth	25 Jan. 1757 at Montauban
Date of rank as general	General of brigade 29 Aug. 1803
Time in the Peninsula	17 Oct. 1808–19 Jun. 1810
Command or post in the Peninsula	Headquarters, Army of Spain 17 Oct.–11 Dec. 1808 Madrid Cavalry Depot 11 Dec. 1808–19 Jun. 1810
Date and place of death	8 Jan. 1832 at Charleville

General Laplanche was another cavalry general who made his reputation during the wars of the French Revolution. He commanded a dragoon brigade in the campaigns in Germany and Eastern Europe from 1805 to 1807. In January 1808 he commanded a light cavalry brigade in General Lasalle's Division, but did not go with him to Spain in February. General Laplanche was assigned to the headquarters of the Army of Spain in the autumn of 1808 and was responsible for setting up the cavalry depot at Laganés, just south of Madrid. He would command it until June 1810, when he returned to France and retired. He came out of retirement upon Napoleon's return in 1815 and was captured while defending Charleville.

Table 8.5   Lasalle, Antoine-Charles-Louis

Awards and honours	Count of the Empire 16 Mar. 1808
Date and place of birth	10 May 1775 at Metz
Regiments commanded	22nd Chasseurs 23 Jul. 1798–10th Hussars 25 Aug. 1800–1 Feb. 1805
Date of rank as general	General of brigade 1 Feb. 1805; General of division 30 Dec. 1806
Time in the Peninsula	18 Feb. 1808–22 Apr. 1809
Command or post in the Peninsula	Light Cavalry Division 18 Feb.–7 Sep. 1808 Light Cavalry Division, 2nd Corps 7 Sep. 1808–19 Feb. 1809; Light Cavalry Division, 1st Corps 19 Feb.–22 Apr. 1809
Date and place of death	6 Jul. 1809 at Wagram, Austria
Cause of death	Shot in head while leading a charge in final moments of battle of Wagram
Place of burial	Crypt, of the Hôtel des Invalides, Paris

Antoine Lasalle was the *beau sabre* of Napoleonic France. He was the ideal light cavalryman – fearless to the point of recklessness, hard-fighting, hard-drinking and possessing a devil-may-care attitude towards life. He was flamboyant, loved fancy uniforms and was fond of theatrics. He often led his men in a charge holding a long-stemmed pipe instead a sabre.

General Lasalle was closely tied to Napoleon, serving under the future emperor as far back as 1796 in Italy. He went to Egypt with Napoleon in 1798. He was promoted to general of brigade in 1805 at the age of 30 and would lead a cavalry brigade in the Austerlitz campaign of 1805 and against Prussia and Russia in 1806 and 1807. Possibly his greatest feat was on 30 October, when he bluffed the commander of the great Prussian fortress of Stettin, garrisoned with 5,000 men, into surrendering it to him. General Lasalle had only the 500 men of the 5th and 7th Hussars with him. Napoleon, hearing of this, wrote to Marshal Murat, 'My compliments on the capture of Stettin; if your light cavalry thus takes fortified towns, I must disband the engineers and melt down my heavy artillery.'*

General Lasalle was promoted to general of division on 30 December 1806 and given command of a new light cavalry division. He would fight at Ziegelhoff on 8 February 1807 and at Heilsberg on 10 June, but stayed in Warsaw for the remainder of the year. On 18 February 1808 he was named commander of a new light cavalry division that was being formed at Poitiers for operations in Spain. By early June he was in Bayonne and received new orders to take a force of four infantry battalions, 700 cavalrymen and six artillery pieces and march to Valladolid. The march was uneventful until his column reached the bridge at Cabezon on 12 June. It was blocked by 5,000 Spaniards of General Cuesta's Army of Castile. The French quickly broke the Spanish force, killing or wounding hundreds of the poorly trained peasants, at a cost of less than 50 French casualties. Lasalle led the cavalry at Medina de Rio Seco on 14 July, hitting the Spanish wing in the flank and creating havoc among the Spanish infantry, who fled as quickly as possible.

General Lasalle and his division were attached to the 2nd Corps under Marshal Soult in early September and then to Marshal Victor's 1st Corps in February 1809. His division was screening the army's flank when the 10th Chasseurs were ambushed by two regiments of Spanish cavalry on 21 March. The tables were turned on the French and the chasseurs lost 63 men killed and another 70 wounded by the time reinforcements had arrived. Lasalle's troopers would get their revenge on 29 March at Medellin. The division was deployed on the left flank of the army and when the French centre and right flank fell back under heavy pressure, Lasalle slowly began to withdraw his men. Under pressure from the advancing Spanish,

---

* Petre, *Napoleon's Conquest of Prussia*, pp. 252–3.

General Lasalle rode proudly and calmly backwards and forwards in front of his division. When the enemy's cavalry came within gunshot, the skirmishers on each side retired and in the space which separated us from the Spaniards, nothing was seen but the horses of the dead, both friends and enemies, running wounded about the plain, some of them struggling to get rid of the cumbersome burden of their masters, whom they were dragging with them.[*]

A charge was ordered and the Spanish were forced back; but the French centre and right was still in danger, so General Lasalle and his men continued slowly to pull back. After about five hours the French dragoons on the right counter-attacked and the light cavalry joined them. The fight was vicious at first, due to the frustration of sitting under fire for so long combined with a desire to avenge what had happened to the 10th Chasseurs a week earlier. Lieutenant de Rocca, an officer in the 2nd Hussars, wrote that

> Our soldiers, who had seen themselves threatened with certain death, had they sunk under the number of their foes and irritated by five hours' resistance, gave no quarter at first. The infantry followed the cavalry at a distance and dispatched the wounded with the bayonet. The fury of our soldiers was particularly directed against such Spaniards as were without military dresses.[†]

General Lasalle was ruthless when dealing with partisans and individuals not in uniform caught fighting. His policy was to hang a Spaniard any time a French national was killed other than in combat. If a village or town was caught harbouring insurgents, he would hang 60 of them. On 5 June Lasalle's troops approached Torquemada. They were fired upon by insurgents barricaded inside the town. After the insurgents were driven off, Lasalle allowed his men to sack the town and then ordered it to be burned. Word quickly spread into the surrounding countryside, especially to Palencia, which was harbouring 4,000 insurgents, City officials convinced them to leave and sent a delegation to General Lasalle asking for amnesty. He agreed upon the payment of a fine and the confiscation of all weapons.[‡]

In March 1809 Lasalle received orders recalling him to France for duty with the French Army in Germany, but he delayed his departure from Madrid for a month, not leaving until 22 April. He did not spend much

---

[*] de Rocca, *In the Peninsula with a French Hussar*, p. 79–80.

[†] Ibid., p. 80.

[‡] Thoumas, *Les Grands Cavaliers*, vol. 2, pp. 31–2.

time in France, arriving in Austria on 19 May, having travelled 1,860 kilometres in 27 days. He immediately took command of the Reserve Cavalry Corps's Light Cavalry Division and was attached to Marshal Masséna's 4th Corps. Three days later, he crossed the Danube River and fought at Aspern-Essling, protecting the French army as it pulled back across the Danube. In June he and his division were part of the covering force during the siege of Raab, but were brought back to the main army for the battle of Wagram on 5 and 6 July. On the first day and most of the second day of the battle, General Lasalle sat in reserve. Legend has it that on the second day General Lasalle sensed that things were not going right for him and had a premonition of his own death.

> The horse which he rode in battle had been carelessly taken at four in the morning to be watered at a stream beyond the forward picquets and had been captured together with the orderly by an enemy patrol. This was the first unpleasant occurrence of the day for the general. A little later when he was looking in his saddle holster for a small bottle of excellent French brandy which his servant never failed to put there, he was disappointed to find only pieces of glass. The bottle had been broken. 'What a wretched day!' said General Lasalle. 'It is the sort of day on which I shall get killed.'*

Towards the end of the day, General Lasalle saw that the battle was almost over and that he and his men had sat out the battle. He requested permission from Marshal Massena to allow him to lead the pursuit of the retreating Austrians. General Lasalle called to his men, 'The battle is ending and we alone have not contributed to victory. Come on!'† He led his division in the last charge of the battle and was killed by a bullet in the brain.

Baron Marbot's description of Antoine Lasalle left no room for any doubt about the qualities of the man:

> He was the best light cavalry officer for outpost duty and had the surest eye. He could take in a whole district in a moment and seldom made a mistake, so that his reports on the enemy's position were clear and precise. He was a handsome man and of a bright wit, but, although well educated, he had adopted the fashion of posing as a swashbuckler. He might always be seen drinking, swearing, singing, smashing everything and possessed by ,a passion for play. He was an excellent horseman and brave to the point of rashness.‡

---

* Parquin, *Napoleon's Army*, pp. 103–4.
† Marbot, *The Memoirs of Baron Marbot*, vol. 2 p. 26.
‡ Ibid., vol. 2, p. 24.

Despite his admiration for General Lasalle, Baron Marbot also gave a sobering assessment on his impact on the French Army:

> His death left a great gap in our light cavalry, which he had trained to a high degree of perfection. In other respects, however, he had done it much harm. The eccentricities of a popular and successful leader are always imitated and his example was long mischievous to the light cavalry. A man did not think himself a chasseur, still less a hussar, if he did not model himself on Lasalle and become, like him, a reckless, drinking, swearing rowdy. Many officers copied the fault of this famous outpost leader, but none of them attained to the merits which in him atoned for the faults.[*]

Part of the mystique of General Lasalle is his famous quote in 1808 'My dear friend, a hussar who is not dead by the time he is thirty is a worthless fucker.'[†] He came close to living up to his own ideal. He died a year later at the age of 34.

Table 8.6   Lefebvre-Desnouettes, Charles

Awards and honours	Count of the Empire 19 Mar. 1808
Date and place of birth	14 Sep. 1773 in Paris
Regiments commanded	18th Dragoons 30 Dec. 1802–19 Sep. 1806; Horse Chasseurs of the Guard 18 Jan. 1808–29 Dec. 1808; Horse Chasseurs of the Guard 6 May 1812–12 May 1814; Horse Chasseurs of the Guard 14 Apr.–24 Jul. 1815
Date of rank as general	General of brigade 19 Sep. 1806; General of division 28 Aug. 1808
Time in the Peninsula	19 Mar.–28 Aug. 1808; 3 Nov.–29 Dec. 1808
Command or post in the Peninsula	Chief-of-Staff, Corps of Observation of the Western Pyrenees 19 Mar.–28 Aug. 1808; Horse Chasseurs of the Guard 3 Nov.–29 Dec. 1808

---

[*] Ibid., vol. 2, p. 26.

[†] Thiébault, *The Memoirs of Baron Thiebault*, vol. 2, p. 79. Général Lasalle actually said '*jean foutre*', which was a very strong pejorative term that cannot be accurately translated into modern English. The translator of Thiebault's memoirs used 'dirty sneak', while others have used blackguard, coward and spineless. Ironically, this quote had nothing to do with combat. It was a retort made by Général Lasalle to Général Thiébault, who had chided him for drinking too much the night before in Salamanca. Général Lasalle was still very drunk or very hung over when he said it.

Table 8.6 continued

Wounds in Peninsula	At Saragossa 4 Aug. 1808; at Benavente 29 Dec. 1808
Date and place of death	22 Apr. 1822 off the coast of Kinsale, Ireland
Cause of death	Drowned at sea

The name was also spelled Lefebvre-Desnoëttes and Lefebvre-Desnoettes. He was a hard-charging cavalry officer with close ties to Napoleon. He served as an aide-de-camp to him during the Marengo campaign in 1800 and joined the Guards of the Consuls (the forerunner of the Imperial Guard) in 1801. He was appointed Master of the Horse to the emperor in July 1804 and was given a house by Napoleon. After being promoted to general of brigade in September 1806, he would serve as an aide-de-camp to Prince Jerome and command a Bavarian cavalry brigade in the 1806 and 1807 campaigns.

In January 1808 General Lefebvre-Desnouettes was appointed major-colonel in the Horse Chasseurs of the Guard. He went to Spain as the chief-of-staff to Marshal Bessières's Corps of Observation of the Western Pyrenees in March 1808 and would serve at Tudela on 7 June 1808, Maillen on 13 June 1808, Alagon on 14 June 1808 and the siege of Saragossa from June–August 1808, where he was wounded. He was recalled to France to prepare his regiment for service in Spain.

General Lefebvre-Desnouettes and his chasseurs entered Spain in early November 1808. In late December he was ordered to take his regiment and pursuit General Moore's retreating British army. They caught up with the British rearguard at Benavente. Lefebvre-Desnouettes did not take time to reconnoitre the British position and ordered his regiment to charge the 18th Hussars on the other side of the river. The attack forced the hussars back, but the commander of the rearguard, Lord Paget, led the British 10th Hussars and the King's German Legion 3rd Hussars in a counter-attack that hit the chasseurs in the flank. The French horses were blown and the regiment broke, fleeing for the river. Lefebvre-Desnouettes and his horse were both wounded in the fight and the horse refused to go into the river. The general was captured by 18-year-old Private Johann Bergmann of the 3rd KGL Hussars. In a disposition given many years later Private Bergmann stated:

> In this affair he cut one French officer from his horse and made another prisoner; the latter was said to be general Lefebvre. If he does not err, three charges were this day made against the enemy; the two first were unsuccessful, but at the third charge the French cavalry were overthrown and driven across the river which runs

near Benavente. It was at the second charge that he came up with the officer whom he cut from his horse. As this officer lay on the ground, he took his sabre and pouch from him. At the third charge, or in reality the pursuit, he came upon the officer whom he made prisoner. He was one of the first in the pursuit and as he came up with this officer, who rode close in rear of the enemy, the officer made a thrust at him with a long straight sword. After, however, he had parried the thrust, the officer called out ' pardon'. He did not trouble himself further about the man, but continued the pursuit; an English hussar, however, who had come up to the officer at the same time with him, led the officer back. When he maintains that he took general Lefebvre prisoner at the combat of Benavente, he must observe that he does not know this general and only makes the assertion because it was said to him after the action that he ought to have held fast the man who thrust at him, for it was general Lefebvre. He was then young and did not trouble himself about the matter; he also never saw the man again; he only remembers that he that day wore a dark green frock, a hat with a feather and a long straight sword[*]

This incident was much debated in the regiment and in 1829, Major General August von dem Bussche, a captain in the 3rd Hussars wrote:

Johann Bergmann, formerly a private in the third hussars of the king's German legion, no doubt took prisoner the general Lefebvre Desnouettes, in the combat in which that regiment was engaged on the 29th of December, 1808, with the French imperial guard, near Benavente, on the Esla. This capture was the same day notorious in the regiment and captain von Kerssenbruch, to whose troop Bergmann belonged, enquired the particulars from him and some of his comrades; and learned, 'that during the individual encounters which took place, the general, being followed by Bergmann, fired a pistol at him, which foiling in its aim, he offered him his sword and made known his wish to be taken to general Stewart; Bergmann, however, did not know general Stewart personally and while he was enquiring where that general was to be found, a hussar of the tenth English regiment joined him and led away the prisoner.[†]

The British hussar who led Lefebvre-Desnouettes into captivity was Private Levi Grisdale of the 10th Hussars. Grisdale took the general's

---

[*] Beamish, *History of the King's German Legion*, vol. 1, p. 358.
[†] Ibid, p. 360.

sword and sabretache and turned them over to General Stewart.* A trooper of the 7th Hussars found General Lefebvre-Desnouettes's watch and pistols. He gave the watch to Sir Richard Vivian, his regimental commander, but kept the pistols. Sir Richard tried to return the watch to the general, however he 'refused to take it, saying the soldier who took him was entitled to it.'† Captain Thomas Wildman of the 7th Hussars ended up with the general's sword belt and scabbard. His sword and sabretache wound up in the Royal United Services Institute Museum.‡ Unfortunately for General Lefebvre-Desnouettes, he went into captivity without any money, having lost it in a card game a few days before. However, a truce was arranged shortly afterwards for the general's baggage to be sent to him.'§

General Lefebvre-Desnouettes was interned at Cheltenham, England, and he soon gave his parole. In January 1812 his wife joined him, carrying with her permission from Napoleon to violate his parole and to return to France. He disguised himself as a Russian count, while his wife dressed in men's clothing and posed as his son. His aide-de-camp, navy Lieutenant Armand le Duc, acted as his valet. They stayed a few nights at Sablonière's in Leicester Square in London and then headed to Dover, where they met up with Waddell, a smuggler from Dymchurch, who was paid £210 to take them to France.¶

On returning to France General Lefebvre-Desnouettes was returned to command of the Guard Chasseurs. He would lead them during the Russian campaign of 1812 and commanded Napoleon's escort when he left the army on 4 December to return to France. During 1813 General Lefebvre-Desnouettes commanded the 1st Guard Cavalry Division until early October, when he took command of 2nd Guard Cavalry Division. When Napoleon abdicated in April 1814, General Lefebvre-Desnouettes had the honour of commanding his escort to Roanne. On 30 July 1814 he was appointed commander of the Royal Corps of Chasseurs.

After Waterloo General Lefebvre-Desnouettes shaved off his moustache and escaped to the United States as a merchant. He was sentenced to death *in absentia*. General Lefebvre-Desnouettes lived in Alabama until 1821, when he decided to return to France. His ship, *L'Albion*, was caught in a storm off Kinsale, Ireland, and sunk. He drowned on 22 April 1822.

---

* The 10th Light Dragoons felt that Grisdale was responsible for the capture and awarded him a silver medal. Legend has it that Private Grisdale would eventually open an inn in Penrith called the 'General Lefebvre'!
† Mollo, *The Princess Dolls*, pp. 67–8.
‡ Ibid. and p. 205.
§ Vivian, *Richard Hussey Vivian*, p. 102.
¶ Abell, *Prisoners of War*, pp. 371, 373, 382.

General Lefebvre-Desnouettes was a brilliant cavalry commander, whose impetuosity cost him three years' imprisonment. He performed superbly as a division commander in the 1813 and 1814 campaigns. He was a dedicated Bonapartist and rather than retreat after Waterloo, he 'wanted to stay and be killed on the field'.*

Table 8.7 Lepic, Louis

Awards and honours	Baron of the Empire 3 May 1809
Date and place of birth	30 Sep. 1765 at Montpellier
Regiments commanded	15th Chasseurs 26 Mar. 1799–18 Dec. 1805
Date of rank as general	General of brigade 13 Feb. 1807; General of division 9 Feb. 1813
Time in the Peninsula	4 Apr. 1808–Mar. 1809; Jun. 1810–7 Aug. 1811
Command or post in the Peninsula	Imperial Guard detachment 18 Feb. 1808–Nov. 1808; Imperial Guard Cavalry Brigade 25 Apr. 1810–7 Aug. 1811
Date and place of death	7 Jan. 1827 at Andrésy
Place of burial	Andrésy

Louis Lepic entered Spain in February 1808 at the head of a detachment of the Imperial Guard that included 1,180 infantry, 1,046 cavalry and 6 artillery pieces. This combined force was stationed in Madrid at the time of the uprising on 1 May. They would remain in the capital until it was evacuated in late July. The Guard detachment would remain along the Ebro River, in the vicinity of Miranda, until the rest of the Imperial Guard entered Spain in early November. The detachment was disbanded and the men joined their regiments. General Lepic was one of the two colonel majors of the Horse Grenadiers of the Imperial Guard and resumed his duties with the regiment. The Horse Grenadiers saw little action in the subsequent campaign and were withdrawn from Spain in March 1809. In June 1810 General Lepic returned to Spain to take command of a composite brigade of Imperial Guard Cavalry that was assigned to the Army of the North. The brigade would conduct counter-insurgency operations in northern Spain until late April 1811, when Marshal Bessières brought it and another cavalry brigade to link up with the Army of Portugal in western Spain. Lepic and his brigade were at the battle of Fuentes de Oñoro on 3–5 May 1811, but were given specific orders by Marshal Bessières that they could not be committed to battle without his permission. The brigade was in reserve. During the massed French cavalry

---

* Lachouque, *The Anatomy of Glory*, pp. 490–1.

attack on 5 May Marshal Masséna (the senior French commander on the field), ordered Lepic to join in the attack.

> But Lepic, biting his swordblade in desperation replied, with much regret, that his immediate chief, Marshal Bessières had forbidden him to take the Guard into action without his order. Ten aides-de-camp went off in every direction to look for Bessières; but he, after being some days always at Masséna's side, had now disappeared.[*]

By the time the marshal was found, the moment had passed and General Lepic and his brigade remained in reserve for the rest of the battle. The brigade returned to northern Spain later in the month and General Lepic returned to France in August.

Although Louis Lepic was a general of brigade, when he served with the Horse Grenadiers of the Guard, his duties were those of a senior regimental officer. In January 1812 Napoleon offered to move him from the regiment and give him command of a division of heavy cavalry. Lepic declined this promotion and subsequent ones, preferring to stay with the regiment.[†] He was seriously wounded in Russia in November 1812. In February 1813 he was promoted to general of division and given command of the 2nd Regiment of the Guards of Honour in April. He rallied to Napoleon in 1815 and served in the army headquarters during the Waterloo campaign. He retired in September 1815 and died in 1827.

An anecdote told by Charles Parquin about General Lepic at the battle of Eylau, probably sums up his character best. After the great charge against the Russians, he had not returned with the rest of the regiment to the French lines:

> It was thought for a short while that General Lepic, who was commanding the Guard mounted grenadiers, had been killed or captured for he did not appear a the head of his regiment when it rallied and the roll was called. Followed by only a few of his men, his eagerness had carried him into the third Russian line. A Russian officer, who spoke perfect French, had then advanced on him with a squadron and had almost completely surrounded him. He addressed the general thus 'Surrender, General. Your courage has carried you too far. You are in our rear lines.' 'Take a look at these faces and see if they want to surrender!' answered the general and shouting to his grenadiers 'Follow me!' he set off at the gallop back through the Russian lines. Half of those who followed him were killed by the

---

[*] Marbot, *The Memoirs of Baron de Marbot*, vol. 2, p. 166.
[†] Pawly, *Mounted Grenadiers of the Imperial Guard*, p. 20.

Russian fire. The Emperor was delighted to see the general return and greeted him saying 'I thought you had been captured, General. I was most worried.' 'The only report of me that you will ever receive will be that of my death, Sire!' answered the fearless commander of the Guard mounted grenadiers.'*

Table 8.8   Lorcet, Jean-Baptiste

Awards and honours	Baron of the Empire 15 Aug. 1810
Date and place of birth	17 Mar. 1768 at Reims
Date of rank as general	General of brigade 3 Jul. 1799
Time in the Peninsula	17 Nov. 1808–Jun. 1811
Command or post in the Peninsula	Light Cavalry Brigade, Ney's 6th Corps 4 Jan. 1809–24 Jul. 1810; 1st Dragoon Brigade, Trelliard's Division 15 Sep. 1810–9 May 1811
Wounds in Peninsula	Shot at Tamames 18 Oct. 1810; hit by shrapnel at Fuentes de Oñoro 5 May 1811
Date and place of death	4 Dec. 1822 at Autry

Jean Lorcet was another cavalry officer who, through skill and bravery, became a general at a relatively young age. He was promoted to general of brigade at 31. He served mostly as a staff officer and never commanded a regiment, though he was wounded nine times between 1793 and 1800. General Lorcet did not command during the Austerlitz campaign, nor during the 1806 and 1807 campaigns against Prussia and Russia, but he was known for his courage. He was sent to Spain in November 1808 and served on the staff of the army's headquarters. On 4 January 1809 he assumed command of the Light Cavalry Brigade of the 6th Corps, after General Colbert was killed at Cacabellos the day before. General Lorcet would lead the brigade, composed of the 3rd Hussars and the 15th Chasseurs, for 19 months. During that time they would fight at Col de Banos on 12 August 1809, Tamames on 18 October 1809, Alba de Tormes on 28 November 1809 and the sieges of Ciudad Rodrigo and Almeida during the summer of 1810. Lorcet was wounded a tenth time at Tamames. On 15 September 1810 he assumed command of the 1st Dragoon Brigade in Trelliard's Division. It consisted of the 3rd and 6th Dragoons. He would lead them into Portugal in September. General Lorcet was seriously wounded at Fuentes de Oñoro in May 1811 and returned to France in June to recover. In 1813 he commanded the Department of Frise and was

---

* Parquin, *Napoleon's Army*, p. 55.

captured by Cossacks in the autumn. He sided with Napoleon in 1815 and was nominated for promotion to lieutenant general, but his rank was never confirmed. General Lorcet was placed on the inactive list in late 1815 and died in 1822.

General Lorcet was not only competent, but also brave beyond belief. He had the misfortune of serving in theatres of operations that were far from Napoleon. Thus, like many other Peninsular generals, he was destined for obscurity. A contemporary biographer of his wrote about him that:

> It is with regret that we cannot find again in the cadre of the French army the names of a few brave souls who have so long shown their valor and this reflection is related primarily to oblivion into which the services of Lorcet fell, who deserved at least an honourable retirement.[*]

Table 8.9   Lorge, Jean-Thomas-Guillaume

Awards and honours	Baron of the Empire 13 Feb. 1811
Date and place of birth	22 Nov. 1767 at Caen
Date of rank as general	General of brigade 25 Sep. 1793; General of division 4 Apr. 1799
Time in the Peninsula	12 Oct. 1808–16 Jul. 1811
Command or post in the Peninsula	5th Dragoon Division 25 May 1807–Apr. 1810 Confederation of the Rhine Division Jul. 1810–Jul. 1811; Governor of La Mancha Province Jul. 1810–Jul. 1811
Date and place of death	29 Nov. 1826 at Chauconin

General Lorge was the third most senior cavalry general to serve in the French army in Spain – junior only to Jacques Tilly and Emmanuel Grouchy. In October 1808 he entered Spain as the commander of the 5th Dragoon Division, which he had commanded for over 17 months. In early January 1809 his division was attached to Marshal Soult's 2nd Corps and led the French Army in the pursuit of the retreating British under General Moore. After the battle of Corunna on 16 January, General Lorge and his division led the 2nd Corps into northern Portugal, where they stayed until forced out by the British in May. In July 1810 General Lorge was reassigned to the Army of the Centre and became governor of La Mancha Province. This was a very important command because the French lines of communications which between Madrid and the Army of the South in Seville ran through his

---

[*] Pascal de Julien, *Galerie historique des contémporaniens*, vol 6, p. 304.

province. His headquarters was in Toledo and among the troops assigned to him was the Confederation of the Rhine Division – an infantry division.

General Lorge was recalled to France in July 1811 and assumed command of the 7th Cuirassier Division of General Tour-Maubourg's 4th Cavalry Corps in March 1812. He fought in the Russian campaign in 1812. He commanded the 5th Light Cavalry Division of General Arrighi's 3rd Corps in Germany in 1813. After the abdication of Napoleon in April 1814, Lorge was appointed to the commission overseeing the repatriation of French prisoners-of-war from Spain and Portugal. He did not side with Napoleon in 1815 and was an inspector general of cavalry in the 13th Military Division until 1818, when he retired.

General Lorge was the quiet professional, competent at what he did, but one overshadowed by his more flamboyant peers. Despite being one of the most senior generals in the French army, twice he was placed in subordinate positions to generals to whom he was many years senior. In 1812 he was seven years senior to General Tour-Maubourg and in 1813 he was nine years senior to General Arrighi.

Table 8.10 Maransin, Jean Pierre

Awards and honours	Baron of the Empire 23 Jun. 1810
Date and place of birth	20 Mar. 1770 at Lourdes
Regiments commanded	1st Legion of the South 27 Jan. 1807–8 Oct. 1808
Date of rank as general	General of brigade 8 Oct. 1808; General of division 30 May 1813
Time in the Peninsula	Aug. 1807–Sep. 1808; 17 Nov. 1808–Apr. 1814
Command or post in the Peninsula	1st Legion of the South 27 Jan. 1807–8 Oct. 1808; 2nd Brigade, Heudelet's Division, 2nd Corps 12 Dec. 1808–16 Mar. 1810; 2nd Brigade, Girard's Division, 5th Corps 10 Apr. 1810–10 Sep. 1811; 2nd Brigade, Barrois's Division, Army of the South 10 Sep.–1 Oct. 1811; Governor of Malaga 1 Oct. 1811–1 Sep. 1812; 2nd Brigade, Barrois's Division, Army of the South 1 Sep.–1 Nov. 1812; 2nd Brigade, Leval's Division, Army of the South 1 Nov. 1812–Feb. 1813; 5th Division, Army of the South Feb.–Mar. 1813; 2nd Light Cavalry Brigade, Soult's Division 6 Apr.–30 May 1813; 6th Division, Army of Spain 22 Jun.–5 Sep. 1813; 5th Division, Army of Spain 5 Sep. 1813–Apr. 1814

Table 8.10 continued

Wounds in Peninsula	Seriously wounded at Albuera 16 May 1811; at Cartama 16 Feb. 1812; in left groin at Saint Pierre 13 Dec. 1813
Date and place of death	16 May 1828 in Paris
Place of burial	Père Lachaise Cemetery

Jean Maransin was unique among French generals in two ways. First, he served continuously in the Peninsula from the very beginning of the war, commanding a brigade during General Junot's invasion of Portugal, in 1807, to the very end in command of a division at Toulouse in April 1814; a total of 81 months. His second distinction was that of being an infantry officer given direct, if brief, command of a cavalry brigade.

General Maransin commanded infantry brigades throughout much of the war, up until October 1811, when he was appointed governor of Malaga, a position he held until the Army of the South was forced to evacuate southern Spain in September 1812. In February 1813 he was appointed provisional commander of the 5th Division. In April he took command of the 2nd Light Cavalry Brigade in Soult's Light Cavalry Division. His new brigade consisted of the 2nd Hussars and the 21st Chasseurs. He would only command it for two months when he was promoted to general of division and reassigned to the headquarters of the Army of Portugal. At Vitoria on 21 June 1813 he commanded an infantry brigade, but after the battle he took temporary command of the 6th Division of the Army of Spain. In September 1813 he assumed command of the 5th Division until the end of the war. General Maransin rallied to Napoleon in 1815, but did not participate in the Waterloo campaign. He was arrested in 1816 and held for four months. He was released and was not given any duties until he retired in 1825.

Captain Andrew Leith Hay, a British exploring officer, was captured by the French in April 1813 and spent several days in the company of General Maransin. He left a vivid description of the general and the frustration he felt after serving six years in the Peninsula.

> I was immediately taken to the palace of the archbishop and pre-
> sented to General Maransin. His manner, at first distant and re-
> served, became softened by degrees and restored to what appeared
> his natural and usual demeanour. The impression occasioned by
> the circumstances under which we had met, became removed and
> in the course of an hour a conversation was in progress with all the
> appearance of confidence existing between officers of the same army
> and long accustomed to familiar discourse. The General had for

some time commanded the vanguard of Marshal Soult's army, had long served in Spain and in the commencement of 1812 was attacked by General Ballesteros, near to Cartamo, and defeated; the troops under his orders, amounting to about 3000, flying in the direction of Malaga. He had an appearance of intelligence and activity, was aged about forty, had the manners of a gentleman and seemed not devoid of information. A baron of the empire, his military rank was that of 'General de Brigade'; but under his immediate orders at this time, were the light cavalry of General Soult (brother to the Marshal), consisting of the Chamboran hussars, the 6me and 10me chasseurs a cheval. The 12me Legere and 45me regiment of the line, composed the infantry of the vanguard and the only French troops now on the banks of the Tagus.

Accompanied by an officer of the etat major, I was permitted to pay visits in the town, returning to the palace at six, where the General was attended by several of his officers and a very sumptuous dinner was served up. In the evening, the other members of his family having retired, I had an unconstrained conversation with the French baron. For upwards of an hour we paced along the spacious and elegant salon of the archbishop, discussing the leading topics, rendered interesting in the progress of the Spanish warfare, with a frankness on his part that occasioned my surprise. Whether it proceeded from having me in his power and consequently conceiving that no detriment, to the imperial cause could result from his open and candid avowal, certainly he was more communicative than either circumstances demanded, or our relative situations warranted. The campaign in Russia, the frightful sufferings of the Grand Army, the hopeless state of affairs in the Peninsula, the imbecility of Joseph Bonaparte, or the military talents of Lord Wellington, were alike subjected to the unreserved remark, the eulogium and, occasionally, to the bitter invective, of the French General. A stranger, overhearing the conversation, would rather have supposed it carried on by officers of the same family, than by a person of rank in one army and a prisoner brought to his quarters, after having instigated the inhabitants of the country to rise and cut off the supplies on which the existence of the other depended.'

General Maransin, without hesitation, admitted the difficulties and losses to which the French armies in the Peninsula were subjected; the faulty arrangements made under existing circumstances and the improbability of reinforcements, at a time when the Guerilla system was of all others most harassing and destructive. The departure of Marshal Soult he considered an event much to be deplored and calculated to have a serious effect on the morale of his army.[*]

Table 8.11   Margaron, Pierre

Awards and honours	Baron of the Empire 29 Jan. 1809
Date and place of birth	1 May 1765 at Lyon
Regiments commanded	1st Cavalry Regiment 23 Dec. 1798–1 Jan. 1801
Date of rank as general	General of brigade 29 Aug. 1803; General of division 16 Aug. 1813
Time in the Peninsula	Aug. 1807–Sep. 1808; Jan.–Dec. 1809
Command or post in the Peninsula	1st Brigade, Kellermann's Division Aug. 1807–Sep. 1808; Staff Officer, 2nd Corps Jan.–Dec. 1809
Date and place of death	16 Dec. 1824 in Paris
Place of burial	Père Lachaise Cemetery

General Margaron was another capable general officer who never seemed to be in the right place at the right time. He was promoted to general of brigade in 1803 and commanded four different cavalry brigades before being given the 1st Brigade in Kellermann's Division in 1807. It was formed with the 1st and 2nd Provisional Cavalry Regiments. He would command the brigade in the French invasion of Portugal. Much of his time was spent in counter-guerrilla operations, but when the British landed in Portugal in August 1808 Margaron was in command of the cavalry that opposed them at Roliça and Vimeiro. His command had expanded to include the 2nd, 3rd and 4th Provisional Cavalry Regiments, about 1,200 men. He commanded them with ability and intelligence at Vimeiro, during which he 'executed some beautiful charges . . . had in three minutes, two horses killed under him by artillery fire'.[†] He would be part of the surrender of the French Army and would return to France in September 1808, after the Convention of Cintra was signed. General Margaron did not stay in France long. In January 1809 he was assigned to the headquarters of Marshal Soult's 2nd Corps and he would be with it, when the corps invaded northern Portugal. He returned to France in December 1809.

Despite having successfully commanded five different cavalry brigades, General Margaron was tainted by the surrender of the French Army in Portugal in 1808. He would not be trusted with a combat command again until September 1813, when he assumed command of the Leipzig Garrison. He would command for less than a month before his command

---

[*] Leith-Hay, *Narrative of the Peninsular War*, vol. 2, pp. 145–8.
[†] Thiébault, *Relation de l'Expédition du Portugal*, pp. 199 and 203.

was destroyed at the battle of Leipzig. When Napoleon returned in 1815, General Margaron was given command of the 12th and 13th Military Districts. After Waterloo he went on the inactive list for a year, but was appointed inspector general of the Gendarmerie in 1816. He retired in 1821.

Table 8.12   Marizy, Frédéric-Christophe-Henri-Pierre-Claude Vagnair dit

Awards and honours	Baron of the Empire 22 Nov. 1808
Date and place of birth	8 Jul. 1765 at Altroff
Regiments commanded	7th Hussars 23 Jun. 1794–24 Mar. 1803
Date of rank as general	General of brigade 24 Mar. 1803
Time in the Peninsula	7 Sep. 1808–1 Feb. 1811
Command or post in the Peninsula	1st Dragoon Brigade, Houssaye's Division 7 Sep. 1808–16 Jan. 1810; Cavalry Division, 5th Corps 16 Jan. 1810–Autumn 1810; 1st Brigade, Houssaye's Division Autumn 1810–11 Feb. 1811
Wounds in Peninsula	Arzobispo 8 Aug. 1809
Date and place of death	11 Feb. 1811 Talavera la Vieja, Spain
Cause of death	Shot by guerrillas in thigh 9 Feb. 1811; died of gangrene on 11 Feb.

Frédéric Marizy's family name was Vagnair. Marizy was the name of his mother. Many histories refer to him as Marisy. He was an experienced brigade commander, having commanded the Light Cavalry Brigade of the 1st Corps in the Austerlitz campaign of 1805, where he was wounded; and the 2nd Dragoon Brigade in Beaumont's Division in the 1806 and 1807 campaigns in Prussia and Poland. In September 1808 he was transferred to Houssaye's Dragoon Division, where he commanded the 1st Dragoon Brigade, consisting of the 17th and 27th Dragoons. In January 1810 General Marizy was given command of the 5th Corps's Cavalry Division, which had Beaurgard's Dragoon Brigade and a light cavalry brigade. He would lead them during the invasion of southern Spain. He served with the 5th Corps until October 1810, when he and his brigade were transferred to the 4th Dragoon Division of the Army of the Centre. In early February 1811 General Marizy received permission to return to France. His escort consisted of the 22nd Dragoons and a small group of the 26th Chasseurs. On 9 February, near the village of Talavera la Vieja, while General Marizy and his aide-de-camp, Commandant Galbaud, rode ahead of the duty company from the 26th Chasseurs, they were ambushed by guerrillas led by four brothers Felicien, François, Felix and Antoine Cuesta. Marizy was shot in the thigh and Commandant Galbaud was killed. The chasseur escort panicked and fled down the road to 22nd Dragoons. The dragoon's advance guard waited for the rest of the regiment to come up before returning to the scene of the ambush. The guerrillas had fled and the arriving dragoons thought Marizy was dead. They immediately looted his baggage and were in process of robbing him of his personal effects when they flipped his body over and noticed that he was still alive. The dragoons carried him to Talavera where the doctor decided to amputate his leg. General Marizy would not let him. Within a day gangrene set in. He died on 11 February. An investigation was ordered and the commander of the advance guard, who refused to ride to the rescue until the regiment arrived, was arrested, along with the commander of the company that looted the general and the twelve dragoons accused of looting him.[*]

It is hard to assess General Marizy's performance in the Peninsula. He was given temporary command of a division, yet the commander of the 13th Dragoons, Colonel Marie Reiset, felt that he was timid and did not show much initiative.[†]

Table 8.13   Maupetit, Pierre-Honoré-Anne

Name	Maupetit, Pierre-Honoré-Anne
Awards and honours	Baron of the Empire 23 Mar. 1808
Date and place of birth	22 Sep. 1772 at Lyon
Regiments commanded	9th Dragoons 31 Aug. 1803–30 Dec. 1806
Date of rank as general	General of brigade 30 Dec. 1806
Time in the Peninsula	18 Sep. 1808–24 Jun. 1809
Command or post in the Peninsula	Light Cavalry Brigade, Lefebvre's 4th Corps 18 Sep. 1808–24 Jun. 1809
Date and place of death	13 Dec. 1811 at Alençon
Cause of death	Numerous wounds received over the years
Place of burial	Cemetery of the Church Our Lady at Alençon

Pierre Maupetit was poured from the same mould as Auguste Colbert and Antoine LaSalle. He was a superb leader of men, fearless in battle and a capable tactician. He fought in ten campaigns from 1792–1800, in the Austerlitz campaign of 1805, the war with Prussia in 1806, the 1807 campaign in Poland and in Spain from 1808–9. He was wounded at least 27 times in three battles multiple times in his right shoulder at Sorigimos in 1793, 12 sabre blows to his head and shot in the right foot at Marengo

---

[*] Derrécagaix, *Le Lieutenant-Général Comte Baillard*, p. 455.
[†] Reiset, *Souvenirs du Lieutenant Général Vicomte de Reiset*, vol. 2, p. 265.

on 14 June 1800 and bayoneted nine times at Wertingen on 8 October 1805. At Wertingen he led the 9th Dragoons in a spectacular charge that captured four artillery pieces and four colours. Colonel Maupetit's horse was killed and he was bayoneted so many times that he was reported killed in the official Bulletin on the battle![*] Marshal Murat, after the battle of Wertingen, visited him in his tent, where he was recovering from being bayoneted nine times said 'Well! Maupetit, you are like a second Bayard,[†] surrounded by your trophies.'[‡] Pierre Maupetit was promoted to general of brigade on 30 December 1806. He commanded the 1st Dragoon Brigade in Milhaud's Division at Eylau and Friedland.

General Maupetit assumed command of the Light Cavalry Brigade of the 4th Corps on 18 September 1808. It consisted of the 5th Dragoons, the 3rd Dutch Hussars and the 1st Vistula Legion Lancers. In June 1809 his health began to fail as a result of his many wounds and he requested permission to return to France for three months to recuperate. He never came back to Spain and died from complications arising from his numerous wounds on 13 December 1813. Napoleon's eulogy on Pierre Maupetit is worth noting: 'I regret his loss, not only as one of my best cavalry general, but as an honest man.'[§]

Table 8.14 Maupoint de Vandeul, Louis-Joseph

Name	Maupoint de Vandeul, Louis-Joseph
Awards and honours	Baron of the Empire with the name Baron de Vandeul 24 Feb. 1809
Date and place of birth	6 Jan. 1766 at Lille
Regiments commanded	16th Chasseurs 13 Jan. 1806–6 Aug. 1811
Date of rank as general	General of brigade 6 Aug. 1811
Time in the Peninsula	Aug. 1811–Aug. 1813
Command or post in the Peninsula	Cavalry Brigade, Army of Aragon Dec. 1811–Aug. 1813
Date and place of death	19 Sep. 1849 at Marseilles

Louis Maupoint was another hard-charging light cavalry officer who was fearless in battle and paid for it with many wounds. He was promoted to general of brigade on 6 August 1811 and sent to command a cavalry

---

[*] Markham, *Imperial Glory*, p. 13.
[†] Pierre Terrail, seigneur de Bayard was a fifteenth-century French soldier who was known as the '*Chevalier sans peur et sans reproche*' Bayard's biographer, Jacques de Mailles, uses the term frequently to describe him.
[‡] Vingtrinier, p. 116.
[§] Arnault, *Biographie Nouvelle*, vol. 20, p. 119.

brigade in the Army of Aragon. He was one of only two French cavalry generals sent to the Peninsula after 1810. Although he was nominally in command of a cavalry brigade, he spent most of his time leading infantry and cavalry in counter-insurgency operations. In July 1812 he was ordered to Cuenca to relieve the garrison, which had been surrounded for 18 days. He had with him about 1,000 men from the 116th Line Infantry Regiment and a company of the 4th Hussars. After successfully relieving the garrison he was attacked by a Spanish force of 4,000 men led by General Villacampa. General Maupoint's command was able to break through the Spanish trap and escape, but not without cost. They suffered 200 men killed and wounded, lost all of the force's baggage and two artillery pieces.

Active campaigning was too much for General Maupoint. He was crippled by the numerous wounds he had received earlier in his career and he returned to France in August 1813. General Maupoint was appointed commandant of the Cavalry School at Saint Germain upon his arrival in France. His time there was so successful that he received the nickname of 'the goose who laid the golden egg for the French cavalry'.* During the Hundred Days he was the commandant of the Department of Var and retired in 1816.

Table 8.15   Maurin, Antoine

Awards and honours	Baron of the Empire 17 Mar. 1808
Date and place of birth	19 Dec. 1771 at Montpellier
Regiments commanded	24th Chasseurs 24 Apr. 1802–25 Jun. 1807
Date of rank as general	General of brigade 25 Jun. 1807; General of division 19 Feb. 1814
Time in the Peninsula	19 Nov. 1807–19 Jun. 1808
Command or post in the Peninsula	2nd Brigade, Kellermann's Division 19 Nov. 1807–Mar. 1808; Commander of Algarve Mar.–Jun. 1808
Date and place of death	4 Oct. 1830 in Paris
Cause of death	Committed suicide
Place of burial	Père Lachaise Cemetery

General Maurin commanded the 2nd Brigade of Kellermann's Division, when the French Army invaded Portugal in late 1807. Under his command were the 3rd Provisional Cavalry (composed of the 4th Squadrons of the 4th and 5th Dragoons) and 4th Provisional Cavalry (made up of the 4th Squadrons of the 9th and 15th Dragoons), serving as the advance guard

---

* Mullié, *Biographie des célébrités militaires*, vol. 2, p. 282.

of the army. In March 1808 he was given command of the province of Algarve. He became very ill and was unable to exercise command. He was recuperating in Faro, with a detachment of about 100 men in June, when the town revolted against the French. Maurin and his men were captured by the insurgents and turned over to the British navy on 19 June 1808.

Instead of being placed in a prison camp, General Maurin was paroled and allowed to live in Wantage, Oxfordshire in England. In September 1812 he violated his parole by paying a smuggler £300 to take him to France.* He served with the Grande Armée in Germany in 1813 and was promoted to general of division in January 1814. He commanded a light cavalry division in the 2nd Cavalry Corps in the 1814 campaign. During the Waterloo campaign Maurin commanded the Light Cavalry Division in Gérard's 4th Corps and was wounded at Ligny. He was placed on inactive duty until 1819 when he commanded the 15th Military Division and then in various positions until he committed suicide in 1830.

General Maurin was another capable commander with bad luck. He was the first French general to be captured in the Peninsula and it took him away from the army for four years. By the time he escaped the end of the Napoleonic Wars was near.

Table 8.16   Merlin, Christophe-Antoine

Awards and honours	Captain General of the Spanish Royal Guard 16 Aug. 1809
Date and place of birth	27 May 1771 in Paris
Regiments commanded	4th Hussars 25 Jan. 1795–1 Feb. 1805
Date of rank as general	General of brigade 1 Feb. 1805; General of division 5 Jan. 1814
Time in the Peninsula	8 Jul. 1808–Jul. 1813
Command or post in the Peninsula	Aide-de-Camp to King Joseph 1808; Light Cavalry Division, 2nd Corps 5 Apr.– Dec. 1809; Spanish Royal Guard 16 Aug. 1809–5 Jan. 1814
Date and place of death	9 Mar. 1839 in Paris

Christophe Merlin and his two brothers were generals in the French Army. Christophe was close to Joseph Bonaparte having served in his government when Joseph was the King of Naples. Christophe received the honorary rank of Master of the Horse to King Joseph in 1807. In 1808 he became an aide-de-camp to King Joseph and served as the commander

---

* Abell, *Prisoners of War*, pp. 295–6, 383.

of his escort when the new king went to Spain to claim his throne in July 1808. On 15 August 1808 General Merlin passed into Spanish service and was promoted to general of division and captain general in the Spanish Army. In April 1809 he took command of General Lasalle's Light Cavalry Division and led them at Talavera on 27 and 28 July, at Almonacid on 11 August 1809 and at Ocaña on 19 November 1809.

With the collapse of the Bonaparte Kingdom of Spain in July 1813, General Merlin was out of a job. He was readmitted into the French Army on 5 January 1814 and was allowed to keep his rank of general of division, but with a date of rank of the day he returned to French service. He commanded a light cavalry division in the 2nd Cavalry Corps during the campaign in France in 1814. During the Hundred Days in 1815 General Merlin commanded the 8th Cavalry Division under General Rapp. After the Second Restoration in July 1815 General Merlin retired for a year. Beginning in 1816 he served in a variety of staff positions until he retired in 1836.

Table 8.17 Mermet, Julien-Augustin-Joseph

Awards and honours	Baron of the Empire 2 Aug. 1811
Date and place of birth	9 May 1772 at Quesnoy
Regiments commanded	8th Hussars 5 Mar. 1797–4 Nov. 1799
Date of rank as general	General of brigade 1 Jan. 1796; General of division 1 Feb. 1805
Time in the Peninsula	1 Sep. 1808–13 Jul. 1811; 12 Sep. 1812–16 Jul. 1813
Command or post in the Peninsula	1st Infantry Division, 6th Corps 1 Sep.–14 Nov. 1808; 2nd Infantry Division, 2nd Corps 14 Nov. 1808–17 Apr. 1810; 2nd Infantry Division, 6th Corps 17 Apr. 1810–13 Jul. 1811; Light Cavalry Division, Army of Portugal 8 Sep.–11 Dec. 1812; Commandant of the Cavalry of the Army of Portugal 11 Dec. 1812–16 Jul. 1813
Wounds in Peninsula	At Corunna on 16 Jan. 1809; in stomach at Foz do Arouce 15 Mar. 1811
Date and place of death	28 Oct. 1837 in Paris

Julien Mermet was one of the bright young stars of the French Revolution, being promoted to general of brigade at the age of 23 in 1796. Despite being a general officer, he became the commander of the 8th Hussars in 1797. He was promoted to general of division in 1805 at the age of 31. General

Mermet was a cavalry officer, yet for his first three years in the Peninsula, he commanded infantry divisions. He distinguished himself at Braga on 20 March 1809 during the invasion of northern Portugal. In April 1810 he was reassigned to the Army of Portugal and took command of the 2nd Division of the 6th Corps. He was seriously wounded in the stomach at Foz do Arouce, in 1811 and returned to France a few months later.

General Mermet was back in Spain in September 1812, after the French disasters that summer. For the first time in four years, he would serve as a cavalry commander. He took command of the Army of Portugal's Dragoon Division, which had been commanded by General Boyer during the Salamanca campaign. In December he was appointed overall commander of the cavalry of the Army of Portugal. He would lead them at Vitoria on 21 June 1813, but when Marshal Soult reorganised the shattered French forces after their defeat at Vitoria, Mermet was not given a command.

General Mermet was sent to the Army of Italy in November 1813. He was without a job during much of the First Restoration, but when Napoleon returned to France in March 1815, Mermet refused to join him. After the defeat of Napoleon he served in a variety of posts until he died in 1837.

General Mermet had the potential to go far in the French army. Of all the cavalry generals who served in the Peninsula, he was the youngest to be promoted to both general of brigade and general of division. Yet he was never noticed by Napoleon. From 1804 to 1814 he never shared the same theatre of war as Napoleon, except for a few short months at the beginning of the Peninsular War. Despite being a cavalry officer, much of his time was spent commanding infantry divisions, which he handled well. By the time he took over command of the Army of Portugal's cavalry, it was only a remnant of what it once was. He did not have the chance to show his abilities as a cavalry general.

Table 8.18   Meyer de Schauensée, Bernard-Meinrad-Fridalin-Joseph-Philippe

Awards and honours	Baron of the Empire 19 Feb. 1812
Date and place of birth	20 Jan. 1777 at Lucerne, Switzerland
Regiments commanded	None
Date of rank as general	General of brigade 28 Jun. 1813
Time in the Peninsula	Oct. 1808–Apr. 1814
Command or post in the Peninsula	Aide-de-camp to Marshal Suchet Oct. 1808–28 Jun. 1813; Cavalry Brigade, Army of Aragon Aug. 1813–Apr. 1814
Date and place of death	5 Sep. 1860
Place of burial	Colmar

General Meyer's full name is Meyer de Schauensée, but he is usually referred to by Meyer. Swiss by birth, he enlisted in the 9th Dragoons in 1799. He became an aide-de-camp to Louis Suchet as a lieutenant in 1805 and by 1810, he was the senior aide-de-camp. Although he never commanded a company, squadron, or regiment his duties as an aide-de-camp often found him leading ad hoc task forces at the command of Marshal Suchet. He distinguished himself at the siege of Tarragona in 1811, when he took command of the assault column that was supposed to take the Prince's Lunette after the previous commander was killed. Ten days later Colonel Meyer was involved in the final assault that secured the breach leading to the capture of the city. He was promoted to general of brigade in June 1813 and two months after being promoted, he took command of one of the Army of Aragon's cavalry brigade. He would command it through the final months of the war. He joined with Napoleon in 1815 and commanded a cavalry division in Marshal Suchet's Army of the Alps. He was forced to retire in September 1815, was given French citizenship in 1817 and in 1819 was called back to active duty. He would serve in various staff positions until he retired in 1848 aged 71. He died in 1860 at the age of 83.

Table 8.19 Milet, Jacques-Louis-François

Awards and honours	Baron of the Empire 26 Oct. 1808
Date and place of birth	30 Nov. 1763 on the island of Martinique
Regiments commanded	8th Dragoons 7 Feb. 1797–5 Jul. 1800
Date of rank as general	General of brigade 5 Jul. 1800
Time in the Peninsula	7 Dec. 1808–4 Jan. 1812
Command or post in the Peninsula	Acting Commander, Kellermann's Dragoon Division 7 Dec. 1808–9 Jan. 1809; 1st Dragoon Brigade, Kellermann's Division 9 Jan. 1809–17 Apr. 1810; 1st Dragoon Brigade, Trelliard's Division 17 Apr.–Sep. 1810; 6th Military Government Sep. 1810–Apr. 1811; Governor of Avila Apr. 1811–Jan. 1812
Date and place of death	18 Sep. 1821 at Fontainebleau

The correct spelling of the name is Milet, but some authors spell it Millet. Jacques Milet was sent to Spain in December 1808. He was the senior general in General Kellermann's 2nd Dragoon Division and had assumed command of the division before it entered Spain, because Kellermann was still in Portugal with the French expedition under General Junot.

Milet commanded the division until January 1809, when Kellermann finally joined it. The 2nd Dragoon Division was assigned to the Army of Portugal. Milet, however, was not part of the invasion force. His brigade was given to General Lorcet and he was attached to the staff of the 6th Military Government under Kellermann. In April 1811 Milet was appointed governor of the province of Avila in northern Spain. On 4 January 1812 he returned to France and retired. He would not serve on active duty again.

Table 8.20 Milhaud, Edouard-Jean-Baptiste

Awards and honours	Count of the Empire 10 Mar. 1808
Date and place of birth	10 Jul. 1766 at Arpajon
Regiments commanded	5th Dragoons 28 Jan. 1796–10 Nov. 1799
Date of rank as general	General of brigade 5 Jan. 1800; General of division 30 Dec. 1806
Time in the Peninsula	7 Sep. 1808–12 Jul. 1811
Command or post in the Peninsula	3rd Dragoon Division 30 Dec. 1806–12 Jul. 1811
Date and place of death	8 Jan. 1833 at Aurillac
Place of burial	Cemetery at Aurillac

Edouard Milhaud was an ardent revolutionary before he joined the army. He was a member of the legislative assembly that voted to execute King Louis XVI and a Representative of the People to the Army. As a People's Representative, he had the power of life and death over the officers in the army that he was assigned to. In 1796 he became the regimental commander of the 5th Dragoons and would command them for 46 months. In late 1799 he became chief-of-staff to the future Marshal Murat and was promoted to general of brigade in early January 1800.

Over the next decade General Milhaud would see much action, commanding light cavalry brigades in the 1805 Austerlitz campaign and the 1806 campaign against Prussia. On 30 December 1806 he was promoted to general of division and given command of the 3rd Dragoon Division, which he would command for the next 55 months.

General Milhaud led his division at Eylau on 7 and 8 February 1807 and was part of the epic charge on the second day of the battle. In the early summer of 1808 he received orders to bring his division to Bayonne in preparation for movement into Spain. On 10 October his division numbered 2,940 men and they crossed the Spanish border in early November. The general and his dragoons would soon make a name for themselves. Within a year they would fight at Ciudad Real on 27 March,

Talavera on 26 and 27 July, Almonacid on 11 August and at Ocaña on 19 November. It was at Ocaña a French army of 32,000 men fought the 51,000 Spaniards of General Areizaga's Army of La Mancha. General Milhaud's dragoons hit the right flank of the Spanish army and destroyed five divisions of Spanish infantry in an hour. The Spanish lost 4,000 men killed or wounded, another 14,000 prisoners, 30 flags and 51 of 60 artillery pieces. Three weeks after the battle, General Areizaga could only muster 24,000 men. Much of the following year would be spent in conquering and holding Andalusia for King Joseph. General Milhaud would lead a combined cavalry and infantry force of 1,300 cavalry and 2,000 infantry in the autumn and, on 3 November 1810, caught Spanish General Blake's army of 1,000 cavalry and 8,000 infantry at Baza. General Milhaud's infantry was too far in the rear, but rather than let the Spaniards escape, he ordered his cavalry to attack. It many ways it was a repeat of Ocaña. The Spanish lost 500 men killed or wounded, another 1,000 taken prisoner, two flags and four artillery pieces were also taken.

The following year the French army in Andalusia spent much of its time pacifying southern Spain. The 3rd Dragoon Division would spend its time combating guerrillas, escorting convoys and protecting lines of communication. In July 1811 General Milhaud requested permission to return to France, because of poor health caused by six years of campaigning and a wound suffered earlier. He was given permission by Marshal Soult on 12 July. Napoleon was not pleased about this and did not give him formal permission to go on convalescence leave until 17 November. Milhaud was recalled to active duty on 20 June to command the 20th Military Division, which had its headquarters in Wesel. On 13 July he received orders to report to the Grande Armée in Russia. There is some question on whether he ever made it. It is possible that he served briefly as the governor of Moscow under Marshal Mortier, but there is no mention of him in any of the major memoirs of the campaign. Charles Thoumas, a biographer of General Milhaud, does not think he ever went.[*] Considering the distance between Wesel and Moscow is over 2,000 kilometres, it is highly unlikely he made it to Moscow in time to join the retreat in October.

In February 1813 Milhaud was ordered to Mainz where he organised a cavalry corps. During the 1813 campaign he commanded the 6th Dragoon Division in General Pajol's 5th Corps and took command of the corps in November. He would command it with distinction throughout the 1814 campaign in eastern France.

After the fall of Napoleon in 1814 Milhaud was an inspector general of the cavalry until forced to resign his position because he was considered a

---

[*] Thoumas, *Les grandes cavaliers*, vol. 2, pp. 171–2.

regicide. He supported Napoleon upon his return in 1815 and commanded the 4th Cuirassier Corps during the Waterloo campaign, during which he was wounded. In August 1815 he was appointed inspector general of cavalry, but was relieved of duties in September, again for being a regicide, and forced to retire in October. He was supposed to go into exile, but received a reprieve two years later and was entered into the reserve cadre of the army headquarters in 1831. He died two years later.

General Milhaud's actions on the battlefield speak for themselves. He was a very capable leader at the regiment, brigade, division and corps level. He was not afraid to speak up to his superiors – a good example was his opposition to the mass cavalry charges at Waterloo – but once the order was given he did his best to fulfill it. What is difficult is to get a feel for his character. His skills were on a par with those of General Montbrun and his name is associated with some of the greatest cavalry actions of the Napoleonic Wars. Yet his personality is a mystery. He is rarely mentioned in memoirs of the period and when he is, it is usually with regard to his command, not him. This was in direct contrast to General Montbrun who was idolised by many. It is as though General Milhaud allowed no one to become close to him.

Table 8.21 Montbrun, Louis-Pierre

Awards and honours	Baron of the Empire 19 Mar. 1808
	Count of the Empire 15 Aug. 1809
Date and place of birth	1 Mar. 1770 at Florensac
Regiments commanded	1st Chasseurs 15 Jun.–26 Oct. 1800;
	8th Dragoons 26 Oct.–28 Nov. 1800;
	1st Chasseurs 28 Nov. 1800–24 Dec. 1805
Date of rank as general	General of brigade 24 Dec. 1805; General of division 9 Mar. 1809
Time in the Peninsula	9 Oct. 1808–23 Jan. 1809; 17 Apr. 1810–9 Jan. 1812
Command or post in the Peninsula	Army HQ 23 Sep. 1808–23 Jan. 1809
	Cavalry of the Army of Portugal 17 Apr. 1810–9 Jan. 1812
Date and place of death	7 Sep. 1812 at the Battle of Borodino
Cause of death	Struck by a 3 pounder cannonball
Place of burial	The Grand Redoubt at Borodino

The most frequently used adjectives that described Louis Montbrun are brave, intrepid and heroic.[*] He was a larger-than-life commander who led

---

[*] Thoumas, *Les grandes cavaliers*, vol. 1, p. 117.

from the front and died leading a charge. He was loved by those who served under him. Marcel Marbot described him as 'a splendid man, in the same style as Murat; lofty stature, a scarred face, a black beard, of soldierly bearing and an admirable horseman.'[*]

General Montbrun was given command of the 1st Corps's Light Cavalry Brigade and ordered to Spain in September 1808. While his brigade was moving from Germany to Bayonne, he went on leave to marry the daughter of General Morand and was absent when the brigade was ordered into Spain. Napoleon was displeased and relieved him from command, giving the brigade to General Beaumont. Montbrun was attached to the headquarters of General Lasalle's Light Cavalry Division and was responsible for the cavalry of the vanguard of the army. On 30 November Napoleon and the vanguard were at the Somosierra Pass, which was fortified and protected by 16 artillery pieces and 7,800 infantry. Napoleon was impatient to move on and ordered the lead squadron of the Polish Light Horse to clear the pass. Montbrun led the attack. The following account of the charge was written by the aide-de-camp who brought the order to attack:

> I arrived at the foot of rock under shelter of which the Polish
> squadron was drawn up alone, in front of the infantry.
> 'Commandant,' I cried to Korjietulski, 'the Emperor orders us
> to charge home and at once!' Upon which Montbrun made an
> exclamation and a gesture of astonishment without venturing to
> contradict me; but Piré answered 'It is impossible!' — 'The Emperor
> has been told that,' I retorted, 'and he will not hear of it.' — 'Very
> well,' resumed Piré, 'come and see for yourself; the devil in person,
> pretty well used to fire as he must be, could hardly stand that!'
> Then to prove the truth of his words, advancing beyond the rock
> through a hail of bullets which rained down upon our equipment, he
> pointed out to me the steep slope of the road up to this amphitheatre
> bristling with rocks, the redoubt of sixteen guns which crowned
> it and twenty battalions deployed in such a manner as to converge
> their front and flank fire on an attack which could only be effected
> in column and along the road . . . 'It does not matter,' I exclaimed;
> 'the Emperor is there and he insists on the thing being settled.
> Come, Commandant, the hour will be ours, advance by squads and
> forward!' . . . I had hardly had time to draw my sword from my
> scabbard, before they had begun their charge in a column . . . We
> charged at full speed, I was about ten paces in front with my head

---

[*] Marbot, *The Memoirs of Baron de Marbot*, vol. 1, p. 349.

bent down, uttering our war cry by way of distracting my attention
from the din of the enemy's fire which was all breaking out at once
and the infernal hiss of their bullets and grape shot. Reckoning on
the rapidity of our impetuous attack, I was hoping that in their
astonishment at our audacity the enemy would aim badly; that we
should have time to dash into the midst of their guns and bayonets
and throw them into disorder. But they aimed only too well! Very
soon, in spite of our clamour and the detonation of so many arms,
I could distinguish behind me the sound of smart reports followed
by groans, with the thud of falling men and horses, which made me
foresee defeat. Our warlike cries were becoming lost in the cries
of pain of the unfortunate Poles; I did not dare to turn my head,
fearing that the sad spectacle would cause me to give up. I knew that
I had been struck several times . . . I was alone within thirty paces
of the redoubt. I had outstripped two battalions of the enemy, place
obliquely, behind a ravine on our right flank. One officer alone was
following me, Rudowski, I believe, a colossus, like most of these
picked men. He was still on horseback, but wounded to death,
staggering and on the point of falling off with his face to the enemy.
Distance and the rocks prevented my seeing anything more. I made
a vain attempt to turn back my horse, which was itself wounded; but
the Spaniards advanced to seize me, shouting cries of victory. Then
I jumped to the ground trying to collect what strength remained to
me . . . Nearly the whole of the squadron was laid low. Out of six
other officers, three were either killed outright or mortally wounded
. . . The three others . . . were wounded. Forty non-commissioned
officers and lancers, killed or mortally wounded, were lying on the
ground. Twelve others were wounded but less serious; twenty alone
had escaped this massacre safe and sound. These had assisted their
wounded to retire, so that, over the whole of the remaining ground
covered by our charge I only saw one trumpeter left standing,
motionless in the midst of the firing which was still going on. The
poor child was weeping for his squadron. . .*

Napoleon recognised the gallantry of General Montbrun and his Poles,
sending him back to Paris in January and promoting him to general de
division in March. He took command of the 2nd Light Cavalry Division
on 12 March and led it through the 1809 campaign against Austria. On 1
April 1810 Montbrun was ordered to return to Spain and take command
of the cavalry of the Army of Portugal. His command would consist of

---

* de Ségur, *An Aide-de-Camp of Napoleon*, pp. 391–3.

the 2nd and 4th Dragoon Divisions, plus three light cavalry brigades. For all practical purposes, his command was a cavalry corps. He led them into Portugal in 1810 and led the pursuit of the retreating enemy to Lisbon. By the time the Army of Portugal was at the Lines of Torres Vedras, the defences built to protect Lisbon, the British and their Portuguese allies had laid waste to the countryside. For the next six months instead of fighting the British army, the French cavalry was entangled in endless patrolling, counter-guerrilla operations and foraging for supplies to keep the men and their mounts alive. The French were preoccupied with finding subsistence because their lines of communications back to Spain had been cut and the only food available was that which they could forage in the ravaged countryside. The difficulty of this is shown by the attrition among the cavalry horses. General Montbrun's cavalry entered Portugal with 7,184 horses. They returned to Spain six months later. During their time in Portugal they did not fight in a single major battle, yet the cavalry lost 2,208 horses. Although this was almost 30 per cent of their mounts,* the losses could have been far worse.

In 1811 General Montbrun achieved considerable success against the British. At Fuentes de Oñoro on 5 May, he was on the left of the French line and through a series of spectacular charges, drove the British right wing back over 5 kilometres, inflicting hundreds of casualties. On 25 September at El Bodon, in a series of attacks he forced Wellington to abandon his forward position, having lost 150 men and 4 artillery pieces. In December 1811 he went to eastern Spain to reinforce Marshal Suchet at the siege of Alicante.

General Montbrun was recalled to France in January 1812 and given command of the 2nd Reserve Cavalry Corps during the 1812 campaign in Russia. His luck ran out on 7 September at the battle of Borodino. He was struck in the left side by a 3-pounder cannonball that passed above the kidneys. Heinrich Roos, a German surgeon

> saw General Montbrun turn pale and fall from his horse . . . The wound wasn't bleeding very much. He'd very quickly turned pale and yellow. His very lively look had been extinguished and we saw his strength gradually failed.[†]

Baron Larrey was called to attend him, but there was nothing he could do. General Montbrun was evacuated to a nearby village, where he died shortly afterwards.

---

* Koch, *Mémoirs de Massena*, vol. 7, pp. 568–70, 590.
† Austin, *Napoleon's Invasion of Russia*, book 1, p. 299.

General Montbrun was buried in the Grand Redoubt. Marshal Lefebvre had a wooden cross erected above the grave. Inscribed on it was:

Here lies
General Montbrun
Passer-by of whatever nation,
Honour his ashes,
They are the remains of one
of one of the Bravest of the Brave,
of General Montbrun.
The Duke of Danzig, Marshal of France,
has erected this modest monument in his honour
His memory will live for ever in the hearts
Of the Great Army.[*]

Lieutenant Vossler, a Württembourg cavalry officer, who recorded the epitaph in his diary, wrote, upon seeing the grave,

So this was where my dear and gracious general had found his last resting place, a man as kind and considerate to his subordinates as he had been brave in war; who had faced death a hundred times and won all his honours and decorations on the field of battle, yet had miraculously escaped injury until the day of his death. A fine and noble person in the flower of his manhood.[†]

General Montbrun was the best of the cavalry generals who served in the Peninsula. His outlook on life was probably best summed up by Captain Charles Parquin who wrote:

The general was the most handsome warrior that I have ever seen. He was famous throughout the whole army for his bravery and for the rather forceful but fairly original comment which he made when he was encamped at Znaym in 1809. Captain Lindsai, his aide-de-camp, galloped up to him, shouting 'Good news General! I have just come from Vienna where peace has been made.' 'What damned use is that to me when I would rather have a good fight!' was the general's reply.[‡]

---

[*] Vossler, *With Napoleon in Russia*, p. 68.
[†] Ibid.
[‡] Parquin, *Napoleon's Army*, p. 130.

Chapter Nine

The Peninsular Cavalry Generals:
Noirot to Watier

Table 9.1   Noirot, Jean-Baptiste

Awards and honours	Baron of the Empire 22 Mar. 1813
Date and place of birth	26 Dec. 1768 at Port-sur-Saône
Regiments commanded	23rd Cavalry Regiment 12 Aug. 1799–30 Dec. 1802
5th Cuirassiers 30 Dec. 1802–31 Dec. 1806	
Date of rank as general	General of brigade 31 Dec. 1806
Time in the Peninsula	12 Dec. 1808–10 Sep. 1811
Command or post in the Peninsula	Cavalry Depot at Burgos, Spain 12 Dec. 1808–7 Apr. 1809; Governor of Santander, Spain; 7 Apr. 1809–Sep. 1809; 1st Dragoon Brigade, Milhaud's Division Sep. 1809–Jul. 1811; 1st Dragoon Brigade, Soult's Division Aug.–Sep. 1811
Date and place of death	18 Sep. 1826 at Chassey-les-Scey
Place of burial	Scey-sur-Saône

Jean Noirot was unusual in the amount of time he spent in regimental command – over seven years. After being promoted to general of brigade in the final days of 1806, he was seriously wounded leading his dragoon brigade at Hoff in February 1807. His initial assignments in Spain were not combat commands, but administrative. In December 1808 he took command of the cavalry depot at Burgos. This was an extremely important command, since all replacements for both men and horses staged through there. In April 1809 he was appointed governor of Santander and would remain there for five months, until he assumed command of the 1st Dragoon Brigade in Milhaud's Division, which was part of the 5th Corps. His brigade consisted of the 5th and 12th Dragoons and he would command it for two years. General Noirot and his brigade distinguished themselves at Ocaña and were mentioned in the after-action report of Marshal Soult to King Joseph. General Noirot relinquished command of his brigade in September 1811 and returned to France. He would continue in administrative positions until April 1813, when he briefly commanded a brigade in Milhaud's Division. In September he assumed command of the Cavalry Depot for the Grande Armée.

Until taking command of the cavalry depot, General Noirot had a good reputation as both a cavalry commander and an administrator. Unfortunately for him, his reputation was shattered in the late summer of 1813. The cavalry depot was located in the vicinity of Leipzig. On 18 September General Noirot was ordered to move the depot west towards the Rhine River.

> Originally some eight thousand men and six thousand more or less injured horses, with a long train of wagons loaded with clothing and equipment, the convoy attracted stragglers, noncombatants, deserters and raiding parties of enemy irregulars. Its commander, General Jean Noirot, panicked and led a stampede to the Rhine, allowing his troops to pillage and abuse the inhabitants along their route and completely disorganising the army's communications.[*]

General Noirot was arrested for negligence on 30 September and dismissed from the army on 28 December 1813. He was restored to active duty in July 1814 and retired in 1825. Two hundred years later, no one recalls General Noirot for his many years of solid service as a regimental and brigade commander. Instead he is remembered, if at all, as the general who lost control of his command and caused serious damage to the army's lines of communication at a critical time.

Table 9.2 Ormancey, François-Léon

Awards and honours	Baron of the Empire 28 Oct. 1808
Date and place of birth	2 Aug. 1754 at Pontailler-sur-Saône
Date of rank as general	General of brigade 30 Dec. 1810
Time in the Peninsula	Nov. 1808–16 Jan. 1814
Command or post in the Peninsula	Headquarters, Milhaud's Dragoon Division Nov. 1808–Dec. 1810; 2nd Brigade, Merlin's Light Cavalry Division Apr. 1809–Dec. 1809; Light Cavalry Brigade, 4th Corps 1 Sep. 1811–7 Feb. 1812; 2nd

---

[*] Elting, *Swords around the Throne*, pp. 318–19.

Table 9.2	continued
Command or post in the Peninsula	Brigade, 2nd Cavalry Division 7 Feb.– Nov. 1812; 2nd Dragoon Brigade, 1st Dragoon Division Nov. 1812–16 Jul. 1813; 2nd Dragoon Brigade, Trelliard's Division 16 Jul. 1813–16 Jan. 1814
Date and place of death	22 Jul. 1824 at Villeron
Place of burial	Villeron

Some sources give his family name as d'Ormancey. François Ormancey was one of the older generation of officers who went to Spain in 1808 and spent virtually the whole war there. He was the chief-of-staff of General Milhaud's Dragoon Division when it was sent to Spain in November 1808. In May 1809 he was given temporary command of the 2nd Brigade of the 4th Corps's Light Cavalry Division and led them through the rest of the year. Upon relinquishing his command he returned to being the chief-of staff until he was promoted to general of brigade on 30 December 1810. He was 54 years old at the time. The average age for promotion to general of brigade among officers serving in the Peninsula was 37 years old. He was the second-oldest colonel to be promoted among all the Peninsular cavalry generals. Nine months later General Ormancey was given command of the 4th Corps's Light Cavalry Brigade, replacing General Perreimond. In February 1812 he was transferred to the 2nd Dragoon Brigade of Pierre Soult's Division. His brigade consisted of the 16th and 21st Dragoons. He would command the brigade until early November when he was transferred to the 2nd Dragoon Brigade of the 1st Dragoon Division. His new brigade was larger than his previous command, having the 14th, 17th and 27th Dragoons. He would command these regiments until the reorganisation of the French army in Spain on 16 July 1813. He was retained in brigade command but assigned to the division commanded by General Trelliard. His new brigade initially only had two regiments, the 14th and 16th Dragoons, but in October there was another reorganisation and consolidation within the division. General Ormancey's 2nd Dragoon Brigade kept the 14th and 16th Dragoons and received the 17th Dragoons from the recently disbanded 3rd Dragoon Brigade.

On 16 January 1814 General Ormancey and his brigade were sent to eastern France with the rest of General Trelliard's Dragoon Division. He was wounded at Bar-sur-Aube on 27 February 1814. He had no active command after the Restoration and when Napoleon returned in 1815, Ormancey was given command of the remount depot for the Armies of the Rhine and the Moselle. He retired on 18 October 1815, after 47 years of service.

Table 9.3   Ornano, Philippe-Antoine

Awards and honours	Count of the Empire 22 Nov. 1808
Date and place of birth	17 Jan. 1784 in Ajaccio
Regiments commanded	25th Dragoons 18 Jan. 1807–5 May 1811
Date of rank as general	General of brigade 16 Jun. 1811; General of division 8 Sep. 1812
Time in the Peninsula	Jan. 1809– 24 Mar. 1812
Command or post in the Peninsula	25th Dragoons 18 Jan. 1807–5 May 1811; 2nd Brigade, 5th Dragoon Division Nov. 1809–Apr. 1810; 3rd Brigade, Trelliard's Division Apr.–May 1810; 3rd Brigade, Trelliard's Division Sep. 1810–Autumn 1811
Date and place of death	13 Oct. 1863 in Paris
Place of burial	Crypt, chapel of the Hôtel des Invalides, Paris

Some references list his name as d'Ornano. He was a outstanding cavalry officer who led the 25th Dragoons into Spain in September 1808 and would command them at the siege of Lugo in May 1809, at Tamames on 18 October 1809, Alba de Tormes on 28 November 1809, the siege of Ciudad Rodrigo in May 1810. He served as the temporary commander of the 2nd Brigade of the 5th Dragoon Division, from November 1809–May 1810. In September 1810 Colonel Ornano assumed command of the 3rd Dragoon Brigade, replacing General Gardanne, who had been named the governor of Ciudad Rodrigo. In March 1811 he was officially appointed the commander of the brigade by Napoleon. His brigade consisted of the 15th and 25th Dragoons and he would lead them at Sabugal on 3 April 1811 and at Fuentes de Oñoro from 3–5 May 1811. During the third day at Fuentes de Oñoro Colonel Ornano was given command of the six elite companies of the 3rd, 6th, 10th, 11th, 15th and 25th Dragoons and ordered to spearhead the French cavalry attack on the British right flank. His attack forced back the British cavalry and the British 7th Infantry Division had to withdraw, covered by the Light Division. After the battle Philippe Ornano received a battlefield promotion to general of brigade, which was confirmed on 16 June 1811. The newly promoted general was 27 years old – the youngest cavalry general in the Peninsula.

General Ornano would command his brigade until the autumn, when he was recalled to France and sent to Germany, where he received command of the 16th Light Cavalry Brigade in General Watier's Division in March 1812. He was promoted to general of division in September 1812 at the age of 28. In 1813 he was promoted to major-colonel in the Empress Dragoons of the Imperial Guard and would serve with them until the abdication of Napoleon in April 1814. In the final days of the Empire he would command the 1st and 2nd Guard Cavalry Divisions.

General Ornano was an ardent Bonapartist who rallied to Napoleon upon his return in 1815. However, on 8 June he fought a duel with General Jean Bonet.* Both officers were seriously wounded and were unable to fight in the Waterloo campaign. Ornano was sent into exile by the Royalists in the summer of 1815 and married Marie Walewski, one of Napoleon's mistresses. He returned to France in 1818 and served in a variety of commands until he retired in 1848. He was promoted to Marshal of France on 2 April 1861 and died two years later.

Philippe Ornano was unique for general officers who served in the Peninsula. Like many of his contemporaries, he was competent and aggressive; however, he had one attribute that they had not: he was a distant cousin of Napoleon. This accounted for his meteoric promotions.

Table 9.4   Oullenbourg, Ignace-Laurent-Joseph-Stanislas d'

Awards and honours	Baron of the Empire 26 Oct. 1808
Date and place of birth	10 Aug. 1766 at Landau
Regiments commanded	1st Dragoons 19 Jun. 1806–4 Apr. 1807
Date of rank as general	General of brigade 4 Apr. 1807
Time in the Peninsula	7 Sep. 1808–9 Nov. 1809
Command or post	3rd Dragoon Brigade, Tour-Maubourg's
in the Peninsula	Division 14 May 1807–9 Nov. 1809
Date and place of death	28 May 1833 at Nancy

General Oullenbourg was another older officer who served in Spain and never went far. He was promoted to general of brigade after 28 years of service, at the age of 41. He took command of the 3rd Dragoon Brigade of Tour-Maubourg's Dragoon Division on 14 May 1807 and would lead them into Spain in September 1808. He commanded them at Ucles on 13 January 1809, Medellin on 28 March 1809 and Talavera from 27–28 July 1809. General Oullenbourg returned to France in November 1809 and commanded the cavalry depot at Versailles until July 1810, when he was appointed commandant of the Department of Seinte-et-Oise. He would command a cuirassier brigade in Russia in 1812 and in 1813 he was reappointed commandant of the Department of Seinte-et-Oise. General Oullenbourg rallied to Napoleon in 1815 and retired in August 1815.

---

* Elting, *Swords around the Throne*, p. 150.

Table 9.5   Paris d'Illins, Antoine-Marie

Date and place of birth	9 Mar. 1746 in Paris
Regiments commanded	6th Hussars 5 Feb.–22 May 1792
Date of rank as general	General of brigade 25 Mar. 1807
Time in the Peninsula	17 Oct. 1808–18 Nov. 1809
Command or post in the Peninsula	Light Cavalry Brigade, 5th Corps 17 Oct.–22 Dec. 1808; Fortress of Retiro in Madrid 22 Dec. 1808–24 Jun. 1809; Light Cavalry Brigade, 4th Corps 17 Oct.–18 Nov. 1809;
Date and place of death	18 Nov. 1809 at Ocaña, Spain
Cause of death	Killed in action, possibly by a lance

General Antoine Paris, who was 62 years old when he entered Spain in 1808, was the oldest cavalry general in the French army there. Prior to serving in the Peninsula, his last active command had been 16 years before, when he led the 6th Hussars for five months, in 1792. He then held a series of staff positions for many years. In August 1808 he was appointed inspector general of the cavalry of the Portuguese Legion. Two months later he assumed command of the Light Cavalry Brigade of Marshal Mortier's 5th Corps. It consisted of the 10th Hussars and the 21st Chasseurs. He would command them for only three months, when he was appointed commander of the Retiro Fortress in Madrid. In June 1809 General Maupetit received permission to return to France on account of poor health and Paris assumed command of the Light Cavalry Brigade of General Sebastini's 4th Corps. His new command was comprised of the 10th and 26th Chasseurs and the 1st Vistula Legion Lancers. On 18 November 1809, in the fighting that led up to the battle of Ocaña, Paris and his brigade were leading the French army when it encountered four divisions of Spanish cavalry under General Freire. General Milhaud brought up his dragoon division in support. It would be the largest cavalry fight of the Peninsular War. The French had 3,000 men in eight regiments, while the Spanish had 4,000 men. Paris broke the first line of the Spanish cavalry and in turn was attacked by the Spanish reserves. General Milhaud and his dragoons hit the Spanish cavalry in the flank, causing them to break. The rout was complete. The Spanish lost hundreds of men killed and wounded and 80 men and 500 horses captured. The French casualties were relatively light, less than 50 men. General Paris was the only officer killed in his brigade. According to one source, he was stabbed by a Spanish lancer.[*]

---

[*] Southey, *History of the Peninsular War*, vol 2, p. 514.

General Paris was 63 years old when he was killed in action. Charles Oman stated that he was 'the not unworthy successor of the adventurous Lasalle'.* In one of the first histories of the Peninsular War Robert Southey wrote about General Paris in 1827 that 'He was an old officer, whom the Spaniards represent as a humane and honourable man, regretting that he should have perished in such a cause.'† Not a bad accolade for an old man!

Table 9.6   Perreimond, André-Thomas

Awards and honours	Baron of the Empire 27 Jul. 1808
Date and place of birth	2 Oct. 1766 at Vidauban
Date of rank as general	General of brigade 13 Jun. 1795
Time in the Peninsula	15 Nov. 1808–10 Jun. 1809; 26 Sep. 1809–9 Nov. 1812
Command or post in the Peninsula	1st Dragoon Brigade, Tour-Maubourg's Division 14 May 1807–10 Jun. 1809; Light Cavalry Brigade, 4th Corps 26 Sep. 1809–1 Jun. 1811; Light Cavalry Brigade, Tour-Maubourg's Division Jun.–Aug. 1811; 2nd Dragoon Brigade, Tour-Maubourg's Division 1 Sep. 1811–7 Feb. 1812; 1st Cavalry Division, Army of the South 7 Feb.–10 Oct. 1812; Light Cavalry Division, Army of the South 10 Oct.–Nov. 1812
Date and place of death	2 Jan. 1844 at Toulon

Variations of his name in different sources include Perreymond and Perreimont.

André Perreimond was another of the older officers who became generals during the Wars of the Revolution. Although promoted to general of brigade in 1795, he held a series of staff positions until 1799, when he was placed in charge of training conscripts. He would hold the job until 1807 when he returned to the Grande Armée. In May 1807 he took command of the 1st Dragoon Brigade in Tour-Maubourg's 1st Dragoon Division. His command consisted of the 1st and 2nd Dragoons. The division entered Spain in November 1808 and General Perreimond commanded his brigade until June 1809, when he was allowed to return to France. His stay in France was cut short when, just three months later, he was ordered back to Spain to assume command of the Light Cavalry Brigade of the 4th Corps. The brigade had the 10th and 27th Chasseurs

---

* Oman, *History of the Peninsular War*, vol. 3, p. 90.
† Southey, *History of the Peninsular War*, vol 2, p. 514.

and the 1st Vistula Legion Lancers. He would command them until June, when he returned to Tour-Maubourg's 1st Dragoon Division and took command of its Light Cavalry Brigade. In September he was transferred to the division's 2nd Dragoon Brigade. This brigade consisted of the 17th and 27th Dragoons. In late autumn of 1811 Perreimond requested permission to retire and by an Imperial Decree dated 16 January 1812, he was authorised to do so. However, before he could retire, permission was withdrawn. Instead Perreimond was given command of the newly formed 1st Cavalry Division, which had three chasseur and two hussar regiments, plus a dragoon regiment. His division was assigned to the Marshal Soult's Army of the South and Perreimond's headquarters was usually in Seville. On 10 October 1812 he received word that he was allowed to retire by the end of the year. He arrived back in France on 9 November. In July 1813 he was recalled to active duty and sent to Italy, where he commanded a cavalry brigade in General Mermet's Division. General Perreimond retired in June 1814 and did not rally to Napoleon in 1815. He died in 1844 at the age of 79.

Table 9.7   Poinsot de Chansac, Pierre

Awards and honours	Baron de Chansac 14 Feb. 1810
Date and place of birth	7 Feb. 1764 at Chalon-sur-Saône
Date of rank as general	General of brigade 7 Aug. 1793
Time in the Peninsula	15 Dec. 1807–24 Oct. 1808; 19 Dec. 1809–2 Jul. 1811
Command or post in the Peninsula	1st Brigade, Vedel's Division, 2nd Corps 15 Dec. 1807–22 Jul. 1808; HQ, Army of Spain 19 Dec. 1809–20 Jun. 1810; 2nd Brigade, Heudelet's Division, 2nd Corps 20 Jun.–15 Sep. 1810; 3rd Prov. Dragoon Brigade, 6th Government 15 Sep. 1810–2 Jul. 1811
Date and place of death	30 Jul. 1833 at Dijon

Pierre Poinsot was one of the young generals of the revolution, being promoted to provisional general of brigade in August 1793 and then provisional general of division a month later. He was relieved from his duties in November, but reinstated as a general of brigade in December 1796. Although General Poinsot had primarily commanded cavalry during his career, he was appointed commander of the 1st Infantry Brigade of General Vedel's Division, in Dupont's Corps. His brigade consisted of the 5th Legion of Reserve and the 3rd Swiss Regiment. Poinsot was part of the surrender at Bailen on 22 July 1808 and was repatriated to France in October 1808. He was assigned to the Army of Italy in November 1808 and was wounded at the battle of Piave on 8 May 1809. In December 1809 General Poinsot was sent back to Spain. What his duties were is unclear. In June 1810 he was given command of the 2nd Brigade of General Heudelet's Division in the 2nd Corps. He would only command this infantry brigade for three months, when he was appointed to command of the 3rd Provisional Dragoon Brigade, which was assigned to the 6th Military Government in Valladolid, Spain. He worked directly for General Kellermann. His brigade consisted of the 6th and 7th Provisional Dragoon Regiments and was responsible for protecting the lines of communications of the Army of Portugal during its invasion of Portugal. l Poinsot would command them until early June 1811 when the provisional regiments were disbanded. He returned to France in July 1811.

General Poinsot was assigned to 11th Corps in the Grande Armée in August 1812 and fought in the 1813 campaign in Germany. He was captured by Russians on 11 March 1813 and returned to France in May 1814. He did not have an active command during the Hundred Days in 1815 and retired in October 1815. He died in 1832.

It is difficult to judge Poinsot's ability as a general. He too was tainted by the disaster at Bailen in 1808 and although given command of an independent dragoon brigade in 1810, he never did anything that made himself stand out. Charles Parquin stated in his memoirs that General Poinsot was '. . . noted for his bravery' and was willing to challenge General Fournier to a duel, despite Fournier's fearsome reputation as a duelist.* General Thiebault, who knew General Poinsot for many years, left an interesting description of his character:

> General Poinsot was a man of extraordinary bravery and a very good
> fellow too; but otherwise ordinary both in style and in manners. He
> was far from being stupid and thus did not fail to justify his name.
> Several things that he said struck me at the time, but I only remember
> one. On my expressing my surprise that he should separate from his
> wife without necessity, this was his answer 'When I get my marching
> orders for active service, I buy a property, the cost to be defrayed
> by the campaign. As soon as the conquest is made, I get a command
> somewhere and when things are pretty quiet again send for my wife.
> Then, when I have got together the sum necessary to pay off the debt
> contracted on the security of the war, Mme Poinsot goes herself to
> effect the payment, clear the new property and sometimes enlarge it.'
> Nothing could be clearer.†

---

* Parquin, *Napoleon's Army*, p. 129. On the duel see p. 144 above.
† Thiebault, *The Memoirs of Baron Thiébault*, vol. 2, p. 48.

Table 9.8   Pryvé, Ythier-Silvain

Awards and honours	Baron of the Empire 19 Mar. 1808
Date and place of birth	19 Jul. 1762 at Vannes-sur-Cosson
Regiments commanded	5th Dragoons 24 Mar.–1 Sep. 1803; 2nd Dragoons 1 Sep. 1803–26 Aug. 1805; 1st Foot Dragoons 26 Aug. 1805–30 Sep. 1805; 2nd Dragoons 1 Oct. 1805–14 May 1807
Date of rank as general	General of brigade 14 May 1807
Time in the Peninsula	Jan. 1808–Oct. 1810
Command or post in the Peninsula	1st Dragoon Brigade, Grouchy's Division, 1st Corps Jan.–21 May 1808; 1st Dragoon Brigade, Fresia's Division, 2nd Corps 21 May–22 Jul. 1808
Date and place of death	13 Feb. 1831 at Passy

The name is often spelled Privé. General Pryvé entered Spain with General Grouchy's Division of Marshal Moncey's Corps in January 1808. He commanded the 1st Dragoon Brigade, which had the 1st and 2nd Provisional Dragoon Regiments, with a strength of about 900 men. In May his brigade was transferred to General Fresia's Division of General Dupont's 2nd Corps. By June it had received enough reinforcements to bring its strength up to over 1,500 men. Pryvé and his brigade played a key role in the campaign that led up the battle of Bailen. At the battle of the Alcolea Bridge on 7 June 1808 they destroyed a column of 3,000 Spanish infantry. General Dupont's Corps marched towards southern Spain, but by late June found his force isolated and out of communications with the French forces in Madrid. He decided that his corps was not strong enough to continue and ordered it to fall back towards central Spain. It was followed closely by General Castaño's Spanish army. During the retreat towards Bailen in mid-July Pryvé commanded the Corps's rearguard, consisting of his brigade, the sailors of the Imperial Guard and six elite infantry companies. At the battle of Bailen on 19 July General Pryvé and his brigade charged the Spanish line several times, breaking the first line and capturing two Spanish flags, but they were too badly outnumbered for these charges to make a difference.

On the night of 19 July General Dupont called a council of war to determine whether he should surrender. Only Pryvé opposed capitulating, wanting to fight on. He proposed abandoning all the baggage and massing the forces on the right of the line to make a breakthrough. General Dupont decided against this move and entered into negotiations with the Spanish. Pryvé was the only French general who refused to sign the capitulation agreement. He would pay for his obstinacy. In September 1808 Dupont and the other senior officers sailed to France, leaving Pryvé in command of the remnants of the 2nd Corps. He and the corps would be imprisoned in the Balearic Islands. Pryvé tried to alleviate the harsh conditions that his men endured. He offered to sign notes of credit drawn on the French treasury to buy food and clothing for his men, but his Spanish captors refused. In July 1810 he was sent to England, where he would remain a prisoner at Chesterfield. He returned to France in June 1814, almost six years after becoming a prisoner.

General Pryvé sided with Napoleon in 1815 but was not given an active command. It was probably because of a combination of several factors, including his age (he was 53), the fact that he had not commanded in seven years and that despite being one of the few general officers who behaved honorably during the Bailen campaign and opposed surrendering, and he was tainted by General Dupont's actions. Pryvé went on the inactive list in the autumn of 1815 and retired in 1818. He died in 1831.

General Pryvé was another experienced cavalry general who had the misfortune of being in the wrong place at the wrong time. His actions during the Bailen campaign and his subsequent captivity demonstrated that he was a capable leader, and moreover one who also cared for his men.

Table 9.9   Rigau, Antoine

Awards and honours	Baron of the Empire 2 Feb. 1809
Date and place of birth	14 May 1758 at Agen
Regiments commanded	8th Dragoons 10 Oct. 1800–Dec. 1801; 16th Cavalry Regiment (25th Dragoons) 23 Dec. 1801–12 Jan. 1807
Date of rank as general	General of brigade 12 Jan. 1807
Time in the Peninsula	5 Nov. 1807–21 May 1808
Command or post in the Peninsula	2nd Heavy Cavalry Brigade, Fresia's Division, Dupont's Corps 5 Nov. 1807–21 May 1808
Date and place of death	4 Sep. 1820 in New Orleans, the United States

---

The name is often spelled Rigaud. Antoine Rigau had the most regimental command experience among the Peninsular cavalry generals, having commanded the 8th and 25th Dragoons for over six years, before being promoted to general of brigade in January 1807. He was seriously wounded at Ostrolenka on 16 February 1807 by a musket ball that traversed the length of his arm and spent the next six months recovering. In November 1807 General Rigau was given command of the 2nd Heavy Cavalry Brigade in General Fresia's Division, which was part of

General Dupont's ill-fated corps. His brigade consisted of the 1st and 2nd Provisional Cuirassier Regiments. These two regiments were composed of companies from 10 different cuirassier and carabinier regiments and had a strength of about 1,100 men. The brigade would stay in Old Castille for the winter and spring of 1808. On 21 May 1808 Rigau was sent back to France, where he would hold a series of administrative commands for the next five years. In late 1813 he was responsible for evacuating the French forces from Kassel before the advancing Russians.

After Napoleon went into exile in 1814, General Rigau became the commander of the Department of the Marne. He immediately declared for Napoleon, when he returned to France in March 1815 and arrested Marshal Victor. After Waterloo he defended Châlons-sur-Marne until 2 July. He was condemned to death *in absentia* on 16 May 1816, but escaped to the United States. He took part in the effort to set up colonies of former French soldiers in Alabama and Texas a few years later. He died in New Orleans in 1820. Napoleon bequeathed him 100,000 francs in his will, not knowing that General Rigau had already died.

Table 9.10   Schwarz, François-Xavier de

Awards and honours	Baron of the Empire 9 Mar. 1808
Date and place of birth	8 Jan. 1762 at Hernwies, Grand Duchy of Baden
Regiments commanded	5th Hussars 3 Sep. 1799–30 Dec. 1806
Date of rank as general	General of brigade 30 Dec. 1806
Time in the Peninsula	Mar. 1808–Sep. 1810
Command or post in the Peninsula	Light Cavalry Brigade, Corps of Observation of the Eastern Pyrenees 19 Mar. 1808–Jun. 1808; Italian Cavalry Brigade, 5th Corps Jun.–Oct. 1808; Italian Cavalry Brigade, 7th Corps Oct. 1808–Jun. 1809; 1st Brigade, Rouyer's German Division, 7th Corps Mar.–Sep. 1810
Date and place of death	9 Oct. 1826 at Sainte-Ruffine
Place of burial	Sainte-Ruffine

François Schwarz was promoted to general of brigade in December 1806 after giving up command of the 5th Hussars. He did not receive command again until he assumed command of the Light Cavalry Brigade of the Corps of Observation of the Eastern Pyrenees. His brigade, known as the Neapolitan Brigade, which initially consisted of the 1st Italian Provisional Regiment, but would become the Italian 2nd Chasseurs and the 2nd Neapolitan Chasseurs. Both units were composed of conscripts and not well trained. On 4 June 1808, at Bruch in Catalonia, General Schwarz was in temporary command of an infantry brigade consisting of 2 Neapolitan, 1 Swiss and 1 Italian infantry battalion with a strength of over 3,000 men. The brigade was attacked by a small force of poorly armed guerrillas. Instead of using his superior numbers to overwhelm the guerrillas, General Schwarz chose to retreat. On the 20-kilometre march back to Barcelona his brigade was under continuous fire by the guerrilla. He eventually lost control of his force, which fled as a disorganised mob to safety. General Schwarz was not relieved for the disaster and would continue to command his cavalry brigade until the autumn of 1809, when it was broken up and the regiments assigned to different infantry divisions.

On 10 March 1810 he was given command of the 1st Brigade of General Royer's German Division. His brigade initially contained the 1st Nassau Infantry Regiment and the 4th Regiment of the Rhine (Saxon Duchies). In early April they were sent to Manresa and on 4 April, they were attacked by a large number of Spanish troops under the command of General O'Donnell. The next morning Schwarz chose to retreat. By the time his brigade reached the safety of Barcelona, they had lost 29 officers and over 950 men killed, wounded, or captured – over 30 per cent of his total force. Later that summer Schwarz was stationed at La Bispal, north of Barcelona. His mission was to protect the line of communications with France. He commanded the 5th and 6th Infantry Regiments of the Rhine and a squadron of the 13th Cuirassiers, a total of about 1,500 men. His brigade was stationed in towns and villages protecting the coast from British landings. He kept a reserve of 700 men with him at La Bispal. On 14 September Schwarz and the garrison at La Bispal were attacked by a large Spanish force under General O'Donnell. After a brief defence Schwarz capitulated rather than trying to hold out until a relief force arrived. He would eventually be sent to England, where he remained until May 1814. He commanded a cavalry depot in 1815 and retired in September of that year.

General Schwarz spent 30 months guarding the French lines of communication in a relatively quiet theatre of the war. During that time he fought three battles and lost all three, with heavy casualties inflicted on his brigade by poorly armed opponents. In every one of the battles he appeared to have lost his nerve and chosen to retreat or surrender, rather than fight. Without a doubt, Schwarz was the most incompetent general in the French army in Spain. Although he was a cavalry general, that does not excuse his consistently poor performance in command of infantry. Most of the counter-insurgency operations in the Peninsula were either combined infantry and cavalry operations or infantry operations. Other cavalry generals also led infantry forces in Spain, none as badly as General Schwarz.

Table 9.11   Soult, Pierre-Benoît

Awards and honours	Baron of the Empire 2 Aug. 1808
Date and place of birth	19 Jul. 1770 at Saint Amans Labastide
Regiments commanded	25th Chasseurs 30 Dec. 1802–12 Mar. 1807
Date of rank as general	General of brigade 11 Jul. 1807; General of division 3 Mar. 1813
Time in the Peninsula	15 Nov. 1808–10 Apr. 1814
Command or post in the Peninsula	HQ, Army of Spain 15 Nov.–28 Nov. 1808 Governor of Santander 28 Nov. 1808–Jun. 1809; Light Cavalry Division, 2nd Corps Jun. 1809–30 Apr. 1811; 3rd Dragoon Division, Army of the South Aug. 1811–Oct. 1811; 3rd Cavalry Division, Army of the South Oct. 1811–10 Oct. 1812; 2nd Dragoon Division, Army of the South 10 Oct. 1812–3 Mar. 1813; 1st Light Cavalry Division, Army of the South 7 Apr.–15 Jul. 1813; 1st Cavalry Division, Army of Spain 16 Jul. 1813–10 Apr. 1814
Wounds in Peninsula	shrapnel in left leg at Bussaco by 27 Sep. 1810; shot in right arm at Alba de Tormes 11 Nov. 1812
Date and place of death	7 May 1843 at Tarbes
Place of burial	Cemetery of Saint Jean in Tarbes

General Pierre Soult was the younger brother of Marshal Jean-de-Dieu Soult and their two careers were closely aligned. After commanding the 25th Chasseurs for four years Pierre Soult became his brother's aide-de-camp a second time, until he was promoted to general of brigade in July 1807. General Soult was assigned to the headquarters of the Army of Spain on 15 November 1808 and would serve in the Peninsula for the next 64 months without a break! After a short time on the army staff General Soult was appointed the governor of Santander, where he would serve for 7 months. In June 1809 he took command of the Light Cavalry Division of the 2nd Corps, his brother's former corps. In the initial days of the invasion of Portugal in September 1810 his division would have almost 1,300 men in four regiments 1st Hussars, 22nd Chasseurs, 8th Dragoons and the Hanoverian Chasseurs. He would command them at Bussaco, where he was hit by shrapnel in the left leg and through the retreat back to Spain. He was released from his command in late April 1811 and sent to the Army of the South, which was commanded by his brother. General

Soult was without a command for three months, when he was made the provisional commander of the 3rd Dragoon Division in August 1811 Although his division was divided into two brigades, only the 1st Brigade was commanded by a general, General Noirot, who returned to France in September.

In the autumn Marshal Soult reorganised the Army of the South and the 3rd Dragoon Division was redesignated the 3rd Cavalry Division. It would have a brigade of chasseurs and a brigade of dragoons. Despite the reorganisation, his division would be plagued by a shortage of general officers to command the brigades. On 7 February 1812 General Soult was officially confirmed as the commander of the division which, in October 1812, was redesignated as the 2nd Dragoon Division. He would command it during the pursuit of the British Army as it retreated back towards Portugal, suffering a wound in the right arm at Alba de Tormes on 11 November 1812. In April 1813 General Soult took command of the Light Cavalry Division of the Army of the South, but would only command it for three months. In July 1813 after the disaster at Vitoria, Marshal Soult, reorganised the new Army of Spain and General Soult was given command of the newly formed 1st Cavalry Division, which had two brigades of chasseurs and one of dragoons. For the first time in two years, he had generals commanding all three of his brigades: General Vinot's 1st Brigade had the 5th, 10th and 22nd Chasseurs; General Berton's 2nd Brigade had the 2nd Hussars and the 13th and 21st Chasseurs; while General Sparre's 3rd Brigade was formed with the 5th and 12th Dragoons. He would command the division through the rest of the war.

After the Restoration General Soult would be an inspector general of cavalry and upon Napoleon's return in 1815, he commanded the 4th Light Cavalry Division in General Pajol's Corps during the Waterloo campaign. He would serve in a variety of staff positions and would retire from active duty in 1836. General Soult died in 1843.

General Soult was the longest-serving cavalry general in the Peninsula – being present almost from the beginning of the war to the final battles in southern France. Being Marshal Soult's brother was both a blessing and a curse for Pierre Soult. It appears that his older brother looked after him, obtaining for him choice commands in the Army of the South. It is difficult to determine how good of a general he was, since he did not fight in any major battles of the Peninsular War until the final campaigns in France in 1814. He led from the front, being wounded four times – twice while a general! Although General Soult enjoyed his older brother's patronage throughout his career, it is doubtful that he would have, if he was not competent. Yet Pierre Soult's career was overshadowed by his brother. Few histories mention him other than in passing.

Andrew Leith Hay, a British exploring officer, who was captured by the French, left a very unflattering portrait of General Soult. He

> had neither a gentlemanlike nor soldierly appearance. Gross and unwieldy in his person, no prepossession of manner tended to remove the extremely unfavourable impression; he had all the look of a parvenu of the vulgarest and lowest description.[*]

King Joseph had an even more unfavorable opinion of Pierre Soult. He wrote in a letter to the Minister of War, dated 20 December 1812, that Marshal Soult,

> knowing the limited capability of his brother, who commands the light cavalry, is afraid of compromising him. For this reason, the light cavalry is always kept near the rest of the army and never sent forward without being closely followed by the rest of the army's cavalry. The Duke of Dalmatia always marches with his brother.[†]

Table 9.12 Sparre, Louis-Ernest-Joseph

Awards and honours	Baron of the Empire 9 May 1811
Date and place of birth	8 Jul. 1780 in Paris
Regiments commanded	5th Dragoons 28 Mar. 1808–11 Apr. 1812
Date of rank as general	General of brigade 11 Apr. 1812; General of division 9 Jul. 1814
Time in the Peninsula	14 Oct. 1808–16 Jan. 1814
Command or post in the Peninsula	5th Dragoons 28 Mar. 1808–11 Apr. 1812; 2nd Dragoon Brigade, 2nd Cavalry Division 7 Feb.–14 Apr. 1812; 2nd Dragoon Brigade, 3rd Cavalry Division 14 Apr. 1812–7 Apr. 1813; 1st Dragoon Brigade, 2nd Dragoon Division 7 Apr.–16 Jul. 1813; 3rd Brigade, Soult's Division 16 Jul. 1813–16 Jan. 1814
Date and place of death	9 Jul. 1845 in Paris
Place of burial	Cimetière du Nord, Montmartre, Paris

Louis Sparre commanded the 5th Dragoons in Spain for 30 months before being promoted to general of brigade in April 1812. During that time he led them in numerous battles and skirmishes, including Medellin on

[*] Leith-Hay, *Narrative of the Peninsular War*, vol. 2, p. 148.
[†] du Casse, Albert, *Mémoires et correspondance politique et militaire*, vol IX; p. 120.

28 March 1809, Talavera on 27–28 July 1809, Ocaña on 19 November 1809 and Baza on 3 November 1810. On 26 January 1812, at Murcia, his regiment attacked a Spanish cavalry brigade led by General Martin La Carrera. The Spanish brigade was destroyed and their commander killed. Colonel Sparre's superb leadership of his regiment was a common theme in many of his superior's after action reports. In February 1812 he was the acting commander of the 2nd Brigade of the 2nd Cavalry Division. On 11 April 1812 he was promoted to general of brigade, at the age of 31. He was one of the youngest generals in the French army.

Three days after being promoted, General Sparre took command of the 2nd Dragoon Brigade in Soult's 3rd Cavalry Division in the Army of the South. It was comprised of the 5th and 12th Dragoons. He would command them until the end of the war. In April 1813 General Digeon took command of the division. In July 1813 General Sparre's and his brigade was redesignated the 3rd Brigade of Soult's Division. It would remain with the division until January 1814, when it was ordered to join the Grande Armée in eastern France. General Sparre was wounded in the thumb at Craone on 7 March 1814. He would rally to Napoleon, upon his return from Elba in 1815, but was assigned to command the 11th Light Cavalry Division in the Pyrenees. He would become an inspector general of cavalry in 1818 and would serve in that role until he died in 1845.

Louis Sparre was in the next generation of talented young officers promoted to general of brigade after the heavy casualties among general officers from 1806 to 1809. He was a superb regimental leader and an outstanding brigade commander. The war ended before he had the chance to demonstrate whether he would have commanded as capably at the division level.

Table 9.13   Strolz, Jean-Baptiste-Alexandre

Awards and honours	1st Master of the Horse to King Joseph of Naples 20 May 1808
Date and place of birth	6 Aug. 1771 at Belfort
Date of rank as general	Lieutenant general in Spanish Service 15 Feb. 1811; General of brigade in French Service 23 Jan. 1814
Time in the Peninsula	9 Jun. 1808–16 Jul. 1813
Command or post in the Peninsula	1st Brigade, Merlin's Light Cavalry Division, 4th Corps May–Nov. 1809
Date and place of death	27 Oct. 1841 in Paris
Place of burial	Montparnasse Cemetery

Jean Strolz was a French colonel who passed into the service of King Joseph of Naples in February 1806 and then followed the king to Spain in 1808. In June 1808 he was authorised to pass from Neapolitan service into Spanish service. He commanded the 1st Brigade of Merlin's Light Cavalry Division at Talavera on 27–28 July where his brigade destroyed the British 23rd Light Dragoons on July 28. He would continue in command until November 1809, having commanded the brigade at Almonacid on 11 August and Ocaña on 19 November. After General Perreimond assumed command of the 4th Corps Cavalry Jean Strolz returned to the court of King Joseph. He was promoted to lieutenant general in the service of Spain in 1811. He returned to French service with the rank of general of brigade in January 1814 and commanded the 9th Dragoon Division during the Waterloo campaign in 1815. General Strolz retired in 1815, but was recalled to active duty in 1821. He died in 1841.

Table 9.14 Tilly, Jacques-Louis-François Delaistre

Awards and honours	Baron of the Empire 23 Apr. 1812
Date and place of birth	2 Feb. 1749 at Vernon
Regiments commanded	14th Dragoons 26 Oct.–29 Nov. 1792; 6th Dragoons 29 Nov. 1792–21 Apr. 1793
Date of rank as general	General of brigade 21 Jun. 1793; General of division 18 Jan. 1795
Time in the Peninsula	17 Oct. 1808–31 Jul. 1813
Command or post in the Peninsula	Staff Officer, HQ Army of Spain 17 Oct.–5 Dec. 1808; Governor of the Province of Segovia 5 Dec. 1808–2 Jun. 1811; HQ, Army of the South Jun. 1811–7 Feb. 1812; Inspector General of the Cavalry of the Army of the South 7 Feb. 1812–1 May 1813; Governor of Xeres 7 Feb. 1812–Spring 1813; 1st Dragoon Division 1 May–16 Jul. 1813
Date and place of death	10 Jan. 1822 in Paris

General Jacques Tilly made his reputation during the wars of the French Revolution. He commanded a cavalry division during the campaigns of 1805–7. He returned to France in July 1807 and in October 1808 he was assigned to the headquarters of the Army of Spain. In December 1808 he was appointed governor of the province of Segovia and was tasked with protecting the French lines of communications. He served as governor for 30 months and then was assigned to the headquarters of the Army of the South. In February 1812 General Tilly became the inspector general of the cavalry for the Army of the South and also served as the governor of Xeres. He was the de facto commander of the 1st Cavalry Division and oversaw the pursuit of the retreating British army in 1812. He outmanoeuvred General Long's Light Cavalry Brigade at Ocaña on 25 October 1812, forcing them to retreat. (French sources state that the British sustained heavy casualties, with many prisoners captured.; however British sources list 30 killed or wounded and another 20 captured.) On 1 May 1813 General Tilly was officially appointed commander of the 1st Dragoon Division and led them at Vitoria on 21 June 1813. In the reorganisation of the French Army in Spain on 16 July, he was not given another command. He helped defend Paris in June and July 1815 and retired after serving 54 years! He died in 1822.

General Tilly was considered one of the best cavalry generals of the French Army prior to 1800.* However, by the time he was assigned to Spain in 1808, he was 59 years old and past his prime. His superiors recognised this. Despite being the senior cavalry general in the Peninsula, most of his duties in Spain were staff positions and it was not until 1813, at the age of 64, did he have an active command.

Table 9.15   Tour-Maubourg, Marie-Victor-Nicolas de Fay, Marquis de La

Awards and honours	Baron of the Empire 3 Jun. 1808; Count of the Empire 22 Mar. 1812; Marquis 21 Jul. 1817
Date and place of birth	22 May 1768 at la Motte-de-Galaure
Regiments commanded	22nd Chasseurs 27 Jul. 1800–24 Dec. 1805
Date of rank as general	General of brigade 24 Dec. 1805; General of division 14 May 1807
Time in the Peninsula	15 Nov. 1808–20 Mar. 1812
Command or post in the Peninsula	1st Dragoon Division 14 May 1807–May 1811; 5th Corps, Army of the South May–Jul. 1811; Dragoon Division Jul. 1811–5 Nov. 1811; Reserve of the Army of the South 5 Nov. 1811–7 Feb. 1812; 2nd Cavalry Division, Army of the South 7 Feb.–20 Mar. 1812
Date and place of death	11 Nov. 1850 at Château de Farey-les-Lys
Place of burial	Danmarie-les-Lys

Many historians refer to him as La Tour-Maubourg, while others as de

---

* Michaud, *Biographie universelle*, vol. 19, p. 205.

Fay. General Tour-Maubourg and his 1st Dragoon Division entered Spain on 15 November 1808. They were part of the cavalry reserve and in the previous month the five regiments that made up the division had a total strength of 3,695 men. They were part of the force that took Madrid in December and were assigned to Marshal Victor's 1st Corps in January 1809. They would fight at Ucles on 13 January, at Medellin on 28 March, at Talavera on 27–28 July and at Ocaña on 19 November. At the beginning of 1810, they were still assigned to the 1st Corps and participated in the invasion of southern Spain and the conquest of Andalusia. It would be their new home for the next three years.

In early 1811 General Tour-Maubourg and the 1st Dragoon Division were reassigned to Marshal Mortier's 5th Corps and served along the southern Portuguese–Spanish border for the next six months. They fought at Gebora on 19 February, captured the fortress at Albuquerque with just two regiments on 15 March and the fortress of Valencia de Alcantara on 17 March and defied a British force under Marshal Beresford at Campo Mayor on 25 March. On 6 April Tour-Maubourg was given temporary command of the 5th Corps, but commanded all of the Army's cavalry at Albuera on 16 May. It caught Colonel Colborne's Brigade of four British battalions in the open and destroyed it. On 25 May the 1st Dragoon Division was covering the withdrawal from Badajoz when Tour-Maubourg saw an opportunity to bloody the British. They drove the advance guard from Villa Garcia and pursued them to Usagre. The British were on the far side of a steep ravine, hidden from view by a high ridge. He sent General Bron's Brigade, which was attached to the 1st Dragoon Division, across the ravine where they were ambushed and took heavy casualties. The British elected not to pursue the French back across the ravine, due to the risk of taking having the tables turned on them. On 23 June Tour-Maubourg's division surprised two British cavalry regiments that were screening Elvas and inflicted very heavy casualties on them.

After Albuera General Tour-Maubourg continued to command the 5th Corps, but in July he and his division reverted back to working directly for the Army of the South. In November 1811 he became commander of the Army of the South's Reserve, which consisted of his Dragoon Division and General Sémellé's Infantry Division. His headquarters was at Seville. In early 1812 Marshal Soult reorganised the Army of the South and abolished the Army Reserve and various army corps. Tour-Maubourg went back to commanding just the 1st Dragoon Division which had been renamed the 2nd Dragoon Division.

General Tour-Maubourg was recalled to France in March 1812 and given command of the 4th Cavalry Corps. He led them in the 1812 campaign in Russia and was wounded at Borodino. During the 1813 campaign in Germany he commanded the 1st Reserve Cavalry Corps and was hit above the left knee by a cannonball at the battle of Wachau on 16 October. Baron Larrey, was called to attend the general and saw that the cannonball had done extensive damage, including to

> most of the lateral condyle peroneal head, the tendons that are inserted into it and a portion of the calf of the leg. The joint was opened at the outer and posterior condyle of the femur was also fractured and the peroneal artery had been broken very near its origin to the popliteal artery.*

The surgeon realised that there was nothing he could do to save the leg and performed battlefield surgery on the spot, amputating the leg in less than three minutes.† General Tour-Maubourg was evacuated to Mainz.

After the abdication of Napoleon General Tour-Maubourg was made a peer of France in June 1814. He did not support Napoleon in 1815. He was a member of the Chamber of Peers when it tried Marshal Michel Ney for treason in November 1815 and was one of the members who found him guilty, thus sentencing him to death. Tour-Maubourg was very busy in 1819. He served as the ambassador to London for ten months and then became the Minister of War in November. He served in the position for two years until he was appointed the Minister of State in December 1821. He went into exile with the Bourbons after the July Revolution of 1830 and only returned to France in 1848. He died in 1850.

General Tour-Maubourg was a superb cavalry commander of the same calibre as Generals Montbrun and Lasalle. Although tactically very competent, what set him apart from them was his personality. He was the cold professional who got the job done, but whose aloof personality did not endear many to him. Unlike Generals Montbrun and Lasalle, he was rarely mentioned, other than in passing, in memoirs. One trait that he did have in common with Generals Montbrun and Lasalle was his personal courage and how it cost him in the end. From the time he was first promoted to colonel in 1800 to his final battle in 1813 he was wounded five times. His character might best be summed up by an anecdote about him after his leg was amputated. According to legend, his valet became hysterical at the sight of his wounded master and General Tour-Maubourg responded, 'What are you complaining about? You no longer have a boot to polish.'‡

---

* Larrey, *Mémoires de chirurgie militaire*, vol. 4, p. 443.
† Ibid.
* Chateaubriand, *Mémoires d'outre-tombe*, vol. 1, p. 445.

Table 9.16   Trelliard, Anne-François-Charles

Awards and honours	Baron of the Empire 9 Mar. 1810
Date and place of birth	9 Feb. 1764 in Parma, Italy
Regiments commanded	11th Chasseurs 1 Sep. 1794–10 Sep. 1799
Date of rank as general	General of brigade 10 Sep. 1799; General of division 30 Dec. 1806
Time in the Peninsula	Oct. 1808–May 1809; 4 Mar. 1810–16 Jan. 1814
Command or post in the Peninsula	Army HQ Oct. 1808; Cavalry Depot at Vitoria 10–28 Nov. 1808; Governor of Alava Province 28 Nov.–15 Dec. 1808; Cavalry Depot at Aranda, Spain 15 Dec. 1808–5 May 1809; 2nd Dragoon Division, Army of Portugal 17 Apr. 1810–Oct. 1811; Confederation of the Rhine Division Oct. 1811–Jul. 1813; Cavalry of the Army of the Centre May 1812–Jul. 1813; Governor of the Province of la Mancha Aug. 1811–Spring 1813; 2nd Dragoon Division, Army of Spain 16 Jul. 1813–16 Jan. 1814
Date and place of death	14 May 1832 at Charonne
Place of burial	Père Lachaise Cemetery

General Anne Trelliard was one of the most experienced cavalry generals in the French army in Spain. Although a general of division, he was too junior to command a division, when he went to Spain in October 1808, so he served on the staff of the army's headquarters. Less than a month later, he was appointed commander of the army's cavalry depot at Vitoria – the forward logistical location for the army. Shortly afterwards, he was appointed governor of Alava Province which sat across the lines of communication to France. Trelliard would serve there for a month, until the cavalry depot relocated to Aranda, Spain. He would command it until 5 May 1809, when he was recalled to France. He joined the Grande Armée in Germany and by the end of the campaign, would command the depot for the carabiniers and cuirassiers at Mautern, Austria.

In March 1810 General Trelliard returned to Spain and took command of the 2nd Dragoon Division in the Army of Portugal on 17 April. On the eve of the invasion of Portugal, in September, his division consisted of three brigades General Lorcet's (3rd and 6th Dragoons), General Cavrois's (10th and 11th Dragoons) and General Gardanne's (15th and 25th Dragoons). It mustered 3,487 dragoons and 3,591 horses in 22 squadrons. The attached artillery would give him another 164 men and 231 horses. During the nine months they spent in Portugal Trelliard and his dragoons would have all the duties a cavalryman could expect to face, except for combat against other organised forces. They served as the advance guard for the army. They screened its flanks and fought numerous skirmishes with guerrillas. Much of the time was spent looking for food and forage in areas that had been picked clean first by the Portuguese who destroyed everything that might help the French and then by their own troops. There was constant attrition of the men and horses, so by the time the division had returned to Spain in April 1811, the dragoon regiments had fit for combat only 2,542 men and 2,509 horses — a loss of 945 men (27 per cent) and 1,082 horses (30 per cent).[*]

In October 1811 General Trelliard was reassigned to the Army of the Centre. He also replaced General Lorge as the governor of La Mancha. His headquarters was in Toledo. In addition to his dragoons he was given command of the Confederation of the Rhine Division. In May 1812 his dragoon division consisted of two brigades – the 1st Brigade, commanded by Colonel Reiset, with the 13th and 18th Dragoons and the 2nd Brigade that had the 19th and 22nd Dragoons. Trelliard had the opportunity to prove his generalship against an organised force on 11 August 1812 at the village of Majahalonda. There he pounced on Wellington's advance guard, a combined arms force of two Portuguese and King's German Legion (KGL) Cavalry Brigades, a KGL light infantry battalion and a Royal Horse Artillery Troop, all under the command of General D'Urban. In less than an hour Trelliard and his cavalry bloodied the force, killing or wounding 200 men, while capturing three artillery pieces, the commander of the KGL Brigade and two of the five regimental commanders (Visconde de Barbaçena and Colonel Lobo). French casualties were probably half that, with one officer killed and 15 wounded, including Colonel Reiset.

After the disaster at the battle of Vitoria on 21 June 1813 Marshal Soult reorganised the French forces in Spain into one army. General Trelliard was given command of one of the two cavalry divisions – the 2nd Dragoon Division. It had three brigades: General Ismert's 1st Brigade (21st and 26th Dragoons), General d'Ormancey's 2nd Brigade (14th and 16th Dragoons) and General Avy's 3rd Brigade (4th and 17th Dragoons). His new division had on paper over 2,300 men and horses, but many were untrained conscripts. In January 1814 Trelliard and his division were ordered to eastern France to fight with the Grande Armée. It took his division a month to traverse France, arriving just in time to turn the tide at Nangis (15 February) where they took 1,200 prisoners and a flag. He and his division made a key charge at Saint Dizier on 26 March, which broke

---

[*] Koch, *Mémoirs de Massena*, vol. 7, pp. 570 and 582.

the Russian line. Within a few weeks, Napoleon would abdicate. Trelliard was the governor of Belle-Isle-en-Mer in 1815 and retired in October of that year. He died in 1832.

General Trelliard was another of the outstanding cavalry generals who served in the Peninsula, but received little or no recognition. He was an able administrator and knew how to handle his division in a myriad of roles that it was assigned during the four years he commanded it. On the two occasions he led them in battle against an organised force, he dispayed his superb skills by inflicting heavy casualties on his enemy, with minimum to his own force.

Table 9.17 Vial, Jacques-Laurent-Louis-Augustin

Name	Vial, Jacques-Laurent-Louis-Augustin
Awards and honours	Baron of the Empire 21 Dec. 1808
Date and place of birth	9 Aug. 1774 at Antibes
Regiments commanded	26th Chasseurs 4 Apr. 1807–22 Jul. 1813
Date of rank as general	General of brigade 22 Jul. 1813
Time in the Peninsula	7 Sep. 1808–Jun. 1813; 27 Dec. 1813–Apr. 1814
Command or post in the Peninsula	26th Chasseurs 7 Sep. 1808–22 Jul. 1812; 2nd Brigade, Curto's Light Cavalry Division Mar.–Sep. 1812; 1st Light Cavalry Brigade, Soult's Division Feb.–Apr. 1814
Date and place of death	20 May 1855

Jacques Vial entered Spain with his regiment in 1807 and would lead them for five years, before being promoted to general of brigade in July 1813. For the first three years, the regiment would be stationed in the vicinity of Madrid. During that time he and the 26th Chasseurs would fight at Medellin on 28 March 1809, Talavera on 27 and 28 July 1809, at d'Almonacid on 11 August 1809 and in numerous counter-insurgency operations in the area. In the autumn of 1811 the regiment was transferred to the Army of Portugal and would fight at La Renda on 2 July 1812, Salamanca on 22 July 1812 and in endless skirmishes against insurgents. He would be the temporary commander of the 1st Brigade of General Curto's Light Cavalry Division through much of 1812. In late June 1813 the 26th Chasseurs were ordered to leave Spain and join the Grande Armée in Germany. On arrival in Germany Jacques Vial was promoted to general of brigade, on 22 July 1813. He would command the 2nd Brigade in General Piré's 9th Light Cavalry Division of General Pajol's 5th Cavalry Corps, leading his brigade in the Leipzig campaign.

After the retreat of the Grande Armée across the Rhine in November

1813 Vial was sent back to the Army of Spain. In February 1814 he assumed command of the 1st Light Cavalry Brigade of General Soult's Division. He would command four regiments the 5th, 10th, 15th and 22nd Chasseurs. Vial led the brigade at Orthez on 27 February 1814 and Toulouse on 10 April 1814. During the Waterloo campaign he commanded a cuirassier brigade under General Delort. He would go on the inactive list after Waterloo and remain retired for 15 years. In 1830 he was appointed the commander of Antibes and then the Department of Basses-Alpes. General Vial died in 1855.

Table 9.18   Vialannes, Jean-Batiste-Théodore

Awards and honours	Baron of the Empire 20 Jul. 1808
Date and place of birth	11 Oct. 1761 at Riom
Regiments commanded	1st Dragoons 21 Mar. 1797–29 Aug. 1803
Date of rank as general	General of brigade 29 Aug. 1803
Time in the Peninsula	Nov. 1808–18 Jul. 1809
Command or post in the Peninsula	1st Dragoon Brigade, Lorge's Dragoon Division Nov.–18 Jul. 1809
Date and place of death	3 Aug. 1826 in Paris

General Vialannes was the commander of the light cavalry brigade assigned to Marshal Davout's 3rd Corps during the 1806 campaign against Prussia. His performance at Auerstädt, on 14 October 1806, was less than satisfactory for the demanding marshal and he was transferred out of the corps shortly afterwards.[*] On 27 November 1806 Vialannes assumed command of the 2nd Brigade of the 5th Dragoon Division. In November 1808 he commanded the 1st Dragoon Brigade when the division was sent to Spain. His brigade contained the 13th and 22nd Dragoons. They would be part of the pursuit of the retreating British Army to Corunna and the subsequent invasion of northern Portugal in 1809. His health began to fail and, on 24 June 1809, Marshal Soult relieved him of his command and sent him to Madrid to recover.[†] On 18 July 1809 General Vialannes returned to France. General Vialannes never held an active combat command again. He would serve in a variety of administrative posts and would support Napoleon upon his return in 1815. General Vialannes retired in September 1815.

---

[*] Bowden, Scott. *Napoleon's Finest*, p. 42.
[*] De Rocca, Albert. *Mémoires sur la guerre des Français in Espagne*, p. 348.

Table 9.19 Vinot, Gilbert-Julien

Awards and honours	Baron of the Empire 15 Aug. 1810
Date and place of birth	17 Jul. 1772 at Soissons
Regiments commanded	2nd Hussars 16 Mar. 1809–3 Mar. 1813
Date of rank as general	General of brigade 3 Mar. 1813
Time in the Peninsula	Mar. 1808–31 Jan. 1814
Command or post in the Peninsula	2nd Hussars 16 Mar. 1809–3 Mar. 1813 1st Brigade, Soult's Light Cavalry Division, Army of the South 3 Mar.–15 Oct. 1812; 1st Brigade, Tilly's Light Cavalry Division, Army of the South 15 Oct. 1812–Apr. 1813; 1st Brigade, Soult's Light Cavalry Division, Army of the South Apr.–16 Jul. 1813; 1st Brigade, Soult's Division, Army of Spain 16 Jul. 1813–1 Mar. 1814
Wounds in Peninsula	Shot in thigh at Medina de Rio Seco 14 Jul. 1808; Vitoria 21 Jun. 1813
Date and place of death	6 Jun. 1838 at Lahontan

Gilbert Vinot was a chief of squadrons with the 22nd Chasseurs, when they were sent to Spain in March 1808. He was wounded in the thigh at the battle of Medina de Rio Seco on 14 July 1808. On 28 August 1808 he was promoted to colonel and assumed command of the 2nd Hussars in March 1809. He would command them for three years, during which he served with distinction at Medellin on 28 March 1809, Alcabon on 26 July 1809, Talavera on 27 and 28 July 1809, Santa-Cruz on 25 January 1810 and Ronda on 9–10 April 1810. On 19 February 1811, during the battle of Gebora, the regiment led the turning movement that outflanked the Spanish army. They broke two Spanish infantry squares and were instrumental in the destruction of the Spanish Army. In April 1811 the regiment captured a squadron of the British 13th Light Dragoons, taking two officers and 50 men by surprise. At Albuera on 16 May 1811 the 2nd Hussars were part of the spectacular charge that destroyed Colborne's Brigade, enduring losses of one officer and four hussars killed and four officers and 57 hussars wounded. (One of the officers would die of his wounds.) Colonel Vinot was mentioned in Marshal Soult's report on the battle. In March 1812 he would be given temporary command of the 1st Brigade of General Soult's Division and would command it until it became the 1st Brigade of General Tilly's Division. During the pursuit of the retreating British army, on 17 November, General Vinot's 2nd Hussars captured Sir Edward Paget, the British lieutenant general who had just arrived in the Peninsula to become Wellington's second-in-command.

On 3 March 1813 Gilbert Vinot was promoted to general of brigade and formally given command of the 1st Brigade of General Tilly's Division. Command of the division would pass to General Soult the following month. The brigade consisted of the 2nd Hussars and the 21st Chasseurs. General Vinot would lead them through the fighting withdrawal to Vitoria, where he was wounded at the battle on 21 June 1813. With the reorganisation of the French Army in Spain in July 1813, Vinot was left in command of the 1st Brigade of Soult's Division, but it was reorganised. The 5th Chasseurs were still under his command, however the 27th Chasseurs were sent to the Grande Armée in Germany and replaced by the 10th and 22nd Chasseurs. He led these three regiments until after the battle of Orthez on 27 February 1814. Shortly after the battle, he was sent to Versailles to command the cavalry depot there. During the Waterloo campaign, he commanded a light cavalry brigade in Domon's Division. In late 1815 Vinot was not given any responsibilities and retired in 1825. He was recalled from retirement in 1830 and served as the commanded of the Department of the Eastern Pyrenees. He retired in 1834 and died four years later.

General Vinot was typical of the generals of brigade who were promoted during the latter part of the Empire. He was a superb, aggressive regimental commander and a competent brigade commander. But like many others who were promoted from the forces stationed in Spain late in the war, he never had the opportunity to demonstrate his ability at higher command.

Table 9.20   Watier de Saint-Alphonse, Pierre

Awards and honours	Count of the Empire 26 Oct. 1808
Date and place of birth	4 Sep. 1770 at Laon
Regiments commanded	4th Dragoons 4 Oct. 1799–24 Dec. 1805
Date of rank as general	General of brigade 24 Dec. 1805; General of division 31 Jul. 1811
Time in the Peninsula	Jun. 1808–Jun. 1809; Oct. 1810–Dec. 1811
Command or post in the Peninsula	Hussar Brigade, Moncey's Corps Jun.–Dec. 1808; Cavalry Brigade, 3rd Corps Dec. 1808–Jun. 1809; Light Cavalry Brigade, Caffarelli's Division of Reserve, Army of the North 4 Oct. 1810–Jan. 1811; Light Cavalry Brigade, Army of the North Jan.–May 1811; Light Cavalry Brigade, Army of Portugal 1 Jun.–31 Jul. 1811; Cavalry of the Army of the North Aug.–Dec. 1811

Date and place of death	3 Feb. 1846 in Paris
Cause of death	'Apoplexy'
Place of burial	Church of Guerquesalles near Vimoutiers

Watier's name is often spelled Wathier and occasionally as Wathiez or Wattier. He was an experienced brigade commander by the time he went to the Peninsula in 1808. He commanded a three regiment light cavalry brigade in the 1806 campaign against Prussia, an independent light cavalry brigade in the winter campaign of 1807 and the 2nd Brigade of Lasalle's Light Cavalry Division in the Friedland campaign of 1807. In June 1808 General Watier was sent to Spain to command the 2nd Hussar Brigade of General Grouchy's Division in Marshal Moncey's 3rd Corps. His brigade had the 1st and 2nd Provisional Hussar Regiments. He would command them at Lerin on 25 October 1808, at Tudela on 23 November 1808 and at the siege of Saragossa in December 1808. Watier was recalled to France in June 1809, to serve in the Austrian campaign. He would return to the Peninsula in October 1810, where he would command a light cavalry brigade in General Caffarelli's Division of Reserve, which had the mission of protecting the French line of communications in northern Spain. His brigade consisted of the 1st Provisional Light Cavalry Regiment and the 9th Hussars. In January 1811 it would become part of the Army of the North. He would remain in northern Spain until April 1811, when Marshal Bessières marched south in support of the French Army of Portugal. Watier's brigade was heavily engaged at Fuentes d'Oñoro on 5 May 1811. In July he would be promoted to general of division and reassigned to the Army of the North. He would be in command of all the cavalry in northern Spain, but had little opportunity to exercise division command, since the operations were mostly at the regimental level. He would lead the Army of the North's cavalry in the final days of the campaign against the British Army in 1811 along the Portuguese border and would fight at Carpio on 25 September 1811 and Aldea da Ponte on 26 September 1811.

In December 1811 General Watier was recalled to France and assumed command of the 2nd Light Cavalry Division at Mainz. He would command the 2nd Cuirassier Division in the 1812 invasion of Russia and then the cavalry of the 13th Corps under Marshal Davout during the long siege of Hamburg. In the Waterloo campaign, he led the 13th Cuirassier Division, which destroyed Ponsonby's cavalry brigade during the battle.

General Watier was a strong supporter of Napoleon and Empress Josephine. The empress was instrumental in arranging his marriage to Antoinette de Mackau, a lady-in-waiting in Josephine's court. After Waterloo Watier was persecuted by the returning Bourbons and went into retirement until 1820, from which time he held a series of staff jobs with the cavalry and the gendarmes. He died in 1846 in Paris.

General Watier was another of those capable cavalry officers who developed his ability as both a brigade and division commander on the battlefields in Spain. He was aggressive and had the commander's instinct for when to commit his men for maximum impact and, conversely, knew when a situation called for caution. General Watier was among the best of the Peninsular cavalry generals who were recalled from Spain to fight with the Grande Armée. He would prove his worth in Russia in 1812, the campaign in Germany in 1813 and at Waterloo.

Part III

The Regiments

Chapter Ten

The Cavalry Regiments

Fifty-four French cavalry regiments had at least one squadron serving in Spain and Portugal at some point during the Peninsular War. Another 17 French cavalry regiments had at least one company fighting there. The majority of the regiments were dragoons and chasseurs, but the hussars, lancers and cuirassiers also fought there. Although only the 13th Cuirassiers served there in strength, twelve other cuirassier regiments and both carabinier regiments had companies deployed to Spain in the early days of the war. In addition to the above regiments, the French also deployed 29 provisional regiments to the Peninsula. By 1812 the French Army had over 100 cavalry regiments, of which half had served in the Peninsula with at least a squadron or more. This was a major commitment of French resources.

Table 10.1   Number of French cavalry regiments serving in the Peninsula with at least one squadron

Type of regiment	No. units that served in the Peninsula
Imperial Guard	4
Cuirassiers	1
Dragoons	25
Chasseurs	17
Hussars	7
Lancers	1
Total	54

But the French were not alone. Thirteen allied cavalry regiments also served in the Peninsula.

Table 10.2   Number of Allied cavalry regiments in the Peninsula

Nationality	No. regiments that served in the Peninsula
Grand Duchy of Berg	2
Kingdom of Holland	1
Hanover	1
Kingdom of Italy	4
Kingdom of Naples	2
Duchy of Nassau	1
Poles	1
Kingdom of Westphalia	1
Total	*13*

During the early years of the war dragoons served in divisions which were assigned to the army's reserve. The light cavalry mostly served in brigades that were assigned to the different corps. By 1812 the French armies in Spain had done away with the corps structure and both the light cavalry and dragoons were assigned to cavalry divisions. Initially, reflecting centuries of European custom, dragoons and light cavalry were in separate divisions, but after July 1813 the mounted divisions were mixed and renamed 'cavalry divisions'. In the Army of the North, which had the mission of protecting the French lines of communications, the cavalry regiments operated in brigades, but it was not uncommon for a regiment to be assigned directly to an infantry division. In the east the Italian and Neapolitan regiments usually operated in direct support of the infantry brigades and rarely served with another cavalry regiment.

Authorised strength of the cavalry regiments
On 24 September 1803 French cavalry regiments were reorganised. Each regiment was authorised four squadrons, of which the first three would be the 'war' squadrons, while the 4th Squadron remained at the regimental depot. Authorised regimental strength depended on the type of regiment. The cuirassier and dragoon regiments had the fewest men in a company, while the light cavalry regiments had the most. The organisation of the regiments stayed the same throughout the Peninsular War, except for some few minor changes. The most notable change in the organisation of the regiments was the number of squadrons a regiment was authorised. By 1813, most regiments had at least six squadrons, but none ever had more than four squadrons serving in the Peninsula at one time.

Table 10.3   Authorised strength of French cavalry regiments, 1808

Type of Regiment	No. Squadrons	Authorised strength
Chasseur	4	1,043
Cuirassier	5	1,040
Dragoon	4	1,124
Hussar	4	948

Table 10.4   Authorised strength of a cuirassier regiment, 1808

Unit	No. men
Regimental Headquarters	20
1st Squadron	204
2nd Squadron	204
3rd Squadron	204
4th Squadron	204
5th Squadron	204
Total	1,040

Table 10.5   Authorised strength of a cuirassier regimental headquarters, 1808

Position	English translation	No. authorised
Colonel	Colonel	1
Major	Major	1
Chef d'escadron	Chief of squadron	2
Adjutans-major	Regimental adjutant	2
Quartier-maitre	Quartermaster	1
Chirurgien-major	Surgeon	1
Chirurgien-aide-major	Assistant surgeon	1
Chirurgien-sous-aide	Subassistant surgeon	2
Adjutans sous-officiers	Assistant sergeant major	2
Brigadier trompette	Trumpeter corporal	1
Artiste vétérinaire	Veterinarian	1
Maître tailleur	Master tailor	1
Maître sellier	Master saddler	1
Maître culottier	Master breechesmaker	1
Maître bottier	Master bootmaker	1
Maître armurier	Master armourer	1
Total		20

Table 10.6 Authorised strength of a cuirassier company, 1808

Position	English translation	No. authorised
Captaine	Captain	1
Lieutenant	Lieutenant	1
Sous-lieutenant	Sublieutenant	2
Maréchal des logis-chef	Sergeant major	1
Maréchal des logis	Sergeant	4
Brigadier-fourier	Blacksmith corporal	1
Brigadier	Corporal	8
Trompette	Trumpeter	2
Cuirassiers	Cuirassiers	82
Total		102

Table 10.7 Authorised strength of a dragoon regiment, 1808

Unit	No. men
Regimental Headquarters	20
1st Squadron	276
2nd Squadron	276
3rd Squadron	276
4th Squadron	276
Total	1,124

Table 10.8 Authorised strength of a dragoon regimental headquarters 1808

Position	English translation	No. authorised
Colonel	Colonel	1
Major	Major	1
Chef d'escadron	Chief of squadron	2
Adjutans-major	Regimental adjutant	2
Quartier-maitre	Quartermaster	1
Chirurgien-major	Surgeon	1
Chirurgien-aide-major	Assistant surgeon	1
Chirurgien-sous-aide	Subassistant surgeon	2
Adjutans sous-officiers	Assistant sergeant major	2
Brigadier trompette	Trumpeter corporal	1
Artiste vétérinaire	Veterinarian	1
Maître tailleur	Master Tailor	1
Maître sellier	Master saddler	1

Table 10.8 continued

Position	English translation	No. authorised
Maître bottier	Master bootmaker	1
Maître armurier	Master armourer	1
Maîtreculottier	Master breechesmaker	1
Total		*20*

Table 10.9 Authorised strength of a dragoon company, 1808

Position	English translation	No. authorised
Captaine	Captain	1
Lieutenant	Lieutenant	1
Sous-lieutenant	Sublieutenant	2
Maréchal des logis-chef	Sergeant major	1
Maréchal des logis	Sergeant	4
Brigadier-fourier	Blacksmith corporal	1
Brigadier	Corporal	8
Trompette	Trumpeter	2
Fourier	Blacksmith	1
Dragon	Dragoon	118
Total		*1138*

Table 10.10 Authorised strength of a light cavalry regiment, 1808

Unit	No. men
Regimental Headquarters	19
1st Squadron	232
2nd Squadron	232
3rd Squadron	232
4th Squadron	232
Total	*948*

Table 10.11 Authorised strength of a light cavalry regimental headquarters, 1808

Position	English translation	No. authorised
Colonel	Colonel	1
Major	Major	1
Chef d'escadron	Chief of squadron	2
Adjutans-major	Regimental adjutant	2
Quartier-maitre	Quartermaster	1
Chirurgien-major	Surgeon	1
Chirurgien-aide-major	Assistant surgeon	1

Position	English translation	No. authorised
Chirurgien-sous-aide	Subassistant surgeon	2
Adjutans sous-officiers	Assistant sergeant major	2
Brigadier trompette	Trumpeter corporal	1
Artiste vétérinaire	Veterinarian	1
Maître tailleur	Master tailor	1
Maître sellier	Master saddler	1
Maître bottier	Master bootmaker	1
Maître armurier	Master armourer	1
Total		*19*

Table 10.12   Authorised strength of a light cavalry company, 1808

Position	No. authorised
Captain	1
Lieutenant	1
Second lieutenant	2
Maréchal des logis-chef	1
Maréchal des logis	4
Brigadier-blacksmith	1
Brigadiers	8
Trumpeter	2
Troopers	96
Total	*116*

The regiment was authorised a chief of squadron for every two squadrons it had. The senior company commander in a squadron (usually a captain) commanded the squadron.

Actual strength of a French cavalry regiment in the Peninsula

It was rare for a cavalry regiment in the Peninsula to be at full strength. Most regiments fielded only three squadrons and they were often at 60–70 per cent strength. A few examples include:

Table 10.13   Effective strength of the 25th Dragoons in Spain February, 1810

Unit	Officers	Men	Horses
1st Squadron and HQ	11	189	206
2nd Squadron	5	184	192
3rd Squadron	4	168	178
4th Squadron	5	201	216
Total	25	742	797

Table 10.14   Effective strength of the 26th Dragoon in Spain, November 1811

Unit	Officers	Men	Horses
1st Squadron and HQ	18	185	122
2nd Squadron	8	167	154
3rd Squadron	5	56	62
Total	*31*	*408*	*338*

Table 10.15   Effective strength of the 5th Chasseurs in Spain, December 1811

Unit	Officers	Men	Horses
1st Squadron and HQ	15	161	195
2nd Squadron	9	176	188
3rd Squadron	7	173	169
Total	*31*	*510*	*552*

Numbering of companies in a regiment

The numbering of the companies in a French cavalry regiment depended on how many squadrons a regiment was authorised. Except for the 1st Squadron, the first company in a squadron was always given the number of the squadron. For example, the first company of the 3rd Squadron would be the 3rd Company. The exception was in the 1st Squadron, where the 1st Company was always the Elite Company. Once the first company in a squadron was identified, the second companies would be numbered based on the last number used to identify the first companies.

Table 10.16   Numbering of companies in a four-squadron regiment

Squadron	1st Company	2nd Company
1st Squadron	Elite Company	5th Company
2nd Squadron	2nd Company	6th Company
3rd Squadron	3rd Company	7th Company
4th Squadron	4th Company	8th Company

This sequencing of company names continued the same way even if there were more than four squadrons in a regiment. By 1812 it was not unusual for a regiment to have five or six squadrons. In 1813 the 13th Chasseurs had nine squadrons!

Explanation of the tables following

Regimental colonels   Most regiments had many colonels over the years. Only those individuals who commanded the regiment while it served in Spain are shown. The reader should be mindful that the colonel may not have been with the regiment during the whole time he commanded it. For example, in 1812 the 25th Dragoons was commanded by Colonel Jean-Pierre-Gauthier Leclerc, who was seriously wounded at Salamanca on 22 July 1812 and had to be evacuated to France. On 22 August 1812 he was replaced by Chief of Squadron Mathis, who commanded the regiment in Spain. On 15 October Major Dumolard arrived with replacements and took command of the regiment. Mathis was transferred to the 15th Dragoons, but would not stay with them long. On 23 October Dumolard was seriously wounded in the leg and had to relinquish command. Mathis moved back to the 25th Dragoons and would command the regiment for eight months until it returned to France in June 1813. Colonel Leclerc did not officially give up the command of the regiment until 12 January 1813. His successor, Colonel Augustin Montigny, was not appointed to command until 25 March 1813, not joining the regiment until after it was withdrawn from Spain in June 1813.

Regimental depots   Replacements, both men and horses were organised and trained at the regimental depots before being sent to the regiment in the field. The depot was usually commanded by the regiment's major and often was where the 4th Squadron was located. During the war it was common for a regiment to send the cadre of a depleted squadron in the field back to the depot to organise recruits there into a new squadron. Meanwhile, the balance of the depleted squadron's men left behind in Spain were integrated into the regiment's squadrons remaining in Spain. As soon as the cadre of the squadron that had been sent back to the depot reformed their new squadron, they would bring it back to the regiment. In addition to the main depot, each regiment also had a small depot at Bayonne where the replacements would stage for movement into Spain. A forward depot was occasionally maintained in Burgos.

Arrival in the Peninsula   This is the date the unit crossed the border into Spain. In many cases I have been able to pinpoint the exact date, but most histories provide only the month and year.

Major commands to which assigned   The higher headquarters to which a regiment was assigned changed from time to time. Although the month and year that this occurred can be determined in most cases, the exact date of the event is difficult to ascertain. A regiment might be in the same garrison as its brigade headquarters, but most of the time it cantonments were not. This caused a time delay between when the order was issued by a higher headquarters and when the brigade or regiment received it. Thus an order could take days or weeks to implement.

Most regiments were assigned to a cavalry brigade. However, for a unit assigned to the Armies of Aragon, Catalonia and the North, it was common for it to be assigned to an infantry brigade for a specific operation and then reverted back to division or army control upon completion of the mission. Occasionally a regiment would be split between two brigades and in one case the regiment had elements serving in two different corps. I have listed the various attachments and detachments when known.

Battles and officer casualties This includes the major battles in which the regiment fought and the officer casualties they sustained. For the cavalryman, the Peninsular War was not often a conventional war fought against an organised army, but one conducted against an elusive guerrilla force. There were numerous combats, skirmishes, ambushes and attacks on convoys and isolated outposts that never made it into the history books, but inflicted casualties nevertheless. These casualties are listed under 'Counter-guerrilla operations'. Unfortunately, most regimental histories do not list casualties the regiment sustained unless it was at a battle in which the regiment distinguished itself. Even then, the casualty toll would not be complete. A regimental history might include the killed and wounded and the soldiers who were killed, but it usually did not list the soldiers who were wounded. On the other hand, thanks to A. Martinien's monumental *Tableuax par corps et par batailles des officiers tués et blessés pendant les Guerres de l'Empire*, a fairly detailed record of officer casualties exists. I used it and the regimental histories to compile the list.

The reader should be careful about making assumptions from any casualty list, for they will not provide an accurate picture of the numberof casualties a regiment took while in the Peninsula. The vast majority of losses were non-combat losses – death through disease, exhaustion, bad food and desertion. This attrition in the strength of the regiment is something that was rarely examined by the regimental histories, yet its impact was significant.

For example, between 1 May 1811 and 10 July 1813 the 13th Chasseurs lost in Spain 201 men either killed, died from disease, made prisoner, or deserted. The regiment also had 982 horses die. Of these 201 men, only 27 were killed in combat and 21 taken prisoner. Non-combat losses thus exceeded combat losses by a ratio of 4 to 1!

Departure from the Peninsula It is rare for a history to give the exact date when a unit crossed the border from Spain into France. Usually it will state that the regiment sent the cadre from the 3rd Squadron back and then give a month and a year. It does not specify whether the date is when they left the regiment to return to the regimental depot or when they arrived there. In 1813 many of the regiments were withdrawn from the Peninsular armies. We know when the orders were given, but not the exact date they were carried out.

Chapter Eleven

The Dragoon Regiments

For the French cavalry, the Peninsular War was a dragoon war. Twenty-five of the 30 French dragoon regiments served in it* and represented nearly half of the all the French regiments in the theatre of operations. Yet this figure is deceiving. The dragoon regiments were there in force, usually with strength of three squadrons, but during 1810 and 1811 the regiments had four squadrons. In early 1811 there were 99 dragoon squadrons in the Peninsula. In contrast, the second largest number of cavalry regiments in the Peninsula was the 17 chasseur regiments; yet only 10 of them were there in regimental strength, i.e. with three or more squadrons. Eight of the chasseur regiments had only one squadron or less at any given time in the Peninsula.

Nineteen of the dragoon regiments went into Spain with three squadrons in late 1808, while five went in with only two squadrons. The 22nd Dragoons brought all four squadrons. In January 1809 Napoleon ordered the regiments to send the cadres of third and fourth squadrons back to France and to incorporate the men from those squadrons into the first and second squadrons. His thinking was that it was better for the regiments to have two full strength squadrons than to have four under-strength ones. Not surprisingly, many of the regimental commanders declined to implement his decree until the initial fighting ended in May and June.

The dragoon regiments would fight at half strength until January 1810, when 12 provisional dragoon regiments arrived in northern Spain. These regiments consisted of the 3rd and 4th Squadrons from 24 of the dragoon regiments serving in Spain.† In February five of the provisional dragoon regiments were disbanded and two more were dissolved the following October. The squadrons were not sent back to France, but instead joined

---

* The 7th, 23rd, 28th, 29th and 30th Dragoons never served in the Peninsula.
† Only the 24th Dragoons did not have to provide squadrons.

their parent regiments. The other five provisional dragoon regiments were not disbanded until the following year. This provided the parent regiments with much need reinforcements and most would have at least three squadrons in country through 1812.

On 18 June 1811 Napoleon ordered nine lancer regiments to be created. Instead raising new regiments, six dragoon regiments were to be converted to lancers. Five of those six dragoon regiments were in the Peninsula. It is probably not an overstatement to say that the army commanders were not happy with this order and delayed its implementation as long as possible. The 9th and 10th Dragoons left for France in August, while the 8th Dragoons left in September. It was not until November did the 1st and 3rd Dragoons depart.

After the disaster in Russia in 1812 Napoleon relied upon his dragoon regiments to rebuild his cavalry. At the end of 1812 there were 20 dragoon regiments still serving in Spain. In the winter and following spring of 1813 thirteen of these regiments were ordered to send cadres back to France to help form new regiments. The 15th Dragoons, which still had its 3rd and 4th Squadrons, was ordered to send the cadre from both of them back. Nine other regiments had to give up the cadre of their 3rd Squadrons. The 18th, 19th and 20th Dragoons, which only had two squadrons in the Peninsula, sent the cadre of their 2nd Squadrons. With the departure of its cadre the squadron was disbanded and the remaining dragoons were incorporated into the other squadrons in the regiment. Upon arriving at their depot, the cadre would reform their squadron from the conscripts there. In June Napoleon ordered ten of the dragoon regiments to return to their depots for refitting for future service with the Grande Armée in Germany. By July only 10 dragoon regiments remained. Six months later, in January 1814, Napoleon ordered the nine dragoon regiments in the Army of Spain to move to eastern France. Only the 24th Dragoons in the Army of Aragon stayed in the Peninsula. They would stay until the end. When peace came in April, they had served for 71 continuous months in the Peninsula.

One of the most noticeable things about the organisation of the dragoons in the Peninsula was the pairing of regiments. It was not unusual for two regiments to serve together in the same brigade for many years. These long-term pairings built mutual trust and esprit de corps based on shared dangers, hardship and glory. Some of the more notable brigading of regiments included the 5th and the 12th Dragoons, the 13th and the 22nd Dragoons, the 15th and the 25th Dragoons and the 18th and 19th Dragoons. The 13th and 22nd Dragoons spent almost four years together in the Peninsula, while the 15th and 25th Dragoons were brigaded together 53 of their 56 months in Spain and Portugal!

Table 11.1   1st Dragoon Regiment

Colonels
Paul-Ferdinand-Stanislas Dermoncourt wounded at Talavera (28 Jul.
    1809) and in an ambush by guerrillas (29 Dec. 1809)
Regimental depot
1810 Chartres
Location of squadrons
 Oct.–Nov. 1807 4th Squadron in Spain
 Nov. 1807–Oct. 1808 4th Squadron in Portugal
 Nov. 1808 HQ, 1st, 2nd and 3rd Squadrons in Spain; 4th Squadron in
    France
 Autumn 1809 HQ, 1st and 2nd Squadrons in Spain; 3rd and 4th
    Squadrons in France
 Autumn 1810 HQ, 1st and 2nd Squadrons in Spain; 3rd and 4th
    Squadrons in Portugal
 Dec. 1811 The regiment is back in France at its depot
Arrival in the Peninsula
 Nov. 1807 4th Squadron
 8 Jan. 1808 1 company
 Nov. 1808 HQ, 1st, 2nd and 3rd Squadrons
 Jan. 1810 3rd and 4th Squadrons
Major commands to which assigned
 Oct. 1807 4th Squadron in 2nd Prov. Cavalry Regiment, Maurin's
    Brigade, Kellermann's Division, Junot's Corps
 Nov. 1807 1 company assigned to 1st Prov. Dragoon Regiment, Pryvé's
    Brigade, Grouchy's Division, Moncey's Corps
 Jul. 1808 1 company assigned to 1st Prov. Dragoon Regiment, Pryvé's
    Brigade, Fresia's Division, Dupont's Corps
 Nov. 1808 HQ, 1st, 2nd and 3rd Squadrons in Perreimond's Brigade,
    Tour-Maubourg's Division
 Summer 1809–spring 1811 HQ, 1st and 2nd Squadrons in
    Dermoncourt's Brigade, Tour-Maubourg's Division
 Jan. 1810 3rd and 4th Squadrons in 1st Prov. Dragoon Regiment, Sainte-
    Croix's Brigade, Caulaincourt's Division
 Apr. 1810 3rd and 4th Squadrons in 1st Prov. Dragoon Regiment,
    Sainte-Croix's Brigade, 8th Corps, Army of Portugal
 Spring 1811 HQ, 1st and 2nd Squadrons in Beaumont's Brigade, 1st
    Corps; 3rd and 4th Squadrons in 1st Prov. Dragoon Regiment,
    ? Brigade, 8th Corps
 Jul. 1811 HQ, 1st and 2nd Squadrons in Bron's Brigade, Tour-
    Maubourg's Division, 1st Corps

Battles and officer casualties
  Vimeiro (21 Aug. 1808) 1 killed
  Tarançon (25 Dec. 1808) 1 killed, 1 wounded
  Villarta (31 Jan. 1809) 1 wounded
  Counter-guerrilla operations 1809–11 2 killed, 3 wounded
  Arzobispo (8 Aug. 1809) 2 wounded
  Gallegos (4 Jun. 1810) 1 wounded
  Ciudad Rodrigo (11 Jul. 1811) 1 wounded
  Barrosa 5 wounded
Departure from the Peninsula
  Autumn 1808 4th Squadron
  May 1809 3rd Squadron
  Summer 1811 3rd and 4th Squadrons
  Nov. 1811 HQ and cadre of all squadrons*

Table 11.2   2nd Dragoon Regiment

Colonels
  Pierre Ismert (14 May 1807–3 Dec. 1812) wounded in counter-guerrilla
    operations (25 Mar. 1809); wounded in right foot by shrapnel at
    Talavera (28 Jul. 1809); at Villa-Martine (21 Mar. 1811); at Tarifa (Jan.
    1812); at Monzarbès (14 Nov. 1812)
  Laurent Hoffmayer (8 Feb. 1813–16 Jan. 1814)
Regimental depot
  1810 Maestricht
Location of squadrons
  Dec. 1807 1 company in Spain
  Autumn 1808 1st, 2nd and 3rd Squadrons in Spain; 4th Squadron at
    depot
  Autumn 1810 HQ, 1st and 2nd Squadrons in Spain; 3rd and 4th
    Squadrons in Portugal
  Autumn 1811 1st, 2nd and 3rd Squadrons in Spain; 4th Squadron at
    Depot
  1812 1st, 2nd and 3rd Squadrons in Spain; 4th Squadron in Russia
  1813 HQ, 1st and 2nd Squadrons in Spain; 3rd Squadron in Bavaria; 4th
    Squadron in Danzig
  Autumn 1813 1st, 2nd and 3rd Squadrons in Germany; 4th Squadron in
    Danzig

---

* On 18 June 1811 the 1st Dragoons were redesignated as the 1st Lancers. The men
were reassigned to other dragoon regiments in the Peninsula and the cadre was sent
back to France to form the new regiment.

Table 11.2 2nd Dragoon Regiment continued

Arrival in the Peninsula

Dec. 1807 1 company

Nov. 1808 1st, 2nd and 3rd Squadrons

Jan. 1810 3rd and 4th Squadrons

Major commands to which assigned

Dec. 1807–Jul. 1808 1 company in the 6th Prov. Dragoons, Boussart's Brigade, Fresia's Division, Dupont's Corps

Nov. 1808 HQ, 1st, 2nd and 3rd Squadrons in Perreimond's Brigade, Tour- Maubourg's Division

Summer 1809 HQ, 1st and 2nd Squadrons in Dermoncourt's Brigade, Tour-Maubourg's Division

Oct. 1810 HQ, 1st and 2nd Squadrons in Dermoncourt's Brigade, Tour-Maubourg's Division; 3rd and 4th Squadrons in 1st Prov. Dragoon Regiment, Sainte-Croix's Brigade, 8th Corps, Army of Portugal

Spring 1811 HQ, 1st and 2nd Squadrons in Bron's Brigade, Tour-Maubourg's Division; 3rd and 4th Squadrons in 1st Prov. Dragoon Regiment, ? Brigade, 8th Corps, Army of Portugal

Jul. 1811 HQ and all squadrons in Bron's Brigade, Tour-Maubourg's Division

Sep. 1811 HQ and all squadrons in Perreimond's Brigade, Tour-Maubourg's Division

Nov. 1811 HQ and all squadrons in Squadrons in Bonnemain's Brigade, 1st Corps

Feb. 1812 HQ and all squadrons in Squadrons in Bonnemain's Brigade, Perreimond's 1st Division

Mar. 1812 HQ, 1st, 2nd and 3rd Squadrons in Bonnemain's Brigade, Perreimond's 1st Division

Oct. 1812 HQ, 1st, 2nd and 3rd Squadrons in Ismert's Brigade, Digeon's Division

Feb. 1813 HQ, 1st and 2nd Squadrons in Ismert's 1st Brigade, Tilly's Division

Late Jun. 1813 Regiment transferred to the Grande Armée

Battles and officer casualties

Tudela (23 Nov. 1808) 1 wounded

Tarragon (25 Dec. 1808) 2 wounded

Ucles (13 Jan. 1809) none

Consuegra (28 Feb. 1809) none

Medellin (28 Mar. 1809) none

Escabon (24 Jul. 1809) 1 wounded

Talavera (28 Jul. 1809) 1 wounded

Fort Conception (4 Jul. 1810) 3 wounded, 1 would die from wounds

Barossa (5 Mar. 1811) 1 wounded
Villa-Martine (21 Mar. 1811) 1 wounded
Gaudelet (16 May 1811) 1 killed, 1 would die from wounds
Alcala (20 Oct. 1811) 1 wounded
Tarifa (Jan. 1812) 1 wounded
Monzarbès (14 Nov. 1812) 1 wounded
Villa-Martine (26 Nov. 1812) 1 wounded
Costromonos (2 Jun. 1813) 1 wounded
Vitoria (21 Jun. 1813) 1 captured
Departure from the Peninsula
   Spring 1809 3rd Squadron
Mar. 1812 4th Squadron
Spring 1813 3rd Squadron
Jun. 1813 HQ, 1st and 2nd Squadrons

Notes During the five years the 2nd Dragoons served in the Peninsula the regiment had only two officers killed and two who died of wounds. However, the 2nd Dragoon's commander, Colonel Pierre Ismert, was wounded five times during his four years in Spain!

Table 11.3   3rd Dragoon Regiment

Colonels
Joseph Grézard (25 Sep. 1806–14 Jul. 1810) wounded at San Carpio (23 Nov. 1809)
Pierre-Marie Berruyer (2 Aug. 1810–18 Jan. 1814)
Denis-Eloi Ludot (9 Oct. 1810–5 Nov. 1810)*
Regimental depot
   1808 Versailles
   1810 Soissons
Location of Squadrons
   Oct.–Nov. 1807 4th Squadron in Spain
   Nov. 1807–Oct. 1808 4th Squadron in Portugal
   Jan. 1809 HQ, 1st, 2nd and 3rd Squadrons in Spain; 4th Squadron in France
   Summer 1809 HQ, 1st and 2nd Squadrons in Spain; 3rd Squadron in Germany; 4th Squadron in France

---

* Colonel Ludot was named colonel of the regiment in August 1810, but never took command. Less than three months after being promoted, he was given command of the 14th Dragoons. Colonel Berruyer was relieved of his command of the regiment on 16 September 1811, for assaulting a commissary officer. He was appointed commander of the 2nd Lancers on 1 January 1812.

Table 11.3   3rd Dragoon Regiment continued

Location of Squadrons

Jan. 1810 HQ and all squadrons in Spain

Autumn 1810 HQ and all squadrons in Portugal

Dec. 1811 The regiment is back in France at its depot

Arrival in the Peninsula

Nov. 1807 4th Squadron

Jan. 1809 HQ, 1st, 2nd and 3rd Squadrons

Jan. 1810 3rd and 4th Squadrons

Major commands to which assigned

Oct. 1807 4th Squadron in 2nd Prov. Cavalry Regiment in Maurin's Brigade, Kellermann's Division, Junot's Corps

Nov. 1808 HQ, 1st, 2nd and 3rd Squadrons in Grézard's Brigade, Milet's Division

Jan. 1809 HQ, 1st, 2nd and 3rd Squadrons in Milet's Brigade, Kellermann's Division

Jun. 1809 HQ, 1st and 2nd Squadrons in Milet's Brigade, Kellermann's Division

Jan. 1810 HQ, 1st and 2nd Squadrons in Milet's Brigade, Kellermann's Division; 3rd and 4th Squadrons part of 4th Prov. Dragoon Regiment, Gardanne's Brigade, Caulaincourt's Division

Jun. 1810 HQ and all squadrons in Milet's Brigade, Trelliard's Division

Sep. 1810–May 1811 HQ and all squadrons in Lorcet's Brigade, Trelliard's Division

Jun.–Aug. 1811 HQ, 1st and 2nd Squadrons in Cavrois's Brigade, Trelliard's Division

Battles and officer casualties

Operations in vicinity of Burgos (Jan.–Oct. 1809) 4 wounded

San Carpio (23 Nov. 1809) 2 wounded

Alba de Tormes (28 Nov. 1809) 1 killed, 1 wounded

Bussaco (27 Sep. 1810) none

Pombal (11 Mar. 1811) none

Fuentes de Oñoro (5 May 1811) none

Departure from the Peninsula

Sep. 1808 4th Squadron

May 1809 3rd Squadron

Jul. 1811 3rd and 4th Squadrons

Nov. 1811 HQ, 1st and 2nd Squadrons*

---

* On 18 June 1811 the 3rd Dragoons were redesignated as the 2nd Lancers. The cadre, the trumpeters and 10 men per company were sent back to France, to form the new regiment. The remaining men were reassigned to the 6th and 11th Dragoon Regiments.

Notes The 3rd Dragoons entered Portugal on 15 September 1810 with 563 horses. On 5 February 1811 they received another 80 horses. However, due to the hardships of the campaign, they could mount only 183 men by 1 May. The regiment lost over 72 per cent of their mounts in 8 months.

Table 11.4   4th Dragoon Regiment

Colonels
  Auguste-Etienne-Marie Lamotte (13 Jan. 1806–21 Mar. 1809)
  Pierre Farine (7 Apr. 1809–25 May 1811) captured at Usagre (25 May 1811)
  Jean-Baptiste Bouquerot des Essarts (28 Oct. 1811–28 Dec. 1815)
Regimental depot
  1810 Moulins
Location of Squadrons
  Oct.–Nov. 1807 4th Squadron in Spain
  Nov. 1807–Oct. 1808 4th Squadron in Portugal
  Nov. 1808 1st, 2nd and 3rd Squadrons in Spain; 4th Squadron in France
  Autumn 1809 1st, 2nd, 3rd and 4th Squadrons in Spain
  Autumn 1810 HQ, 1st and 2nd Squadrons in Spain; 3rd and 4th Squadrons in Portugal
  1811 1st, 2nd and 3rd Squadrons in Spain; 4th Squadron in France
  Autumn 1813 1st, 2nd and 3rd Squadrons in France; 4th Squadron in Germany
  Jan. 1814 HQ and all squadrons in France
Arrival in the Peninsula
  23 Oct. 1807 4th Squadron
  Nov. 1808 1st, 2nd and 3rd Squadrons
  Jan. 1810 3rd and 4th Squadrons
Major commands to which assigned
  Oct. 1807 4th Squadron in 3rd Prov. Dragoon Regiment, Maurin's Brigade, Kellermann's Division, Junot's Corps
  Nov. 1808 1st, 2nd and 3rd Squadrons in Oullenbourg's Brigade, Tour-Maubourg's Division
  Jul. 1809 HQ, 1st and 2nd Squadrons in Cavrois's Brigade, Tour-Maubourg's Division
  Jan. 1810 HQ, 1st and 2nd Squadrons in Cavrois's Brigade, Tour-Maubourg's Division; 3rd and 4th Squadrons in 2nd Prov. Dragoon Regiment, Sainte-Croix's Brigade, Caulaincourt's Division
  Oct. 1810 HQ, 1st and 2nd Squadrons in Queunot's Brigade, Tour-Maubourg's Division; 3rd and 4th Squadrons in 2nd Prov. Dragoon Regiment, Sainte-Croix's Brigade, 8th Corps

Table 11.4 continued

Major commands to which assigned

May 1811 HQ, 1st and 2nd Squadrons in Bron's Brigade, Tour-Maubourg's Division; 3rd and 4th Squadrons in 2nd Prov. Dragoon Regiment, ? Brigade, 8th Corps

Sep. 1811 HQ and 3 squadrons in Bouvier des Eclaz's Brigade, Tour-Maubourg's Division; 1 squadron assigned to Perreimond's Brigade in 1st Corps

Nov. 1811 HQ, 1st, 2nd and 3rd Squadrons in Perreimond's Brigade, Tour-Maubourg's Division

Feb. 1812 HQ, 1st, 2nd and 3rd Squadrons in Lallemand's Brigade, Perreimond's Division

Apr. 1812 HQ, 1st, 2nd and 3rd Squadrons in Briche's Brigade, Tour-Maubourg's Division

Mar. 1812 HQ, 1st, 2nd and 3rd Squadrons in Sparre's Brigade, Digeon's Division

Jul. 1812 HQ, 1st, 2nd and 3rd Squadrons in Bouquerot des Essarts's Brigade, Digeon's Division

Oct. 1812 HQ, 1st, 2nd and 3rd Squadrons in Ismert's 1st Brigade, Digeon's Division

Mar. 1813 HQ, 1st and 2nd Squadrons, Ismert's Brigade, Tilly's Division

Jul. 1813 Avy's Brigade Trelliard's Division

Sep. 1813–Jan. 1814 HQ, 1st and 2nd Squadrons, Ismert's Brigade, Trelliard's Division

Battles and officer casualties

Vimeiro (21 Aug. 1808) 1 wounded

Ucles (13 Jan. 1809) none

Medellin (28 Mar. 1809) none

Talavera (27–28 Jul. 1809) 3 wounded

Ocaña (19 Nov. 1809) none

Alcanizas (7 Jun. 1810) none

Pombal (11 Mar. 1811) none

Fuentes de Oñoro (5 May 1811) none

Badajoz (25 Jan.–1 Mar.1811) none

Albuera (16 Apr. 1811) 3 killed, 1 wounded*

Usagre (25 May 1811) 1 killed, 1 wounded, regimental commander captured

Vitoria (21 Jun. 1813) 1 wounded

Departure from the Peninsula

Aug. 1808 4th Squadron

---

* The regimental history states that at Albuera 2 officers and 25 dragoons were killed and 9 officers wounded.

May 1809 3rd Squadron
Oct. 1811 4th Squadron
Spring 1813 3rd Squadron
Jan. 1814 HQ, 1st and 2nd Squadrons

Table 11.5 5th Dragoon Regiment

Colonels
Louis-Ernest-Joseph de Sparre (28 Mar. 1808–11 Apr. 1812)
Jean-Baptiste-Louis Morin (1 Jun. 1812–12 Mar. 1814) was shot twice
  and received multiple sabre cuts at Vitoria (21 Jun. 1813), wounded at
  Saint Pierre d'Irube (13 Dec. 1813)
Regimental depot
Mar. 1807 Kulm
Jul. 1807 Saint-Germain
1810 Provins
Location of squadrons
Oct.–Nov. 1807 4th Squadron in Spain
Nov. 1807–Nov. 1808 4th Squadron in Portugal
Nov. 1808 HQ, 1st and 2nd Squadrons in Spain; 3rd Squadron in
  France; 4th Squadron in Portugal
Jan. 1811 HQ, 1st and 2nd Squadrons in Spain; 3rd and 4th Squadrons
  in Portugal
Aug. 1813 HQ, 1st and 2nd Squadrons in France; 3rd Squadron in
  Germany; 4th Squadron in Danzig; 5th and 6th Squadrons in depot at
  Provins
Jan. 1814 Regiment sent to Eastern France
Arrival in the Peninsula
18 Oct. 1807 4th Squadron
14 Oct. 1808 HQ, 1st, 2nd and 3rd Squadrons
Oct. 1810 3rd and 4th Squadrons
Major commands to which assigned
Oct. 1807 4th Squadron in 3rd Prov. Dragoon Regiment, Maurin's
  Brigade, Kellermann's Division, Junot's Corps
Oct. 1808 HQ, 1st, 2nd and 3rd Squadrons in Maupetit's Brigade, 4th
  Corps
Jun. 1809 HQ, 1st and 2nd Squadrons in Barthélemi's Brigade,
  Milhaud's Division
Sep. 1809 HQ, 1st and 2nd Squadrons in Noirot's Brigade, Milhaud's
  Division
Jan. 1810 HQ, 1st and 2nd Squadrons in Noirot's Brigade, Milhaud's
  Division; 3rd and 4th Squadrons part of 8th Prov. Dragoon Regiment,
  Bron's Brigade, Caulaincourt's Division

Table 11.5 continued

Major commands to which assigned

May 1810 HQ, 1st and 2nd Squadrons in Noirot's Brigade, Milhaud's Division; 3rd and 4th Squadrons part of 8th Prov. Dragoon Regiment, Bron's Brigade, 6th Military Government

Jan. 1811 HQ and all Squadrons in Noirot's Brigade, Milhaud's Division

Oct. 1811 HQ and all squadrons in 1st Brigade, Soult's Division

Nov. 1811 HQ and all squadrons in Ormancey's Brigade, Soult's Division

Feb. 1812 HQ, 1st, 2nd and 3rd Squadrons in Briche's Brigade, Soult's Division

Mar. 1812 HQ, 1st, 2nd and 3rd Squadrons in Briche's Brigade, Soult's Division

Jul. 1812 HQ, 1st, 2nd and 3rd Squadrons in Bouquerot des Essarts's Brigade, Digeon's Division

Oct.1812 HQ, 1st, 2nd and 3rd Squadrons in Sparre's Brigade, Soult's Division

Apr. 1813 1st and 2nd Squadrons in Sparre's Brigade, Digeon's Division

Jul. 1813–Jan. 1814 HQ, 1st and 2nd Squadrons in Sparre's Brigade, Soult's Division

Jan. 1814 Regiment transferred to the Grande Armée

Battles and officer casualties

Medellin (28 Mar. 1809) 1 wounded

Talavera (27–28 Jul. 1809) none

Ocaña (19 Nov. 1809) 2 wounded

Counter-guerrilla operations (1809–13) 2 killed, 7 wounded

Baza (3 Nov. 1810) 2 wounded

Vitoria (21 Jun. 1813) 6 wounded, 1 would die from wounds

St. Pierre d'Irrube (13 Dec. 1813) 1 wounded

Departure from the Peninsula

8 Dec. 1808 4th Squadron sails from Lisbon

May 1809 3rd Squadron

Mar. 1812 4th Squadron

Jan. 1813 3rd Squadron

Jan. 1814 HQ, 1st and 2nd Squadrons

Table 11.6   6th Dragoon Regiment

Colonels

Cyrille-Simon Picquet (13 Feb. 1808–8 Mar. 1813) wounded at Salamanca (22 Jul. 1812)

Claude Mugnier (29 Mar. 1813–26 Jan. 1816)

Regimental depot
1809 Pau
1810 Namur
1811 Limoges
Location of squadrons
Dec. 1807 1 company in Spain; rest of regiment in France
29 Dec. 1808 HQ, 1st, 2nd and 3rd Squadrons at Bayonne; 4th Squadron in depot
Jan. 1809 HQ, 1st, 2nd and 3rd Squadrons in Spain; 4th Squadron in France
Autumn 1809 HQ, 1st and 2nd Squadrons in Spain; 3rd and 4th Squadron in France
Spring 1810 HQ and all squadrons in Spain
Autumn 1810 HQ and all squadrons in Portugal
Jun. 1811 HQ, 1st, 2nd and 3rd Squadrons in Spain; 4th Squadron in France
Autumn 1811 HQ and all squadrons in Spain
Summer 1812 HQ, 1st and 2nd Squadrons in Spain; 3rd and 4th Squadrons in France
Autumn 1813 1st, 2nd and 4th Squadrons in Germany
Arrival in the Peninsula
Dec. 1807 1 company
Jan. 1809 HQ, 1st, 2nd and 3rd Squadrons
Spring 1810 3rd and 4th Squadrons
Autumn 1811 4th Squadron
Major commands to which assigned
Dec. 1807–Jul. 1808 1 company part of 6th Prov. Dragoons, Boussart's Brigade, Fresia's Division, Dupont's Corps
Nov. 1808 HQ, 1st, 2nd and 3rd Squadrons in Grézard's Brigade, Milet's Division
Jan. 1809 HQ, 1st, 2nd and 3rd Squadrons in Milet's Brigade, Kellermann's Division
Jul. 1809–Apr. 1810 HQ, 1st and 2nd Squadrons in Milet's Brigade, Kellermann's Division
Jan. 1810 3rd and 4th Squadrons part of 4th Prov. Dragoon Regiment, Garndanne's Brigade, Caulaincourt's Division
Apr. 1810 HQ and all 4 squadrons in Milet's Brigade, Trelliard's Division
Jul. 1810–Apr. 1811 HQ and all 4 squadrons in Lorcet's Brigade, Trelliard's Division
Apr. 1811 HQ and all 4 squadrons in Lorcet's Brigade, Trelliard's Division

Table 11.6 continued

Major commands to which assigned

Jul.–Oct. 1812 HQ, 1st, 2nd and 3rd Squadrons in Ornano's Brigade, Trelliard's Division

Nov. 1811–Feb. 1812 HQ and all Squadrons in Piquet's Brigade, Cavrois's Division

Mar. 1812 HQ and all squadrons in Picquet's Brigade, Boyer's Division

Jul. 1812 HQ, 1st and 2nd Squadrons in Picquet's Brigade, Boyer's Division

Oct. 1812–Jun. 1813 HQ, 1st and 2nd Squadrons in Thévenez d'Aoust's Brigade, Boyer's Division

Late Jun. 1813 Regiment transferred to the Grande Armée

Battles and officer casualties

Medina de Rio Seco (14 Jul. 1808) 1 wounded

Counter-guerrilla operations 1808–13 1 killed, 11 wounded

Alba de Tormes (28 Nov. 1809) 1 killed

Apesta (10 Mar. 1811) 1 killed, 1 wounded

Fuentes de Oñoro (5 May 1811) 3 wounded, 1 would die from wounds

El Bodon (25 Aug. 1811) 1 killed, 1 wounded

Salamanca (22 Jul. 1812) 9 wounded, 1 would die from wounds

Villadrigo (23 Oct. 1812) 1 wounded

Vitoria (21 Jun. 1813) 1 wounded

Departure from the Peninsula

Feb. 1809 3rd Squadron

May 1811 4th Squadron

Winter 1812 3rd and 4th Squadrons

Jun. 1813 HQ, 1st and 2nd Squadrons

Table 11.7 8th Dragoon Regiment

Colonels

Alexandre-Louis-Robert Girardin d'Ermenonville (7 Dec. 1806–22 Jun. 1811)

Regimental depot

1810 Molsheim

Location of squadrons

Dec. 1807 1 company in Spain;

Nov. 1808 HQ, 1st, 2nd and 3rd Squadrons in Spain; 4th Squadron in depot

Autumn 1809 HQ, 1st and 2nd Squadrons in Spain; 3rd and 4th Squadrons in France

Jan. 1810 HQ and all squadrons in Spain

Oct. 1810 HQ, 1st and 2nd Squadrons in Portugal; 3rd and 4th

Squadrons in Spain
Dec. 1811 The regiment was back in France at its depot
Arrival in the Peninsula
8 Jan. 1808 1 company
Nov. 1808 HQ, 1st, 2nd and 3rd Squadrons
Major commands to which assigned
Nov. 1807 1 company assigned to 2nd Prov. Dragoon Regiment, Pryvé's
Brigade, Grouchy's Division, Moncey's Corps
Jun. 1808 1 company assigned to 2nd Prov. Dragoon Regiment, Pryvé's
Brigade, Fresia's Division, Dupont's Corps
Nov. 1808 HQ, 1st, 2nd and 3rd Squadrons in Debelle's Brigade,
Lasalle's Division, 2nd Corps
Dec. 1808 HQ, 1st, 2nd and 3rd Squadrons in Debelle's Brigade, 2nd
Corps
Jan. 1809 HQ, 1st, 2nd and 3rd Squadrons in Debelle's Brigade,
Francheschi's Division, 2nd Corps
Jul. 1809 HQ, 1st and 2nd Squadrons in Debelle's Brigade, Soult's
Division, 2nd Corps
Aug. 1809–Aug. 1811 HQ, 1st and 2nd Squadrons in d'Ermenomville's
Brigade, Soult's Division, 2nd Corps
Jan. 1810 3rd and 4th Squadrons part of 8th Prov. Dragoon Regiment,
Bron's Brigade, Caulaincourt's Division
Apr.–Oct. 1810 3rd and 4th Squadrons part of 8th Prov. Dragoon
Regiment, Bron's Brigade, 6th Military Government
Aug. 1811 HQ, 1st and 2nd Squadrons in Cavrois's Brigade, Trelliard's
Division
Battles and officer casualties
Sahagun (21 Dec. 1808) 3 wounded
Counter-guerrilla operations (1809–11) 1 killed, 2 wounded
Ocaña (19 Nov. 1809) 1 wounded
Bussaco (27 Sep. 1810) 1 wounded
Departure from the Peninsula
May 1809 3rd Squadron
Oct. 1810 3rd and 4th Squadron*
Sep. 1811 HQ, 1st and 2nd Squadrons†

---

* The 8th Provisional Dragoons was disbanded in October 1810. I can find no information on what happened to the 3rd and 4th Squadrons of the 8th Dragoons. The
regimental headquarters and the 1st and 2nd Squadrons were deep in Portugal, so they
did not join the regiment. They probably returned to France.
† On 18 June 1811 the 8th Dragoons were redesignated as the 3rd Lancers. The cadre,
the trumpeters and 10 men per company were sent back to France to form the new
regiment, the remaining men were reassigned to other regiments in the Peninsula.

Table 11.8   9th Dragoon Regiment

Colonels
Mathieu Queunot (31 Dec. 1806–13 Oct. 1811)
Regimental depot
1808 Versailles
1810 Chateaudun
Location of squadrons
Oct.–Nov. 1807 4th Squadron in Spain
Nov. 1807–Jul. 1808 4th Squadron in Portugal
14 Jul. 1808 HQ, 1st and 2nd Squadrons at Rennes, 3rd Squadron at
  Versailles, 4th Squadron at Elvas, Portugal.
Nov. 1808 HQ, 1st and 2nd Squadrons in Spain; 3rd and 4th Squadrons
  in France
Apr. 1809 HQ, 1st and 2nd Squadrons in Portugal, 3rd Squadron in
  Germany, 4th Squadron at depot
Jul. 1811 HQ, 1st, 2nd, 3rd and 4th Squadrons in Spain
Arrival in the Peninsula
17 Oct. 1807 4th Squadron
Oct. 1808 HQ, 1st and 2nd Squadrons
Spring 1810 3rd and 4th Squadrons
Major commands to which assigned
Oct. 1807 4th Squadron in 4th Prov. Cavalry Regiment, Maurin's
  Brigade, Kellermann's Division, Junot's Corps
Sep. 1808 HQ, 1st and 2nd Squadrons in Milhaud's Division, 2nd Corps
Oct. 1808 HQ, 1st and 2nd Squadrons in Bordessoulle's Brigade,
  Lasalle's Division, 2nd Corps
Jan. 1809 HQ, 1st and 2nd Squadrons in Montbrun's Brigade, Lasalle's
  Division, 2nd Corps
Apr. 1809 HQ, 1st and 2nd Squadrons in Franceschi's Division, 2nd
  Corps
Jul. 1809–Apr. 1810 HQ, 1st and 2nd Squadrons in Cavrois's Brigade,
  Tour-Maubourg's Division
Jan. 1810 3rd and 4th Squadrons part of 2nd Prov. Dragoon Regiment,
  Sainte-Croix's Brigade, Caulaincourt's Division
Apr. 1810 HQ, 1st and 2nd Squadrons in Queunot's Brigade, Tour-
  Maubourg's Division; 3rd and 4th Squadrons part of 2nd Prov.
  Dragoon Regiment, Sainte-Croix's Brigade, 8th Corps
Oct. 1810–Jun. 1811 HQ, 1st and 2nd Squadrons in Queunot's Brigade,
  Tour-Maubourg's Division; 3rd and 4th Squadrons part of 2nd Prov.
  Dragoon Regiment, ? Brigade, 8th Corps
Jul.–Aug. 1811 HQ, 1st and 2nd Squadrons in Bouvier des Eclaz's

Brigade, Tour-Maubourg's Division
Battles and officer casualties
 Beja (26 Jun. 1808) none
 Talavera (27–28 Jul. 1809) 1 would die from wounds
 Ocaña (19 Nov. 1809) none
 Counter-guerrilla operations 1809–11 3 killed, 6 wounded
Departure from the Peninsula
 Dec. 1808 4th Squadron
 Jun. 1811 3rd and 4th Squadrons
 Aug. 1811 HQ and cadre of 1st and 2nd Squadrons*

Table 11.9 10th Dragoon Regiment

Colonels
 Jean-Baptiste Dommanget (20 Sep. 1806–6 Aug. 1811)
Regimental depot
 1810 Amiens
Location of squadrons
 Dec. 1807 4th Squadron in Spain
 Jun. 1808 4th Squadron in Portugal
 Jan.1809 HQ, 1st and 2nd Squadrons in Spain; 3rd and 4th Squadrons in
  France†
 Jan. 1810–Jun. 1811 HQ and all squadrons in Spain
 Jun.–Nov. 1811 HQ, 1st and 2nd Squadrons in Spain; 3rd and 4th
  Squadrons in France
Arrival in the Peninsula
 Jan. 1809 HQ, 1st and 2nd Squadrons
 Jan. 1810 3rd and 4th Squadrons
Major commands to which assigned
 Dec. 1807 4th Squadron was part of the 6th Prov. Dragoon Regiment,
  Boussart's Brigade, Grouchy's Division, Dupont's Corps
 Nov. 1808–Jan. 1809 HQ, 1st and 2nd Squadrons and 7th Company in
  Carrié's Brigade, Milet's Division
 Jan.–Nov. 1809 HQ, 1st and 2nd Squadrons and 7th Company in
  Carrié's Brigade, Kellermann's Division
 Nov. 1809–Apr. 1810 HQ, 1st and 2nd Squadrons in Dommanget's
  Brigade, Kellermann's Division

---

* On 18 June 1811 the 9th Dragoons were redesignated the 4th Lancers. The men were reassigned to other dragoon regiments in the Peninsula and the cadre was sent back to France to form the new regiment.
† The 4th Squadron was captured at Bailen in July 1808 and was being reconstituted.

Table 11.9 continued

Major commands to which assigned

Jan. 1810 3rd and 4th Squadrons part of the 5th Prov. Dragoon Regiment, Gardanne's Brigade, Caulaincourt's Division

Apr.–Aug. 1810 HQ and all squadrons in Cavrois's Brigade, Trelliard's Division

Aug. 1810–Mar. 1811 HQ and all squadrons part of the garrison of Cuidad Rodrigo

Apr.–Jun. 1811 HQ and all squadrons in Cavrois's Brigade, Trelliard's Division

Jun.–Aug. 1811 HQ, 1st and 2nd Squadrons in Cavrois's Brigade, Trelliard's Division

Battles and officer casualties

Carprio (23 Nov. 1809) 1 killed, 1 wounded

Counter-guerrilla operations (1809–11) 6 wounded, 1 would die from wounds

Alba de Tormes (28 Nov. 1810) 1 wounded

Fuentes de Oñoro (5 May 1811) 4 wounded

Departure from the Peninsula

Dec. 1808 4th Squadron

Jun. 1811 3rd and 4th Squadrons

Aug.1811 HQ, 1st and 2nd Squadrons*

Notes Unlike the most of the other dragoon regiments, the 10th Dragoons did not take its 3rd Squadron when it went to Spain in January 1809. The 4th Squadron was still in Portugal when the plans were being made for the move to Spain, so the 3rd Squadron was left at the depot in order to help rebuild the 4th Squadron when it returned.

Table 11.10 11th Dragoon Regiment

Colonels

Pierre-François-Marie Dejean (13 Feb. 1807–16 Aug. 1811)

François-Alexandre Thévenez d'Aoust (14 Oct. 1811–19 Apr. 1815) wounded in the eyes by a ricochet at Villadrigo (22 Oct. 1812) and in the neck at Vitoria (21 Jun. 1813)

Regimental depot

1808 Hesdin

1811 Limoges

---

* On 18 June 1811 the 10th Dragoons were redesignated as the 5th Lancers. The men were reassigned to the 17th and 27th Dragoon Regiments and the cadre was sent back to France, to form the new regiment.

Location of squadrons

Dec. 1807 Regiment in France; 1 company in Spain

Jan.–Mar. 1809 HQ, 1st, 2nd and 3rd Squadrons in Spain; 4th Squadron in France

Mar. 1809–Jan. 1810 HQ, 1st and 2nd Squadrons in Spain; 3rd and 4th Squadrons in France

Jan. 1810 HQ and all squadrons in Spain

Autumn 1810 HQ and all squadrons in Portugal

Summer 1811 HQ, 1st and 2nd Squadrons in Spain; 3rd and 4th Squadrons in France

Aug. 1811–Mar. 1813 HQ, 1st and 2nd Squadrons in Spain; 3rd and 4th Squadrons in France

Mar.–Jun. 1813 HQ, 1st and 2nd Squadrons in Spain; 3rd and 4th Squadrons in Germany

Summer 1813 Regiment was in Germany

Arrival in the Peninsula

Jan. 1808 1 company

Nov. 1808 HQ, 1st, 2nd and 3rd Squadrons

Spring 1810 3rd and 4th Squadrons

Major commands to which assigned

Aug. 1807–May 1808 1 company assigned to 1st Prov. Dragoon Regiment, Pryvé's Brigade, Grouchy's Division, Moncey's Corps

Jun. 1808 1 company assigned to 1st Prov. Dragoon Regiment, Pryvé's Brigade, Fresia's Division, Dupont's Corps

Nov. 1808–Jan. 1809 HQ, 1st, 2nd and 3rd Squadrons in Carrié's Brigade, Milet's Division

Jan.–May 1809 HQ, 1st, 2nd and 3rd Squadrons in Carrié's Brigade, Kellermann's Division

May–Nov. 1809 HQ, 1st and 2nd Squadrons in Carrié's Brigade, Kellermann's Division

Nov. 1809–Apr. 1810 HQ, 1st and 2nd Squadrons in Dommanget's Brigade, Kellermann's Division

Jan. 1810 3rd and 4th Squadrons part of the 5th Prov. Dragoon Regiment, Gardanne's Brigade, Caulaincourt's Division

Apr. 1810–Jun. 1811 HQ and all squadrons in Cavrois's Brigade, Trelliard's Division

Jun.–Oct. 1811 HQ, 1st and 2nd Squadrons in Ornano's Brigade, Trelliard's Division

Oct. 1811–Feb. 1812 HQ, 1st and 2nd Squadrons in Cavrois's Brigade, Army of Portugal

Feb.–Oct. 1812 HQ, 1st and 2nd Squadrons in Piquet's Brigade, Boyer's Division

---

Table 11.10 continued

Major commands to which assigned
  Oct.1812–Jun. 1813 HQ, 1st and 2nd Squadrons in Thévenez d'Aoust's
    Brigade, Boyer's Division
  Late Jun. 1813 Regiment transferred to the Grande Armée
Battles and officer casualties
  Bailen (19 Jul. 1808) 1 wounded
  Alba de Tormes (29 Nov. 1809) none
  Fuentes de Oñoro (5 May 1811) 1 killed, 3 wounded
  Salamanca (22 Jul. 1812) 2 officers; 2 wounded
  Alba de Tormes (23 Jul. 1812) 2 wounded
  Villadrigo (22 Oct. 1812) 1 wounded
  Vitoria (21 Jun. 1813) 1 wounded
Departure from the Peninsula
  Mar. 1809 3rd Squadron
  Aug. 1811 3rd and 4th Squadrons
  Jun. 1813 HQ, 1st and 2nd Squadrons

Table 11.11   12th Dragoon Regiment

Colonels
  Girault de Martigny wounded by guerrillas 26 Mar. 1809, died of
    wounds 30 Mar. 1809.
  Jean Merlhes (14 Aug. 1809–Dec. 1811)*
  Alexis Bessard-Graugniard (9 Aug. 1812–19 Apr. 1815)
Regimental depot
  1810 Schelestatt
Location of squadrons
  Jan. 1808 1 company in Spain
  Nov. 1808 HQ, 1e and 2nd Squadrons in Spain ; 3rd and 4th Squadrons
    in France
  Jan. 1810 HQ and all squadrons in Spain
  Aug. 1811 HQ, 1st and 2nd Squadron in Spain; 3rd and 4th Squadrons
    in France
  Autumn 1813 HQ, 1st and 2nd Squadron in France; 3rd Squadron in
    Germany; 4th Squadron in Danzig
  Arrival in the Peninsula 8 Jan. 1808 1 company
  Nov. 1808 HQ, 1st and 2nd Squadrons
  Jan. 1810 3rd and 4th Squadrons
Major commands to which assigned
  Nov. 1807–Jun. 1808 1 company assigned to 2nd Prov. Dragoon
    Regiment, Pryvé's Brigade, Grouchy's Division, Moncey's Corps

---

* Colonel Merlhes returned to France in late 1811 because of poor health.

Jun. 1808 1 company assigned to 2nd Prov. Dragoon Regiment, Pryvé's Brigade, Fresia's Division, Dupont's Corps

Oct. 1808 HQ, 1st and 2nd Squadrons in Debelle's Brigade, Milhaud's Division

Nov. 1808–Aug. 1809 HQ, 1st and 2nd Squadrons in Barthélemi's Brigade, Milhaud's Division

Sep. 1809–Sep. 1811 HQ, 1st and 2nd Squadrons in Noirot's Brigade, Milhaud's Division

Jan. 1810 3rd and 4th Squadrons part of 6th Prov. Dragoon Regiment, Bessières's Brigade, Caulaincourt's Division

Feb.–May 1810 3rd and 4th Squadrons part of 6th Prov. Dragoon Regiment, Bessières's Brigade, Kellermann's Division

Jun.–Aug. 1810 3rd and 4th Squadrons part of 6th Prov. Dragoon Regiment, Bessières's Brigade, 6th Military Government

Aug. 1810–Jul. 1811 3rd and 4th Squadrons part of 6th Prov. Dragoon Regiment, Poinsot's Brigade, 6th Military Government

Oct. 1811–Feb. 1812 HQ and all squadrons in 1st Brigade, Soult's Division Feb.–Apr. 1812 HQ, 1st, 2nd and 3rd Squadrons in Bouillé's Brigade, Soult's Division

Apr. 1812–Jan. 1813 HQ, 1st, 2nd and 3rd Squadrons in Sparre's Brigade, Soult's Division

Jan.–May 1813 HQ, 1st and 2nd Squadrons, Sparre's Brigade, Digeon's Division

May–Jul. 1813 HQ, 1st and 2nd Squadrons in Grouvel's Brigade, Digeon's Division

Jul. 1813–Jan. 1814 HQ, 1st and 2nd Squadrons in Sparre's Brigade, Soult's Division

Jan. 1814 Regiment transferred to the Grande Armée

Battles and officer casualties

Counter-guerrilla operations (1809–13) 1 killed, 11 wounded, 1 would die from wounds

Almonacid (11 Aug. 1809) 1 killed

Ocaña (19 Nov. 1809) 3 killed, 1 would die from wounds

Vitoria (21 Jun. 1813); 1 wounded

Nive 1 wounded

Departure from the Peninsula

Mar. 1812 4th Squadron

Jan. 1813 3rd Squadron

Jan. 1814 HQ, 1st and 2nd Squadrons

Notes Except for six weeks in May and June 1813, the 12th Dragoons were in the same brigade as the 5th Dragoons from August 1809 until they left the Peninsula in January 1814.

Table 11.12   13th Dragoon Regiment

Colonels

Pierre-Victor Laroche (20 Sep. 1806–18 Dec. 1809) died from a putrid fever at 7:00 p.m. on 18 Dec. 1809.

Marie-Antoine Reiset (20 Jan. 1810–9 Sep. 1812) shot in the left foot at Astorga (Mar. 1810); by multiple sabre cuts at Las Rosas (11 Aug. 1812); and at Majalahonda (15 Aug. 1812)

Marie-Frederic Monginot (29 Mar. 1813–8 Sep. 1813)*

Regimental depot

1810 Namur

Location of squadrons

Nov. 1808 HQ, 1st, 2nd and 3rd Squadrons in Spain; 4th Squadron in France

Autumn 1813 1st, 2nd, 3rd and 5th Squadrons in Germany; 4th Squadron in Danzig

Arrival in the Peninsula

8 Jan. 1808 1 company

Dec. 1808 HQ, 1st, 2nd and 3rd Squadrons

Jan. 1810 3rd and 4th Squadrons

Major commands to which assigned

Dec. 1807 1 company assigned to 1st Prov. Dragoon Regiment, Pryvé's Brigade, Grouchy's Division, Moncey's Corps

Jun. 1808 1 company assigned to 1st Prov. Dragoon Regiment, Pryvé's Brigade, Fresia's Division, Dupont's Corps

Dec. 1808–Jun. 1809 HQ, 1st, 2nd and 3rd Squadrons in Viallannes's Brigade, Lorge's Division,

Jun.–Nov. 1809 HQ, 1st and 2nd Squadrons in Cambacérès's Brigade, Lorge's Division

Nov. 1809–Feb. 1810 HQ, 1st and 2nd Squadrons in Beaurgard's Brigade, Lorge's Division

Jan. 1810 3rd and 4th Squadrons part of 11th Prov. Dragoon Regiment, Lamotte's Brigade, Caulaincourt's Division

Feb.–Oct. 1810 HQ and all squadrons in Reiset's Brigade, Marizy's Division, 5th Corps

Oct. 1810–Feb. 1811 HQ and all squadrons in Marizy's Brigade, Houssaye's Division

Feb.–Jul. 1811 HQ and all squadrons in Reiset's Brigade, Houssaye's Division,

Oct. 1811–Spring 1812 HQ and all squadrons in Reiset's Brigade,

---

* Colonel Monginot died on 8 September 1813, after being wounded in the arm at the combat of Pirna on 22 August 1813.

Trelliard's Division

Mar.–Aug. 1812 HQ, 1st, 2nd and 3rd Squadrons in Reiset's Brigade, Trelliard's Division

Aug. 1812–Deccember 1812 HQ, 1st, 2nd and 3rd Squadrons in Dard's Brigade, Trelliard's Division

Jan.–Jun. 1813 HQ, 1st and 2nd Squadrons in Dard's Brigade, Trelliard's Division

Late Jun. 1813 Regiment transferred to the Grande Armée

Battles and officer casualties

Counter-guerrilla operations (1808–13) 11 wounded

Bailen (19 Jul. 1808) 1 wounded

Oporto (29 Mar. 1809) 1 wounded

Arzobispo (8 Aug. 1809) 1 wounded

Valverde (19 Feb. 1810) 2 wounded

Villafranca (29 Mar. 1812) 4 wounded

Las Rosas (11 Aug. 1812) 1 killed, 6 wounded

Majalahonda (15 Aug. 1812) 1 wounded

Vitoria (21 Jun. 1813) 1 wounded

Departure from the Peninsula

Mar. 1809 3rd Squadron

Mar. 1812 4th Squadron

Dec. 1812 3rd Squadron

Jun. 1813 HQ, 1st and 2nd Squadrons

Table 11.13   14th Dragoon Regiment

Colonels

Joseph Bouvier des Eclaz (12 Sep. 1806 -4 Nov. 1810)

Denis-Eloi Ludot (5 Nov. 1810–29 May 1813)

Alphonse-Alexandre Séguier (25 Nov. 1813–10 Aug. 1814)

Regimental depot

Dec. 1808 Maëstricht, small depot at Valdemoro

Location of squadrons

Jan. 1808 Regiment was in Niebusch; 8th Company was in Spain

Jan. 1809 HQ, 1st, 2nd and 3rd Squadrons in Spain, 4th Squadron in depot

Aug. 1809 HQ, 1st and 2nd Squadrons in Spain, 3rd Squadron in depot, 4th Squadron in the Tyrol

1810 HQ and all squadrons in Spain

1811 3rd Squadron rejoins regiment; 4th Squadron in the Army of the Center

Summer 1813 HQ, 1st and 2nd Squadrons in Spain, 3rd Squadron in Germany; 4th Squadron in Danzig

Table 11.13 continued

Location of squadrons
 Jan. 1814 Eastern France
Arrival in the Peninsula
 8 Jan. 1808 8th Company
 Nov. 1808 1st, 2nd and 3rd Squadrons
 Jan. 1810 3rd and 4th Squadrons
Major commands to which assigned
 Nov. 1807 8th Company assigned to 1st Prov. Dragoon Regiment,
   Pryvé's Brigade, Grouchy's Division, Moncey's Corps
 Jan. 1808 8th Company assigned to 1st Prov. Dragoon Regiment,
   Pryvé's Brigade, Grouchy's Division, Moncey's Corps
 Jun. 1808 8th Company assigned to 1st Prov. Dragoon Regiment,
   Pryvé's Brigade, Fresia's Division, Dupont's Corps
 Nov. 1808–Apr. 1809 HQ,1st, 2nd and 3rd Squadrons in Oullenbourg's
   Brigade, Tour-Maubourg's Division
 Apr.–7 Nov.1809 HQ, 1st and 2nd Squadrons in Oullenbourg's Brigade,
   Tour-Maubourg's Division
 7 Nov. 1809–Jun. 1811 HQ, 1st and 2nd Squadrons in Bouvier des
   Eclaz's* Brigade, Tour-Maubourg's Division
 Nov. 1809–Feb. 1810 3rd and 4th Squadrons part of 3rd Prov. Dragoon
   Regiment, Sainte-Croix's Brigade, Caulaincourt's Division
 Mar.–Oct. 1810 3rd and 4th Squadrons part of 3rd Prov. Dragoon
   Regiment, Sainte-Croix's Brigade, 8th Corps
 Oct. 1810–Jun. 1811 3rd and 4th Squadrons part of 3rd Prov. Dragoon
   Regiment, ? Brigade, 8th Corps
 Jun.–Oct. 1811 HQ, 1st, 2nd and 3rd Squadrons in Bouvier des Eclaz's
   Brigade, Tour-Maubourg's Division
 Oct. 1811–Feb. 1812 HQ, 1st, 2nd, 3rd Squadrons in Perreimond's
   Brigade, Tour-Maubourg's Division
 Feb.–Mar. 1812 HQ, 1st, 2nd and 3rd Squadrons in Lallemand's Brigade,
   Digeon's Division
 Feb.–Oct. 1812 HQ, 1st, 2nd and 3rd Squadrons in Lallemand's Brigade,
   Digeon's Division
 Oct.–Nov. 1812 HQ, 1st, 2nd and 3rd Squadrons in Ludot's Brigade,
   Digeon's Division
 Nov. 1812–Apr. 1813 HQ, 1st, 2nd and 3rd Squadrons† in Ormancey's

---

* Colonel Bouvier des Eclaz, the 14th Dragoon's commander, took command of the
brigade on 7 November 1809. He was promoted to general of brigade in October 1810.
He would continue to command the brigade until October 1811, when he was recalled
to France.
† The 3rd Squadron departed for France in March.

Brigade, Digeon's Division

May–Jul. 1813 HQ, 1st and 2nd Squadrons in Ormancey's Brigade, Tilly's Division

Jul. 1813–Jan. 1814 HQ, 1st and 2nd Squadrons in Ormancey's Brigade, Trelliard's Division

Jan. 1814 Regiment transferred to the Grande Armée

Battles and officer casualties

Counter-guerrilla operations (1808–13) 3 killed, 6 wounded

Madrid (2 May 1808) 1 wounded

Bailen (19 Jul. 1808) 3 captured*

Ledrija (7 Dec. 1808) 2 murdered

Medellin (28 Mar. 1809) 3 killed, 4 wounded

Talavera (27 Jul. 1809) 2 wounded

Gebora (19 Feb. 1811) 1 wounded

Albuera (16 May 1811) 1 wounded

Departure from the Peninsula

Apr. 1809 3rd Squadron

Oct. 1812 4th Squadron

Mar. 1813 3rd Squadron

Jan. 1814 HQ, 1st and 2nd Squadrons

Notes Sergeant Damien of the 14th Dragoons, who captured a Swiss colonel at Valselle on 24 February 1809, was himself captured on 3 May 1811 and imprisoned on the Balearic island of Cabrera. In 1813 he was in a group of soldiers who seized a Spanish guard boat and sailed it to Algiers. He was able to enlist the aid of Barbary Corsairs and return to France. He rejoined the 14th Dragoons that December. Denis Smith writes at length about this escape, although he does not mention Damien by name.[†]

In May 1809 the 14th Dragoons and the 5th Dragoons were formed temporarily into a new brigade commanded by General Maupetit. The 14th Dragoons returned to General Oullenbourg's Brigade on 15 June.

Table 11.14   15th Dragoon Regiment

Colonels
Jean-Baptiste Treuille de Beaulieu (14 Feb. 1807–13 Aug. 1809)
Jean Claude Boudinhon-Valdec (14 Aug. 1809–3 Feb. 1814)
Regimental depot
1808 Versailles

---

* The 8th Company had 130 officers and dragoons assigned to it when it joined the 2nd Provisional Dragoon Regiment. All were either killed or captured when General Dupont surrendered at Bailen.

† Smith, Denis, *The Prisoners of Cabrera*, pp. 151–6.

Table 11.14   continued

Regimental depot

1810 Laon

1811 Soissons

Location of squadrons

Oct.–Nov. 1807 4th Squadron in Portugal

Nov. 1807–Oct. 1808 4th Squadron in Portugal

Dec. 1808 HQ, 1st, 2nd and 3rd Squadrons in Spain; 4th Squadron in France

May 1809 HQ, 1st and 2nd Squadrons in Spain; 3rd and 4th Squadrons in France

Spring 1810 HQ and all squadrons in Spain

Autumn 1810 HQ and all squadrons in Portugal

Spring 1811–Dec. 1812 HQ and all squadrons in Spain

May 1813 HQ, 1st and 2nd Squadrons in Spain, 3rd and 4th Squadrons in France

Autumn 1813 1st, 2nd, 3rd and 4th Squadrons in Germany

Arrival in the Peninsula

Nov. 1807 4th Squadron

Dec. 1808 HQ, 1st, 2nd and 3rd Squadrons

Jan. 1810 3rd and 4th Squadrons

Major commands to which assigned

Autumn 1807 1 company of the 4th Squadron in 4th Prov. Cavalry Regiment, Maurin's Brigade, Kellermann's Division, Junot's Corps

Dec. 1808–May 1809 HQ, 1st, 2nd and 3rd Squadrons in Fournier-Sarlovèse's Brigade, Lorge's Division

May–Dec. 1809 HQ, 1st and 2nd Squadrons in Fournier-Sarlovèse's Brigade, Lorge's Division

Dec. 1809–Feb. 1810 HQ, 1st and 2nd Squadrons in Ornano's Brigade, Lorge's Division

Jan.–Feb. 1810 3rd and 4th Squadrons in 12th Prov. Dragoon Regiment, Lamotte's Brigade, Caulaincourt's Division

Feb.–May 1810 HQ and all squadrons in Ornano's Brigade, Lorge's Division

May–Aug. 1810 HQ and all squadrons in Gardanne's Brigade, Trelliard's Division

in Cavrois's Brigade

Sep. 1810–Jul. 1811 HQ and all squadrons in Ornano's Brigade, Trelliard's Division

Jul.–Sep. 1811 HQ and all squadrons in Cavrois's Brigade, Trelliard's Division

Oct. 1811–Feb. 1812 HQ, 1st and 2nd Squadrons in Boyer's Brigade,

Cavrois's Division

Nov. 1811–Oct. 1813 3rd and 4th Squadrons attached to 5th Military Government in Burgos

Mar.–Jul. 1812 HQ and all squadrons in Carrié's Brigade, Boyer's Division

Jul. 1812–Jun. 1813 HQ, 1st and 2nd Squadrons in Boudinhon-Valdec's Brigade, Boyer's Division

Jun. 1813 Regiment transferred to the Grande Armée

Battles and officer casualties

Lugo (19 May 1809) 1 killed, 1 wounded

Doucos (8 Jun. 1809) 3 wounded

Tamames (18 Oct. 1809) 2 wounded

Alba de Tormes (28 Nov. 1809) 3 wounded, 1 would die from wounds

Counter-guerrilla operations (1809–13) 2 killed, 3 wounded

Fuentes de Oñoro (5 May 1811) none

El Bodon (25 Sep. 1811) 1 killed, 1 wounded

Castrillo (18 Jul. 1812) 1 killed, 1 wounded

Salamanca (22 Jul. 1812) 1 wounded

Vitoria (21 Jun. 1813) 1 killed, 4 wounded

Departure from the Peninsula

Dec. 1808 4th Squadron

May 1809 3rd Squadron

May 1813 3rd and 4th Squadrons

Jun. 1813 HQ, 1st and 2nd Squadrons

Table 11.15　16th Dragoon Regiment

Colonels

Sebastien Vial (19 Jul. 1799–19 Nov. 1809) killed at Ocaña.

François Grouvel (20 Jan. 1810–30 May 1813)

Alexandre-Pierre Gery (31 May 1813–7 Oct. 1814)

Regimental depot

1810 Strasbourg

1811 Saintes

Location of squadrons

Dec. 1807 1 company in Spain

Nov. 1808 HQ, 1st and 2nd Squadrons in Spain; 3rd and 4th Squadrons in France

Summer 1809 HQ, 1st and 2nd Squadrons in Spain; 3rd and 4th Squadrons in Germany

Autumn 1810 HQ, 1st and 2nd Squadrons in Spain; 3rd and 4th Squadrons in Portugal

Table 11.15 continued

Location of squadrons

Dec. 1812 HQ, 1st, 2nd and 3rd Squadrons in Spain; 4th Squadron in France

Apr. 1813 HQ, 1st and 2nd Squadrons in Spain; 3rd and 4th Squadrons in France

Aug. 1813 HQ, 1st and 2nd Squadrons in France; 3rd and 4th Squadrons in Germany; 5th Squadron at Saintes

Arrival in the Peninsula

Nov. 1808 HQ, 1st and 2nd Squadrons

Jan. 1809 3rd Squadron

Jan. 1810 3rd and 4th Squadrons

Major commands to which assigned

Dec. 1807–Jul. 1808 1 company in the 6th Prov. Dragoons, Boussart's Brigade, Fresia's Division, Dupont's Corps

Nov. 1808–Jun. 1809 HQ, 1st and 2nd Squadrons in Barthélemi's Brigade, Milhaud's Division

Jul.–Nov. 1809 HQ, 1st and 2nd Squadrons in Digeon's Brigade, Milhaud's Division

7–19 Nov. 1809 HQ, 1st and 2nd Squadrons in Vial's Brigade, Milhaud's Division

19 Nov. 1809–Jul. 1811 HQ, 1st and 2nd Squadrons in Corbineau's Brigade, Milhaud's Division

Jan. 1810 3rd and 4th Squadrons part of 6th Prov. Dragoon Regiment, Bessières's Brigade, Caulaincourt's Division

Feb.–May 1810 3rd and 4th Squadrons part of 6th Prov. Dragoon Regiment, Bessières's Brigade, Kellermann's Division

Jun.–Aug. 1810 3rd and 4th Squadrons part of 6th Prov. Dragoon Regiment, Bessières's Brigade, 6th Military Government

Aug. 1810–Jul. 1811 3rd and 4th Squadrons part of 6th Prov. Dragoon Regiment, Poinsot's Brigade, 6th Military Government

Jul.–Oct. 1811 HQ and all squadrons in Noirot's Brigade, Soult's Division

Oct. 1811–Feb. 1812 HQ and all squadrons in 1st Brigade, Soult's Division

Feb.–Apr. 1812 HQ and all squadrons in Bouillé's Brigade, Soult's Division

Apr. 1812–Aug. 1812 HQ and all squadrons in Sparre's Brigade, Soult's Division

Aug.–Nov. 1812 HQ and all squadrons in Squadrons in Ormancey's Brigade, Soult's Division

Dec. 1812–Jan. 1813 HQ, 1st, 2nd and 3rd Squadrons in Ruat's Brigade,

Soult's Division

Jan.–Apr. 1813 HQ, 1st, 2nd and 3rd Squadrons in Sparre's Brigade, Digeon's Division

Apr.–May 1813 HQ, 1st and 2nd Squadrons in Sparre's Brigade, Digeon's Division

May–Jul. 1813 HQ, 1st and 2nd Squadrons in Grouvel's Brigade, Digeon's Division

Jul. 1813–Jan. 1814 HQ, 1st and 2nd Squadrons in Ormancey's Brigade, Trelliard's Division

Jan. 1814 Regiment transferred to the Grande Armée

Battles and officer casualties

Talavera (27–28 Jul. 1809) none

Arzobispo (8 Aug. 1809) 1 killed

Ocaña (19 Nov. 1809) 1 killed, 1 wounded

Alcala Real (20 Jan. 1810) no casualties

Counter-guerrilla operations (1810–12) 2 killed, 3 wounded

Screening the Duero (31 May–2 Jun. 1813) 1 wounded

Vitoria (21 Jun. 1813) 1 killed

Departure from the Peninsula

Dec. 1807 1 company

Apr. 1809 3rd Squadron

29 Nov. 1812 4th Squadron*

15 Apr. 1813 3rd Squadron†

Jan. 1814 HQ, 1st and 2nd Squadrons

Table 11.16   17th Dragoon Regiment

Colonels

Frédéric-Auguste Beurmann (27 Feb. 1806–6 Aug. 1811)

Albert-François-Joseph Larcher (14 Oct. 1811–18 Jul. 1812)‡

Joachim Hyppolyte Lepic (6 Feb. 1813–14 Apr. 1815) wounded in the left knee at Leipzig (19 Oct. 1813) and the left leg at Arcis-sur Aube (20 Feb. 1814)

Regimental depot

Haguenau

---

* The 4th Squadron was disbanded, and its men were incorporated into the other squadrons. It was reformed at the depot in Saintes.

† The 3rd Squadron was disbanded and its men were incorporated into the 1st and 2nd Squadrons.

‡ Colonel Larcher was killed in a duel on 18 July 1812.

Table 11.16   continued

Location of squadrons

Dec. 1807 1 company in Spain

Nov. 1808 HQ, 1st, 2nd and 3rd Squadrons in Spain; 4th Squadron in France

Autumn 1810 HQ and all squadrons in Spain

Jul. 1811 HQ, 1st, 2nd and 3rd Squadrons in Spain; 4th Squadron in France

Autumn 1812 HQ, 1st, 2nd and 3rd Squadrons in Spain; 4th Squadron in France

Sep. 1813 HQ, 1st and 2nd Squadrons in France; 3rd Squadron in Germany; 4th Squadron in Danzig

Arrival in the Peninsula

Dec. 1807 1 company

Nov. 1808 HQ, 1st, 2nd and 3rd Squadrons

Jan. 1810 3rd and 4th Squadrons

Major commands to which assigned

Dec. 1807–Jul. 1808 1 company part of 6th Prov. Dragoons, Boussart's Brigade, Fresia's Division, Dupont's Corps

Nov. 1808–May 1809 HQ, 1st, 2nd and 3rd Squadrons in Marizy's Brigade, Houssaye's Division

May 1809–May 1810 HQ, 1st and 2nd Squadrons in Marizy's Brigade, Houssaye's Division

Jan.–Feb. 1810 3rd and 4th Squadrons in 9th Prov. Dragoon Regiment, Bron's Brigade, Caulaincourt's Division

Feb.–Apr. 1810 3rd and 4th Squadrons in 9th Prov. Dragoon Regiment, Bron's Brigade, Kellermann's Division

Apr.–Oct. 1810 3rd and 4th Squadrons in 9th Prov. Dragoon Regiment, Bron's Brigade, 6th Military Government

Jun.–Oct. 1810 HQ, 1st and 2nd Squadrons in Digeon's Brigade, Houssaye's Division

Oct.–Nov. 1810 HQ and all squadrons in Bron's Brigade, Houssaye's Division

Nov. 1810–Apr. 1811 HQ and all squadrons in Bron's Brigade, Tour-Maubourg's Division

May–Jun. 1811 HQ and all squadrons in Bouvier des Eclaz's Brigade, Tour-Maubourg's Division

Jul.–Sep. 1811 HQ and all squadrons on independent duty in the Army of the South

Sep.–Nov. 1811 HQ and all squadrons in Bron's Brigade, Army of the South's Reserve

Nov. 1811–Feb. 1812 HQ and all squadrons in Lallemand's Brigade,

Army of the South's Reserve

Feb.–Mar. 1812 HQ and all squadrons in Lallemand's Brigade, Perreimond's Division

Mar.–Oct. 1812 HQ, 1st, 2nd and 3rd Squadrons in Lallemand's Brigade, Digeon's Division

Oct.–Nov. 1812 HQ, 1st, 2nd and 3rd Squadrons in Ludot's Brigade, Digeon's Division

Nov. 1812–Apr. 1813 HQ, 1st, 2nd and 3rd Squadrons in Ormancey's Brigade, Digeon's Division

Apr.–Jul. 1813 HQ, 1st and 2nd Squadrons, Ormancy's Brigade, Tilly's Division

Jul.–Sep. 1813 HQ, 1st and 2nd Squadrons in Avy's Brigade, Trelliard's Division

Oct. 1813–Jan. 1814 HQ, 1st and 2nd Squadrons in Ormancy's Brigade, Trelliard's Division

Jan. 1814 Regiment transferred to the Grande Armée

Battles and officer casualties

Madrid (2 Dec. 1808) 3 wounded

Corunna (15 Jan. 1809) 1 wounded

Braga (26 Mar. 1809) 2 wounded

Oporto (28 Mar. 1809) 1 wounded

Amarante (12 May 1809) 1 wounded

Arzobispo (8 Aug. 1809) 2 wounded

Counter-guerrilla operations 1810–13 6 wounded

Albuera (16 May 1811) 3 wounded, 1 would die from wounds

Maguilla (11 Jun. 1812) 2 wounded

Departure from the Peninsula

May 1809 3rd Squadron

Feb. 1812 4th Squadron

Winter 1813 3rd Squadron

Jan. 1814 HQ, 1st and 2nd Squadrons

Notes The only officer in the 17th Dragoons to die from the result of combat during the 5 years the regiment was in the Peninsula was Lieutenant Petit, who was severely wounded at Albuera on 16 May 1811 and would die from wounds on 23 July.

Table 11.17   18th Dragoon Regiment

Colonels

Justin Lafitte (30 Sep. 1806–10 Oct. 1812)

Benoist-François Dard (11 Oct. 1812–1 Aug. 1814)

Table 11.17 continued

Regimental depot

1808 Haguenau

1811 Angoulême

Location of squadrons

Nov. 1808 HQ, 1st, 2nd and 3rd Squadrons in Spain, 4th Squadron in France

Mar. 1809 HQ, 1st, 2nd and 3rd Squadrons in Portugal, 4th Squadron in France

Jun. 1809 3rd and 4th Squadrons in France

Jan. 1810 HQ and all squadrons in Spain

Jan. 1811 HQ and all squadrons in Spain

Jan. 1813 HQ, 1st and 2nd Squadrons in Spain, 3rd and 4th Squadrons in France

Jun. 1813 HQ and all squadrons in France; 3rd Company in Germany

Arrival in the Peninsula

8 Jan. 1808 1 company

16 Nov. 1808 HQ, 1st, 2nd, 3rd and 4th Squadrons

Jan. 1810 3rd and 4th Squadrons

Major commands to which assigned

Oct. 1807 1 company assigned to 1st Prov. Dragoon Regiment, Pryvé's Brigade, Grouchy's Division, Moncey's Corps

Jan. 1808 Company assigned to 1st Prov. Dragoon Regiment, Pryvé's Brigade, Grouchy's Division, Moncey's Corps

Jun. 1808 1 company assigned to 1st Prov. Dragoon Regiment, Pryvé's Brigade, Fresia's Division, Dupont's Corps

Nov. 1808 HQ, 1st, 2nd and 3rd Squadrons in Davenay's Brigade, Houssaye's Division

Dec. 1808–Jun. 1809 HQ, 1st, 2nd and 3rd Squadrons in Caulaincourt's Brigade, Houssaye's Division

Jun.–Sep. 1809 HQ, 1st and 2nd Squadrons in Caulaincourt's Brigade, Houssaye's Division

Sep. 1809–Oct. 1811 HQ, 1st and 2nd Squadrons in Saint-Genies's Brigade, Houssaye's Division

Jan.–Feb. 1810 3rd and 4th Squadrons in 9th Prov. Dragoon Regiment, Bron's Brigade, Caulaincourt's Division

Feb.–Apr. 1810 3rd and 4th Squadrons in 9th Prov. Dragoon Regiment, Bron's Brigade, Kellermann's Division

Apr.–Oct. 1810 3rd and 4th Squadrons in 9th Prov. Dragoon Regiment, Bron's Brigade, 6th Military Government

Oct. 1811–Jan. 1812 HQ and all squadrons in Mermet's Brigade, Trelliard's Division

Jan. 1812–Aug. 1812 HQ and all squadrons in Reiset's Brigade, Trelliard's Division

Sep. 1812–Jan. 1813 HQ, 1st, 2nd and 3rd Squadrons in Dard's Brigade, Trelliard's Division

Jan.–Apr. 1813 HQ, 1st and 2nd Squadrons in Dard's Brigade, Trelliard's Division

Apr. 1813 1st Squadron in Dard's Brigade, Trelliard's Division

Late Jun. 1813 Regiment transferred to the Grande Armée

Battles and officer casualties

Bailen (19 Jul. 1808) 4 captured, 3 murdered*

Somosierra (30 Nov. 1808) none

Corunna (16 Jan. 1809) none

Oporto (29 Mar. 1809) 1 wounded

Canaveles (30 Mar. 1809) 1 killed, 2 wounded

Amarante (18 Apr. 1809) none

Arzobispo (8 Aug. 1809) 3 wounded,

Majahalonda (11 Aug. 1812) 4 wounded

Vitoria (21 Jun. 1813) none

Departure from the Peninsula

Jun. 1809 3rd Squadron

Oct. 1812 4th Squadron

Jan. 1813 3rd Squadron

Apr. 1813 2nd Squadron

Jun. 1813 HQ and 1st Squadron

Table 11.18   19th Dragoon Regiment

Colonels

Jean-Marie-Noel Delisle de Falcon Saint-Genies (20 Sep. 1806–6 Aug. 1811)

Joseph Antoine Mermet (14 Oct. 1811–16 May 1816)

Regimental depot

1810 Strasbourg

Location of squadrons

Nov. 1808 HQ, 1st, 2nd and 3rd Squadrons in Spain; 4th Squadron in France

---

* On 7 December, when word reached the local Spaniards that the prisoners would be moved to the prison hulks at Cadiz, a mob led by priests, attacked the officers outside their quarters. Among those who were killed were three officers the 18th Dragoons: Major Baron the commander of the 1st Provisional Dragoon Regiment, Captain Martin and Lieutenant Marignol.

Table 11.18 continued

Location of squadrons

Autumn 1809 HQ, 1st and 2nd Squadrons in Spain; 3rd and 4th
  Squadrons in Austria

Jan. 1810–Jan. 1812 HQ and all squadrons in Spain

Feb.–Dec. 1812 HQ, 1st, 2nd and 3rd Squadrons in Spain; 4th Squadron
  in France

Jan.–Mar. 1813 HQ, 1st and 2nd Squadrons in Spain; 3rd Squadron in
  France; 4th Squadron in Germany

May 1813 HQ and 1st Squadron in Spain; 3rd and 4th Squadrons in
  Germany

Arrival in the Peninsula

8 Jan. 1808 1 company

Nov. 1808 HQ, 1st, 2nd and 3rd Squadrons

Spring 1810 3rd and 4th Squadrons

Major commands to which assigned

Oct. 1807–Jun. 1808 1 company assigned to 1st Prov. Dragoon
  Regiment, Pryvé's Brigade, Grouchy's Division, Moncey's Corps

Jun. 1808 1 company assigned to 1st Prov. Dragoon Regiment, Pryvé's
  Brigade, Fresia's Division, Dupont's Corps

Nov. 1808 HQ, 1st, 2nd and 3rd Squadrons in Davenay's Brigade,
  Houssaye's Division

Dec. 1808–Jun. 1809 HQ, 1st, 2nd and 3rd Squadrons in Caulaincourt's
  Brigade, Houssaye's Division

Jun.–Sep. 1809 HQ, 1st and 2nd Squadrons in Caulaincourt's Brigade,
  Houssaye's Division

Sep. 1809–Oct. 1810 HQ, 1st and 2nd Squadrons in Squadrons in Saint-
  Genies's Brigade, Houssaye's Division

Jan.–Feb. 1810 3rd and 4th Squadrons in 10th Prov. Dragoon Regiment,
  Bron's Brigade, Caulaincourt's Division

Feb.–Apr. 1810 3rd and 4th Squadrons in 10th Prov. Dragoon Regiment,
  Bron's Brigade, Kellermann's Division

Apr.–Oct. 1810 3rd and 4th Squadrons in 10th Prov. Dragoon Regiment,
  Bron's Brigade, 6th Military Government

Oct. 1810–Oct. 1811 HQ and all squadrons in Saint-Genies's Brigade,
  Houssaye's Division

Oct. 1811–Oct. 1812 HQ and all squadrons in Mermet's Brigade,
  Trelliard's Division

Oct. 1812–Apr. 1813 HQ and all squadrons in Rozat's Brigade,
  Trelliard's Division

Apr.–Jun. 1813 1st Squadron in Rozat's Brigade, Trelliard's Division

Late Jun. 1813 Regiment transferred to the Grande Armée

Battles and officer casualties
Bailen (19 Jul. 1808) 3 captured
Somosierra (30 Nov. 1808) none
Corunna (16 Jan. 1809) none
Portugal (Jan.–Mar. 1809) 4 wounded
Canaveles (30 Mar. 1809) 2 wounded
Counter-guerrilla operations (1810–11) 1 killed, 3 wounded
Arzobispo (8 Aug. 1809) 3 killed, 7 wounded
Majahalonda (11 Aug. 1812) 5 wounded
Departure from the Peninsula
Autumn 1809 3rd Squadron
Jan. 1812 4th Squadron
Dec. 1812 3rd Squadron
13 Apr. 1813 2nd Squadron
Jun. 1813 HQ and 1st Squadron

Table 11.19 20th Dragoon Regiment

Colonels
Jean-Baptiste-Juvénal Corbineau (7 Jan. 1807–6 Aug. 1811)
Pierre Jean Baptiste Martin Desargus (14 Oct. 1811–19 Apr. 1815)
Regimental depot
Maestricht
Location of squadrons
Jan. 1808 1 company in Spain; HQ and all squadrons in France
Nov. 1808 HQ, 1st, 2nd and 3rd Squadrons in Spain; 4th Squadron in France
Autumn 1809 HQ, 1st and 2nd Squadrons in Spain; 3rd and 4th Squadrons in France
Autumn 1810 HQ and all squadrons in Spain
Jul. 1811 HQ, 1st and 2nd Squadrons in Spain; 3rd and 4th Squadrons in France
Autumn 1812 HQ, 1st, 2nd and 3rd Squadrons in Spain; 4th Squadron in France
Autumn 1813 HQ, 1st and 2nd Squadrons in France; 3rd Squadron in Germany; 4th Squadron in Danzig
Arrival in the Peninsula
8 Jan. 1808 1 company
Nov. 1808 HQ, 1st, 2nd and 3rd Squadrons
Spring 1810 3rd and 4th Squadrons

Table 11.19 continued

Major commands to which assigned

Nov. 1807–Jun. 1808 1 company assigned to 2nd Prov. Dragoon Regiment, Pryvé's Brigade, Grouchy's Division, Moncey's Corps

Jun. 1808 1 company assigned to 2nd Prov. Dragoon Regiment, Pryvé's Brigade, Fresia's Division, Dupont's Corps

Nov. 1808 HQ, 1st, 2nd and 3rd Squadrons in Digeon's Brigade, Tour-Maubourg's Division, attached to Marshal Lannes's force

Dec. 1808 HQ, 1st, 2nd and 3rd Squadrons in Digeon's Brigade attached to 6th Corps

Jan.–Jun. 1809 HQ, 1st, 2nd and 3rd Squadrons in Digeon's Brigade, Tour-Maubourg's Division

Jul. 1809–Apr. 1811 HQ, 1st and 2nd Squadrons in Corbineau's Brigade, Milhaud's Division

Jan. 1810 3rd and 4th Squadrons part of 7th Prov. Dragoon Regiment, Bessières's Brigade, Caulaincourt's Division

Feb.–May 1810 3rd and 4th Squadrons part of 7th Prov. Dragoon Regiment, Bessières's Brigade, Kellermann's Division

Jun.–Aug. 1810 3rd and 4th Squadrons part of 7th Prov. Dragoon Regiment, Bessières's Brigade, 6th Military Government

Aug. 1810–Jul. 1811 3rd and 4th Squadrons part of 7th Prov. Dragoon Regiment, Poinsot's Brigade, 6th Military Government

May–Oct. 1811 HQ and all squadrons in Bron's Brigade, Tour-Maubourg's Division

Nov. 1811–Feb. 1812 HQ and all squadrons in Lallemand's Brigade, Tour-Maubourg's Division

Feb. 1812 HQ and all squadrons were ordered back to France but in the Spring it was diverted to the Army of the North

Autumn 1812–Feb. 1813 HQ, 1st, 2nd and 3rd Squadrons in Cassan's Brigade, Abbé's Division

Mar.–Apr. 1813 HQ, 1st and 2nd Squadrons in Cassan's Brigade, Abbé's Division

Apr.–Jun. 1813 1st Squadron in Cassan's Brigade, Abbé's Division

Late Jun. 1813 Regiment transferred to the Grande Armée

Battles and officer casualties

Bailen (19 Jul. 1808) 3 wounded

Albuera (16 May 1811) 3 killed, 9 wounded, 1 would die from wounds

Usagre (25 May 1811) 2 wounded

Counter-guerrilla operations May 1811–Jun. 1813 1 killed, 1 wounded

Departure from the Peninsula

May 1809 3rd Squadron

Summer 1812 4th Squadron

Feb. 1813 3rd Squadron
Mar. 1813 HQ and 2nd Squadron
Jun. 1813 1st Squadron

Table 11.20 21st Dragoon Regiment

Colonels
Jean-Baptiste-Charles-René-Joseph Mas de Polart (22 Dec. 1801–2 Mar.
  1809)
Jean-François-Noel Ruat (3 Mar. 1809–17 Jan. 1813)
Jean-Baptiste Saviot (29 Mar. 1813–25 Aug. 1814)
Regimental depot
  1810 Belfort
  1811 Saintes
Location of squadrons
Nov. 1808 HQ, 1st and 2nd Squadrons in Spain; 3rd and 4th Squadrons
  in France
Jan. 1810 HQ and all squadrons in Spain
Jun. 1813 HQ, 1st and 2nd Squadrons in France; 3rd and 4th Squadrons
  in Germany
Arrival in the Peninsula
8 Jan. 1808 1 company
Nov. 1808 HQ, 1st and 2nd Squadrons
Spring 1810 3rd and 4th Squadrons
Major commands to which assigned
Nov. 1807–Jun. 1808 1 company assigned to 2nd Prov. Dragoon
  Regiment, Pryvé's Brigade, Grouchy's Division, Moncey's Corps
Jun. 1808 1 company assigned to 2nd Prov. Dragoon Regiment, Pryvé's
  Brigade, Fresia's Division, Dupont's Corps
Nov. 1808–Jun. 1809 HQ, 1st and 2nd Squadrons in Barthélemi's
  Brigade, Milhaud's Division
Jul.–Nov. 1809 HQ, 1st and 2nd Squadrons in Digeon's Brigade,
  Milhaud's Division
7–19 Nov. 1809 HQ, 1st and 2nd Squadrons in Vial's Brigade, Milhaud's
  Division
19 Nov. 1809–Jul. 1811 HQ, 1st and 2nd Squadrons in Corbineau's
  Brigade, Milhaud's Division
Major commands to which assigned
Jan. 1810 3rd and 4th Squadrons part of 7th Prov. Dragoon Regiment,
  Bessières's Brigade, Caulaincourt's Division
Feb.–May 1810 3rd and 4th Squadrons part of 7th Prov. Dragoon
  Regiment, Bessières's Brigade, Kellermann's Division

Table 11.20 continued

Major commands to which assigned

Jun.–Aug. 1810 3rd and 4th Squadrons part of 7th Prov. Dragoon Regiment, Bessières's Brigade, 6th Military Government

Aug. 1810–Jul. 1811 3rd and 4th Squadrons part of 7th Prov. Dragoon Regiment, Poinsot's Brigade, 7th Military Government

Jul.–Oct. 1811 HQ and all squadrons, 2nd Brigade, Soult's Division

Oct.–Nov. 1811 HQ and all squadrons, attached to Barrois's Division

Nov. 1811–6 Feb. 1812 HQ and all squadrons, Ruat's Brigade, Soult's Division

7 Feb.–14 Apr. 1812 HQ, 1st, 2nd and 3rd Squadrons in Bouillé's Brigade, Soult's Division

Apr. 1812–Aug. 1812 HQ, 1st, 2nd and 3rd Squadrons in Sparre's Brigade, Soult's Division

Aug.–Nov. 1812 HQ, 1st, 2nd and 3rd Squadrons in Ormancey's Brigade, Soult's Division

Dec. 1812–Jan. 1813 HQ, 1st, 2nd and 3rd Squadrons in Ruat's Brigade, Soult's Division

Jan.–Apr. 1813 HQ, 1st, 2nd and 3rd Squadrons in Sparre's Brigade, Digeon's Division

Apr.–Jul. 1813 HQ, 1st and 2nd Squadrons in Sparre's Brigade, Digeon's Division

Jul. 1813–Jan. 1814 HQ, 1st and 2nd Squadrons in Ismert's Brigade, Trelliard's Division

Jan. 1814 Regiment transferred to the Grande Armée

Battles and officer casualties

Bailen (19 Jul. 1808) 2 wounded

Operations (Nov. 1808–Jul. 1809) 4 wounded

Almoncid (11 Aug. 1809) 1 killed

Huete (24 Dec. 1809) 2 wounded

Counter-guerrilla operations Jan. 1810–May 1813 1 killed, 9 wounded

Vitoria (21 Jun. 1813) 3 wounded

Bayonne (13 Dec. 1813) 1 wounded

Departure from the Peninsula

Mar. 1812 4th Squadron

Winter 1813 3rd Squadron

Jan. 1814 1st and 2nd Squadrons

Notes The 21st Dragoons took very few casualties in the 6 years the regiment spent in the Peninsula: only 2 officers were killed and 21 wounded. After they joined the French army in eastern France in 1814, they had 2 killed and 9 wounded in two months.

Table 11.21   22nd Dragoon Regiment

Colonels
 François-Xavier Frossard (5 Apr. 1807–29 Aug. 1809)
 Claude-Basile-Gaspard Blancheville (28 Dec. 1809–2 Mar. 1810)
 Nicolas-Felix Rozat (29 Jun. 1810–22 Sep. 1813)*

Regimental depot
 1810 Namur
 1811 Saintes

Location of squadrons
 Dec. 1807–Jul. 1808 1 company in Spain
 Dec. 1808 HQ and all squadrons in Spain
 Feb.–May 1809 HQ and all squadrons in Portugal
 Jun. 1809 HQ, 1st and 2nd Squadrons in Spain; 3rd and 4th Squadrons
  in France
 Autumn 1813 3rd Squadron in Germany

Arrival in the Peninsula
 8 Jan. 1808 1 company
 Dec. 1808 HQ, 1st, 2nd, 3rd and 4th Squadrons
 Jan. 1810 3rd and 4th Squadrons

Major commands to which assigned
 Oct. 1807–Jun. 1808 1 company assigned to 1st Prov. Dragoon
  Regiment, Pryvé's Brigade, Grouchy's Division, Moncey's Corps
 Jun. 1808 1 company assigned to 1st Prov. Dragoon Regiment, Pryvé's
  Brigade, Fresia's Division, Dupont's Corps
 Dec. 1808–Jun. 1809 HQ, 1st, 2nd and 3rd Squadrons in Viallannes's
  Brigade, Lorge's Division,
 Jun.–Nov. 1809 HQ, 1st and 2nd Squadrons in Cambacérès's Brigade,
  Lorge's Division
 Nov. 1809–Feb. 1810 HQ, 1st and 2nd Squadrons in Beaurgard's
  Brigade, Lorge's Division
 Jan. 1810 3rd and 4th Squadrons part of 11th Prov. Dragoon Regiment,
  Lamotte's Brigade, Caulaincourt's Division
 Feb.–Oct. 1810 HQ and all squadrons in Reiset's Brigade, Marizy's
  Division, 5th Corps
 Oct. 1810–Feb. 1811 HQ and all squadrons in Marizy's Brigade,
  Houssaye's Division
 Feb.–Jul. 1811 HQ and all squadrons in Reiset's Brigade, Houssaye's
  Division,
 Oct. 1811–Spring 1812 HQ and all squadrons in Reiset's Brigade,
  Trelliard's Division

---

* Colonel Rozat retired on 22 September 1813, due to chronic rheumatism.

Table 11.21   continued

Major commands to which assigned

Mar.–Jan. 1813 HQ, 1st, 2nd and 3rd Squadrons in Rozat's Brigade, Trelliard's Division

Jan.–Jun. 1813 HQ, 1st and 2nd Squadrons in Rozat's Brigade, Trelliard's Division

Late Jun. 1813 Regiment transferred to the Grande Armée

Battles and officer casualties

Ledrija (7 Dec. 1808) 2 (prisoners) murdered by a mob

Portugal (Mar. and Apr. 1809) 4 wounded, 1 would die from wounds

Counter-guerrilla operations (1809) 1killed, 2 wounded

Valverde (19 Feb. 1810) 1 killed

Counter-guerrilla operations (1810–12) 1 killed, 8 wounded, 1 would die from wounds

Majahalonda (11 Aug. 1812) 1 wounded

Irun (3 Apr. 1813) 1 wounded

Vitoria (21 Jun. 1813) none

Departure from the Peninsula

Jun. 1809 3rd and 4th Squadrons

Winter 1812 4th Squadron

Jan. 1813 3rd Squadron

1813 HQ, 1st and 2nd Squadrons

Notes In December 1809 Colonel Charles Blancheville was appointed commander of the 22nd Dragoons, but he never had the opportunity to command them. On 2 March 1810, while en route to join his new command, he was killed by guerrillas from the villages of El Ronquillo and Santa Olalla.

Table 11.22   24th Dragoon Regiment

Colonels

Jacques Delort (8 May 1806–21 Jul. 1811) shot in the right thumb at Valls (25 Feb. 1809); seriously wounded by many sabre blows at Valls (15 Jan. 1811)

Jean Baptiste Dubessy (14 Oct. 1811–Apr. 1814)

Regimental depot

1810 Castres

Location of squadrons

Dec. 1808–Aug. 1813 HQ, 1st, 2nd and 3rd Squadrons in Spain

Apr. 1814 HQ, 1st, 2nd and 3rd Squadrons in France

Arrival in the Peninsula

Nov. 1808

Major commands to which assigned
  Nov. 1808–Jul. 1811 HQ, 1st, 2nd and 3rd Squadrons in 7th Corps
  Jul. 1811–Jul. 1813 HQ, 1st, 2nd and 3rd Squadrons in Delort's Brigade
    Army of Aragon
  Jul. 1813–Jan. 1814 HQ, 1st, 2nd and 3rd Squadrons in Meyer's Brigade,
    Digeon's Division
  Jan.–Apr. 1814 HQ, 1st, 2nd and 3rd Squadrons in Meyer's Brigade,
    Army of Aragon
Battles and officer casualties
  Counter-guerrilla operations (1808–13) 5 wounded
  Vals (25 Feb. 1809) 1 killed, 4 wounded
  Vich (10 Feb. 1810) 1 killed, 4 wounded
  Villafranca (8 Apr. 1810) 1 wounded
  Vals (15 Jan. 1811) 2 wounded
  Figueres (3 May 1811) 2 wounded
  Sagonte (25 Oct. 1811) 1 wounded
  Castalla (21 Jul. 1812) 1 killed, 1 wounded
  Villafranca (13 Sep. 1813) 1 killed, 3 wounded
Departure from the Peninsula
  The regiment and its three squadrons served the whole war in the
    Peninsula.

Notes Although many regiments had three or four of their squadrons serving in
Spain at one time, few had all of their squadrons there for the whole war. The general
practice was to send the 3rd or 4th Squadron back to the regimental depot to rebuild
the unit, when casualties or attrition reduced its combat effectiveness. The 24th
Dragoons is the exception. The regiment arrived in the Peninsula in November 1808
and when the war ended in April 1814, it still had itss three squadrons with it. This
was most likely due to the fact that the regimental depot was at Castres, France–less
than 400 kilometres from the area where the 24th Dragoons operated throughout
much of the war. This made it much easier for it to receive replacements than
regiments serving at a greater distance from their depot, especially those serving in
the Army of the South.

Table 11.23   25th Dragoon Regiment

Colonels
  Antoine-Philippe d'Ornano (18 Jan. 1807–22 Aug. 1811)
  Jean-Pierre-Gauthier dit Leclerc (23 Aug. 1811–12 Jan. 1813) wounded
    at Salamanca (22 Jun. 1812)
  Augustin-Jean-Louis Montigny (25 Mar. 1813–30 Jan. 1814)
Regimental depot
  1810 Strasbourg

Table 11.23   continued

Regimental depot

  1812 Montauban

Location of squadrons

  Dec. 1808 HQ, 1st, 2nd and 3rd Squadrons in Spain; 4th Squadron in
    France

  Summer 1809 HQ, 1st and 2nd Squadrons in Spain; 3rd and 4th
    Squadrons in Germany

  Jan. 1810 HQ and all squadrons in Spain

  Jan. 1811 HQ and all squadrons in Portugal

  Summer 1812 HQ, 1st and 2nd Squadrons in Spain; 3rd and 4th
    Squadrons in France

  Jun. 1813 HQ, 1st and 2nd Squadrons in Spain; 3rd and 4th Squadrons
    in Germany; 5th Squadron in France

  12 Oct. 1813 HQ, 1st, 2nd, 3rd and 4th Squadrons together in Germany

Arrival in the Peninsula

  8 Jan. 1808 1 company of the 4th Squadron

  Jan. 1809 HQ, 1st, 2nd and 3rd Squadrons

  Jan. 1810 3rd and 4th Squadrons

Major commands to which assigned

  Nov. 1807–Jun. 1808 1 company assigned to 2nd Prov. Dragoon
    Regiment, Pryvé's Brigade, Grouchy's Division, Moncey's Corps

  Jun. 1808 1 company assigned to 2nd Prov. Dragoon Regiment, Pryvé's
    Brigade, Fresia's Division, Dupont's Corps

  Dec. 1808–May 1809 HQ, 1st, 2nd and 3rd Squadrons in Fournier-
    Sarlovèse's Brigade, Lorge's Division

  May–Dec. 1809 HQ, 1st and 2nd Squadrons in Fournier-Sarlovèse's
    Brigade, Lorge's Division

  Dec. 1809–Feb. 1810 HQ, 1st and 2nd Squadrons in Ornano's Brigade,
    Lorge's Division

  Jan.–Feb. 1810 3rd and 4th Squadrons in 12th Prov. Dragoon Regiment,
    Lamotte's Brigade, Caulaincourt's Division

  Feb.–May 1810 HQ and all squadrons in Ornano's Brigade, Lorge's
    Division

  May–Aug. 1810 HQ and all squadrons in Gardanne's Brigade, Trelliard's
    Division

  Sep. 1810–May 1811 HQ and all squadrons in Ornano's Brigade,
    Trelliard's Division

  Jun.–Nov. 1811 HQ, 1st, 2nd and 3rd Squadrons in Ornano's Brigade,
    Montbrun's Division

  Nov. 1811–Feb. 1812 HQ, 1st and 2nd Squadrons in Boyer's Brigade,
    Cavrois's Division

Feb.–Jul. 1812 HQ, 1st and 2nd Squadrons in Carrié's Brigade, Boyer's
  Division
Jul. 1812–Jun. 1813 HQ, 1st and 2nd Squadrons in Boudinhon-Valdec's
  Brigade, Boyer's Division
Late Jun. 1813 Regiment transferred to the Grande Armée
Battles and officer casualties
Alcolea (7 Jun. 1808) 1 wounded
Capitulation at Bailen (19 Jul. 1808) losses uncertain*
Siege of Lugo (May 1809) 1 wounded
Tamames (18 Oct.e 1809) none
Alba de Tormes (28 Nov. 1809) 1 killed, 1 wounded
Siege of Ciudad Rodrigo (1 May 1810) 1 killed
Portugal (Sep. 1810–Apr. 1811) 3 dragoons killed, 1 wounded
Sabugal (3 Apr. 1811) none
Fuentes de Oñoro (5 May 1811) 2 wounded
El Bodon (25 Sep. 1811) 2 killed, 1 wounded
Villanova (8 Feb. 1812) 1 killed
San Cristoval (12 Jun. 1812) 1 wounded
Salamanca (18–22 Jun3 1812) 10 wounded
Villadiego (23 Oct. 1812) 3 wounded
Vitoria (21 Jun. 1813) 1 wounded
Departure from the Peninsula
Mar. 1809 3rd Squadron
Jun. 1811 4th Squadron
Sep. 1811 3rd Squadron
27 Jun. 1813 HQ, 1st and 2nd Squadrons

Notes The commander of the 25th Dragoons in 1809, Colonel d'Ornano, had his
17-year-old brother serving as a second lieutenant in the regiment. The teenager was
killed on 28 November 1809 at Alba de Tormes, in the charge that broke the Spanish
Army. The younger d'Ornano was trying to capture a Spanish gun, when he was
killed in hand-to-hand combat with a gunner.

Table 11.24 26th Dragoon Regiment

Colonels
Vital Joachim Chamorin (16 Feb. 1807–25 Mar. 1811) killed at Campo-
  Mayor on 25 Mar. 1811

---

* The 25th Dragoons had 120 officers and men assigned to Dupont's Corps. All 120
were either killed or captured at Bailen. The company was immediately reconstituted
from new dragoons at the depot.

Table 11.24 continued

Colonels

Gabriel Gaspard-Achille-Adolphe Montélégier (19 Apr. 1811–30 May 1813)

Louis Pierre Besnard (19 Sep. 1813–19 Sep. 1814)

Regimental depot

1810 Maestricht

1811 Saintes

Location of squadrons

Jan. 1808 1 company in Spain

Nov. 1808 HQ, 1st, 2nd and 3rd Squadrons in Spain; 4th Squadron in France

Summer 1809 HQ, 1st and 2nd Squadrons in Spain; 3rd and 4th Squadron in Germany

Jan. 1810 HQ and all squadrons in Spain

Autumn 1810 HQ, 1st and 2nd Squadrons in Spain; 3rd and 4th Squadron in Portugal

Spring 1811 HQ and all squadrons in Spain

Summer 1811–Summer 1813 HQ, 1st, 2nd and 3rd Squadrons in Spain; 4th Squadron in France

Jul. 1813 HQ, 1st and 2nd Squadrons in France; 3rd and 4th Squadron in Germany

Arrival in the Peninsula

8 Jan. 1808 1 company

4 Nov. 1808 HQ, 1st, 2nd and 3rd Squadrons

Spring 1810 3rd and 4th Squadrons

Major commands to which assigned

Nov. 1807–Jun. 1808 1 company assigned to 2nd Prov. Dragoon Regiment, Pryvé's Brigade, Grouchy's Division, Moncey's Corps

Jun. 1808 1 company assigned to 2nd Prov. Dragoon Regiment, Pryvé's Brigade, Fresia's Division, Dupont's Corps

Nov. 1808 HQ, 1st, 2nd and 3rd Squadrons in Digeon's Brigade, Tour-Maubourg's Division, attached to Marshal Lannes's force

Dec. 1808 HQ, 1st, 2nd and 3rd Squadrons in Digeon's Brigade attached to 6th Corps

Jan.–Feb. 1809 HQ, 1st, 2nd and 3rd Squadrons in Digeon's Brigade, Tour-Maubourg's Division

Feb.–Jun. 1809 HQ, 1st and 2nd Squadrons in Digeon's Brigade, Tour-Maubourg's Division

Jul.–7 Nov. 1809 HQ, 1st and 2nd Squadrons in Oullenbourg's Brigade, Tour-Maubourg's Division

7 Nov. 1809–Apr. 1811 HQ, 1st and 2nd Squadrons in Bouvier des

Eclaz's Brigade, Tour-Maubourg's Division

Nov. 1809–Feb. 1810 3rd and 4th Squadrons part of 3rd Prov. Dragoon Regiment, Sainte-Croix's Brigade, Caulaincourt's Division

Mar.–Oct. 1810 3rd and 4th Squadrons part of 3rd Prov. Dragoon Regiment, Sainte-Croix's Brigade, 8th Corps

Oct. 1810–Jun. 1811 3rd and 4th Squadrons part of 3rd Prov. Dragoon Regiment, ? Brigade, 8th Corps

May–Jul. 1811 HQ, 1st and 2nd Squadrons in Bron's Brigade, Tour-Maubourg's Division

Jul.–Oct. 1811 HQ, 1st and 2nd Squadrons in Bouvier des Eclaz's Brigade, Tour-Maubourg's Division (Cavalry Reserve of the Army of the South)

Oct. 1811–7 Feb. HQ, 1st and 2nd Squadrons in Perreimond's Brigade, Tour-Maubourg's Division (Cavalry Reserve of the Army of the South)

7 Feb.–Mar. 1812 HQ, 1st, 2nd and 3rd Squadrons in Lallemand's Brigade, Perreimond's Division

Mar.–Oct. 1812 HQ, 1st, 2nd and 3rd Squadrons in Vinot's Brigade, Perreimond's Division

Oct. 1812–Apr. 1813 HQ, 1st, 2nd and 3rd Squadrons in Ismert's Brigade, Digeon's Division

May–Jul. 1813 HQ, 1st, 2nd and 3rd Squadrons in Ismert's Brigade, Tilly's Division

Jul. 1813 HQ, 1st and 2nd Squadrons in Ismert's Brigade, Trelliard's Division

Jan. 1814 Regiment transferred to the Grande Armée

Battles and officer casualties

Bailen (19 Jul. 1808) 1 wounded

Tudela (23 Nov. 1808) 2 killed, 1 wounded

Medellin (28 Mar. 1809) 1 killed, 7 wounded

Talavera (28 Jul. 1809) 1 wounded

Ocaña (19 Nov. 1809) 2 wounded

Operations 1809–10 5 wounded, 1 would die from wounds

Gebora (19 Feb. 1811) 1 killed, 1 wounded, 1 would die from wounds

Campo-Mayor (25 Mar. 1811) 1 killed, 6 wounded

Albuera (16 May 1811) 1 killed, 2 wounded

Usagre (25 May 1811) none

Operations 1811–12 6 wounded

Ubeda (12 Jun. 1812) 2 wounded

Departure from the Peninsula

Feb. 1809 3rd Squadron

Jun. 1811 4th Squadron

Jul. 1813 3rd Squadron

Jan. 1814 HQ, 1st and 2nd Squadrons

Table 11.25   27th Dragoon Regiment

Colonels
François Antoine Lallemand (20 Nov. 1806–6 Aug. 1811)
Louis Charlemagne Prévost (14 Oct. 1811–21 Aug. 1814)
Regimental depot
1810 Haguenau
1811 Saintes
Location of squadrons
Nov. 1808 HQ, 1st, 2nd and 3rd Squadrons in Spain; 4th Squadron in France
Jan. 1810–Feb. 1812 HQ and all squadrons in Spain
Feb.–Dec. 1812 HQ, 1st, 2nd and 3rd Squadrons in Spain; 4th Squadron in France
Jan. 1813 HQ, 1st and 2nd Squadrons in Spain; 3rd and 4th Squadrons in France
Jun. 1813 HQ, 1st and 2nd Squadrons in France; 3rd and 4th Squadrons in Germany
Arrival in the Peninsula
Nov. 1808 HQ, 1st, 2nd and 3rd Squadrons
Jan. 1810 3rd and 4th Squadrons
Major commands to which assigned
Nov. 1808 HQ, 1st, 2nd and 3rd Squadrons in Marizy's Brigade, Houssaye's Division
Dec. 1808 HQ, 1st, 2nd and 3rd Squadrons in Marizy's Brigade, attached to 1st Corps
Jan.–Jun. 1809 HQ, 1st, 2nd and 3rd Squadrons in Marizy's Brigade, Houssaye's Division
Jul. 1809–Apr. 1810 HQ, 1st and 2nd Squadrons in Marizy's Brigade, Houssaye's Division
Jan.–Feb. 1810 3rd and 4th Squadrons in 10th Prov. Dragoon Regiment, Bron's Brigade, Caulaincourt's Division
Feb.–Apr. 1810 3rd and 4th Squadrons in 10th Prov. Dragoon Regiment, Bron's Brigade, Kellermann's Division
Apr.–Oct. 1810 3rd and 4th Squadrons in 10th Prov. Dragoon Regiment, Bron's Brigade, 6th Military Government
May–Oct. 1810 HQ, 1st and 2nd Squadrons in Digeon's Brigade, Houssaye's Division
Nov. 1810–Apr. 1811 HQ and all squadrons in Bron's Brigade, Tour-Maubourg's Division
May–Jun. 1811 HQ and all squadrons in Bouvier d'Escaz's Brigade, Tour-Maubourg's Division

Jul.–Sep. 1811 HQ and all squadrons attached to the Army of the South's Reserve

Sep.–Nov. 1811 HQ and all squadrons in Bron's Brigade, Army of the South's Reserve

Nov. 1811–7 Feb. 1812 HQ and all squadrons in Lallemand's Brigade, Army of the South's Reserve

Feb.–Mar. 1812 HQ and all squadrons in Digeon's Brigade, Tour-Maubourg's Division

Mar.–Oct. 1812 HQ, 1st, 2nd and 3rd Squadrons in Lallemand's Brigade, Digeon's Division

Oct. 1812–Jan. 1813 HQ, 1st, 2nd and 3rd Squadrons in Ludot's Brigade, Digeon's Division

Jan.–Apr. 1813 HQ, 1st and 2nd Squadrons in Ludot's Brigade, Digeon's Division

May–Jul. 1813 HQ, 1st and 2nd Squadrons in Ormancey's Brigade, Tilly's Division

Jul.–Dec. 1813 HQ, 1st and 2nd Squadrons in Sparre's Brigade Soult's Division

Jan. 1814 HQ, 1st and 2nd Squadrons in Sparre's Brigade Trelliard's Division

Jan. 1814 Regiment transferred to the Grande Armée

Battles and officer casualties

Operations in Portugal (1809) 1 killed, 2 wounded

Operations in Spain (1809–11) 1 killed, 5 wounded

Albuera (16 May 1811) 4 wounded

Valencia de Las Torres (11 Jun. 1812) 1 killed, 2 wounded

Salamanca (22 Jul. 1812) 1 wounded

Operations 1812 3 wounded

Departure from the Peninsula

Spring 1809 3rd Squadron

Feb. 1812 4th Squadron

Jan. 1813 3rd Squadron

Jan. 1814 HQ, 1st and 2nd Squadrons

Chapter Twelve

The Chasseur Regiments

By 1814 Napoleon had 31 chasseur regiments, of which 22 had elements serving in the Peninsula. Unlike the dragoon regiments which were usually committed with three or four of their squadrons, only 10 of the chasseur regiments had three or four of their squadrons in the Peninsula. Most of the other regiments were not there in strength. Four regiments sent only their 3rd and 4th Squadrons, usually as part of provisional regiments; and these were often without their regimental headquarters. Three other regiments had only a single squadron in the Peninsula. The remaining five regiments were only tasked to provide a single company in 1807.

In the early years of the war the chasseurs were assigned to the corps light cavalry. Only after the reorganisation of the French armies in 1811 and 1812 were the chasseur regiments considered an army asset. By the final year of the war the chasseurs were the most common regiment in the French armies in the Peninsula and in 1814, seven of the nine cavalry regiments were chasseurs.

Table 12.1   5th Chasseur Regiment

Colonels
  Pierre Bonnemains (20 Sep. 1806–6 Aug. 1811)
  Joseph Baillot (5 Sep. 1811–1 Aug. 1814)
Regimental depot
  1808 Clèves; small depot in Bayonne
  15 Feb. 1812 La Rochelle; small depot in Burgos
  1814 Small depot in Orthez
Location of squadrons
  Dec. 1807 1 company in Spain
  1808 HQ, 1st, 2nd and 3rd Squadrons in Spain; 4th Squadron at Clèves
  1813 3rd Squadron in Germany

Dec. 1813 1st Squadron and 1 company of 2nd Squadron at Orthez;
   HQ, 3rd and 4th Squadrons and 1 company of 2nd Squadron on the
   Rhine River; 5th and 6th Squadrons at La Rochelle
Arrival in the Peninsula
22 Nov. 1807 1 company
16 Nov. 1808 HQ, 1st, 2nd and 3rd Squadrons
Major commands to which assigned
   Nov. 1807 1 company assigned to 1st Prov. Chasseur Regiment, Fresia's
   Division, Dupont's Corps
   Nov. 1808 Franceschi's Brigade, 2nd Corps
   Dec. 1808–Jan. 1809 Montbrun's Brigade, Lasalle's Division
   Jan. 1809–Mar. 1809 Bordessoulle's Brigade, Lasalle's Division
   Apr. 1809–Sep. 1811 Beaumont's Brigade, 1st Corps
   Oct.–Nov. 1811 Attached to the Army of the South Reserve
   Nov. 1811–Feb. 1812 Bonnemains's Brigade, 1st Corps
   7 Feb.–Oct. 1812 Bonnemains's Brigade, Perreimond's Division
   Oct.–Nov. 1812 Bonnemains's Brigade, Tilly's Division
   Nov.–Mar. 1813 1st Squadron in Bonnemains's Brigade, Tilly's Division
   Apr.–May 1813 1st Squadron in Marazin's Brigade, Soult's Division
   Jun. 1813 1st Squadron in Houssin de Sainte-Laurent's Brigade, Soult's
   Division
   Jul. 1813 1st Squadron in Vinot's Brigade, Soult's Division
   Feb.–Apr. 1814 1st Squadron in Vial's Brigade, Soult's Division
Battles and officer casualties
   Bailen (19 Jun. 1808) 1 killed, 1 wounded
   Truxillo (20 Feb. 1809) 1 wounded
   Medellin (28 Mar. 1809) 5 wounded, 1 would die from wounds
   Talavera (28 Jul. 1809) 4 wounded
   Villamerique (30 Dec. 1809) 1 wounded
   Arcos (27 Mar. 1810) none
   Montellano (22 Apr. 1810) 2 wounded, 1 would die from wounds
   Bornos (20 Sep. 1810) none
   Bornos (1 Jun. 1811) 2 killed, 3 wounded
   Anti-Guerrilla Operations (1810–13) 1 killed, 10 wounded
   Vitoria (21 Jun. 1813) 2 wounded
   Orthez (27 Feb. 1814) 1 wounded
   Tarbes (27 Mar. 1814) 1 wounded
   Toulouse (10 Apr. 1814) 1 wounded
Departure from the Peninsula
   Nov. 1812 HQ, 1 company of the 2nd Squadron and 3rd Squadron

Table 12.2   7th Chasseur Regiment

Colonels

Hippolyte-Marie-Guillaume de Rosnyvinen Pire (25 Jun. 1807–30 Nov. 1808)

François-Joseph Bohn (16 Mar.–21 Jun. 1809) died at Acs from wounds received at Raab (14 Jun. 1809)

Alexandre Montbrun (15 Jul. 1809–26 Jul. 1811) wounded at Fuentes de Oñoro (5 May 1811)

Antoine-Charles-Bernard Delaitre (27 Jul. 1811–9 Feb. 1812)

Alfred Amand Saint-Chamans (10 Feb. 1812–16 Oct. 1813) wounded and taken prisoner at Leipzig (16 Oct. 1812)

Auguste Colin de Verdière (16 Dec. 1813–13 Nov. 1815)

Regimental depot

1810 Strasbourg

Location of squadrons

Dec. 1807–Jul. 1808 1 company in Spain

Sep. 1810–Nov. 1811 1st, 2nd and 5th Squadrons in France; 3rd and 4th Squadrons in Spain

Arrival in the Peninsula

Dec. 1807 1 company

21 Aug. 1810 3rd and 4th Squadrons

Major commands to which assigned

Dec. 1807–Jul. 1808 Dupré's Brigade, Fresia's Division, Dupont's Corps

Aug. 1810–Nov. 1811 3rd and 4th Squadrons in Fournier's Brigade, Army of Portugal

Battles and officer casualties

Maçanarès (10 Jun. 1808) 1 killed

Fuentes de Oñoro (5 May 1811) 5 wounded, 1 would die from wounds

Notes In Nov. 1811 General Fournier's Brigade was disbanded. The 7th Chasseurs were ordered to turn their squadrons over to the 13th Chasseurs, the 3rd and 4th Squadrons of the 7th Chasseurs were designated the 5th and 6th Squadrons of the 13th Chasseurs. The cadre of the squadrons were also transferred with their men, including Colonel Jean Poiré, who would be given command of the 13th Chasseurs on 1 Dec. 1811.

Table 12.3   10th Chasseur Regiment

Colonels

Jacques-Gervais Protais Subervie (27 Dec. 1806–6 Aug. 1811)

Auguste Houssin de Saint-Laurent (14 Oct. 1811–12 May 1814)

Regimental depot

1810 Brussels

Location of squadrons

May 1808–Sep. 1810 HQ, 1st and 2nd Squadrons in Spain; 3rd and 4th Squadrons in France

Oct. 1810–Jan. 1813 HQ and all squadrons in Spain

Jan.–Mar. 1813 HQ, 1st, 2nd and 3rd Squadrons in Spain; 4th Squadron in France

Mar.–Jun. 1813 HQ, 1st, 2nd and Squadrons in Spain; 3rd and 4th Squadrons in France

Jun. 1813 HQ, 1st and 2nd Squadrons in France; 3rd and 4th Squadrons in Germany

Arrival in the Peninsula

1 May 1808 HQ, 1st and 2nd Squadrons

Oct. 1810 3rd and 4th Squadrons

Major commands to which assigned

May–Nov. 1808 HQ, 1st and 2nd Squadrons in Lasalle's Brigade, Bessières's Corps of the Pyrenees

Nov. 1808 HQ, 1st and 2nd Squadrons in Bordessoulle's Brigade, Lasalle's Division, 2nd Corps

Jan. 1809–Mar. 1809 Bordessoulle's Brigade, Lasalle's Division

Apr. 1809–Dec. 1810 HQ, 1st and 2nd Squadrons in Strolz's Brigade, Merlin's Division, 4th Corps

Dec. 1809–Oct. 1810 HQ, 1st and 2nd Squadrons in Perreimond's Brigade, 4th Corps

Oct. 1810–Aug. 1811 HQ and all Squadrons in Perreimond's Brigade, 4th Corps

Aug. 1811–6 Feb. 1812 HQ and all squadrons in Ormancey's Brigade 4th Corps

7 Feb.–Oct. 1812 HQ and all squadrons in Ormancey's Brigade, Soult's Division

Oct. 1812–Jan. 1813 HQ and all squadrons in Vinot's Brigade, Tilly's Division

Jan.–Apr. 1813 HQ, 1st, 2nd and 3rd Squadrons in Vinot's Brigade, Tilly's Division

Apr.–May 1813 HQ, 1st and 2nd Squadrons in Marazin's Brigade, Soult's Division

Jun. 1813 HQ, 1st and 2nd Squadrons in Houssin de Sainte-Laurent's Brigade, Soult's Division

Jul. 1813–Jan. 1814 HQ, 1st and 2nd Squadrons in Vinot's Brigade, Soult's Division

Jan.–Apr. 1814 HQ, 1st and 2nd Squadrons and 9th Company in Vial's Brigade, Soult's Division

Table 12.3 continued

Battles and officer casualties
 Medina de Rio Seco (14 Jul. 1808) 4 wounded
 Burgos (10 Nov. 1808) 1 wounded
 Medellin (27 Mar. 1809) 2 killed
 Talavera (28 Jul. 1809) 1 wounded
 Ocaña (19 Nov. 1809) 3 wounded
 Counter-guerrilla operations (1810–13) 6 killed, 5 wounded
 Ribeira (1 Aug. 1812) 2 wounded
 Toulouse (10 Apr. 1814) 2 killed
Departure from the Peninsula
 4th Squadron Jan. 1813
 3rd Squadron Spring 1813

Table 12.4   11th Chasseur Regiment

Colonels
 Charles-Claude Jacquinot (13 Jan. 1806–10 Mar. 1809)
 Mathieu Désirat (16 Mar. 1809–7 Sep. 1812) killed at Borodino (7 Sep.
  1812)
Regimental depot
 1811 Verdun
Location of squadrons
 Dec. 1807–Jul. 1808 1 company in Spain
 Nov. 1810–Sep. 1811 4th Squadron in Spain
Arrival in the Peninsula
 Dec. 1807 1 company
 Nov. 1810 4th Squadron
Major commands to which assigned
 Nov. 1807–Jul. 1808 1 company assigned to 1st Prov. Chasseur
  Regiment, Fresia's Division, Dupont's Corps
 Sep. 1810–Jul. 1811 4th Squadron part of 1st Prov. Light Cavalry
  Regiment, Watier's Brigade, Army of the North
 Jul.–Sep. 1811 4th Squadron assigned to 6th Military Government
Battles and officer casualties
 Tudela (23 Nov. 1808) 1 wounded
 Counter-guerrilla operations (1810–11) 2 wounded
 Salamanca (22 Jul. 1812) 1 wounded

Notes When the 4th Squadron of the 11th Chasseurs joined the 1st Provisional Light
Cavalry Regiment in Sept. 1810, it consisted of 10 officers, 237 chasseurs and 271
horses. The squadron was commanded by Captain Dominique Guyon. In Sept. 1811
the 4th Squadron was used to help form the new 31st Chasseur Regiment.

Table 12.5   12th Chasseur Regiment

Colonels
  Claude-Raymond Guyon (24 Mar. 1805–6 Aug. 1811)
  Charles-Etienne Ghigny (14 Oct. 1811–9 Oct. 1814)
Regimental depot
  1811 Niort
Location of squadrons
  Jan. 1808–Jul. 1808 1 company in Spain
  Nov. 1810–Sep. 1811 4th Squadron in Spain
Arrival in the Peninsula
  Jan. 1808 1 company
  Nov. 1810 4th Squadron in Spain
Major commands to which assigned
  Nov. 1807–Jul. 1808 1 company assigned to 2nd Prov. Chasseur
    Regiment, Fresia's Division, Dupont's Corps
  Sep. 1810–Jul. 1811 4th Squadron part of 1st Prov. Light Cavalry
    Regiment, Watier's Brigade, Army of the North
  Jul.–Sep. 1811 4th Squadron assigned to 6th Military Government
Battles and officer casualties
  Bailen (19 Jul. 1808) 2 killed
  Fuentes de Oñoro (5 May 1811) 3 wounded
  Salamanca (22 Jul. 1812) 1 wounded
Departure from the Peninsula
  Sep. 1811 4th Squadron

Table 12.6   13th Chasseur Regiment

Colonels
  Jean-Baptiste Demêngeot (5 Sep. 1806–31 Aug. 1809)
  Eugène de Montesquiou (23 Aug. 1809–12 Dec. 1810) died at Cuidad
    Rodrigo
  Eugène-Redmond Shée (9 Jun. 1811–1 Aug. 1814)
  Nicolas Poiré (1 Dec. 1811–1 Aug. 1814)*
Regimental depot
  1806 Belfort
  1811 Niort
Location of squadrons
  1808 1 Company was in Spain
  1809 Regiment was in Germany
  1810 Regiment was in France

---

* Was the 2nd Colonel but commanded the squadrons in Spain December 1811–14.

Table 12.6   continued

Location of squadrons

Autumn 1810 HQ, 3rd and 4th Squadrons in Spain; 1st and 2nd
Squadrons in France

Nov. 1811 HQ, 3rd, 4th, 6th, 7th and 8th Squadrons in Spain; 1st, 2nd
and 5th Squadrons in France

Feb. 1812 HQ, 1st, 2nd, 3rd and 4th Squadrons in Spain; 5th, 6th, 7th
and 8th Squadrons in France

Jan. 1813 HQ, 1st, 2nd and 3rd Squadrons in Spain; 4th, 5th, 6th, 7th,
8th, 9th Squadrons in France

Jul. 1813 1st and 2nd Squadrons in southern France; 3rd and 4th
Squadrons at depot; 5th, 6th, 7th and 8th Squadrons in Germany

Dec. 1813 1st, 2nd and 3rd Squadrons in southern France; 4th, 7th and
8th Squadrons in Niort; 5th and 6th Squadrons in Germany

Arrival in the Peninsula

Jan. 1808 1 company

25 Sep. 1810 3rd and 4th Squadrons

Nov. 1813 3rd Squadron

Major commands to which assigned

Nov. 1807–Jul. 1808 1 company assigned to 2nd Prov. Chasseur
Regiment, Fresia's Division, Dupont's Corps

Aug. 1810–Nov. 1811 HQ, 3rd and 4th Squadrons in Fournier's Brigade,
Army of Portugal

Nov. 1811–Jan. 1812 HQ, 3rd, 4th, 6th, 7th and 8th Squadrons in
Curto's Light Cavalry Brigade, Army of Portugal

Feb.–Sep. 1812 HQ, 1st, 2nd, 3rd, 4th and 5th Squadrons in Desfossés's
Brigade, Curto's Division

Sep.–Oct. 1812 HQ, 1st, 2nd, 3rd, 4th and 5th Squadrons in Shée's
Brigade, Mermet's Division

Oct. 1812–Mar. 1813 HQ, 1st, 2nd, 3rd and 4th Squadrons in Shée's
Brigade, Mermet's Division

Apr.–Jul. 1813 1st and 2nd Squadrons in Shée's Brigade, Mermet's
Division

Jul.–Dec. 1813 1st and 2nd Squadrons in Berton's Brigade, Soult's
Division

Jan.–Apr. 1814 1st, 2nd and 3rd Squadrons in Berton's Brigade, Soult's
Division

Battles and officer casualties

Bailen (19 Jun. 1808) 1 wounded

Fuentes de Oñoro (5 May 1811) 5 wounded

Jun.–Jul. 1812 1 wounded

Tordesillas (18 Jul. 1812) 1 killed, 1 wounded

Salamanca (22 Jul. 1812) 1 wounded, 2 would die from wounds
Rio Hermanza (23 Oct. 1812) none
May–Dec. 1813 2 killed
Orthez (27 Feb. 1814) none
Toulouse (8 Apr. 1814) 1 wounded
Departure from the Peninsula
Oct. 1812 4th Squadron
Mar. 1813 3rd and 4th Squadrons

Notes In Feb. 1812 the five squadrons of the 13th Chasseurs in Spain were re-organised into three squadrons and numbered the 1st, 2nd and 3rd. The regiment had a strength in Spain of 716 men and 618 horses at this time. The 1st and 2nd Squadrons were already in existence and were back in France. Three months later, the old 2nd Squadron and a march squadron arrived with 381 men and 332 horses. They would be designated the 4th and 5th Squadrons. In mid-May the 13th Chasseurs had 56 officers, 940 chasseurs and 708 horses in Spain.

Table 12.7   14th Chasseur Regiment

Colonels
Pierre Frederic Sachs (8 May 1806–22 Apr. 1809) killed charging an
  artillery battery at Eckmühl (22 Apr. 1809)
Jean-Dieudonné Lion (30 Apr. 1809–10 Aug. 1809)
Hilaire Lemoyne (10 Aug. 1809–1 May 1815)
Regimental depot
1810 Pigernol
Location of squadrons
Nov. 1811–Jun. 1813 1st and 2nd Squadrons in France; 3rd and 4th
  Squadrons in Spain
Autumn 1813 HQ and all squadrons in Germany
Arrival in the Peninsula
Feb. 1808 1 company
Nov. 1811 3rd and 4th Squadrons
Major commands to which assigned
Dec. 1807–Oct. 1808 1 company in 3rd Prov. Chasseur Regiment,
  Bessières's Brigade, Corps of the Eastern Pyrenees
Nov. 1808–16 Jan. 1809 1 company in 3rd Prov. Chasseur Regiment,
  Bessières's Brigade, 7th Corps
Mar.–Sep. 1812 3rd and 4th Squadrons in Vial's Brigade, Curto's
  Division
Sep. 1812–Jun. 1813 3rd and 4th Squadrons in Shée's Brigade, Mermet's
  Division

Table 12.7 continued

Battles and officer casualties

Bridge of Camaye (21 Jul. 1808) 1 wounded

Counter-guerrilla operations (1809–13) 1 killed, 3 wounded

Tordesillas (18 Jul. 1812) 3 wounded

Salamanca (22 Jul. 1812) 5 wounded

Monasterio (19 Oct. 1812) 2 wounded, 1 would die from wounds

Villadrigo (23 Oct. 1812) 2 wounded

Vitoria (21 Jun. 1813) 2 wounded

Departure from the Peninsula

Jun. 1813 3rd and 4th Squadrons

Notes In December 1811 the 3rd and 4th Squadrons of the 14th Chasseurs arrived in Spain. They would be the last cavalry regiment to be sent to the Peninsula.

Table 12.8 15th Chasseur Regiment

Colonels

Pierre Mourier (21 Aug. 1805–6 Aug. 1811)

François-Jacques-Guy Faverot de Kerbrech (14 Oct. 1811–2 Aug. 1815) wounded by 3 sabre cuts – to the head, the shoulder and the right arm, on 23 Oct. 1812, at Villadrigo

Regimental depot

1808 Parma

1811 Auch; the small depot was in Avila, Spain

1813 Montauban

Location of squadrons

1807 1 company in Spain

Oct. 1808–Aug. 1810 HQ, 1st, 2nd and 3rd Squadrons in Spain; 4th Squadron in France

Aug. 1810–Mar. 1811 HQ, 1st, 2nd and 3rd Squadrons in Portugal; 4th Squadron in France

Apr. 1811–Apr. 1813 HQ, 1st, 2nd and 3rd Squadrons in Spain; 4th Squadron in France

Apr.–Jun. 1813 HQ, 1st and 2nd Squadrons in Spain; 3rd Squadron in France; 4th Squadron in Germany

Aug. 1813 1st, 2nd and 3rd Squadrons in France; 4th Squadron in France

Arrival in the Peninsula

22 Nov. 1807 1 company

Oct. 1808 HQ, 1st, 2nd and 3rd Squadrons

Oct. 1811 3rd Squadron

Nov. 1811 4th Squadron

Nov. 1813 3rd Squadron

Major commands to which assigned

Dec. 1807–Oct. 1808 1 company in 3rd Prov. Chasseur Regiment, Bessières's Brigade, Corps of the Eastern Pyrenees

Nov. 1808–16 Jan. 1809 1 company in 3rd Prov. Chasseur Regiment, Bessières's Brigade, 7th Corps

Oct. 1808–3 Jan. 1809 HQ, 1st, 2nd and 3rd Squadrons in General Colbert's Brigade, 6th Corps

4 Jan. 1809–Jun. 1810 HQ, 1st, 2nd and 3rd Squadrons in General Lorcet's Brigade, 6th Corps

Jul. 1810–Mar. 1811 HQ, 1st, 2nd and 3rd Squadrons in Lamotte's Brigade, 6th Corps

Mar.–Jun. 1811 HQ, 1st, 2nd and 3rd Squadrons in Mourier's Brigade, 6th Corps

Jul.–Oct. 1811 HQ, 1st, 2nd and 3rd Squadrons in Laferrière's Brigade, Army of the North

Nov. 1811–Nov. 1812 HQ, 1st, 2nd, 3rd and 4th Squadrons in Laferrière's Brigade, Army of the North

Dec. 1812–Feb. 1813 HQ, 1st, 2nd and 3rd Squadrons in Laferrière's Brigade, Army of the North

Feb.–Apr. 1813 HQ, 1st, 2nd and 3rd Squadrons in Merlin's Brigade, Army of the North

Apr.–Jul. 1813 HQ, 1st and 2nd Squadrons in Merlin's Brigade, Army of the North

Jul.–Aug. 1813 HQ, 1st and 2nd Squadrons in Berton's Brigade, Soult's Division

Sep. 1813–Feb. 1814 HQ, 1st and 2nd Squadrons in Vinot's Brigade, Soult's Division

Feb.–Apr. 1814 HQ, 1st, 2nd and 3rd Squadrons in Vial's Brigade, Soult's Division

Battles and officer casualties

Tudela (23 Nov. 1808) none

Cacabellos (3 Jan. 1809) 1 wounded

Tamames (18 Oct. 1809) 1 killed, 1 wounded

Alba de Tormes (28 Nov. 1809) 2 killed, 2 wounded

Siege of Almeida (Jul.–Aug. 1810) 1 wounded

Fuentes de Oñoro (3–5 May 1811) none

Sanguessa (5 Feb. 1812) 1 killed, 2 wounded

Villadrigo (23 Oct. 1812) 11 wounded, 1 would die from wounds

Orthez (27 Feb. 1814) 1 killed, 1 wounded

Toulouse (10 Apr. 1814) 2 wounded

Table 12.8 continued

Departure from the Peninsula
  Sep. 1811 3rd Squadron
  Nov. 1812 4th Squadron
  Apr. 1813 3rd Squadron

Notes The 15th Chasseurs was a hard-charging regiment and it showed in the number of men killed. The regiment lost 5 officers and 191 chasseurs in combat between 1808 and 1814. Over half of the casualties were in 1809, where 3 officers and 120 chasseurs were killed. The heaviest losses occurred on 1 February 1809, when a detachment of 24 men were wiped out in the village of San Clodio. The regiment returned four months later and on 14 June extracted revenge for the massacre by burning the village.

Table 12.9 20th Chasseur Regiment

Colonels
  Betrand-Pierre Castex (20 Oct. 1806–21 Jul. 1809)
  Jean-Baptiste-Alexandre Cavrois (10 Aug. 1809–23 Nov. 1811)
  Auguste-François-Joseph de la Grange (23 Nov. 1811–1 Jun. 1814)
Regimental depot
  1810 Bonn
Location of squadrons
  Jan.–Jul. 1808 1 company in Spain
  Aug. 1810–Mar. 1811 HQ, 1st and 2nd Squadrons in Nantes; 3rd and
    4th Squadrons in Spain
  Mar.–Nov. 1811 HQ, 1st and 5th Squadrons in Bonn; 2nd, 3rd and 4th
    Squadrons in Spain
  Jan.–Mar. 1812 1st, 3rd, 4th and 5th Squadrons in Bonn; 2nd Squadron
    in Spain
Arrival in the Peninsula
  18 Aug. 1810 3rd and 4th Squadrons
  Mar. 1811 2nd Squadron
Major commands to which assigned
  Nov. 1807–Jul. 1808 1 company assigned to 2nd Prov. Chasseur
    Regiment, Fresia's Division, Dupont's Corps
  Aug. 1810–5 Dec. 1811 3rd and 4th Squadrons in Fournier's Brigade,
    Army of Portugal
  Mar. 1811 2nd Squadron assigned to General Gareau's Brigade, General
    Quesnel's Division of the Army of Catalonia
Battles and officer casualties
  Villa Rosa (6 Nov. 1810) none
  Fuentes de Oñoro (5 May 1811) 1 wounded*

---

* The officer was the noted memoirist, Charles Parquin, who was shot in the face; he lost six of his teeth.

Departure from the Peninsula
 Mar. 1812 2nd Squadron

Notes In November 1811 General Fournier's Brigade was disbanded. The 20th
Chasseurs were ordered to turn their squadrons over to the 13th Chasseurs. The 3rd
and 4th Squadrons of the 20th Chasseurs were designated the 7th and 8th Squadrons
of the 13th Chasseurs. Major de Vérigny and Captain Parquin did not transfer.
On 3 March 1812 Major de Vérigny was killed by a drunken French gendarme at
Valladolid. He was given a full military funeral and buried in the cathedral.

Table 12.10 21st Chasseur Regiment

Colonels
 Charles-François Steenhaudt (29 Jan. 1808–16 Feb. 1811) wounded on
  the Tagus River (6 Aug. 1809)
 Louis-Charles-Barthelémy Sopransi (17 Feb. 1811–13 Jun. 1811)
 Louis Claude Duchastel (31 Mar. 1812–12 May 1814) wounded in the
  chest at Espartina (5 Apr. 1812)
Regimental depot
 1810 Colmar
Location of squadrons
 Jan.–Jul. 1808 1 company in Spain
 Dec. 1808–Jul. 1813 HQ, 1st, 2nd and 3rd Squadrons in Spain
 Autumn 1813 HQ, 1st and 2nd Squadrons in France; 3rd Squadron in
  Germany
Arrival in the Peninsula
 Jan. 1808 1 company
 8 Dec. 1808 HQ, 1st, 2nd and 3rd Squadron
 ? 4th Squadron
Major commands to which assigned
 Nov. 1807–Jul. 1808 1 company assigned to 2nd Prov. Chasseur
  Regiment, Fresia's Division, Dupont's Corps
 Nov. 1808–Jun. 1809 HQ, 1st, 2nd and 3rd Squadrons in Boussart's
  Brigade, 5th Corps
 Jun.–Nov. 1809 HQ, 1st, 2nd and 3rd Squadrons in Beaurgard's Brigade,
  5th Corps
 Dec. 1809–Feb. 1810 HQ, 1st, 2nd and 3rd Squadrons in Steenhaudt's
  Brigade, 5th Corps
 Feb.–May 1810 HQ, 1st, 2nd and 3rd Squadrons in Briche's Brigade, 5th
  Corps
 May–Oct. 1810 HQ, 1st, 2nd and 3rd Squadrons in Briche's Brigade,
  Marizy's Division, 5th Corps

Table 12.10 continued

Major commands to which assigned

Nov. 1810–7 Feb. 1812 HQ, 1st, 2nd and 3rd Squadrons in Briche's Brigade, 5th Corps

7 Feb.–Mar. 1812 HQ, 1st, 2nd and 3rd Squadrons in Bouillé's Brigade, Soult's Division

Mar.–Oct. 1812 HQ, 1st, 2nd and 3rd Squadrons in Vinot's Brigade, Perreimond's Division

Oct. 1812–Dec. 1812 HQ, 1st, 2nd and 3rd Squadrons in Vinot's Brigade, Tilly's Division

Dec. 1812–Mar. 1813 HQ, 1st and 2nd Squadrons in Vinot's Brigade, Tilly's Division

Mar.–Jul. 1813 HQ, 1st and 2nd Squadrons in Vinot's Brigade, Soult's Division

Jul. 1813–Apr. 1814 HQ, 1st and 2nd Squadrons in Berton's Brigade, Soult's Division

Battles and officer casualties

Medina de Rio Seco (14 Jul. 1808) 1 wounded

Valladolid (10 Jun. 1809) 1 wounded

Talavera (28 Jul. 1809) 1 wounded

Ocaña (19 Nov. 1809) 1 wounded

Counter-guerrilla operations (1809–12) 2 killed, 4 wounded

Valverde (19 Feb. 1810) 2 wounded

Villagarcia (11 Aug. 1810) 1 killed, 2 wounded

Fuente de Cantos (19 Sep. 1810) 1 wounded

Gebora (19 Feb. 1811) 3 wounded

Albuera (16 May 1811) 6 wounded

Espartina (5 Apr. 1812) 2 wounded

Vitoria (21 Jun. 1813) 2 captured

Maubourguet (10 Mar. 1814) 1 wounded

Toulouse (10 Apr. 1814) 2 wounded

Departure from the Peninsula

Dec. 1812 3rd Squadron

Table 12.11   22nd Chasseur Regiment

Colonels

Jean-Baptiste Piéton-Prémale (25 Jun. 1807–14 Jul. 1808) died from multiple wounds he received at Medina de Rio Seco (14 Jul. 1808)

François Michel dit Desfossés (28 Aug. 1808–12 May 1814) wounded at Salamanca (22 Jul. 1812)

Regimental depot

1810 Ghent

Location of squadrons

Mar. 1808–Aug. 1810 HQ, 1st, 2nd and 3rd Squadrons in Spain; 4th Squadron in France

Sep. 1810–Apr. 1811 HQ, 1st, 2nd and 3rd Squadrons in Portugal; 4th Squadron in France

Apr. 1811–Jan. 1813 HQ, 1st, 2nd and 3rd Squadrons in Spain; 4th Squadron in France

Jul. 1813 HQ, 1st and 2nd Squadrons in France; 3rd, 4th and 5th Squadrons in Germany

Arrival in the Peninsula

Mar. 1808 HQ, 1st, 2nd and 3rd Squadrons

Major commands to which assigned

Mar.–Oct. 1808 HQ, 1st, 2nd and 3rd Squadrons in Lasalle's Brigade, Bessières's Corps

Nov. 1808 HQ, 1st, 2nd and 3rd Squadrons in Lasalle's Division

Dec. 1808 HQ, 1st, 2nd and 3rd Squadrons in Franceschi's Division

Jan.–Jun. 1809 HQ, 1st, 2nd and 3rd Squadrons in Defossés's Brigade, Franceschi's Division, 2nd Corps

Jul. 1809–Apr. 1811 HQ, 1st, 2nd and 3rd Squadrons in Defossés's Brigade, Soult's Division, 2nd Corps

May–Jun. 1811 HQ, 1st, 2nd and 3rd Squadrons in d'Ermenoville's Brigade, 2nd Corps

Jul.–Oct. 1811 HQ, 1st, 2nd and 3rd Squadrons in Defossés's Brigade, Army of Portugal

Oct. 1811–Feb. 1812 HQ, 1st, 2nd and 3rd Squadrons in Curto's Brigade, Army of Portugal

Feb.–Sep. 1812 HQ, 1st and 2nd Squadrons in Defossés's Brigade, Curto's Division

Sep. 1812–Jun. 1813 HQ, 1st and 2nd Squadrons in Curto's Brigade, Mermet's Division

Jul. 1813–Feb. 1814 HQ, 1st and 2nd Squadrons in Vinot's Brigade, Soult's Division

Feb.–Apr. 1814 HQ, 1st and 2nd Squadrons in Vial's Brigade, Soult's Division

Battles and officer casualties

Medina de Rio Seco (14 Jul. 1808) 2 killed, 3 wounded

Niou (23 Jul. 1808) 1 killed

Burgos (10 Nov. 1808) 3 wounded

Counter-guerrilla operations (1808 –13) 2 killed, 9 wounded, 1 would die from wounds

Sabugal (3 Apr. 1811) 1 killed, 1 wounded

El Bodon (25 Sep. 1811) 1 killed, 3 wounded

Aldea da Ponte (27 Sep. 1811) 1 killed

Table 12.11   continued

Battles and officer casualties
  Salamanca (22 Jul. 1812) 4 wounded
  Vitoria (21 Jun. 1813) 1 wounded
  Orthez (27 Feb. 1814) 1 wounded
  Toulouse (10 Apr. 1814) 1 wounded
Departure from the Peninsula
  Winter 1812 3rd Squadron

Table 12.12   24th Chasseur Regiment

Colonels
  Vivant Jean Brunet-Denon (25 Jun. 1807–22 May 1809) lost his right
    arm at Essling (22 May 1809)
  Auguste-Jean-Joseph-Gilbert Ameil (12 Jun. 1809–21 Nov. 1812)
  Pierre Henri Schneit (11 Mar. 1813–12 May 1814) wounded in the left
    foot at Leipzig (18 Oct. 1813)
Regimental depot
  1811 Joigny
Location of squadrons
  Sep. 1810–Jul. 1811 HQ, 1st and 2nd Squadrons in France; 3rd and 4th
    Squadrons in Spain
  Aug. 1811–Spring 1813 HQ, 1st, 2nd and 3rd Squadrons in France; 4th
    Squadron in Spain
Arrival in the Peninsula
  Dec. 1807 1 company
  Sep. 1810 3rd and 4th Squadrons
Major commands to which assigned
  Dec. 1807–Oct. 1808 1 company in 3rd Prov. Chasseur Regiment,
    Bessières's Brigade, Corps of the Eastern Pyrenees
  Nov. 1808–16 Jan. 1809 1 company in 3rd Prov. Chasseur Regiment,
    Bessières's Brigade, 7th Corps
  Sep. 1810–Jul. 1811 3rd and 4th Squadrons part of 1st Prov. Light
    Cavalry Regiment, Watier's Brigade, Army of the North
  Aug. 1811–Spring 1813 4th Squadron assigned to 7th Military
    Government
Battles and officer casualties
  Barcelona (8 Nov. 1808) 1 wounded
  Figuières (21 Jul. 1808) 2 wounded
  Oporto (1 Mar. 1809) 1 wounded
  Fuentes de Oñoro (5 May 1811) 1 wounded
  Santo-Domingo (8 Feb. 1813) 1 wounded

Departure from the Peninsula
Jul. 1811 3rd Squadron
Spring 1813 4th Squadron

Table 12.13   26th Chasseur Regiment

Colonels
Jacques-Laurent-Louis-Augustin Vial (4 Apr. 1807–22 Jul. 1813)
Jacques François Joseph Miller (5 Aug. 1813–27 Jan. 1814) killed at
   Saint-Dizier (27 Jan. 1814)
Regimental depot
1810 Saumur
Location of squadrons
Oct.–Nov. 1807 4th Squadron in Portugal
Nov. 1807–Oct. 1808 4th Squadron in Portugal
Nov. 1808 HQ, 1st, 2nd and 3rd Squadrons
Arrival in the Peninsula
Jan. 1808 1 squadron
Oct. 1808 HQ, 1st, 2nd and 3rd, Squadrons
Major commands to which assigned
Sep. 1807 1 squadron assigned to Magaron's Brigade, Kellermann's
   Division
Nov. 1808 HQ, 1st, 2nd and 3rd Squadrons attached to the 4th Corps
Dec. 1808 HQ, 1st, 2nd and 3rd Squadrons in Beaumont's Brigade,
   attached to the 6th Corps
Jan.–May 1808 HQ, 1st, 2nd and 3rd Squadrons in Beaumont's Brigade,
   1st Corps
May — Sep. 1809 HQ, 1st, 2nd and 3rd Squadrons in Strolz's Brigade,
   Merlin's Division, 4th Corps
Sep. 1809–Feb. 1812 HQ, 1st, 2nd and 3rd Squadrons in the Army
   Reserve in Madrid
Feb.–Sep. 1812 HQ, 1st and 2nd Squadrons in Vial's Brigade, Curto's
   Division
Sep. 1812–Jun. 1813 HQ, 1st and 2nd Squadrons in Curto's Brigade,
   Mermet's Division
Battles and officer casualties
Roliça (17 Aug. 1808) 1 wounded
Vimeiro (21 Aug. 1808) 1 wounded
Medellin (28 Mar. 1809) 2 wounded
Talavera (28 Jul. 1809) 2 wounded
d'Almonacid (11 Aug. 1809) 1 wounded
Counter-guerrilla operations (1809–13) 2 killed, 6 wounded

Table 12.13   continued

Battles and officer casualties
  La Renda (2 Jul. 1812) 1 killed, 2 wounded
  Salamanca (22 Jul. 1812) 4 wounded
Departure from the Peninsula
  Feb. 1812 3rd Squadron
  Jun. 1813 HQ, 1st and 2nd Squadrons

Note The 26th Chasseurs may have been assigned to the Army of the North in the
autumn of 1811.

Table 12.14   27th Chasseur Regiment

Colonels
  Prosper Louis d'Arenberg (30 Sep. 1806 –28 Oct. 1811) wounded in the
    arm at Gibraleon (4 Jun. 1810) and captured at Arroyo dos Molinos
    (28 Oct. 1811)
  François-Xavier Strub (8 Feb. 1813 –7 Oct. 1813) captured at Domburg
    (7 Oct. 1813)
Regimental depot
  1810 Liege
Location of squadrons
  Jan. 1809 HQ, 1st, 2nd and 3rd Squadrons in Spain; 4th Squadron in
    France
  Sep. 1810 HQ, 1st, 2nd and 3rd Squadrons in Spain; 4th Squadron in
    France
  Autumn 1811 HQ and all squadrons in Spain
  Jun. 1812 HQ, 1st, 2nd and 3rd Squadrons in Spain; 4th Squadron in
    France
  Apr. 1813 HQ, 1st and 2nd Squadrons in Spain; 3rd and 4th Squadrons
    in France
Arrival in the Peninsula
  Jan. 1809 HQ, 1st, 2nd and 3rd Squadrons
  Sep. 1811 4th Squadron
Major commands to which assigned
  Jan. 1809 –Jan. 1810 HQ, 1st, 2nd and 3rd Squadrons in Army Reserve
    in Madrid
  Jan. 1810 –Apr. 1811 HQ, 1st, 2nd and 3rd Squadrons in Perreimond's
    Brigade, 4th Corps
  Apr. –Aug. 1811 HQ, 1st, 2nd and 3rd Squadrons in Army Reserve,
    Army of the South
  Sep. 1811–7 Feb. 1812 HQ, 1st, 2nd, 3rd and 4th Squadrons in Briche's
    Brigade, 5th Corps

7 Feb.–May 1812 HQ, 1st, 2nd, 3rd and 4th Squadrons in Ormancey's
   Brigade, Soult's Division
May–Oct. 1812 HQ, 1st, 2nd and 3rd Squadrons in Ormancey's
   Brigade, Soult's Division
Oct. 1812–Mar. 1813 HQ, 1st, 2nd and 3rd Squadrons in Bonnemains's
   Brigade, Tilly's Division
Apr.–May 1813 HQ, 1st and 2nd Squadrons in Marazin's Brigade,
   Soult's Division
Jun. 1813 HQ, 1st and 2nd Squadrons in Houssin de Sainte-Laurent's
   Brigade, Soult's Division
Battles and officer casualties
  Guadalajara (15 Nov. 1809) 1 killed
  Counter-guerrilla operations (1809–12) 4 killed, 8 wounded
  Albuera (16 May 1811) 2 wounded
  Montijo (17 Sep. 1811) 2 wounded
  Arroyo dos Molinos (28 Oct. 1811) 2 killed, 2 wounded
Departure from the Peninsula
  Spring 1812 4th Squadron
  Mar. 1813 3rd Squadron
  Jun. 1813 HQ, 1st and 2nd Squadrons

Note The Duke of Arenberg's Belgian Light Horse were redesignated the 27th
Chasseurs on 29 May 1808.

Table 12.15   28th Chasseur Regiment

Colonels
  Pierre Victor Laroche (20 Jul. 1811–21 Apr. 1813)
Regimental depot
  1811 Orleans
Location of squadrons
  Jul. 1808–Winter 1813 1st Squadron in Spain
Arrival in the Peninsula
  Jul. 1808 1st Squadron
Major commands to which assigned
  Jul.–Nov. 1808 1st Squadron assigned to Duhesme's Corps
  Nov. 1808–Jan. 1810 1st Squadron assigned to Reille's Division, 7th
   Corps
  Jan. 1810–Apr. 1811 1st Squadron assigned to Bonet's Division 4th
   Military Government
Major commands to which assigned
  Apr.–Jun. 1811 1st Squadron assigned to Watier's Brigade, Army of the
   North

Table 12.15   continued

Major commands to which assigned
 Jun.–Jul. 1811 1st Squadron assigned to Watier's Brigade, Army of
  Portugal
 Aug. 1811–Jun. 1812 1st Squadron assigned to Bonet's Division, Army
  of the North
 Jul.–Sep. 1812 1st Squadron assigned to Vial's Brigade, Curto's Division
 Sep. 1812–Winter 1813 1st Squadron assigned to Curto's Brigade,
  Mermet's Division
Battles and officer casualties
 Fuentes de Oñoro (3–5 May 1811) 1 would die from wounds
 Salamanca (22 Jul. 1812) 2 wounded
Departure from the Peninsula
 Winter 1813 1st Squadron

Notes The 1st Squadron of the 28th Chasseurs spent most of its time fighting insurgents in north-western Spain. They worked closely with General Jean Bonet's Infantry Division trying to pacify the Asturias.

Table 12.16   29th Chasseur Regiment

Colonels
 Jean-François-Nicolas Maucomble 7 Oct. 1810–18 Jun. 1813
 François Gabriel Dornier 14 Aug. 1813–Apr. 1814
Regimental depot
 1811 Carcassone
Location of squadrons
 Sep. 1810 HQ, 1st, 2nd, 3rd and 4th Squadrons in Spain
 Mar. 1812 HQ, 1st, 2nd and 3rd Squadrons in Spain; 4th Squadron in
  France
 Autumn 1813 HQ, 1st, 2nd and 3rd Squadrons in France; 4th and 5th
  Squadrons in Germany
Arrival in the Peninsula
 Sep. 1810 HQ, 1st, 2nd, 3rd and 4th Squadrons
Major commands to which assigned
 Sep. 1810–Summer 1811 HQ, 1st, 2nd, 3rd and 4th Squadrons in 7th
  Corps
 Sep. 1811–Winter 1812 HQ, 1st, 2nd, 3rd and 4th Squadrons in Army of
  Catalonia
 Winter 1812–Aug. 1813 HQ, 1st, 2nd and 3rd Squadrons in Army of
  Catalonia
 Sep.–Dec. 1813 HQ, 1st, 2nd and 3rd Squadrons in Army of Aragon
  and Catalonia

Jan.–Apr. 1814 HQ, 1st, 2nd and 3rd Squadrons in Meyers's Brigade,
   Army of Aragon and Catalonia
Battles and officer casualties
   Tarrega (3 Jan. 1811) 3 wounded
   Counter-guerrilla operations 1811–13 1 killed, 4 wounded
   Altafulla (24 Jan. 1812) 1 killed, 2 wounded
   Notre Dame de la Salud (9 Jul. 1813) 5 wounded
Departure from the Peninsula
   Winter 1812 4th Squadron

Notes The 29th Chasseur Regiment traces its origin to the 3rd Provisional Chasseur
Regiment, which was formed on 10 Mar. 1808. By the Decree of 22 August 1810, it
was renamed the 29th Chasseurs. The regiment would serve its whole existence in
the Peninsula, until disbanded in May 1814. While there, it was usually divided into
company- and squadron-size detachments and was responsible for securing the lines
of communication with France.

Table 12.17   31st Chasseur Regiment

Colonels
   Louis Alexis Desmichels 11 Dec. 1811–Apr. 1814
Regimental depot
   1813 Annecy
Location of squadrons
   Sep. 1811–Jun. 1813 HQ, 1st, 2nd and 3rd Squadrons in Spain
Arrival in the Peninsula
   Sep. 1811 HQ, 1st, 2nd and 3rd Squadrons
Major commands to which assigned
   Sep. 1811–Feb. 1813 HQ, 1st, 2nd and 3rd Squadrons in Laferrière's
      Brigade, Army of the North
   Feb.–Jun. 1813 HQ, 1st, 2nd and 3rd Squadrons in Merlin's Brigade,
      Army of the North
Battles and officer casualties
   Counter-guerrilla operations 1811–13 1 killed, 2 wounded
   Salamanca (22 Jul. 1812) 2 wounded
   Villadrigo (23 Oct. 1812) 2 wounded
Departure from the Peninsula
   Jun. 1813 HQ, 1st, 2nd and 3rd Squadrons

Notes The 31st Chasseurs were formed on 7 September 1811, when the 1st Provisional Light Cavalry Regiment was dissolved. The new regiment would consist
of the 4th Squadrons from the 11th and 12th Chasseurs and the 5th Hussars. In
November 1813, while the regiment was in Italy, one of its squadrons was armed
with a lance.

Chapter Thirteen

The Hussar Regiments

By March 1814 the French Army had 14 hussar regiments, 11 of which had served in Spain over the years. Only the 6th, 13th and 14th Hussars never served in the Peninsula. The 1st, 2nd, 3rd, 4th, 9th, 10th and 12th Hussars had served in there in strength with three or more squadrons. The 5th Hussars had one squadron that served there for 11 months from November 1810 to September 1811. The 7th and 8th Hussars each had only one company in the early days of the war. Both were in the 2nd Provisional Hussar Regiment. The Dutch 3rd Hussars also served in Spain from November 1808 to September 1810. They would be incorporated into the French Army as the 11th Hussars. In February 1812 the 10th Hussars were ordered back to France. A year later, in February 1813, the 9th Hussars (bis) were renamed the 12th Hussars. Four months later, in June, the 1st and 3rd Hussars were withdrawn from the Peninsula for service with the Grande Armée in Germany. In January 1814 the 4th and 12th Hussars were ordered to eastern France. Only the 2nd Hussars remained with the Peninsular Armies until the end of the war.

Table 13.1   1st Hussar Regiment

Colonels
 Jacques Bégougne de Juniac (6 Jan. 1807–31 Aug. 1810)
 Antoine-François-Eugène Merlin (1 Sep. 1810–14 Jul. 1813)
 François-Joseph-Marie Clary (17 Jul. 1813–1814)
Regimental depot
 1808 Fontenay-le-Comte
 1810 Liege
 1811 Fontenay-le-Comte
Location of squadrons
 Jan. 1809 HQ, 1st, 2nd, 3rd and 4th Squadrons in Spain

Mar.–May 1809 HQ, 1st, 2nd, 3rd and 4th Squadrons in Portugal
Jan.–Aug. 1810 HQ, 1st, 2nd, 3rd and 4th Squadrons in Spain
Sep. 1810–Apr. 1811 HQ, 1st, 2nd, 3rd and 4th Squadrons in Portugal
Jul. 1811–Apr. 1813 HQ, 1st, 2nd and 3rd Squadrons in Spain; 4th
  Squadron in France
May 1813 HQ, 1st and 2nd Squadrons in Spain; 3rd Squadron in France;
  4th Squadron in Germany
Arrival in the Peninsula
Dec. 1808 HQ, 1st, 2nd, 3rd and 4th Squadrons
Major commands to which assigned
Jan.–Jun. 1809 HQ, 1st, 2nd, 3rd and 4th Squadrons in Debelle's
  Brigade, Franceschi's Divisions, 2nd Corps
Jun.–Aug. 1809 HQ, 1st, 2nd, 3rd and 4th Squadrons in Debelle's
  Brigade, Soult's Division
Aug. 1809–Mar. 1811 HQ, 1st, 2nd, 3rd and 4th Squadrons in
  d'Ermenoville's Brigade, Soult's Division
Apr. 1811 HQ, 1st, 2nd, 3rd and 4th Squadrons in Desfossés's Brigade,
  Soult's Division
Jul. 1811–Oct. 1812 HQ, 1st, 2nd and 3rd Squadrons in Laferrière's
  Brigade, Army of the North
Oct. 1812–Jun. 1813 HQ, 1st and 2nd Squadrons in Merlin's Brigade,
  attached to the Army of Portugal until Mar. 1813
Oct. 1812–Apr. 1813 3rd Squadron in Gareau's Brigade, Quesnel's
  Division, Army of Catalonia
Battles and officer casualties
Braga (20 Mar. 1809) 1 killed, 1 wounded
Ciudad Rodrigo (31 Jul. 1809) 2 wounded
Sabugal (3 Apr. 1811) 3 wounded, 1 would die from wounds
Fuentes de Oñoro (5 May 1811) none
Counter-guerrilla operations in Spain 1811–14 7 wounded
Villadrigo (23 Oct. 1812) 1 wounded
Departure from the Peninsula
Jul. 1811 4th Squadron
Apr. 1813 3rd Squadron
27 Jun. 1813 HQ, 1st and 2nd Squadrons

Notes In June 1811 the men from the Hanoverian Chasseurs were transferred to the
1st Hussars, when their regiment was disbanded. This would bring the strength of the
1st Hussars to over 500 men.

Table 13.2   2nd Hussar Regiment

Colonels

François-Joseph Gérard (7 Oct. 1806–10 Mar. 1809)

Gilbert-Julien Vinot (16 Mar. 1809–2 Mar. 1813) wounded at Vitoria (21 Jun. 1813)

Alexandre-Louis de Séganville (21 Apr. 1813–10 Dec. 1815)

Regimental depot

1810 Maestricht

Location of squadrons

Dec. 1807 1 company in Spain

Oct. 1808 HQ and all squadrons in Spain

May 1813 HQ, 1st and 2nd Squadrons in Spain; 3rd Squadron in France; 4th Squadron in Germany

Oct. 1813 May 1813 HQ, 1st and 2nd Squadrons in France; 3rd and 4th Squadrons in Germany

Jan. 1814 HQ and all squadrons in France

Arrival in the Peninsula

Dec. 1807 1 company

Oct. 1808 HQ, 1st, 2nd, 3rd and 4th Squadrons

Oct. 1811 4th Squadron

Major commands to which assigned

Dec. 1807–Aug. 1808 1 company in the 1st Prov. Hussar Regiment, Watier's Brigade, Grouchy's Division, Moncey's Corps

Sep. 1808–Jan. 1809 1 company in the 1st Prov. Hussar Regiment, Watier's Brigade, 3rd Corps

Sep.–Nov. 1808 HQ, 1st, 2nd, 3rd and 4th Squadrons in Beaumont's Brigade, 1st Corps

Dec. 1808 HQ, 1st, 2nd, 3rd and 4th Squadrons in Beaumont's Brigade, 1st Corps attached to the 6th Corps

Jan. 1809–Apr. 1811 HQ, 1st, 2nd, 3rd and 4th Squadrons in Beaumont's Brigade, 1st Corps

May 1811 HQ, 1st, 2nd and 3rd Squadrons in Briche's Brigade, Latour-Maubourg's Division

Jun.–Aug. 1811 HQ, 1st, 2nd and 3rd Squadrons in Perreimond's Brigade, Latour-Maubourg's Division, 1st Corps

Sep. 1811 HQ, 1st, 2nd and 3rd Squadrons in Vinot's Brigade, Latour-Maubourg's Reserve Division, Army of the South

Oct. 1811–Feb. 1812 HQ, 1st, 2nd and 3rd Squadrons in Briche's Brigade, 5th Corps

Feb.–Mar. 1812 HQ, 1st, 2nd and 3rd Squadrons in Lallemand's Brigade, Perreimond's Division

Mar.–Oct. 1812 HQ, 1st, 2nd and 3rd Squadrons in Vinot's Brigade, Perreimond's Division

Oct. 1812–Feb. 1813 HQ, 1st, 2nd and 3rd Squadrons in Vinot's Brigade, Tilly's Division

Mar. 1813–Jul. 1813 HQ, 1st and 2nd Squadrons in Vinot's Brigade, Soult's Division

Jul. 1813–Apr. 1814 HQ, 1st and 2nd Squadrons in Berton's Brigade, Soult's Division, Army of Spain

Battles and officer casualties

Medellin (28 Mar. 1809) 2 wounded

Alcabon (26 Jul. 1809) 1 wounded

Talavera (27–28 Jul. 1809) 1 wounded

Santa-Cruz (25 Jan. 1810) none

Ronda (9–10 Apr. 1810) 1 killed, 3 wounded

Gebora (19 Feb. 1811) 1 killed, 1 wounded

Albuera (16 May 1811) 1 killed, 4 wounded, 1 would die from wounds

Vitoria (21 Jun. 1813) 1 wounded

Saint-Pierre d'Irube (13 Dec. 1813) none

Aire (2 Mar. 1814) none

Toulouse (10 Apr. 1814) none

Departure from the Peninsula

Winter 1811 4th Squadron

Feb. 1813 3rd Squadron

Notes The 2nd Hussars often referred to themselves by their old regimental name–the Chamborant Hussars. On 17 November 1812, during the retreat of the British army to the Portuguese border, the 2nd Hussars captured the British army's second-in-command, Lieutenant General Sir Edward Paget.

Table 13.3   3rd Hussar Regiment

Colonels

Louis Laferrière-Levesque (8 Mar. 1807–12 May 1811) wounded at Col de Banos (12 Aug. 1809), shot in the left arm at Alba de Tormes (28 Nov. 1809) and shot twice in the right arm at Redinha (12 Mar. 1811)

Louis Paulin Rousseau (14 Oct. 1811–21 Feb. 1814) wounded in the head by two sabre cuts at Salamanca (22 Jul. 1812)

Regimental depot

1810 Venloo

1812 Pamiers

Location of squadrons

Dec. 1807 1 company in Spain

Table 13.3   continued

Location of squadrons

Nov. 1808 HQ, 1st, 2nd, 3rd and 4th Squadrons in Spain

Sep. 1810–Mar. 1811 HQ, 1st, 2nd, 3rd and 4th Squadrons in Portugal

Apr.–Jun. 1811 HQ, 1st, 2nd, 3rd and 4th Squadrons in Spain

Autumn 1811–Jun. 1813 HQ, 1st and 2nd Squadrons in Spain; 3rd and 4th Squadron in France

Arrival in the Peninsula

Dec. 1807 1 company

Nov. 1808 HQ and all squadrons

Oct. 1811 3rd and 4th Squadrons

Major commands to which assigned

Dec. 1807–Aug. 1808 1 company in the 1st Prov. Hussar Regiment, Watier's Brigade, Grouchy's Division, Moncey's Corps

Sep. 1808–Jan. 1809 1 company in the 1st Prov. Hussar Regiment, Watier's Brigade, 3rd Corps

Nov. 1808–Jan. 1809 HQ, 1st, 2nd, 3rd and 4th Squadrons in Colbert's Brigade, 6th Corps

Jan. 1809–Jul. 1810 HQ, 1st, 2nd, 3rd and 4th Squadrons in Lorcet's Brigade, 6th Corps

Jul. 1810–7 Mar. 1811 HQ, 1st, 2nd, 3rd and 4th Squadrons in Lamotte's Brigade, 6th Corps

Mar.–Jun. 1811 HQ, 1st, 2nd, 3rd and 4th Squadrons in Mourier's Brigade, 6th Corps

Jul.–Nov. 1811 HQ, 1st and 2nd Squadrons in Desfossés's Brigade, Army of Portugal

Nov. 1811–Jan. 1812 HQ, 1st and 2nd Squadrons in Curto's Brigade, Army of Portugal

Feb.–Sep. 1812 HQ, 1st and 2nd Squadrons in Desfossés's Brigade, Curto's Division

Sep. 1812–Jun. 1813 HQ, 1st and 2nd Squadrons in Squadrons in Curto's Brigade, Mermet's Division

Battles and officer casualties

Madrid (2 May 1808) 1 wounded

Tudela (22 Nov. 1808) 4 wounded

Cacabellos (3 Jan. 1809) none

Col de Banos (12 Aug. 1809) 1 killed, 6 wounded

Tamames (18 Oct. 1809) none

Alba de Tormes (28 Nov. 1809) 2 wounded

Siege of Almeida (Jul.–Aug. 1810) 1 killed, 1 wounded

Bussaco (27 Sep. 1810) none

Leria (7 Oct. 1810) 3 wounded

Alcoluto (9 Oct. 1810) 1 wounded
Redinha (12 Mar. 1811) 5 wounded
Fuentes de Oñoro (3–5 May 1811) none
Salamanca (22 Jul. 1812) 3 wounded
Vitoria (21 Jun. 1813) 3 wounded
Departure from the Peninsula
Jun. 1811 3rd and 4th Squadrons
Jun. 1813 HQ, 1st and 2nd Squadrons

Notes After the death of their brigade commander, General Colbert, in January 1809, the 3rd Hussars changed their white *'flammes'* to black and draped their standard with a black mourning veil for three years. A *flamme* was the white ribbon wrapped around the mirliton, the headgear that was replaced by the shako. Most regiments did not use the *flamme* on their shako. The 3rd Hussars was one of those that did.

Table 13.4   4th Hussar Regiment

Colonels
Andre Burthe (1 Feb. 1805–30 Dec. 1810)
Jean-François Christophe (9 Jan. 1811–30 Mar. 1815)
Regimental depot
1810 Malines
1811 Niort
Location of squadrons
Nov. 1808–Nov. 1813 HQ, 1st, 2nd, 3rd and 4th Squadrons in Spain
Arrival in the Peninsula
Dec. 1807 1 company
Nov. 1808 HQ, 1st, 2nd, 3rd and 4th Squadrons
Major commands to which assigned
Dec. 1807–Aug. 1808 1 company in the 1st Prov. Hussar Regiment,
    Watier's Brigade, Grouchy's Division, Moncey's Corps
Sep. 1808–Jan. 1809 1 company in the 1st Prov. Hussar Regiment,
    Watier's Brigade, 3rd Corps
Nov. 1808 HQ, 1st, 2nd, 3rd and 4th Squadrons in Beaumont's Brigade,
    1st Corps
Dec. 1808–Apr. 1809 HQ, 1st, 2nd, 3rd and 4th Squadrons in Watier's
    Brigade, 3rd Corps
Apr. 1809–May 1810 HQ, 1st, 2nd, 3rd and 4th Squadrons in Boussart's
    Brigade, 3rd Corps
May 1810–Dec. 1811 HQ, 1st, 2nd, 3rd and 4th Squadrons in Boussart's
    Brigade, Army of Aragon
Dec. 1811 HQ, 1st, 2nd, 3rd and 4th Squadrons in Maupoint's Brigade,
    Army of Aragon

Table 13.4 continued

Major commands to which assigned

Jan. 1812–Sep. 1813 HQ, 1st, 2nd, 3rd and 4th Squadrons in Delort's
  Brigade, Army of Aragon

Sep. 1813–Jan. 1814 HQ, 1st, 2nd, 3rd and 4th Squadrons in Delort's
  Brigade, Digeon's Division, Army of Aragon

Battles and officer casualties

Medellin (28 Mar. 1809) 1 wounded

Maria (15 Jun. 1809) 3 wounded

Counter-guerrilla operations (1809–13) 4 killed, 13 wounded

Saguntum (25 Oct. 1811) 2 wounded, 1 would die from wounds

Yecla (11 Apr. 1813) 2 wounded, 1 would die from wounds

Carcagenta (13 Jun. 1813) 2 wounded, 1 would die from wounds

Departure from the Peninsula

Jan. 1814 HQ, 1st, 2nd, 3rd and 4th Squadrons

Notes The 4th Hussars was one of the few cavalry regiments that Napoleon did not draw on in 1813 to rebuild his depleted forces in Germany. In early 1814 it had a strength of 650 men and was one of the strongest cavalry regiments in the Peninsula. Napoleon finally ordered it to eastern France in January 1814.

Table 13.5   5th Hussar Regiment

Colonels

Pierre-César Dery (30 Dec. 1806–20 Sep. 1809)

Claude Meuziau (21 Sep. 1809–14 May 1813) wounded at Borodino (7
  Sep. 1812) and Winkowo (18 Oct. 1812)

Regimental depot

1811 Stenay

Location of squadrons

Dec. 1807–Jan. 1809 1 company in Spain

Jul. 1810–Sep. 1811 4th Squadron in Spain

Arrival in the Peninsula

Dec. 1807 1 company

Nov. 1810 4th Squadron

Major commands to which assigned

Dec. 1807–Aug. 1808 1 company in the 1st Prov. Hussar Regiment,
  Watier's Brigade, Grouchy's Division, Moncey's Corps

Sep. 1808–Jan. 1809 1 company in the 1st Prov. Hussar Regiment,
  Watier's Brigade, 3rd Corps

Sep.–Dec. 1810 4th Squadron part of the 1st Prov. Light Cavalry
  Regiment, Watier's Brigade, Army of Spain

Jan.–Jun. 1811 4th Squadron part of the 1st Prov. Light Cavalry
Regiment, Watier's Brigade, Army of the North
Jul.–Aug. 1811 4th Squadron in 7th Military Government, Army of the
North
Sep. 1811 4th Squadron incorporated into 31st Chasseurs, General
Laferrière's Brigade, Army of the North
Battles and officer casualties
Tudela (23 Nov. 1808) 1 wounded
Saragossa (19 Mar. 1809) 1 wounded
Fuentes de Oñoro (3–5 May 1811) 1 wounded
On reconnaissance in Spain (Jun. 1811) 1 killed

Notes In September 1811 the 4th Squadron had 10 officers and 197 hussars serving in
Spain. Eight of the officers were transferred into the newly formed 31st Chasseurs,
instead of returning to France.[*]

Table 13.6   9th Hussar Regiment

Colonels
Pierre-Edme Gauthrin (16 Oct. 1806–21 Sep. 1809) shot at Friedland 14
Jun. 1807
Louis Charles Grégoire Maignet (21 Sep. 1809–9 Feb. 1812)
Louis-Pierre-Alphonse Colbert (15 Jan. 1812–17 Feb. 1813)
Regimental depot
1811 Schelestatt
1812 Niort
Location of squadrons
Dec. 1807–Jan. 1809 1 company in Spain
Arrival in the Peninsula
Dec. 1807 1 company
Jun. 1808 2nd Squadron
Jul. 1810 3rd and 4th Squadrons
Winter 1811 4th Squadron
Major commands to which assigned
Dec. 1807–Aug. 1808 1 company in the 2nd Prov. Hussar Regiment,
Watier's Brigade, Grouchy's Division, Moncey's Corps
Sep. 1808–Jan. 1809 1 company in the 2nd Prov. Hussar Regiment,
Watier's Brigade, 3rd Corps
Jun. 1808–Jul. 1810 2nd Squadron, Pamplona Garrison, Army of Spain
Jul.–Nov. 1810 2nd, 3rd and 4th Squadrons in 3rd Military Government,
Army of Spain

---

[*] Massoni, *Histoire d'un regiment de cavalerie légère*, p. 351

Table 13.6 continued

Major commands to which assigned

Nov. 1810–Jan. 1811 2nd and 3rd Squadrons in Watier's Brigade, Army
of Spain

Jan.–Oct. 1811 2nd, 3rd and 4th Squadrons in Watier's Brigade, Army of
Spain

Nov.–Dec. 1811 2nd, 3rd and 4th Squadrons attached to Reille's
Division, Army of Aragon

Jan. 1812–Feb. 1813 2nd Squadron attached to Reille's Division, Army
of Aragon; 3rd and 4th Squadrons in 3rd Military Government, Army
of Spain

Battles and officer casualties

Counter-guerrilla operations 1810–12 11 wounded

Tarragona (24 Jun. 1811) 1 wounded

Saguntum (25 Oct. 1811) 1 wounded

River Ebro (8 Nov. 1812) 2 killed, 2 wounded

Notes When the 3rd and 4th Squadrons deployed to Spain in July 1810, they were
commanded by Major Marc. Colonel Colbert would command them in 1811 and
1812. The 9th Hussars were redesignated as the 9th Hussars (bis)* on 9 January 1812.
For all practical purposes, the three squadrons in Spain were a separate regiment from
the 9th Hussars, which were located in Alsace. On 17 February 1813 the 9th Hussars
(bis) were redesignated as the 12th Hussars.

Table 13.7   10th Hussar Regiment

Colonels

Andre-Louis-Elisabeth-Marie Briche (13 Jan. 1806–17 Dec. 1809)

François-Marie De Laval (17 Dec. 1809–17 Apr. 1812)

Regimental depot

1810 Schelestatt

1811 Niort

Location of squadrons

Nov. 1807 1 company in Spain

Dec. 1808–May 1812 HQ, 1st, 2nd, 3rd and 4th Squadrons in Spain

---

* Bis is a curious term used by the French Army to designate units that were originally
part of another unit, but acted independently from its parent unit. Many times it would
evolve into a unit of similar size and organisation as the parent unit. To help identify
the detached unit, but to show that it was still considered part of the parent unit, it
would have (bis) after its name. By January 1812, the 9th Hussars had 7 squadrons,
three of which (the 2nd, 3rd and 4th) were in Spain. When the 9th Hussars (bis) were
formed, the 5th, 6th and 7th Squadrons, which were stationed in Alsace, were renamed
the 2nd, 3rd and 4th Squadrons, 9th Hussars. The original 2nd, 3rd and 4th Squadrons
kept their names, but were named 9th Hussars (bis).

Arrival in the Peninsula
Nov. 1807 1 company
Dec. 1808 HQ, 1st, 2nd, 3rd and 4th Squadrons
Major commands to which assigned
Dec. 1807–Aug. 1808 1 company in the 2nd Prov. Hussar Regiment, Watier's Brigade, Grouchy's Division, Moncey's Corps
Sep. 1808–Jan. 1809 1 company in the 2nd Prov. Hussar Regiment, Watier's Brigade, 3rd Corps
Dec. 1808–Jun. 1809 HQ, 1st, 2nd, 3rd and 4th Squadrons in Boussart's Brigade, 5th Corps
Jun.–Nov. 1809 HQ, 1st, 2nd, 3rd and 4th Squadrons in Beaurgard's Brigade, 5th Corps
Nov. 1809–Feb. 1810 HQ, 1st, 2nd, 3rd and 4th Squadrons in Steenhaudt's Brigade, 5th Corps
Feb.–May 1810 HQ, 1st, 2nd, 3rd and 4th Squadrons in Briche's Brigade, 5th Corps
May–Oct. 1810 HQ, 1st, 2nd, 3rd and 4th Squadrons in Briche's Brigade, Marizy's Division, 5th Corps
Nov. 1810–7 Feb. 1812 HQ, 1st, 2nd, 3rd and 4th Squadrons in Briche's Brigade, 5th Corps
Feb. 1812 HQ, 1st, 2nd, 3rd and 4th Squadrons in Lallemand's Brigade, Perreimond's Division
Battles and officer casualties
Counter-guerrilla operations (1808–12) 2 killed, 6 wounded, 1 would die from wounds
Valverde (19 Feb. 1810) 1 wounded
Gebora (19 Feb. 1811) 1 killed, 1 wounded
Albuera (16 May 1811) 7 wounded, 1 would die from wounds
Departure from the Peninsula
May 1812 HQ, 1st, 2nd, 3rd and 4th Squadrons

Notes The 10th Hussars were brigaded with the 21st Chasseurs from the time the regiment entered Spain in December 1808 until they departed for France in March 1812.

Table 13.8   12th Hussar Regiment

Colonels
Louis-Pierre-Alphonse Colbert (17 Feb. 1813–11 Mar. 1814)
Location of squadrons
Feb.–Dec. 1813 HQ, 1st, 2nd and 3rd Squadrons in Spain
Jan. 1814 HQ, 1st, 2nd and 3rd Squadrons in France

Table 13.8   continued

Arrival in the Peninsula

  17 Feb. 1813 HQ, 1st, 2nd and 3rd Squadrons

  Feb.–Jul. 1813 HQ, 1st, 2nd and 3rd Squadrons in Bourgeois's Brigade,
    Paris's Division, Army of Aragon

Major commands to which assigned

  Jul. 1813–Jan. 1814 HQ, 1st, 2nd and 3rd Squadrons in Meyer's Brigade,
    Digeon's Division

Battles and officer casualties

  Sos (1 Mar. 1813) 1 wounded

  Catalonia (16 Dec. 1813) 1 wounded

Departure from the Peninsula

  Jan. 1814 HQ, 1st, 2nd and 3rd Squadrons

Notes On 17 February 1813 the 9th Hussars (bis) were renamed the 12th Hussars. Colonel Colbert, the commander of the 9th Hussars (bis), was appointed its new commander. In the 11 months that the 12th Hussars fought in the Peninsula, they only had 2 officers wounded.

Chapter Fourteen

The Imperial Guard, Cuirassier and Lancer Regiments

The Imperial Guard Cavalry served in Spain during three distinct periods. They were among the first cavalry to enter Spain, when a detachment of 1,340 under the command of Colonel Jean Friederichs arrived on 18 February 1808. This detachment was formed by the contribution of a squadron from every Guard cavalry regiment. It initially garrisoned Madrid and was heavily involved in suppressing the uprising there on 2 May 1808. The detachment had 14 wounded, most from among the Chasseurs and Mamelukes. Six months later, in November 1808, Napoleon arrived in Spain with the five cavalry regiments of his guard. The cavalry regiments saw little action, though the Polish Light Horse covered itself with glory with a charge against the Spanish batteries in response to the Emperor's order to clear the Somosierra Pass. A month later, on 29 December, the Chasseurs and the Mamelukes were mauled at Benavente by British cavalry. In addition to having 2 killed and 6 wounded, the Chasseurs' regimental commander, General Charles Lefebvre-Desnouettes was captured! In March 1809 Napoleon ordered the Imperial Guard to return to France in anticipation of needing them against an increasingly belligerent Austria.

In June 1810 Napoleon ordered the Imperial Guard to send troops to northern Spain to help secure the lines of communication with France. They would be garrisoned in Burgos. The cavalry consisted of two composite formations – a regiment of heavy cavalry and one of light cavalry. The brigade would initially be commanded by General Louis Lepic. The heavy cavalry regiment consisted of two squadrons from the Empress Dragoons and one squadron from the Horse Grenadiers. The light cavalry regiment had two squadrons of Polish Lancers, one squadron of Horse Chasseurs, the company of Mamelukes and a company of Velites. The two regiments were at Fuentes de Oñoro from 3–5 May 1808, but were not engaged. General Lepic give up command of the brigade in

August 1811. In December 1811 Napoleon ordered the cavalry to return to France so they would be available for the upcoming invasion of Russia. Their departure was not implemented until four months later and the Light Cavalry Regiment was still involved in combat operations in early April 1812.

Although the Imperial Guard cavalry regiments had colonels who commanded them on paper, these officers were generals and they were often assigned other duties, such as command of a brigade or division. The regiments also had two colonel-majors assigned to them and they would command the regiment on campaign.

Table 14.1   Horse Grenadiers of the Imperial Guard

Colonels
Frédéric-Henri Walther (20 May 1806–30 Nov. 1813)
Regimental depot
Paris
Arrival in the Peninsula
Apr. 1808 1 squadron
Nov. 1808 3 squadrons
Jun. 1810 1 squadron
Major commands to which assigned
Apr.–Nov. 1808 1 squadron assigned to Lepic's Division
Nov. 1808–Mar. 1809 The regiment was assigned to the Imperial Guard Cavalry Division
Jun. 1810–Jan. 1811 1 squadron in the Guard Heavy Cavalry Regiment, Lepic's Brigade, Army of Spain
Jan.–Aug. 1811 1 squadron in the Guard Heavy Cavalry Regiment, Lepic's Brigade, Army of the North
Sep. 1811–Mar. 1812 1 squadron in the Guard Heavy Cavalry Regiment, Army of the North
Battles and officer casualties
Madrid (2 May 1808) 1 wounded
Departure from the Peninsula
Mar. 1809 The whole regiment
Mar. 1812 1 squadron

Table 14.2   Horse Chasseurs of the Imperial Guard

Colonels
Charles Lefebvre-Desnouettes (18 Jan. 1808–12 May 1814) Captured by the British at Benavente on 29 Dec. 1809

Regimental depot
 Paris
Arrival in the Peninsula
 Apr. 1808 1 squadron
 Nov. 1808 3 squadrons
 Jun. 1810 1 squadron
Major commands to which assigned
 Apr.–Nov. 1808 1 squadron assigned to Lepic's Division
 Nov. 1808–Mar. 1809 The regiment was assigned to the Imperial Guard
  Cavalry Division
 Jun. 1810–Jan. 1811 1 squadron in the Guard Light Cavalry Regiment,
  Lepic's Brigade, Army of Spain
 Jan.–Aug. 1811 1 squadron in the Guard Light Cavalry Regiment,
  Lepic's Brigade, Army of the North
 Sep. 1811–Apr. 1812 1 squadron in the Guard Light Cavalry Regiment,
  Army of the North
Battles and officer casualties
 Madrid (2 May 1808) 8 wounded
 Benavente (29 Dec. 1808) 1 killed, 5 wounded
 Counter-guerrilla operations (1810–12) 4 wounded
Departure from the Peninsula
 Mar. 1809 The whole regiment
 Apr. 1812 1 squadron

Notes Although General Lefebrvre-Desnouettes was captured on 29 December 1809,
he was kept on as the regimental commander despite being a prisoner of the British
until 1812.

Table 14.3   The Empress Dragoons

Colonels
 Jean Toussaint Arrighi de Casanova (19 May 1806–12 Jul. 1809)
 Raymond Saint-Sulpice (12 Jul. 1809–21 Jan. 1813)
Regimental depot
 Paris
Arrival in the Peninsula
 Apr. 1808 1 squadron
 Nov. 1808 3 squadrons
 Jun. 1810 2 squadrons
Major commands to which assigned
 Apr.–Nov. 1808 1 squadron assigned to Lepic's Division
 Nov. 1808–Mar. 1809 The regiment was assigned to the Imperial Guard
  Cavalry Division

Table 14.3   continued

Major commands to which assigned

Jun. 1810–Jan. 1811 2 squadrons in the Guard Heavy Cavalry Regiment, Lepic's Brigade, Army of Spain

Jan.–Aug. 1811 2 squadrons in the Guard Heavy Cavalry Regiment, Lepic's Brigade, Army of the North

Sep. 1811–Mar. 1812 2 squadrons in the Guard Heavy Cavalry Regiment, Army of the North

Battles and officer casualties

Medina del Rio Seco (14 Jul. 1808) 3 wounded

Counter-guerrilla operations (5 Dec. 1810) 1 killed

Departure from the Peninsula

Mar. 1809 The whole regiment

Mar. 1812 2 squadrons

Table 14.4   The Mamelukes

Chiefs of Squadrons Antoine-Charles-Bernard Delaitre (18 Dec. 1805 – 27 Jan. 1811)

François-Antoine Kirmann (Feb. 1811–14)

Regimental depot

Paris

Arrival in the Peninsula

Apr. 1808 1 company

Nov. 1808 1 company

Jun. 1810 1 company

Major commands to which assigned

Apr.–Nov. 1808 1 company assigned to Lepic's Division

Nov. 1808–Mar. 1809 The Mamelukes were assigned to the Imperial Guard Cavalry Division

Jun. 1810–Jan. 1811 1 company in the Guard Light Cavalry Regiment, Lepic's Brigade, Army of Spain

Jan.–Aug. 1811 1 company in the Guard Light Cavalry Regiment, Lepic's Brigade, Army of the North

Sep. 1811–Apr. 1812 1 company in the Guard Light Cavalry Regiment, Army of the North

Battles and officer casualties

Madrid (2 May 1808) 5 wounded

Saragossa (4 Aug. 1808) 1 wounded

Benavente (29 Dec. 1808) 1 killed, 1 wounded

Counter-guerrilla operations (1810–12) 4 wounded

Departure from the Peninsula
Mar. 1809 1 company
Apr. 1812 1 company

Notes The Mamelukes were a company that was usually attached to the Horse Chasseurs of the Imperial Guard. It was commanded by a chief of squadron.

Table 14.5   The Polish Light Horse/Lancers of the Imperial Guard

Colonels
Vincent Corvin Krasinksi (7 Apr. 1807—?), the regiment's only
  commander, was wounded at Madrid on 2 May 1808
Regimental depot
Chantilly
Arrival in the Peninsula
Apr. 1808 2 squadrons
Nov. 1808 2 squadrons
Jun. 1810 2 squadrons
Major commands to which assigned
Apr.–Nov. 1808 1 squadron assigned to Lepic's Division
Nov. 1808–Mar. 1809 The regiment was assigned to the Imperial Guard
  Cavalry Division
Jun. 1810–Jan. 1811 2 squadrons in the Guard Light Cavalry Regiment,
  Lepic's Brigade, Army of Spain
Jan.–Aug. 1811 2 squadrons in the Guard Light Cavalry Regiment,
  Lepic's Brigade, Army of the North
Sep. 1811–Apr. 1812 2 squadrons in the Guard Light Cavalry Regiment,
  Army of the North
Battles and officer casualties
Madrid (2 May 1808) 8 wounded
Benavente (29 Dec. 1808) 1 killed, 5 wounded
Counter-guerrilla operations (1810–11) 4 wounded
Departure from the Peninsula
Mar. 1809 the whole regiment
Apr. 1812 2 squadrons

Notes In late 1809 the Polish Light Horse Regiment was redesignated as the 1st Lancer Regiment of the Imperial Guard.

The Cuirassiers

Three regiments of provisional cuirassiers were formed in 1808 for duty in Spain. Each cuirassier regiment and the two carabinier regiments were tasked to provide a company to the new regiments. In July 1808 the 2nd Provisional Cuirassiers surrendered at Bailen. In December the 1st Provisional Cuirassiers was designated as the 13th Cuirassiers. The 3rd Provisional Cuirassiers served in the east in Aragon and was finally disbanded in January 1811. (For more detail on the service of these regiments, see chapter 15.)

Table 14.6   13th Cuirassier Regiment

Colonels
 Guillaume-François d'Aigremont (13 Feb. 1809–10 Apr. 1813)
 François Bigarne (28 Jun. 1813–Jul. 1814)
Regimental depot
 Niort
Location of squadrons
 Dec. 1808–Jul. 1813 HQ, 1st, 2nd, 3rd and 4th Squadrons in Spain
 Jul. 1813–Jan. 1814 HQ, 1st, 2nd, 3rd and 4th Squadrons in France; 5th
  Squadron in Germany
Arrival in the Peninsula
 Dec. 1808 HQ, 1st, 2nd, 3rd and 4th Squadrons
Major commands to which assigned
 Dec. 1808–Jun. 1809 HQ, 1st, 2nd, 3rd and 4th Squadrons in Watier's
  Brigade, 3rd Corps
 Jun. 1809–Jul. 1811 HQ, 1st, 2nd, 3rd and 4th Squadrons in Boussart's
  Brigade, 3rd Corps
 Aug.–Dec. 1811 HQ, 1st, 2nd, 3rd and 4th Squadrons in Boussart's
  Brigade, Army of Aragon
 Dec. 1811–Aug. 1813 HQ, 1st, 2nd, 3rd and 4th Squadrons in
  Maupoint's Brigade, Army of Aragon
 Sep. 1813–Jan. 1814 HQ, 1st, 2nd, 3rd and 4th Squadrons in Delort's
  Brigade, Digeon's Division, Army of Aragon
Battles and officer casualties
 Maria (15 Jun. 1809) 2 wounded
 Barcelona (12 Jul. 1809) 1 wounded
 Lerida (23 Apr. 1810) 1 killed
 Barcelona (15 Jul. 1810) 1 wounded
 Oldeconna (12 Apr. 1811) 2 wounded
 Mora (19 Jun. 1811) 1 wounded
 Saguntum (25 Oct. 1811) 3 wounded
 Counter-guerrilla operations 1809–13 3 wounded, 1 would die from
  wounds
 Col d'Ordal (13 Sep. 1813) 1 wounded

Departure from the Peninsula
Jan. 1814 HQ, 1st, 2nd, 3rd and 4th Squadrons

Notes The 13th Cuirassiers were formed in December 1808 from the 1st Provisional Cuirassiers and elements from the 2nd Provisional Cuirassiers who were in Madrid when the regiment surrendered at Bailen. The exact date that the regiment was created is unknown. Even the regimental history does not provide anything other than the month. However, Danielle and Bernard Quintin give the date of creation as 2 October 1808.*

The Lancers

One regiment of lancers served in the French Army in Peninsula. It was the 1st Vistula Legion Lancers, which would enter Spain in June 1808 and would not be withdrawn until January 1813. On 18 June 1811 the 1st Vistula Legion Lancers were redesignated as the 7th Lancers.

Table 14.7   1st Vistula Legion Lancer Regiment / 7th Lancers

Colonels
Jan Konopka (15 Jul. 1807–6 Aug. 1811) wounded at Saragossa on 4 Aug. 1808
Ignace Ferdinand Stokowski (13 Oct. 1811–9 Jun. 1813) wounded at Dresden and captured by Prussian guerrillas on 9 Jun. 1813
Regimental depot
1811 Sedan
Location of squadrons
12 Jun. 1808–Jan. 1813 HQ, 1st, 2nd, 3rd and 4th Squadrons in Spain
Arrival in the Peninsula
12 Jun. 1808 HQ, 1st, 2nd, 3rd and 4th Squadrons
Major commands to which assigned
12 Jun.–Sep. 1808 HQ, 1st, 2nd, 3rd and 4th Squadrons in Marshal Lannes's Force
Sep. 1808–Jan. 1809 HQ, 1st, 2nd, 3rd and 4th Squadrons in Watier's Brigade, 3rd Corps
Jan. 1809 HQ, 1st, 2nd, 3rd and 4th Squadrons in Montbrun's Brigade, Lasalle's Division
Feb.–Apr. 1809 HQ, 1st, 2nd, 3rd and 4th Squadrons in Watier's Brigade, 3rd Corps
Apr.–Dec. 1809 HQ, 1st, 2nd, 3rd and 4th Squadrons in Ormancey's Brigade, Merlin's Division, 4th Corps

---

* Quintin, *Dictionnaire des Colonels de Napoléon*, p. 906.

Table 14.7   1st Vistula Legion Lancer Regiment/7th Lancers continued

Major commands to which assigned

Dec. 1809–18 Jun. 1811 HQ, 1st, 2nd, 3rd and 4th Squadrons in Perreimond's Brigade, 4th Corps

Jul.–Aug. 1811 HQ, 1st, 2nd, 3rd and 4th Squadrons in Perreimond's Brigade, 4th Corps

Aug.–Oct. 1811 HQ, 1st, 2nd, 3rd and 4th Squadrons in Bron's Brigade, Tour-Maubourg's Reserve Corps of the Army of the South

Nov. 1811–Jan. 1812 HQ, 1st, 2nd, 3rd and 4th Squadrons in Konopka's Brigade, Tour-Maubourg's Reserve Corps of the Army of the South

7 Feb.–Mar. 1812 HQ, 1st, 2nd, 3rd and 4th Squadrons in Digeon's Brigade, Tour-Maubourg's Division

Mar.–10 Oct. 1812 HQ, 1st, 2nd, 3rd and 4th Squadrons in Lallemand's Brigade, Digeon's Division

10 Oct. 1812–7 Jan. 1813 HQ, 1st, 2nd, 3rd and 4th Squadrons in Sparre's Brigade, Soult's Division

Battles and officer casualties

Saragossa (15 Jun. 1808) 1 killed

Saragossa (4 Aug. 1808) 5 wounded

Tudela (23 Nov.e 1808) 1 wounded

Operations 1808–10 6 wounded

Juvenez (24 Mar. 1809) 1 killed, 3 wounded, 1 would die from wounds

Ciudad Real 1 wounded

Talavera (28 Jul. 1809) 2 wounded

Almonacid (11 Aug. 1809) 1 wounded

Baza (2 Nov. 1810) 2 wounded

Albuera (16 May 1811 1 killed, 13 wounded, 2 would die from their wounds

Between Jun. 1811 and Dec. 1812, the 7th Lancers had three wounded in action.

Departure from the Peninsula

7 Jan. 1813

Chapter Fifteen

The Provisional Cavalry Regiments

In 1807 Napoleon realised that he would have to do something to keep the Iberian Peninsula under his control. He also knew he did not have enough regiments to accomplish the mission, since most of his cavalry was still deployed in eastern Europe. As a temporary measure Napoleon authorised the formation of 20 provisional cavalry regiments. These regiments would not be part of the formal establishment of the French army, but were to fill in until regular troops could be sent. This allowed him to send troops that were available in various regimental depots throughout France, rather than having to draw on the regiments with the Grande Armée. The first four of these regiments were created in July 1807 and assigned to General Junot's 1st Corps of Observation of the Gironde.

The new regiments were formed by instructing existing regiments to send their 4th Squadrons to the new regiments. In October Napoleon authorised the formation of 16 additional provisional regiments, including 3 cuirassier, 7 dragoon, 3 chasseur and 3 hussar regiments. The tasking for these regiments was done differently from that of the first four regiments. Now, instead of giving up a squadron, the regiment provided a company with the appropriate number of officers. Some regiments were also tasked to provide a major to command the new provisional regiment. By December 1807 the regiments were formed and all but the 3rd, 4th, 5th and 7th Provisional Dragoons, as well as the 3rd Provisional Hussars, deployed to Spain by January 1808.

The Provisional Cavalry Regiments

The cavalry regiments assigned to General Junot's Corps were known as Provisional Cavalry Regiments and never received a designation of Dragoon or Chasseur. Although the regiments were in General Kellermann's Division and nominally organised into two brigades commanded by Generals Margaron and Maurin, they usually operated as independent regiments or were even assigned as individual squadrons to infantry regiments for operations.

Table 15.1   The Provisional Cavalry Regiments in 1807–8

Regiment	Commander	Comprised of
1st	Major Weiss (26th Chasseurs)	4th Squadron of the 26th Chasseurs
2nd	Major Contant (3rd Dragoons)	4th Squadrons of the 1st and 3rd Dragoons
3rd	Major Théron (4th Dragoons)	4th Squadrons of the 4th and 5th Dragoons
4th	Major Jean Gauthier dit Leclerc (9th Dragoons)	4th Squadrons of the 9th and 15th Dragoons

---

The four provisional cavalry regiments were disbanded upon their return to France in November 1808.

Major Weiss, commander of the 1st Provisional Cavalry Regiment, was wounded at Vimeiro on 21 August 1808 and died three months later on 8 November. Major Théron was also wounded at Vimeiro. Major Leclerc would go on to command the 25th Dragoons and be promoted to general of brigade in 1813.

The Provisional Cuirassier Regiments

Three provisional cuirassier regiments were formed in the autumn of 1807. These regiments were sometimes known as provisional heavy cavalry regiments. Initially the 1st and 2nd Provisional Cuirassiers served in the same brigade, but in May 1808 the 1st Provisional Cuirassier Regiment was transferred to General Watier's Brigade in General Grouchy's Division, in Marshal Moncey's Corps, where it performed superbly. In December 1808 it was formally incorporated into the French Army as the 13th Cuirassiers. The 2nd Provisional Cuirassiers surrendered at Bailen and was disbanded. The 3rd Regiment fought in eastern Spain until January 1811, when it was sent back to France and disbanded.

Table 15.2   1st Provisional Cuirassier Regiment 1807–8

When Formed
16 Oct. 1807
Commander
Colonel Guillaume-François d'Aigremont (6 Dec. 1807–Dec. 1808)

Composition and strength
  1 company from the 1st Carabiniers (4 officers and 119 carabiniers)
  1 company from the 2nd Carabiniers (4 officers and 118 carabiniers)
  1 company from the 1st Cuirassiers (4 officers and 142 cuirassiers)
  1 company from the 2nd Cuirassiers (2 officers and 138 cuirassiers)
  1 company from the 3rd Cuirassiers (2 officers and 100 cuirassiers)
Arrival in Spain
  Dec. 1807
Major commands to which assigned
  Dec. 1807–May 1808 Rigaud's Brigade, Fresia's Division, Dupont's 2nd
    Corps of Observation of the Gironde
  May–Sep. 1808 Watier's Brigade, Grouchy's Division, Moncey's Corps
  Sep.–Dec. 1808 Watier's Brigade, 3rd Corps
Battles and officer casualties
  Tudela (23 Nov. 1808) 4 wounded, 1 would die from wounds

Notes In a decree dated 21 October 1808 Napoleon ordered the disbanding of the
1st Provisional Cuirassiers. In December 1808 it was combined with the soldiers of
the 2nd Provisional Cuirassiers who had been in the hospital and missed the Bailen
campaign, to form the 13th Cuirassiers. Colonel d'Aigremenot was appointed the
commander of the new 13th Cuirassiers.

Table 15.3   2nd Provisional Cuirassier Regiment 1807–8

When Formed
  16 Oct. 1807
Commander
  Major Philippe-Albert Christophe (Dec. 1807–Jul. 1808)
Composition and strength
  1 company from the 5th Cuirassiers (2 officers and 109 cuirassiers)
  1 company from the 9th Cuirassiers (2 officers and 64 cuirassiers)
  1 company from the 10th Cuirassiers (2 officers and 96 cuirassiers)
  1 company from the 11th Cuirassiers (3 officers and 120 cuirassiers)
  1 company from the 12th Cuirassiers (2 officers and 100 cuirassiers)
Arrival in Spain
  Dec. 1807
Major commands to which assigned
  Dec. 1807–May 1808 Rigaud's Brigade, Fresia's Division, Dupont's 2nd
    Corps of Observation of the Gironde
  Jun.–Jul. 1808 Fresia's Division, Dupont's Corps
Battles and officer casualties
  Madrid (2 May 1808) 1 wounded
  Bailen (19 Jul. 1808) 4 killed, 2 wounded, 1 would die from wounds

Notes The 2nd Provisional Cuirassiers were disbanded when Dupont's Corps sur-rendered at Bailen in July 1808. Two-thirds of the officers (8 of 12 officers) assigned to the 2nd Provisional Cuirassiers would be either killed or wounded in the 9 months the regiment existed. A number of cuirassiers were in the hospital in Madrid and were not part of the surrender at Bailen. They were merged with the 1st Provisional Cuirassiers to become the 13th Cuirassiers when it was formed in December 1808.

Table 15.4   3rd Provisional Cuirassier Regiment 1807–11

When Formed
  13 Jan. 1808
Commander
  Antoine-Didier Guéry (Dec. 1807–Jul. 1811) Captured at Mollet on 21 Jan. 1810
Composition and strength
  1 company from the 4th Cuirassiers (2 officers and 100 cuirassiers)
  1 company from the 6th Cuirassiers (2 officers and 100 cuirassiers)
  1 company from the 7th Cuirassiers (2 officers and 80 cuirassiers)
  1 company from the 8th Cuirassiers (2 officers and 80 cuirassiers)
Arrival in Spain
  Feb. 1808
Major commands to which assigned
  Feb.–Sep. 1808 Bessières's Brigade, Duhesme's Corps of Observation of the Eastern Pyrenees
  Sep.–Oct. 1808 Bessières's Brigade, 5th Corps
  Oct. 1808–Jan. 1809 Bessières's Brigade, 7th Corps
  Jan. 1809–Jan. 1811 Unattached, 7th Corps
Battles and officer casualties
  Counter-guerrilla operations in 1808 1 killed, 3 wounded
  Mollet (21 Jan. 1810) 1 killed 2 taken PoW
Departure from the Peninsula Jan. 1811

Notes The 3rd Provisional Cuirassiers was disbanded in January 1811, three years after it was formed. It was the last of all the provisional cavalry regiments formed in 1807 for operations in the Peninsula to be disbanded.

The Provisional Dragoons in 1807–8

Initially seven regiments of provisional dragoons were organised for service in Spain, though only the 1st, 2nd and 6th Provisional Dragoon Regiments were sent. They arrived in Spain in late December 1807. They were assigned to General Fresia's Division in General Dupont's Corps. The 1st and 2nd Provisional Dragoons fought at Bailen. The 6th Provisional Dragoons were not present at the battle. All three regiments were included in the surrender and went into captivity in southern Spain. They would eventually be sent to the prison hulks at Cadiz and then on to the Balearic island of Cabrera, where they would remain until 1814. The three regiments ceased to exist after the surrender.

Table 15.5   1st Provisional Dragoon Regiment 1807–8

When Formed
 16 Oct. 1807
Commander
 Major Baron (18th Dragoons) Killed by a mob on 7 Dec. 1808
Composition and strength
 1 company from the 11th Dragoons (1 officer and 80 dragoons)
 1 company from the 13rd Dragoons (2 officers and 56 dragoons)
 1 company from the 14th Dragoons (3 officers and 82 dragoons)
 1 company from the 18th Dragoons (2 officers and 50 dragoons)
 1 company from the 19th Dragoons (3 officer and 80 dragoons)
 1 company from the 22nd Dragoons (2 officers and 52 dragoons)
Arrival in Spain
 Dec. 1807
Major commands to which assigned
 Dec. 1807–May 1808 Pryvé's Brigade, Grouchy's Division, Moncey's
  Corps of Observation of the Ocean Coasts
 May–Jul. 1808 Pryvé's Brigade, Fresia's Division, Dupont's Corps
Battles and officer casualties
 Madrid (2 May 1808) 1 wounded
 Tudela (11 Jun. 1808) 1 wounded
 Bailen (19 Jul. 1808) 1 wounded
 Lebrija (7 Dec. 1808) 11 (prisoners) murdered by a mob, 1 wounded

Notes The 1st Provisional Dragoons were disbanded after the surrender of Dupont's Corps at Bailen on 19 July 1808 and were initially interred at Lebrija. On 7 December, when word reached the local Spaniards that the prisoners would be moved to the prison hulks at Cadiz, a mob led by priests, attacked the officers outside their quarters.[*] Eleven officers were killed, including Major Baron, the commander of the 1st Provisional Dragoons.

Table 15.6   2nd Provisional Dragoon Regiment 1807–8

When Formed
 16 Oct. 1807

---

[*] Smith, Denis, *The Prisoners of Cabrera*, p. 30.

Table 15.6 continued

Commander

Major Alexis Bessard-Graugniard (21st Dragoons) wounded by a sabre blow to the head at Bailen (19 Jul. 1808)

Composition and strength

1 company from the 8th Dragoons (2 officers and 55 dragoons)
1 company from the 12th Dragoons (4 officers and 108 dragoons)
1 company from the 20th Dragoons (4 officers and 119 dragoons)
1 company from the 21st Dragoons (4 officers and 80 dragoons)
1 company from the 25th Dragoons (1 officer and 50 dragoons)
1 company from the 26th Dragoons (2 officers and 78 dragoons)

Arrival in Spain

Dec. 1807

Major commands to which assigned

Dec. 1807–May 1808 Pryvé's Brigade, Grouchy's Division, Moncey's Corps of Observation of the Ocean Coasts
May–Jul. 1808 Pryvé's Brigade, Fresia's Division, Dupont's Corps

Battles and officer casualties

Alcolea (7 Jun. 1808) 2 wounded
Bailen (19 Jul. 1808) 5 wounded
Lebrija (25 Dec. 1808) 1 (prisoner) murdered by a mob

Table 15.7 6th Provisional Dragoon Regiment 1807–8

When Formed

29 Mar. 1808

Commander

Major Jean Ruat (21st Dragoons)

Composition and strength

4th Squadron 10th Dragoons (4 officers and 345 dragoons)
1 company from the 2nd Dragoons
1 company from the 6th Dragoons (80 men)
1 company from the 16th Dragoons
1 company from the 17th Dragoons
1 company from the 27th Dragoons

Arrival in Spain

Dec. 1808

Major commands to which assigned

Dec. 1807–Jul. 1808 Boussart's Brigade, Fresia's Division, Dupont's 2nd Corps of Observation of the Gironde

Battles and officer casualties

Medina del Rio Seco (14 Jul. 1808) 1 wounded

The Provisional Chasseur Regiments

Three regiments of provisional chasseurs were formed and sent to Spain by January 1808. The 1st and 2nd Provisional Chasseurs were part of Fresia's Division, while the 3rd Provisional Chasseurs served in General Duhesme's Division in eastern Spain. The 1st and 2nd Provisional Chasseur Regiments were part of the surrender after Bailen and the regiments cease to exist. The 3rd Provisional Chasseurs would serve in Catalonia until 1810.

Table 15.8   1st Provisional Chasseur Regiment 1807–8

When Formed
  16 Oct. 1807
Composition and strength
  1 company from the 1st Chasseurs (2 officers and 52 chasseurs)
  1 company from the 2nd Chasseurs (4 officers and 89 chasseurs)
  1 company from the 5th Chasseurs (4 officers and 116 chasseurs)
  1 company from the 7th Chasseurs (3 officers and 83 chasseurs)
  1 company from the 11th Chasseurs (1 officer and 58 chasseurs)
Arrival in Spain
  Dec. 1807
Major commands to which assigned
  Dec. 1807–Jul. 1808 Dupré's Brigade, Fresia's Division, Dupont's 2nd
    Corps of Observation of the Gironde
Battles and officer casualties
  Val de Penas (6 Jun. 1808) 1 wounded
  Cordoba (7 Jun. 1808) 1 wounded
  Maçanarès (10 Jun. 1808) 1 wounded
  Mobile Column (5 Jul. 1808) 1 wounded
  Bailen (19 Jul. 1808) 1 killed, 3 wounded

Table 15.9   2nd Provisional Chasseur Regiment 1807–8

When Formed
16 Oct. 1807
Commander
Major Jean Baptiste Bureau (12th Chasseurs)
  1 company from the 12th Chasseurs (3 officers and 125 chasseurs)
  1 company from the 13th Chasseurs (6 officers and 96 chasseurs)
  1 company from the 16th Chasseurs (2 officers and 85 chasseurs)
  1 company from the 20th Chasseurs (4 officers and 100 chasseurs)
  1 company from the 21st Chasseurs (4 officers and 115 chasseurs)

Table 15.9   continued

Arrival in Spain
  Dec. 1807
Major commands to which assigned
  Dec. 1807–Jul. 1808 Dupré's Brigade, Fresia's Division, Dupont's 2nd
    Corps of Observation of the Gironde
  Bailen (19 Jul. 1808) none

Notes Lieutenant Maurice de Tascher volunteered for service in the 2nd Provisional Chasseurs. He served as an aide-de-camp to General Louis Liger-Belair until right before the battle of Bailen, when he rejoined the 2nd Provisional Chasseurs. He was allowed to return to France in September instead of suffering the fate of the rest of the regiment.*

Table 15.10   3rd Provisional Chasseur Regiment 1808–10

When Formed
  13 Jan. 1808
Composition and strength
  1 company from the from the 14th Chasseurs
  1 company from the from the 15th Chasseurs
  1 company from the from the 19th Chasseurs
  1 company from the from the 23rd Chasseurs
  1 company from the from the 24th Chasseurs
Arrival in Spain
  Apr. 1808
Major commands to which assigned
  Feb.–Sep. 1808 Bessières's Brigade, Duhesme's Corps of Observation of
    the Eastern Pyrenees
  Sep.–Oct. 1808 Bessières's Brigade, 5th Corps
  Oct. 1808–Jan. 1809 Bessières's Brigade, 7th Corps
  Jan. 1809–Aug. 1810 Unattached, 7th Corps
Battles and officer casualties
  Counter-guerrilla operations 1808–10 1 killed, 2 wounded
  Figuières (21 Jul. 1808) 2 wounded

Notes On 22 August 1810 the 3rd Provisional Chasseurs were redesignated as the 29th Chasseurs.

---

* Mauice de Tascher's diary was edited by Rosemary Brindle and published under the name *Campaigning for Napoleon*.

Table 15.11   Auxiliary Chasseur Regiment

When Formed
 1807?
Commander
 Jean Henry Tascher de la Pagerie
Composition and strength
 ?
Arrival in Spain
 Apr. 1808
Major commands to which assigned
 Nov. 1808–Jan. 1809 Debelle's Brigade, 2nd Corps
Battles and officer casualties
 Sahagun (21 Dec. 1809) 13 captured.

Notes Little is known about this regiment. It is sometimes confused with the 1st Provisional Chasseurs, which surrendered at Bailen. Its composition is a mystery. The regiment was poorly handled at Sahagun and had 20 men killed and 11 officers and 157 men captured. Napoleon removed it from General Debelle's Brigade after the debacle and placed it on garrison duty in Leon. It was dissolved by June 1809. Considering the extent of its casualties at Sahagun, at least one officer should have been killed or wounded. This would provide a possible clue of its composition, yet Martinien does not list any chasseur or hussar regiment with casualties at the battle.

The Provisional Hussar Regiments

Three provisional hussar regiments were formed for duty in Spain in 1807. The 1st and 2nd Regiments were part of Marshal Moncey's 2nd Corps of the Observation of the Ocean Coasts and would fight in northern Spain until March 1809, when they were disbanded. The 3rd Provisional Hussars were never sent to Spain.

Table 15.12   1st Provisional Hussar Regiment 1807–9

When Formed
 16 Oct. 1807
Composition and strength
 1 company from the 2nd Hussars (4 officers and 111 hussars)
 1 company from the 3rd Hussars (1 officer and 85 hussars)
 1 company from the 4th Hussars (2 officers and 70 hussars)
 1 company from the 5th Hussars (3 officers and 72 hussars)
Arrival in Spain
 Dec. 1807

Table 15.12   continued

Major commands to which assigned
  Dec. 1807–Sep. 1808 Watier's Brigade, Grouchy's Division, Moncey's
    2nd Corps of the Observation of the Ocean Coasts
  Sep. 1808–Mar. 1809 Watier's Brigade, 3rd Corps
Battles and officer casualties
  Valence (26 Jun. 1808) 2 wounded
  Almanza (3 Jul. 1808) 1 wounded
  Tudela (5 Sep. 1808) 1 wounded
  Saragossa (19 Mar. 1809) 1 wounded
Departure from the Peninsula
  Disbanded in Mar. 1809

Table 15.13   2nd Provisional Hussar Regiment 1807–9

When Formed
  16 Oct. 1807
Composition and strength
  1 company from the 7th Hussars (2 officers and 80 hussars)
  1 company from the 8th Hussars (2 officer and 86 hussars)
  1 company from the 9th Hussars (4 officers and 110 hussars)
  1 company from the 10th Hussars (3 officers and 80 hussars)
Arrival in Spain
  Dec. 1807
Major commands to which assigned
  Dec. 1807–Sep. 1808 Watier's Brigade, Grouchy's Division, Moncey's
    2nd Corps of the Observation of the Ocean Coasts
  Sep. 1808–Mar. 1809 Watier's Brigade, 3rd Corps
Battles and officer casualties
  Saragossa (6 Feb. 1809) 2 wounded
Departure from the Peninsula
  Disbanded in Mar. 1809

Notes After the regiment was disbanded in 1809 the soldiers from the 7th Hussars were reassigned to the 10th Hussars, rather than being returned to France.

The Provisional Dragoon Regiments in 1810 and 1811

On 12 March 1809 Napoleon wrote a letter to General Clarke, his minister of war, on his plans to form 12 new provisional dragoon regiments to supplement the forces in France. Each of the 24 dragoon regiments serving in Spain were to be tasked to provide their 3rd and 4th Squadrons to the new regiments. Initially only six of the regiments were created and because the 3rd Squadrons from most dragoon regiments were still serving in Spain, these new provisional regiments were formed from 4th Squadrons and individual companies and detachments. On 3 November 1809 Napoleon authorised the formation of an additional six regiments. He also changed the composition of the provisional regiments. Each provisional regiment would have the 3rd and 4th Squadrons from two different dragoon regiments, making each of the provisional regiments a four-squadron regiment. The regiment would have a colonel, a major, two chiefs of squadrons, eight captains, eight lieutenants and eight sub-lieutenants.*

The creation of these new regiments would allow Napoleon to reinforce his armies in Spain with another 12,000 cavalrymen. On the surface the formation of the provisional regiments did not make much sense. If there was such a shortage of the troops in the Peninsula, why not use the 3rd and 4th Squadrons to bring the regiments already serving there back up to strength? Although this would appear to be the more logical course of action, it would limit where Napoleon could deploy the troops. Creating new regiments allowed him more flexibility on where to send the troops, but at a cost. These provisional regiments' operations inevitably suffered from a lack of the trust and cohesion that units obtain only through long association with each other; there were also internal administrative problems with such things as pay, clothing, equipment and remounts. Napoleon used most of the regiments to secure the lines of communication in northern Spain. However, several of the regiments were disbanded within a few months of their arrival in Spain and the squadrons sent to their parent regiments.

Little is known about the operations of the provisional dragoon regiments from 1809 to 1811. Even officer casualties are difficult to determine, because Martinien did not provide a separate citing for them. Instead Martinien incorporated the provisional dragoon regiments' officer casualties into the parent regiments' figures

---

Table 15.14 1st Provisional Dragoon Regiment 1809–11

When Formed
12 Mar. 1809
Commander
Colonel Jean Baptiste Dubessy
Composition
3rd and 4th Squadrons of the 1st and 2nd Dragoons

---

* Bonaparte, Napoleon, *Correspondance de Napoléon*, vol. 18, p. 395; vol. 19, p. 648; Detaille, *L'Armée française*, pp. 106–16.

Table 15.14   continued
Arrival in Spain
 Jan. 1810
Major commands to which assigned
 Nov. 1809–Feb. 1810 Sainte-Croix's Brigade, Caulaincourt's Division,
  8th Corps
 Mar.–17 Apr. 1810 Sainte-Croix's Brigade, Kellermann's Division
 17 Apr.–11 Oct. 1810 Sainte-Croix's Brigade, 8th Corps
 11 Oct. 1810–Jul. 1811 8th Corps
Areas of Operation
 Portugal
Departure from the Peninsula
 Disbanded 16 Jul. 1811

Table 15.15   2nd Provisional Dragoon Regiment 1809–11

When Formed
 12 Mar. 1809
Commander
 Colonel Denis Eloi Ludot
Composition
 3rd and 4th Squadrons of the 4th and 9th Dragoons
Arrival in Spain
 Jan. 1810
Major commands to which assigned
 Nov. 1809–Feb. 1810 Sainte-Croix's Brigade, Caulaincourt's Division,
  8th Corps
 Mar.–17 Apr. 1810 Sainte-Croix's Brigade, Kellermann's Division
 17 Apr.–11 Oct. 1810 Sainte-Croix's Brigade, 8th Corps
 11 Oct. 1810–Jul. 1811 8th Corps
Area of operations
 Portugal
Departure from the Peninsula
 Disbanded 16 Jul. 1811

Table 15.16   3rd Provisional Dragoon Regiment 1809–11

When Formed
 12 Mar. 1809
Commander
 Colonel Joseph Antoine Mermet shot in the chest at Alcaniz, Spain
  (7 Jun. 1810)

Composition
3rd and 4th Squadrons of the 14th and 26th Dragoons
Arrival in Spain
Jan. 1810
Major commands to which assigned
 Nov. 1809–Feb. 1810 Sainte-Croix's Brigade, Caulaincourt's Division,
  8th Corps
 Mar.–17 Apr. 1810 Sainte-Croix's Brigade, Kellermann's Division
 17 Apr.–11 Oct. 1810 Sainte-Croix's Brigade, 8th Corps
 11 Oct. 1810–Jul. 1811 8th Corps
Area of operations
 Portugal
Departure from the Peninsula
 Disbanded 16 Jul. 1811

Table 15.17   4th Provisional Dragoon Regiment 1809–10

When Formed
 12 Mar. 1809
Commander
 ?
Composition
 3rd and 4th Squadrons of the 3rd and 6th Dragoons
Arrival in Spain
 31 Jan. 1810
Major commands to which assigned
 Nov. 1809–Feb. 1810 Gardanne's Brigade, Caulaincourt's Division,
  8th Corps
Area of operations
 Valladolid
Departure from the Peninsula
 Disbanded 8 Feb. 1810

Table 15.18   5th Provisional Dragoon Regiment 1808–10

When Formed
 12 Mar. 1809
Commander
 Colonel Jacques-Charles de Béthisy,
Composition
 3rd and 4th Squadrons of the 10th and 11th Dragoons

Table 15.18 continued

Arrival in Spain
31 Jan. 1810
Major commands to which assigned
Nov. 1809–Feb. 1810 Gardanne's Brigade, Caulaincourt's Division, 8th Corps
Area of operations
Valladolid
Departure from the Peninsula
Disbanded 8 Feb. 1810

Table 15.19   6th Provisional Dragoon Regiment 1809–11

When Formed
12 Mar. 1809
Commander
Colonel Pierre Alexis Pinteville
Composition
3rd and 4th Squadrons of the 12th and 16th Dragoons
Arrival in Spain
Jan. 1810
Major commands to which assigned
Nov. 1809–Feb. 1810 Bessière's Brigade, Caulaincourt's Division, 8th Corps
Mar.–17 Apr. 1810 Bessière's Brigade, Kellermann's Division
17 Apr.–Jun. 1810 Bessière's Brigade, Trelliard's Division
Jul. 1810–Jul. 1811 Poinsot's Brigade, 6th Military Government
Area of operations
Leon
Departure from the Peninsula
Disbanded Jul. 1811

Table 15.20   7th Provisional Dragoon Regiment 1809–10

When Formed
3 Nov. 1809
Commander
Colonel Louis Charlemagne Prévost
Composition
3rd and 4th Squadrons of the 20th and 21st Dragoons
Arrival in Spain
Jan. 1810

Major commands to which assigned
Nov. 1809–Feb. 1810 Bessière's Brigade, Caulaincourt's Division,
   8th Corps
Mar.–17 Apr. 1810 Bessière's Brigade, Kellermann's Division
17 Apr.–Jun. 1810 Bessière's Brigade, Trelliard's Division
Jul. 1810–Jul. 1811 Poinsot's Brigade, 6th Military Government
Area of operations
Medina del Campo
Departure from the Peninsula
Disbanded Jul. 1811

Table 15.21   8th Provisional Dragoon Regiment 1809–10

When Formed
3 Nov. 1809
Commander
Colonel François-Alexandre Thévenez d'Aoust
Composition
3rd and 4th Squadrons of the 5th and 8th Dragoons
Arrival in Spain
Jan. 1810
Major commands to which assigned
Nov. 1809–Feb. 1810 Bron's Brigade, Caulaincourt's Division,
   8th Corps
Mar.–17 Apr. 1810 Bron's Brigade, Kellermann's Division
17 Apr.–Jun. 1810 Bron's Brigade, Trelliard's Division
Jun.–Sep. 1810 Bron's Brigade, 6th Military Government
Area of operations
Zamora
Departure from the Peninsula
Disbanded Sep. 1810

Table 15.22   9th Provisional Dragoon Regiment 1809–10

When Formed
3 Nov. 1809
Commander
Colonel François Grouvel (31 Dec. 1809–20 Jan. 1810)
Jean Pierre Gauthier dit Leclerc (15 Mar.–29 May 1810)
Composition
3rd and 4th Squadrons of the 17th and 18th Dragoons
Arrival in Spain
Jan. 1810

Table 15.22 continued

Major commands to which assigned
 Nov. 1809–Feb. 1810 Bron's Brigade, Caulaincourt's Division,
  8th Corps
 Mar.–17 Apr. 1810 Bron's Brigade, Kellermann's Division
 17 Apr.–Jun. 1810 Bron's Brigade, Trelliard's Division
 Jun.–Sep. 1810 Bron's Brigade, 6th Military Government
Area of operations
 Salamanca
Departure from the Peninsula
 Disbanded Sep. 1810

Table 15.23   10th Provisional Dragoon Regiment 1809–10

When Formed
 3 Nov. 1809
Commander
 Colonel Nicolas-Felix Rozat
Composition
 3rd and 4th Squadrons of the 19th and 27th Dragoons
Arrival in Spain
 Jan. 1810
Major commands to which assigned
 Nov. 1809–Feb. 1810 Bron's Brigade, Caulaincourt's Division,
  8th Corps
 Mar.–17 Apr. 1810 Bron's Brigade, Kellermann's Division
 17 Apr.–Jun. 1810 Bron's Brigade, Trelliard's Division
 Jun.–Sep. 1810 Bron's Brigade, 6th Military Government
Area of operations
 Benavente
Departure from the Peninsula
 Disbanded Sep. 1810

Table 15.24   11th Provisional Dragoon Regiment 1809–10

When Formed
 3 Nov. 1809
Commander
 ?
Composition
 3rd and 4th Squadrons of the 13th and 22nd Dragoons
Arrival in Spain
 23 Jan. 1810

Major commands to which assigned
  Nov. 1809–Feb. 1810 Lamotte's Brigade, Caulaincourt's Division,
    8th Corps
Area of operations
  Valladolid
Departure from the Peninsula
  Disbanded Feb. 1810

Table 15.25   12th Provisional Dragoon Regiment 1809–10

When Formed
  3 Nov. 1809
Commander
  Major Pierre Holdrinet
Composition
  3rd and 4th Squadrons of the 15th and 25th Dragoons
Arrival in Spain
  23 Jan. 1810
Major commands to which assigned
  Nov. 1809–Feb. 1810 Lamotte's Brigade, Caulaincourt's Division,
    8th Corps
Area of operations
  Valladolid
Departure from the Peninsula
  Disbanded Feb. 1810

The Provisional Light Cavalry Regiments in 1810 and 1811

In the summer of 1810 General Fournier-Sarlovès was ordered to organise two provisional light cavalry regiments for service in Spain. The 1st Provisional Light Cavalry Regiment was assigned to the Army of the North, while the 2nd Provisional Light Cavalry Regiment was sent to the Army of Portugal. Both of these regiments were extremely strong, with the 1st having five squadrons, while the 2nd had six! The 2nd Provisional Light Cavalry Regiment was the only regiment assigned to General Fournier's Brigade.

Table 15.26   1st Provisional Light Cavalry Regiment 1810–11

When Formed
  Sep. 1810
Commander
  Colonel Auguste Houssin de Saint-Laurent

Table 15.26   continued

Composition
 4th Squadron of the 11th Chasseurs
 4th Squadron of the 12th Chasseurs
 3rd and 4th Squadrons of the 24th Chasseurs
 4th Squadron of the 5th Hussars
Arrival in Spain
 Nov. 1810
Major commands to which assigned
 Nov. 1810–Jan. 1811 Watier's Brigade, Army of Spain
 Jan.–Aug. 1811 Watier's Brigade, Army of the North
Area of operations
 Asturias
Departure from the Peninsula
 Disbanded Aug. 1811

Table 15.27   2nd Provisional Light Cavalry Regiment 1810–11

When Formed
 Sep. 1810
Commander
 Colonel Auguste Houssin de Saint-Laurent
Composition and strength
 3rd and 4th Squadrons of the 7th Chasseurs
 3rd and 4th Squadrons of the 13th Chasseurs
 3rd and 4th Squadrons of the 20th Chasseurs
Arrival in Spain
 21 Aug. 1810
Major commands to which assigned
 Nov. 1810–Nov. 1811 Fournier's Brigade, Army of Portugal
Area of operations
 Spanish–Portuguese border in the vicinity of Cuidad Rodrigo
Departure from the Peninsula
 Disbanded Aug. 1811

Notes The 2nd Provisional Light Cavalry Regiment had an estimated strength of 1,500 men when it entered Spain in 1810. It was stronger than most cavalry brigades serving there at the time. There is some doubt that it ever operated as a single regiment. Furthermore the 2nd Provisional Light Cavalry was the only regiment assigned to General Fournier's Brigade. It was more likely that the 3rd and 4th Squadrons from each regiment operated together as a separate regimental entity. In addition to providing two squadrons to the 2nd Provisional Light Cavalry Regiment, the 13th Chasseurs also brought its regimental headquarters.

Chapter Sixteen

The Foreign Regiments

In addition to the many French cavalry regiments, there were 13 regiments drawn from the satellite kingdoms and duchies of the Napoleonic Empire. The service of most of these regiments is not well known, for they served in areas of operation that were not close to the British army under the Duke of Wellington. Their war was a thankless one, with little glory to gain. Their mission was generally one of counter-insurgency, trying to instill a measure of security in a very hostile land. Despite their relative anonymity, the record of these regiments was good. They fought hard against an implacable foe and took many casualties.

Two of the regiments (the Berg Light Horse and the Berg Lancers) became part of the Imperial Guard. Two (the 3rd Dutch Hussars and the 1st Vistula Legion Lancers) were renamed and formally incorporated into the French Army, while the men of a third (the Hanoverian Chasseurs) were transferred into the 1st French Hussars and the 30th Chasseurs, when their regiment was disbanded. Despite five years of loyal service, two regiments, the Nassau and Westphalian Light Horse, were disarmed and imprisoned when their countries turned against Napoleon in December 1813.

By 1814 no foreign regiments still fought with the French in Spain or southern France.

The Grand Duchy of Berg

Table 16.1   Berg Light Horse Regiment

Colonel
Major Johann Maximilian Friedrich Franz Graf von Nesselrode-
   Reichenstein (21 May 1807–11 Jan. 1809)

Table 16.1   continued

Location of squadrons

Apr. 1808–Jan. 1809 HQ, 1st and 2nd Squadrons in Spain

Arrival in the Peninsula

Apr. 1808 HQ, 1st and 2nd Squadrons

Major commands to which assigned

Apr. 1808–Jan. 1809 HQ, 1st and 2nd Squadrons attached to the
Imperial Guard

Battles and officer casualties

Benavente (29 Dec. 1808) 1 wounded

Burgos (25 Jan. 1809) 1 wounded

Departure from the Peninsula

Disbanded on 11 Jan. 1809

Notes Although Major Nesselrode was the commander of the two squadrons, he never entered Spain with them. The actual commander was most likely Chief of Squadron Etienne Honoré de Lanougarède. On 11 January 1809 Napoleon ordered the regiment to be disbanded and the men to be incorporated into the Imperial Guard Chasseurs.

Table 16.2   Berg Lancer Regiment

Colonel

Franz von Goltstein (1809–Feb. 1812)

Major Aug. von Witzleben (Feb. 1812–Sep. 1812)

Stanislaus Trautwein von Belle (Sep. 1812–Dec. 1813

Location of squadrons

Apr. 1810 HQ, 1st, 2nd and 3rd Squadrons in Spain; 4th, 5th and 6th
Squadrons in Germany

Arrival in the Peninsula

Jun. 1810 HQ, 1st, 2nd, 3rd Squadrons

Major commands to which assigned

Jun.–Dec. 1810 HQ, 1st, 2nd and 3rd Squadrons in Lepic's Brigade,
Imperial Guard, Army of Spain

Jan.–Aug. 1811 HQ, 1st, 2nd and 3rd Squadrons in Lepic's Brigade,
Army of the North

Sep.–Dec. 1811 HQ, 1st, 2nd and 3rd Squadrons in Watier's Brigade,
Army of the North

Jan. 1812–Feb. 1813 HQ, 1st, 2nd and 3rd Squadrons in Laferrière's
Brigade, Army of the North

Battles and officer casualties

Counter-guerrilla operations 1810–11) 5 wounded

Villadrigo (23 Oct. 1812) 2 wounded
Vitoria (21 Jun. 1813) 1 wounded
Departure from the Peninsula
5 Mar. 1813 HQ and all squadrons

Notes The regiment was first raised as a chasseur regiment, but on 17 December 1809, it was armed with lances and redesignated the Berg Lancers. It was attached to the French Imperial Guard in 1810. Colonel von Goltstein commanded it in Spain, until he was promoted to general of brigade. He was replaced by Major von Witzleben, who served with the regiment until September 1812, when he returned to Germany to raise more squadrons. Upon his departure, Chief of Squadron von Toll, commander of the 1st Squadron, assumed command of the sqaudrons still in Spain.

The Kingdom of Holland

One Dutch cavalry regiment, the 3rd Hussars, deployed to Spain in 1808. It would serve there for two years until it was withdrawn in the summer of 1810. Most of its time was spent in central Spain protecting lines of communications.

Table 16.3   3rd Dutch Hussar Regiment

Colonels
Otto Fredrik van Goes 1806–6 Jan. 1809) wounded at Toro (6 Jan. 1809), he was 64 years old when he was wounded
Antoine Roest d'Alkemade (6 Jan.–27 Mar. 1809) shot in the chest at Ciudad Real (27 Mar. 1809) died from the wound on 18 Dec. 1811
Jean-Baptiste van Merlen (Mar. 1809–Sep. 1810)
Regimental depot
1808 Bois-le-Duc
Location of squadrons
Oct. 1808–Jul. 1809 HQ, 1st, 2nd, 3rd and 4th Squadrons in Spain
Jul. 1809–Feb. 1810 HQ, 1st, 2nd and 3rd Squadrons in Spain; 4th Squadron in Holland
Feb.–Sep. 1810 1st Squadron in Spain; HQ, 2nd, 3rd and 4th Squadrons in Holland
Arrival in the Peninsula
Oct. 1808 HQ, 1st, 2nd, 3rd and 4th Squadrons
Major commands to which assigned
Oct.–21 Dec. 1808 HQ, 1st, 2nd, 3rd and 4th Squadrons in Maupetit's Brigade, 4th Corps
21 Dec. 1808–Jan. 1809 HQ, 1st, 2nd, 3rd and 4th Squadrons in Davenay's Brigade, Army Reserve
Jan.–Jun. 1809 HQ, 1st, 2nd, 3rd and 4th Squadrons in Maupetit's Brigade, 4th Corps

---

Table 16.3   continued

Major commands to which assigned

Jun.–Dec. 1809 HQ, 1st, 2nd, 3rd and 4th Squadrons in Montbrun's
   Division

Dec. 1809–Sep. 1810 1st Squadron part of the Madrid Garrison

Battles and officer casualties

Sierra Morena (28 Nov. 1808) 1 wounded

Toro (6 Jan. 1809) 1 killed, 1 wounded

Mesas de Ibor (17 Mar. 1809) 1 wounded

Ciudad Real (27 Mar. 1809) 2 wounded

Departure from the Peninsula

Jul. 1809 4th Squadron

Feb. 1810 HQ, 2nd and 3rd Squadrons

Sep. 1810 1st Squadron

Notes On 1 September 1810 the cadre of the 1st Squadron was ordered back to
Holland. Its troopers were incorporated into the 1st French Hussars. The Dutch
regiment was designated as France's 11th Hussars upon its return to Holland.

Hanover

The Hanoverian Legion deployed to Spain in November 1808 and with
it came the Hanoverian Mounted Chasseurs. The cavalry was in almost
continuous combat operations in north-west Spain and Portugal until it
was disbanded in August 1811.

Table 16.4   Hanoverian Chasseur Regiment

Colonel

Charles Joseph Evers (26 Oct. 1803–Aug. 1811)

Regimental depot

Hamburg

Location of squadrons

Nov. 1808–Aug. 1810 HQ, 1st, 2nd and 3rd Squadrons in Spain

Aug. 1810–Mar. 1811 HQ, 1st, 2nd and 3rd Squadrons in Portugal

Apr.–Aug. 1811 HQ, 1st, 2nd and 3rd Squadrons in Spain

Arrival in the Peninsula

Nov. 1808–Aug. 1811 HQ, 1st, 2nd and 3rd Squadrons

Major commands to which assigned

Nov. 1808 HQ, 1st, 2nd and 3rd Squadrons in Franceschi's Brigade, 2nd
   Corps

Dec. 1808–Jan. 1809 HQ, 1st, 2nd and 3rd Squadrons in Franceschi's
   Division, Army Reserve

Jan.–Jun. 1809 HQ, 1st, 2nd and 3rd Squadrons in Desfossés Brigade,
Franceschi's Division, 2nd Corps
Jun. 1809–Mar. 1811 HQ, 1st, 2nd and 3rd Squadrons in Desfossés
Brigade, Soult's Division, 2nd Corps
Apr.–Aug. 1811 HQ, 1st, 2nd and 3rd Squadrons in d'Ermenonville's
Brigade, Soult's Division, 2nd Corps
Battles and officer casualties
Astorga (2 Jan. 1809) 2 wounded, 1 would die from wounds
Corunna (16 Jan. 1809) 1 wounded
Braga (20 Mar. 1809) 1 killed, 2 wounded
Sabugal (3 Apr. 1809) 1 wounded
Coimbra (10 May 1809) 2 wounded
Rocca (5 Mar. 1810) 1 wounded
Operations 1808–1811 1 killed, 6 wounded
Villadrigo (6 May 1811) 1 wounded
Departure from the Peninsula
Disbanded Aug. 1811

Notes When the Hanoverian Chasseurs were disbanded June 1811, the first three
squadrons were incorporated into the 1st Hussars. The 4th Squadron, at the depot in
Hamburg, was incorporated into the 30th Chasseurs.

The Kingdom of Italy

Four Italian regiments served in the Peninsula. From 1808 to 1812 they
were stationed in eastern Spain. In 1813 one squadron of the Napoleon
Dragoons was reassigned to the Army of the North for operations in
north central Spain. After 1808 the regiments were usually attached to
infantry brigades, where they often operated in company- and squadron-
size formations in support of the infantry.

Table 16.5   1st Italian Chasseur Regiment

Colonel
Francesco Villata (1807–30 Dec. 1810) wounded at Mora on 4 Apr. 1810
Claude Odier (1810–1812)
Antonio Gasparinetti (1813–1814)
Regimental depot
Crema
Location of squadrons
Oct. 1808–Jun. 1813 HQ, 1st, 2nd and 3rd Squadrons in Spain
Jul. 1813–Jan. 1814 HQ, 1st and 2nd Squadrons in Spain; 3rd Squadron
in Italy

Table 16.5   continued

Arrival in the Peninsula

Oct. 1808 HQ, 1st, 2nd and 3rd Squadrons

Major commands to which assigned

Oct. 1808–Apr. 1811 HQ, 1st, 2nd and 3rd Squadrons in Pino's Division, Army of Catalonia

May–Mar. 1811 HQ, 1st, 2nd and 3rd Squadrons in Severoli's Division, Army of Catalonia

Mar. 1811–Jul. 1811 HQ, 1st, 2nd and 3rd Squadrons in Pino's Division, Army of Aragon

Jul. 1811–Oct. 1812 HQ, 1st, 2nd and 3rd Squadrons in Maupoint's Brigade, Army of Aragon

Oct. 1812–Jul. 1813 HQ, 1st, 2nd and 3rd Squadrons in the Army of Aragon

Jul. 1813–Winter 1814 HQ, 1st and 2nd Squadrons in the Army of Aragon

Battles and officer casualties

Hostalrich (Jun. 1809) 1 wounded

Girona (3 Dec. 1809) 1 wounded

Combat in Catalonia (Mar. 1810) 1 killed

Mora (4 Apr. 1810) 1 wounded

Combat in Catalonia (Sep. 1810) 2 killed

On reconnaissance in Catalonia (20 Dec. 1810) 1 wounded

Lerida (3 Jan. 1811) 1 wounded, would die from wounds 24 Jan. 1811

Daroca (26 Oct. 1811) 1 killed, 2 wounded

Departure from the Peninsula

Jul. 1813 3rd Squadron

Winter 1814 HQ, 1st and 2nd Squadrons

Notes The regiment was also known as the Royal Chasseurs.

Table 16.6   2nd Italian Chasseur Regiment

Colonel

Antonio Banco (30 Mar. 1808–3 Nov. 1812) killed at Wiasma on 3 Nov. 1812.

Regimental depot

Crema

Location of squadrons

Mar. 1808–Mar. 1810 HQ, 1st and 2nd Squadrons in Spain; 3rd and 4th Squadrons in Italy.

Arrival in the Peninsula
  24 Mar. 1808 HQ, 1st and 2nd Squadrons in Spain; HQ, 1st and 2nd
  Squadrons
Major commands to which assigned
  May 1808–Jun. 1809 HQ, 1st and 2nd Squadrons in Schwarz's Brigade,
  Lechi's Division
  Jul.–Mar. 1810 HQ, 1st and 2nd Squadrons in 7th Corps
Battles and officer casualties
  Sans (8 Nov. 1808) 1 wounded, would die from wounds the next day
Departure from the Peninsula
  Mar. 1810 HQ, 1st and 2nd Squadrons

Notes The regiment was also known as the Royal Prince's Chasseurs. It was formed
when the 1st Provisional Italian Cavalry Regiment was redesignated as the 2nd
Chasseurs on 24 March 1808.

Table 16.7   Italian Napoleon Dragoon Regiment

Colonel
  Giuseppe Palombini (4 Feb. 1805–14 Feb. 1809)
  Fortunate Schiazzetti (Feb. 1809–7 Feb. 1812)
  Pietro Maranesi (1812–1813)
Location of squadrons
  Oct. 1808–Feb.1813 HQ, 1st, 2nd and 3rd Squadrons in Spain
  Feb.–Jun. 1813 1st Squadron in Spain; HQ, 2nd and 3rd Squadrons in
  Italy
Arrival in the Peninsula
  Oct. 1808 HQ, 1st, 2nd and 3rd Squadrons
Major commands to which assigned
  Oct. 1808–Apr. 1811 HQ, 1st, 2nd and 3rd Squadrons in Pino's
  Division, Army of Catalonia
  May–Mar. 1811 HQ, 1st, 2nd and 3rd Squadrons in Severoli's Division,
  Army of Catalonia
  Mar. 1811–Jul. 1811 HQ, 1st, 2nd and 3rd Squadrons in Pino's Division,
  Army of Aragon
  Aug. 1811–Aug. 1812 HQ, 1st, 2nd and 3rd Squadrons in the Army of
  Aragon
  Aug. 1812–Feb. 1813 HQ, 1st, 2nd and 3rd Squadrons in the Army of
  the Centre
  Feb.–Jun. 1813 1st Squadron in Schiazetti's Brigade, Palombini's
  Division, Army of the North

Table 16.7 continued

Battles and officer casualties
  Near the border (Oct. 1808) 1 wounded
  Catalonia (6 Dec. 1808) 1 wounded
  Vich (20 Feb. 1810) 1 killed, 1 wounded
  Boria-Blancas (20 Dec. 1810) 1 killed, 4 wounded
  Tarragona (3 Jan. 1811) 1 wounded
  Llobregat (9 Apr. 1811) 2 wounded
  Tarres-Torre (29 Sep. 1811) 1 wounded
  Saguntum (25 Oct. 1811) 1 wounded
  Guadarama (11 Aug. 1812) 1 wounded
  Castro-Urdiale (24 Mar. 1813) 1 killed, 6 wounded
Departure from the Peninsula
  Feb. 1813 HQ, 2nd and 3rd Squadrons
  Jun. 1813 1st Squadron

Notes The Napoleon Dragoons were disbanded on 24 July 1814.

Table 16.8 1st Provisional Italian Cavalry Regiment

When Formed
  24 Nov. 1807
Commander
  Major Gabriel Rambourgt (24 Nov. 1807–1 May 1808)
Composition and strength
  Dragoon Squadron 1 company from the Queen's Dragoon and 1
    company from the Napoleon Dragoons
  Chasseur Squadron 1 company from the 1st Italian Chasseurs and 1
    company from the 2nd Neapolitan Chasseurs
Arrival in Spain
  9 Feb. 1808 Dragoon and Chasseur Squadrons
Major commands to which assigned
  Feb.–May 1808 both squadrons in Bessières's Brigade, Duhesme's
    Division
Battles and officer casualties
  None

Notes The 1st Provisional Italian Cavalry Regiment was renamed the 2nd Italian
Chasseurs on 30 March 1808. Not until 1 May 1808 did the regiment in Spain receive
word of its new name.

The Kingdom of Naples

Two regiments of Neapolitan Chasseurs served in the Peninsula. They were often understrength and in December 1809, most of the 2nd Chasseurs were withdrawn to France in order for them to rebuild their strength. By December 1811 only the 1st Squadrons from the two regiments were still in Spain. The rest had returned to Naples.

Table 16.9   1st Neapolitan Chasseur Regiment

Colonel
 Vincenzo Pignatelli Strongoli (25 May 1806–Nov. 1808)
 Nicolas Philibert Desvernois (2 Dec. 1808–3 Jul. 1813)
Location of Squadrons
 Feb. 1810 HQ, 1st and 2nd Squadrons in Spain
Arrival in the Peninsula
 12 Feb. 1810
Major commands to which assigned
 Feb. 1810–Mar. 1811 HQ, 1st and 2nd Squadrons in 7th Corps, Army of
  Catalonia
 Mar.–Sep. 1811 HQ, 1st and 2nd Squadrons in Army of Aragon
 Sep.–Dec. 1811 HQ, 1st and 2nd Squadrons in Delort's Brigade, Army
  of Aragon
 Dec. 1811–May 1813 1st Squadron in Maupoint's Brigade, Army of
  Aragon
Battles and officer casualties
 On reconnaissance in Spain (6 Jun. 1811) 1 wounded
 Mora (12 Aug. 1811) 1 wounded
 Valencia (26 Dec. 1811) 2 wounded
Departure from the Peninsula
 Autumn 1811 HQ and 2nd Squadron
 May 1813 1st Squadron

Notes In March 1813 the 1st Chasseurs Regiment was renamed the 1st Light Cavalry Regiment.

Table 16.10   2nd Neapolitan Chasseur Regiment

Colonel
Giuseppe Scarlata Xibilia Platamone Zenardi (7 Nov. 1806–Apr. 1809)
 Michel Victor Briges (7 Apr. 1809–14 Sep. 1809) died at Gerona from
  typhoid on 14 Sep. 1809

Table 16.10 continued

Colonel

 Corrado Malaspina of Fosdinovo (10 Oct. 1809–Mar. 1812)

 Antonio Napoletano (13 Mar. 1812 — ?)

Location of squadrons

 9 Feb. 1808 1 company in Spain

Arrival in the Peninsula

 Feb. 1808 1 company

 Apr. 1808 HQ, 1st and 3rd Squadrons

 Apr. 1809 2nd Squadron

 Jul. 1810 HQ, 1st and 2nd Squadrons

Major commands to which assigned

 Apr. 1808–Apr. 1809 HQ, 1st and 3rd Squadrons in Schwarz's Brigade,
   Lechi's Division

 Apr.–Jun. 1809 HQ, 1st and 3rd Squadrons in Schwarz's Brigade,
   Lechi's Division

 Jun.–Autumn 1809 HQ, 1st, 2nd and 3rd Squadrons in 7th Corps,
   Army of Catalonia

 Dec. 1809–Jul. 1810 2nd Squadron in Guillot's Division, 7th Corps,
   Army of Catalonia

 Aug. 1810–Jul. 1811 HQ, 1st and 2nd Squadron in Pignatelli's Division,
   7th Corps, Army of Catalonia

 Jul.–Dec. 1811 HQ, 1st and 2nd Squadron in Army of Aragon

 Dec. 1811–May 1813 1st Squadron in Maupoint's Brigade, Army of
   Aragon

Battles and officer casualties

 Combat in Catalonia (2 Jan. 1809) 2 wounded – one would die from
   wounds 4 Jan., the other 6 Jan.

Departure from the Peninsula

 Dec. 1809 HQ, 1st and 3rd Squadrons

 Jan. 1812 HQ and 2nd Squadron

 May 1813 1st Squadron

Notes In March 1813 the 2nd Chasseurs Regiment was renamed the 2nd Light
Cavalry Regiment.

The Duchy of Nassau

The Nassau Light Horse was not a regiment, but consisted of two
independent squadrons. In 1808 the Duchy of Nassau sent the 2nd Light
Horse Squadron to Spain. It would be stationed in central Spain and
spent most of its time conducting counter-insurgency operations. In May
1813 it was joined by the 1st Light Horse Squadron. Despite five years of

honorable service, the squadrons were disarmed on 22 December 1813, after the 2nd Nassau Infantry Regiment defected to the British 11 days earlier.

Table 16.11 Nassau Light Horse

Commander
1st Squadron Major Oberkamp
2nd Squadron Major Reineck (Nov. 1808–17 Jul. 1811) shot and killed at Lezuza on 17 Jul. 1811
Regimental depot
Biebrich
Location of squadrons
Nov. 1808–Jul. 1813
Arrival in the Peninsula
Nov. 1808 2nd Squadron
17 May 1813 1st Squadron
Major commands to which assigned
Oct. 1808–Jun. 1809 2nd Squadron in Maupetit's Brigade, 4th Corps
Jul. 1809–Jun. 1810 2nd Squadron in the 4th Corps
Jul.–Sep. 1810 2nd Squadron in the German Division, Army of the South
Sep. 1810–Aug. 1812 2nd Squadron in the German Division, Army of the Centre
Aug. 1812–Mar. 1813 2nd Squadron in the Army of the Centre
Mar. 1813–May 1813 2nd Squadron in Avy's Brigade, Abbé's Division, Army of the Centre
May–Jul. 1813 1st and 2nd Squadrons in the German Brigade, Army of the Centre
Jul.–Oct. 1813 1st and 2nd Squadrons in Vinot's Brigade, Soult's Division
Nov.–22 Dec. 1813 1st and 2nd Squadrons in Digeon's Division, Army of Aragon
Battles and officer casualties
Lezuza (17 Jul. 1811) 3 killed
Departure from the Peninsula
22 Dec. 1813 1st and 2nd Squadrons

The Poles

Two regiments of Polish cavalry, the Polish Light Horse/Lancers of the Imperial Guard and the 1st Vistula Legion Lancers, served in the Peninsula. In June 1811 1st Vistula Legion Lancers were incorporated into the French Army as the 7th Lancers. For information on the lancers, see tables 14.5 and 14.7.

The Kingdom of Westphalia

The Westphalian Light Horse Regiment was one of the strongest cavalry regiments in the Peninsula. It was a three squadron regiment for most of the years it was in Spain. Not until the winter of 1813 did the regiment's presence drop to a single squadron, when the rest of the squadrons were withdrawn to Germany.

Table 16.12   Westphalian Light Horse (Westphalian Lancers) Regiment[*]

Colonel
  Karl Christoph Wilhelm Hildesheim (28 Aug. 1808–Sep. 1809)
  Karl Christoph Wilhelm Hessberg (1809–1810)
  Ferdinand Silvius Heinrich Karl von Stein (16 Jul. 1810–Dec. 1813)
Regimental depot
  Melsungen
Location of Squadrons
  Nov. 1808–Feb. 1813 HQ, 1st, 2nd and 3rd Squadrons in Spain
  Mar.–Dec. 1813 1st Squadron in Spain; HQ, 2nd and 3rd Squadrons in Germany
Arrival in the Peninsula
  Nov. 1808 HQ, 1st, 2nd and 3rd Squadrons
Major commands to which assigned
  Nov. 1808–Jan. 1809 HQ, 1st, 2nd and 3rd Squadrons in Maupetit's Brigade, 4th Corps
  Jan.–Jun. 1809 HQ, 1st, 2nd and 3rd Squadrons in Beaumont's Brigade 1st Corps
  Jun.–Sep. 1809 HQ, 1st, 2nd and 3rd Squadrons in Ormancey's Brigade, Merlin's Division, 4th Corps
  Sep.–Dec. 1809 HQ, 1st, 2nd and 3rd Squadrons in 4th Corps
  Jan.–Sep. 1810 HQ, 1st, 2nd and 3rd Squadrons in the German Division, Army of Spain
  Sep. 1810–Jul. 1812 HQ, 1st, 2nd and 3rd Squadrons in the German Division, Army of Centre
  Jul.–Sep. 1812 HQ, 1st, 2nd and 3rd Squadrons in Merlin's Division, Army of the Centre
  Oct. 1812–Feb. 1813 HQ, 1st, 2nd and 3rd Squadrons in Trelliard's Division, Army of the Centre

---

[*] Renamed Westphalian Lancers on 9 October 1811.

Mar.–May 1813 1st Squadron in Avy's Brigade, Army of the Centre
May–Jul. 1813 1st Squadron in Maupoint's Brigade, Army of Aragon
Jul.–Dec. 1813 1st Squadron in Meyer's Brigade, Digeon's Division, Army of Aragon
Battles and officer casualties
Hynojola (11 Mar. 1809) 5 wounded
Talavera (28 Jul. 1809) 2 wounded
Counter-guerrilla operations (1809–12) 1 killed, 2 wounded, 1 would die from wounds
Departure from the Peninsula
Feb. 1813 HQ, 2nd and 3rd Squadrons
Dec. 1813 1st Squadron disarmed

Notes When the regiment was disarmed by the French in December 1813, their horses were given to the 29th Chasseurs.

Appendix

Sources

The format of this study does not lend itself to using footnotes to cite every source used in compiling the tables. The following is a listing by table of the major sources used for them. Every major source, such as an order-of-battle from Oman's *History of the Peninsular* War, was then cross-checked with the numerous regimental histories and memoirs. These were too many to cite, so when this occurred, I noted it with 'various regimental histories'. Sources cited in the narrative are not included in the list below.

'Author's analysis of data' means other tables or major sources that were already listed (such as Six and Martinein) were used them as the basis for the information, usually occurring when no regimental histories were available.

1.1 Grasset, *La guerre*, vol. I, p. 431
1.2 Ibid, p. 123
1.3 Ibid, p. 438
1.4 Ibid, pp. 451–8
1.5 Ibid, *État G*
1.6 Oman, vol. I, p. 613
1.7 Ibid, p. 468
1.8 Grasset, *La guerre*, vol. I, État G
1.9 Oman, vol. I, pp. 612–15
1.10 Balagny, vol. I, pp. 6–10
1.11 Oman, vol. I, pp. 640–2
2.1 Balagny, vol. I, pp. 470–3
2.2 Balagny, vol. II, pp. 707–10
2.3 Balagny, vol. V; Oman, vol. II, pp. 620–7; var. regimental histories
2.4 Author's analysis of data
2.5 Oman, vol. II, p. 624–7; var. regimental histories
2.6 Oman, vol. II, p. 648; var. regimental histories
2.7 Ilari, 'La Truppe Italiane'; 'La Truppe napoletani', p. 55; var. regimental histories

2.8 Author's analysis of data and var. regimental histories
2.9 Oman, vol. III, pp. 93, 532–9
3.1 Balagny, vol. V, pp. 418–19
3.2 Balagny, vol. V, p. 420
3.3 Balagny, vol. V, p. 419
3.4 Bonaparte, *Confidential Correspondence*, vol. II, p. 148; Ibid. vol. III, pp. 104, 108; *Unpublished Correspondence*, vol. III, pp. 584–5
3.5 Bonaparte, *Confidential Correspondence*, vol. II, pp. 114, 129, 150, 151
3.6 Bonaparte, *Correspondance de Napoléon Ier*, vol. XX, p. 117; Nafziger, 'French Army & the Armies of Client States', pp. 23–4
3.7 Koch, vol. VII, pp. 564–7; Oman, vol. III, pp. 532–9; var. regimental histories
3.8 Koch, vol. VII, pp. 581–2; Oman, vol. III, pp. 532–9; var. regimental histories
3.9 du Casse, *Mémoires,* vol. VII, p. 148
3.10 Author's analysis of data; var. regimental histories

3.11 Koch, vol. VII, p. 590

3.12 Koch, vol. VII, pp. 579–82

3.13 Koch, vol. VII, pp. 600–2

3.14 Oman, vol. IV, pp. 610, 612, 635; Dempsey, *Albuera*, pp. 270–1; var. regimental histories

3.15 Dempsey, *Albuera*, pp. 270–1

3.16 Oman, vol. IV, pp. 638–42; var. regimental histories

3.17 Var. regimental histories

3.18 Oman, vol. IV, pp. 638–42; var. regimental histories; author's analysis of data

3.19 Ibid.

3.20 Ibid.

3.21 Grasset, *Malaga Province*, pp. 573–7

3.22 Ibid., pp. 579–82

3.23 Ibid., pp. 586–9

3.24 Ibid., pp. 590–3

3.25 Ibid., p. 594

3.26 Grasset, *Malaga*, pp. 590–8; vari. regimental histories; author's analysis of data

3.27 Author's analysis of data

3.28 Grasset, *Malaga*, pp. 590–8; Nafziger, 'French Armée du Centre'; Oman, vol. V, pp. 601–5; var. regimental histories

4.1 Oman, vol. VI, pp. 741–5; var. regimental histories

4.2 Oman, vol. VI, pp. 741–5; 754–6; var. regimental histories

4.3 Var. regimental histories

4.4 Oman, vol. VI, pp. 754–6; var. regimental histories

4.5 Nafziger, 'French Units Ordered from Spain to France June 1813'

4.6 Oman, vol. VI, pp. 765-768; various regimental histories

4.7 Nafziger, 'French Army of Spain 1 September 1813'; Oman, vol. VI, pp. 765–8; var. regimental histories

4.8 Nafziger, 'French Army of Spain 16 January 1814.'; var. regimental histories

4.9 Nafziger, 'French Forces'; var. regimental histories

4.10 Nafziger, 'French Cavalry', 'French Army of Catalonia', 'French Units'; Oman, vol. VII, pp. 557–8

5.1 to 5.5 Author's analysis of data in tables

6.1 Chappet, p. 123; Mullié, vol. I, pp. 23–4; Six, vol. I, pp. 23–4

6.2 Charaway, pp. 171–4; Six, vol. I, p. 36

6.3 Alexandre, p. 57; Six, vol. I, p. 58

6.4 Mullié, vol. I, pp. 49–50; Six, vol. I, p. 67

6.5 Charaway, pp. 62–3; Six, vol. I, p. 70

6.6 Mullié, vol. I, pp. 67–8; Six, vol. I, pp. 90–1

6.7 Chappet, p. 141; Mullié, vol. I, pp. 70–1; Six, vol. I, pp. 95–6; Timmermans

6.8 Chappet, p. 70; Mullié, vol. I, pp. 207–8; Six, vol. I, pp. 126–7

6.9 Chappet, p. 85; Mullié, vol. I, pp. 209–11; Six, vol. I, pp. 130–1

6.10 Mullié, vol. I, p. 218; Six, vol. I, pp. 138–9

6.11 Chappet, p. 135; Mullié, vol. I, pp. 223–4; Six, vol. I, pp. 147–8; Timmermans

6.12 Six, vol. I, pp. 149–50

6.13 Chappet, p. 140; Mullié, vol. I, pp. 225–6; Six, vol. I, pp. 153–4; Timmermans

6.14 Mullié, vol. I, pp. 234–6; Six, vol. I, pp. 158–9

6.15 de Bonnières de Wierre, pp. 280–1; Mullié, vol. I, p. 238; Six, vol. I, pp. 160–1; Timmermans

6.16 Mullié, vol. I, pp. 256–7; Six, vol. I, p. 181

6.17 Six, vol. I, pp. 194–5

6.18 Charaway, pp. 91–3; Six, vol. I, pp. 204–5; Mullié, vol. I, pp. 278–81;

6.19 Chappet, p. 148; Six, vol. I, pp. 207–8

6.20 Mullié, vol. I, pp. 290–3; Six, vol. I, p. 207; Charaway, pp. 71–3; du Courthial pp. 255–6; Six, vol. I, pp. 216–17

6.21 Charaway, pp. 31–2; Mullié, vol.

I, pp. 318–19; Six, vol. I, p. 252;
Thoumas, pp. 265–383

6.22 de Bonnières de Wierre, pp. 285–6;
Six, vol. I, pp. 276–7; Timmermans

7.1 Charaway, pp. 40–1; Six, vol. II, p. 272

7.2 Chappet, p. 55; Mullié, vol. I, pp.
371–2; Six, vol. I, pp. 299–300

7.3 Six, vol. I, pp. 322–3

7.4 Chappet, p. 78; Mullié, vol. I, pp.
430–1; Six, vol. I, pp. 356–7

7.5 Charaway, pp. 25–7; Six, vol. I, p. 407

7.6 Charaway, pp. 65–6; Six, vol. I, pp.
426–7

7.7 Mullié, vol. I, pp. 536–7; Six, vol. I,
p. 461

7.8 Chappet, p. 38; Six, vol. I, pp. 462–3

7.9 Six, vol. I, pp. 465–6

7.10 Mullié, vol. I, pp. 543–4; Six, vol. I,
p. 469; Timmermans

7.11 Chappet, p. 5; Mullié, vol. I, pp.
553–4; Six, vol. I, pp. 481–2

7.12 Mullié, vol. II, pp. 28–31. Six, vol. I,
pp. 531–3; Timmermans

7.13 Six, vol. I, pp. 533–4

7.14 Mullié, vol. II, pp. 147-149; Six, vol.
I, pp. 577-578

7-15 Chappet, p. 58; Mullié, vol. II,
pp. 70-71; Six, vol. I, p. 588

7.16 Mullié, vol. II, pp. 111-116; Six, vol.
II, pp. 2–4; Thoumas, pp. 51–115;
Timmermans

7.17 Six, vol. II, pp. 13–14

8.1 Six, vol. II, pp. 118–19

8.2 Chappet, p. 139; Mullié, vol. II, pp.
151–2; Six, vol. II, pp. 39–40

8.3 Chappet, p. 137; Six, vol. II, pp. 48–9

8.4 Six, vol. II, p. 57

8.5 Mullié, vol. II, pp. 183–6; Six, vol.
II, pp. 64–5; Thoumas, pp. 1–49;
Timmermans

8.6 Cuel, p. 161; Mullié, vol. II, p. 205;
Six, vol. II, pp. 92–4

8.7 Mullié, vol. II, p. 214; Six, vol. II, pp.
107–8; Timmermans

8.8 Six, vol. II, p. 131

8.9 Mullié, vol. II, pp. 239–40; Six, vol.
II, pp. 132–3

8.10 Chappet, p. 135; Mullié, vol. II, pp.
255–8 Six, vol. II, p. 148

8.11 Chappet, p. 140; Mullié, vol. II, pp.
263–4; Six, vol. II, pp. 154–5

8.12 Charaway, pp. 69–70; Six, vol. II,
pp. 157–8

8.13 Mullié, vol. II, pp. 280–1; Six, vol.
II, pp. 172–3

8.14 Mullié, vol. II, pp. 281–2; Six, vol.
II, p. 173

8.15 Mullié, vol. II, pp. 282–4; Six, vol.
II, p. 174; Timmermans

8.16 Mullié, vol. II, pp. 288–90; Six, vol.
II, pp. 183–4

8.17 Mullié, vol. II, pp. 291–2; Six, vol.
II, pp. 185–6

8.18 Six, vol. II, pp. 192–3

8.19 Six, vol. II, p. 198

8.20 Chappet, p. 21; Mullié, vol. II, pp.
300–3; Six, vol. II, pp. 199–200

8.21 Charaway, pp. 89–91; Mullié, vol.
II, pp. 322–4; Six, vol. II, p. 215;
Thoumas, pp. 117–75

9.1 Six, vol. II, pp. 259–60

9.2 Six, vol. II, p. 270

9.3 Chappet, p. 123; Six, vol. II, pp. 271–2

9.4 Six, vol. II, pp. 277–8

9.5 Charaway, pp. 61–2; Six, vol. II, pp.
287–8

9.6 Six, vol. II, pp. 302–3

9.7 Mullié, vol. II, pp. 456–8; Six, vol. II,
pp. 319–20

9.8 Mullié, vol. II, pp. 466–9; Six, vol. II,
pp. 334–5

9.9 Six, vol. II, pp. 370–1

9.10 Six, vol. II, p. 440

9.11 Six, vol. II, pp. 474–5

9.12 Chappet, p. 135; Six, vol. II, pp.
476–7

9.13 Chappet, p. 131; Six, vol. II, pp.
479–80; Timmermans

9.14 Six, vol. II, pp. 500–1

9.15 Chappet, p. 144; Mullié, vol. II, pp.
192–3; Six, vol. II, pp. 505–6

9.16 Mullié, vol. II, pp. 556–7; Six, vol.
II, pp. 510–11; Timmermans

9.17 Six, vol. II, p. 546

9.18 Chappet, p. 139; Six, vol. II, p. 547
9.19 Six, vol. II, p. 560
9.20 Six, vol. II, p. 566

The Regiments
Unless otherwise noted, certain sources
were used in all the tables
Colonels: Quintin and Quintin; Six
*Regimental Depot and all tables for
Provisional Dragoon Regiments 1808–11*
Nafziger 'French Army & Mobilized
Forces of Client States 15 October 1811'
Battles and officer casualties: Martinien
10.1 Author's analysis of data
10.2 Author's analysis of data
10.3 Author's analysis of data
10.7 Bukhari, pp. 13–14; Lemaitre,135–7;
    Nafziger *The French Army*, pp. 30–1
10.8 Ibid.
10.9 Ibid.
10.10–10.12 Ibid., p. 28
10.13 de Bourqueney, p. 165
10.14 Du Courthial, p. 172
10.15 Courtès-Lapeyrat, p. 139
10.16 Descaves, p. 19
11.1 Author's analysis of data
11.2 Bruyère, pp. 114–22, 167–76
11.3 de Bonnières de Wierre, pp. 73–89,
    208–14, 249–52, 280–99, 315–16
11.4 Lemaitre pp. 180–252, 351–72
11.5 de Saint-Just, pp. 241–307, 397
11.6 *Historique du 6e Régiment de
    Dragons*, pp. 127–47, 253–4, 279–95
11.7 Author's analysis of data
11.8 Martinet, pp. 93–172
11.9 d'Ollone, pp. 335–59, 531
11.10 Savin de Larclause, pp. 161, 215–24
11.11 Author's analysis of data
11.12 *Historique du 13e Régiment de
    Dragons*, pp. 81–143, 213–307
11.13 Menuau, pp. 211–83
11.14 Alexandre, pp. 41–52, 57, 61–3
11.15 de Castéras-Villemartin, pp. 123–53
11.16 Author's analysis of data
11.17 Cuel, pp. 53–85, 161
11.18 Sauzey, Camille pp. 149–219
11.19 Author's analysis of data

11.20 Author's analysis of data
11.21 Dupont-Delporte, pp. 112–44,
    212–18
11.22 Author's analysis of data
11.23 de Bourqueney, pp. 148–251,
    269–77
11.24 du Courthial, pp. 119–276
11.25 d'Ollone, p. 532
12.1 Courtès-Lapeyrat, pp. 75–168
12.2 *Historique du 7e Régiment de
    Chasseurs*, pp. 35, 42–7, 120–21,
    134–5, 140
12.3 Wolf, pp. 132–188
12.4 Le Moine de Margon, pp. 114–15
12.5 Author's analysis of data
12.6 Descaves, pp. 17–37, 82–109, 167–
    76, 186–9, 210–17
12.7 Author's analysis of data
12.8 Magon, pp. 84–183, 225–7, 236–40,
    251–5, 267–9
12.9 Aubier, pp. 218–54, 377, 382, 435–8,
    454–5,
12.10 d'Ars, pp. 137–307
12.11–12.14 Author's analysis of data
12.12 Author's analysis of data
12.13 Author's analysis of data
12.14 Author's analysis of data
12.15 de Conchard, pp. 160–2, 165,
    180–1, 196–7, 215–16, 223–4, 237, 241,
    253–8
12.16 Author's analysis of data
12.17 Author's analysis of data
13.1 Staub, pp. 117–39
13.2 Buisson, pp. 99–128, 266–8
13.3 Dupuy, pp. 42–61, 126–40
13.4 Author's analysis of data
13.5 de Castillon de Saint-Victor, pp.
    91–4, 204–5; Massoni, pp. 350–2
13.6 Ogier d'Ivry, pp. 68–88
13.7 Author's analysis of data
13.8 Ogier d'Ivry, pp. 77–88
14.1 Pawley, *Mounted Grenadiers*, pp.
    16–21
14.2 Author's analysis of data
14.3 Pawley, *Napoleon's Mounted
    Chasseurs*, pp. 20–35; Pawley,
    Mounted Grenadiers, p. 21

14.4 Pawley, *Mounted Grenadiers,* p. 21

14.5 Pawley, *Napoleon's Polish Lancers,* pp. 13–35

14.6 Yvert, pp. 10–38

14.7 Dempsey, *Napoleon's Mercenaries.* pp. 123–8; Kirkor, pp. 32–177, 259–301, 525–52, 562–3

15.1 de Bonnières de Wierre, pp. 73–8; Grasset, *La Guerre,* vol. I, p. 431; de Saint-Just, pp. 242–50; Lemaitre, pp. 182–9

15.2 Grasset, *La Guerre,* vol. I, État D

15.3 Ibid.

15.4 Ibid. p. 460

15.5 Dupont-Delporte, pp. 112–13; Grasset, *La Guerre,* vol. I, État E

15.6 Ibid; de Bourqueney, pp. 149–51

15.7 Bruyère, p. 114; Grasset, *La Guerre,* vol. II, p. 76; *Historique du 6e Régiment de Dragons,* p. 127

15.8 Grasset, *La Guerre,* vol. I, État E

15.9 Ibid.

15.10 Ibid. vol. I, p. 460

15.11 Oman, vol. I, pp. 535–8, 645

15.12 Grasset, *La Guerre,* vol. I, État E

15.13 Ibid.

15.14 Bruyère, pp. 117–18

15.15 Lemaitre, pp. 212–21; Martinet, pp. 116–18; Menuau, pp. 232–42

15.16 Du Courthial de Lassuchette, p. 168

15.17 *Historique du 6e Régiment de Dragons,* p. 133; de Bonnières de Wierre, pp. 78–9, 84

15.18 de Bonnières de Wierre, p. 79; d'Ollone, p. 347; Savin de Larclause, pp. 169, 175

15.19 Castéras-Villemartin, pp. 139–42; de Conchard, pp. 215–16

15.20 Ibid.

15.21 de Saint-Just, pp. 276–7

15.22 Cuel, p. 75

15.23 Sauzey, *Historique,* pp. 181–3

15.24 *Historique du 13e Régiment de Dragons,* p. 105

15.25 Alexandre, p. 42; de Bourqueney, pp. 163–5

15.26 Detaille, p. 11; Le Moine de Margon, pp. 114–15; de Castillon de Saint-Victor, pp. 91–4, 204–5; Massoni, pp. 350–2

15.27 Aubier, pp. 218–54, 377, 382, 435–8, 454–5; Descaves, pp. 24–5; 86–90; *Historique du 7e Régiment de Chasseurs,* pp. 35, 42–7, 134–5, 140; Parquin, pp. 111–50

16.1 Dempsey, *The Berg Regiment,* Nafziger, *The Armies of Westphalia and Cleves-Berg;* Thomas, pp. 20–103

16.2 Dempsey, *The Berg Regiment;* Nafziger, *The Armies of Westphalia and Cleves-Berg;* Thomas, pp. 20–103

16.3 de Lassus, pp. xviii–xx, 145–64

16.4 Dempsey, *Napoleon's Mercenaries.* pp. 167–9

16.5 Ilari, 'La Truppe Italiane in Spagna', tables 2.4, 6.11, 14, 15

16.6 Ibid., tables 2, 4, 5, 6

16.7 Ibid., tables 2.4, 6.11, 14, 15

16.8 Ibid., pp. 13–16

16.9 Ibid., tables 12, 14, 15; Ilari, 'La Truppe napoletane in Spagna', pp. 1–63

16.10 Ilari, 'La Truppe Italiane in Spagna', tables 2, 4, 5, 6, 10, 11, 12, 14, 15; 'La Truppe napoletani in Spagna', pp.1–63

16.11 Nafziger, *The Armies of Germany;* Sauzey, *Les Allemands*

16.12 Lünsmann; Nafziger, *The Armies of Westphalia and Cleves-Berg;* Nafziger, *The Bavarian and Westphalian Armies*

References

Abell, Francis   *Prisoners of War in Britain 1756 to 1815*, Humphrey Milford, Oxford 1914

Alexandre, Léon   *Historique du 15e Dragons*, G. Maleville, Libourne 1885

Amonville, Marie François d'   *Les cuirassiers du roy, le 8e cuirassiers: journal historique du régiment, 1638–1892*, A. Lahure, Paris 1892

Arnault, Antoine-Vincent et al.   *Biographie nouvelle des contemporains*, 20 vols, Librairie Historique, Paris 1824

d'Ars, Anatole de Bremond   *Historique du 21e Régiment de Chasseurs à Cheval 1792–1814*, Honoré Champion, Paris 1903

Aubier, Achille   *Un Régiment de cavalerie légère de 1793 à 1815*, Berger-Levrault, Paris 1891

Austin, Paul B.   *1812: Napoleon's Invasion of Russia*, Greenhill Books, London 2000

Balagny, Dominique   *Campagne de l'Empereur Napoléon en Espagne (1808–1809)*, 5 vols, Berger–Levrault, Paris 1902–7

Barbieux, le Père   *Manuel du soldat belge: recueil patriotique et religieux*, J. Casterman, Tournai 1836

Beamish, N. Ludlow   *History of the King's German Legion*, 2 vols, Buckland & Brown, London 1993

Beauvais, Charles-Théodore   *Victoires, conquêtes, désastres, revers et guerres civiles des Français, de 1792 à 1815*, 27 vols, C. L. F. Panckoucke, Paris 1820.

Berriat, Honoré   *Législation militaire: ou, recueil methodique et raisonné des lois, décrets, arrêtés, réglemens et instructiona actuellement en vigueur sur toutes les branches de l'état militaire*, 2 vols, Louis Caprioloe, Paris 1812

Blakeney, Robert   *A Boy in the Peninsular War*, Greenhill Books, London 1989

Bloch, E.   *Historique du 95e Régiment d'Infanterie de Ligne: 1734–1888*, Typ. Tardy-Pigelet, Bourges 1888

Bonaparte, Napoleon   *Correspondance de Napoléon Ier*, 28 vols, Imprimerie Impériale, Paris 1858–69

— *The Confidential Correspondence of Napoleon Bonaparte with His Brother Joseph*, 2 vols, D. Appleton & Company, New York 1856

— *The Unpublished Correspondence of Napoleon I*, 3 vols, Duffield & Company, New York 1913

Bonnières de Wierre, André de   *Historique du 3e Régiment de Dragons*, Bourgeois, Nantes 1892

Bouillé du Chariol, Louis-Joseph Amour, Marquis de   *Souvenirs et fragments pour servir aux mémoires de ma vie et de mon temps*, 3 vols, Alphonse Picard, Paris 1911

Bourqueney, Marie V. de   *Historique du 25e Régiment de Dragons*, A. Mame et Fils, Tours 1890

Bowden, Scotty and Charlie Tarbox   *Armies on the Danube*, Empire Games Press, Arlington 1980

Bowden, Scott   *Napoleon's Grande Armée of 1813* Emperor's Press, Chicago 1990

—   (translator and annotater)   *Napoleon's Finest: Marshal Davout and His 3rd Corps Combat Journal of Operations 1805–1807*, Military History Press, 2006

Bruyère, Paul   *Historique du 2e Régiment de Dragons*, Imprimerie Garnier, Chartres 1885

Brye, P. de   *Historique du 6e Régiment de Cuirassiers*, np 1893

Buisson, Émile   *Les Hussards de Chamborant (2e Hussards)*, Maison Didot, Paris 1897

Bukhari, Emir   *Napoleon's Dragoons and Lancers*, Osprey, London 1976

Cannon, Richard   *Historical Record of the Thirteenth Regiment of Light Dragoons*, John W. Parker, London 1842

Casse, Albert du   *Le Général Arrighi de Casanova: duc de Padoue*, 5 vols, Dentu, Paris 1866

—   *Mémoires et correspondance politique et militaire du roi Joseph*, 10 vols, Perrotin, Paris 1854

Castéras-Villemartin, Jacques de   *Historique du 16e Régiment de Dragons*, Éditions Artistiques Militaires, Paris 1892

de Castillon de Saint-Victor, Marie   *Historique du 5e Régiment de Hussards*, Editions Artistiques Militaires, Paris 1889

Caulaincourt, Armand de   *With Napoleon in Russia: The Memoirs of General de Caulaincourt, Duke of Vicenza*, William Morrow, New York 1935

Chandler, David G. *On the Napoleonic Wars*, Greenhill Books, London 1994

Chappet, Alain and et al.   *Guide Napoléonien*, Charles-Lavauzelle, Paris 1981

Charaway, Noel   *Les généraux morts pour la patrie*, Au Siège de la Société, Paris 1893

Chartrand, René   *Spanish Guerrillas in the Peninsular War 1808–14*, Osprey, Oxford 2004

Clerc, Captaine   *Historique du 79e Régiment d'Infanterie*, Berger-Levrault, Paris 1896

Chateaubriand, François-René   *Mémoires d'outre-tombe*, 42 vols, P. Arpin, New York 1848

Colbert, N. J.   *Traditions et souvenirs ou mémoires touhant le temps et la vie du Général Auguste Colbert*, Librairie de Firmin Didot, Paris 1873

Conchard, Vermeil de   *Historique du 120e Régiment d'Infanterie 1808–1814–1870–1892*, Imprimerie Albert Dury, Givet 1892

Corret, A.   *Histoire pittoresque et anecdotique de Belfort et ses environs*, J.-B Clerc, Belfort 1855

Courcelles, Jean Baptiste de   *Dictionnaire historique et biographique des généraux français, depuis le onzième siècle jusqu'en 1820*, Arthus Bertrand, Paris 1821

Courtès-Lapeyrat, Joseph-Pierre-Eugène   *Historique du 5e Régiment de Chasseurs*,

Librairie Militaire de L. Baudoin, Paris 1888

Crociani, Piero and Massimo Brandani   *La Cavalleria di Linea di Murat 1808–15*, Edizioni La Roccia, Rome 1978

Courthial de Lassuchette, Jules du   *Historique du 26e Dragons*, Hachette, Paris 1890

Cuel, Fernand Louis   *Historique du 18e Régiment de Dragons 1744–1894*, Noizette & cie, Paris 1894

Dempsey, Guy   *The Berg Regiment of Light Horse 1807–1808*, unpublished manuscript, 2002

—   *Napoleon's Mercenaries: Foreign units in the French army under the Consulate and Empire, 1799 to 1814*, Greenhill Books, London 2002

—   *Albuera 1811*, Frontline Books, London 2008

Derrécagaix, Victor Bernard   *Le Lieutenant-général comte Balliard, chef d'état-major de Murat*, Libraire Militaire Chapelot, Paris 1809

Descaves, Paul   *Historique du 13me Régiment de Chasseurs et des Chasseurs a Cheval de la Garde*, A. Bouineau, Beziers 1891

Desvernois, Nicolas P.   *Mémoires du General Bon. Desvernois*, Librairie Plon, Paris 1898

Detaille, Edouard   *L'Armée Française: An illustrated history of the French army, 1790–1885*, Waxtel & Hasenauer, New York 1992

Devimes, Jacques   *Manuel historique du département de l'Aisne*, Le Blan-Courtois, Laon 1826

Dupont-Delporte, Henri   *Historique du 22e Régiment de Dragons*, Typographie Georges Chamerot, Paris 1889

Dupuy, Raoul   *Historique du 3e Régiment de Hussards*, Paris Librairie Française, 1887

D'Urban, Benjamin   *The Peninsular Journal, 1808–1817*, Greenhill Books, London 1988

Dyneley, Thomas   *Letters Written by Lieutenant General Thomas Dyneley While on Active Service between the Years 1806 and 1815*, Ken Trotman, London 1984

Elting, John   *Swords around the Throne: Napoleon's Grande Armée*, Free Press, London 1988

Epstein, Robert M.   *Prince Eugene at War 1809*, Empire Games Press, Arlington 1984

Gärtner, Markus and Edmund Wagner   *Westphälisches Militär*, Herausgegeben im Auftrag, Beckum 1990

Gill, John   'Vermin, Scorpions and Mosquitoes: the Rheinbund in the Peninsula', *The Peninsular War: Aspects of the Struggle for the Iberian Peninsula*, ed. Ian Fletcher, Spellmount, Staplehurst 1998

—   *With Eagles to Glory Napoleon and His German Allies in the 1809 Campaign*, Greenhill Books, London 1992

Girod de l'Ain, Maurice   *Vie militaire du Général Foy*, Libraire Plon, Paris 1900

Gonneville, Aymar de   *Recollections of Colonel de Gonneville*, 2 vols, Worley Publications, Felling 1988

Gordon, Alexander   *A Cavalry Officer in the Corunna Campaign: 1808–1809*, Worley Productions, Felling 1990

Grasset, A.   *La Guerre d'Espagne (1807–1813)*, 3 vols, Berger-Levrault, Paris 1914

—   *Malaga: Province française (1802–1812)*. Henri-Charles Lavauzelle, Paris 1910.

References

Grémillet, Paul   *Un Régiment pendant deux siècles: historique du 81e Ligne, ancien 6e Légèr*, Paul Viala, Paris 1899

Griffith, Edwin   *From Corunna to Waterloo: The letters and journals of two Napoleonic Hussars, 1801–1816*, ed. Gareth Glover, Greenhill Books, London 2006

Hall, John A.   *A History of the Peninsular War, Vol. VIII: The biographical dictionary of British officers killed and wounded, 1808–1814*, Greenhill Books, London 1998

Hay, Andrew Leith   *Narrative of the Peninsular War*, 2nd edn, 2 vols, Ken Trotman, Godmanchester 2008

Haythornthwaite, Philip   *British Cavalryman 1792–1815*, Osprey, London 1994

Historique du 6e Régiment de Dragons Marengo 1800, Austerlitz 1805, Friedland 1807 Kanghil 1855, Librairie Ch. Delagrave, Paris 1898

Historique du 7e Régiment de Chasseurs, Imprimerie Jules Céas, Valence 1891

Historique du 13e Régiment de Dragons, Librairie Hachette, Paris 1891

Horricks, Raymond   *In Flight with the Eagle: A guide to Napoleon's elite*, Costello, Tunbridge Wells 1988

Horward, Donald   *Napoleon and Iberia: The twin sieges of Ciudad Rodrigo and Almeida, 1810*, Greenhill Books, London 1984

Ilari, Virgilio   'Cinque Reggimenti Napoletani dell'Armee d'Espagne (1808–1813)', *Storia Militare del Regno Murattiano*, Widerholdt Frères, Invorio (NO), 2007, vol. II, pp. 175–247

— 'GLI Italiani in Spagna', *Gli italiani in Spagna nella Guerra napoleonica (1807–1813)*, Edizioni dell'Orso, Alessandria 2006

— 'La Cavalleria Italiana', *Storia militare del Regno Italico*, vol. 1, USSME, Rome 2001

— 'La Truppe Italiane in Spagna', *Gli italiani in Spagna nella Guerra napoleonica (1807–1813)*, Edizioni dell'Orso, Alessandria 2006

— 'La Truppe napoletane in Spagna', *Gli italiani in Spagna nella Guerra napoleonica (1807–1813)*, Edizioni dell'Orso, Alessandria 2006

Jones, B. T. (editor)   *Charles Parquin*, Longmans, Green, London 1969

Koch, Jean Baptiste   *Mémoirs de Massena*, 5 vols, Paulin et Lechevalier, Paris 1848–50

Kirkor, Stanisław   *Legia Nadwislanska 1808–1814* Oficyna Poetów i Malarzy, Londyn 1981

Lachouque, Henry and Anne S. K. Brown   *The Anatomy of Glory: Napoleon and his Guard*, Hippocrene Books, New York 1978

Lapène, Edouard   *Conquête de l'Andalousie campagne de 1810 et 1811 dans le Midi de l'Espagne*, Anselin et Pochard, Paris 1823

Larrey, Dominique J.   *Mémoires de chirurgie militaire, et campagnes*, 4 vols, Chez J. Smith, Paris 1817

Lassus, H. de   *Historique du 11e Régiment de Hussards*, Jules Ceas et Fils, Valence 1890

Lejeune, Louis François   *Memoirs of Baron Lejeune*, 2 vols, Worley, Tyne & Wear 1987

Lemaitre, Louis   *Historique du 4e Régiment de Dragons (1672–1894)*, Charles-Lavauzelle, Paris 1894

Le Moine de Margon, Gabriel   *Historique du 11e Régiment de Chasseurs*, Librairie de Louis Bon, Vesoul 1896

Lombroso, Giacomo *Biografie dei Primarii Generali ed Ufficiali: La maggior parte italiani, che si distinsero nelle guerre napoleoniche in ogni angolo d'Europa*, Franceso Sanvito, Milan 1843

Long, Robert *Peninsular Cavalry General (1811–13): The correspondence of Lieutenant-General Robert Ballard Long*, ed. T. H. McGuffie George G. Harrap, London 1951

Lünsmann, Fritz *Die Armee des Königreichs Westfalen, 1807–1813*, Leddihn, Berlin 1935

Magon, Henri Georges Marie *Historique du 15e Régiment de Chasseurs à Cheval*, Berger-Levrault, Paris 1895

Mailles, Jacques de *History of Bayard the Good*, Chapman & Hall, London 1883

Marbot, Jean *The Memoirs of Baron de Marbot*, 2 vols, Greenhill Books, London 1990

Markham, J. David *Imperial Glory: The bulletins of Napoleon's Grande Armée 1805–1814*, Greenhill Books, London 2003

Martinet, François *Historique du 9e Régiment de Dragons*, Henry Thomas Hamel, Paris 1888

Martinien, A. *Tableaux par corps et par batailles des officiers tués et blessés pendant les guerres de l'Empire (1805–1815)*, Editions Militaires Européennes, Paris nd

— *Tableaux par corps et par batailles des officiers tués et blessés pendant les guerres de l'Empire (1805–1815)*, supplement, Librairie L. Fournier, Paris 1909

Massoni, Gérard-Antoine *Histoire d'un regiment de cavalerie légère: Le 5e Hussards de 1783 à 1815*, Archives & Culture, Paris nd

Menuau, Maurice *Historique du 14e Régiment de Dragons*, Boussod, Valadon, Paris 1889

Michaud, Joseph *Biographie universelle, ancienne et modern*, Chez H. Ode, Brussels 1847

Mollo, John *The Prince's Dolls: Scandals, skirmishes and splendours of the first British Hussars, 1793–1815*, Leo Cooper, London 1997

Mullié, M. C. *Biographie des célébrités militaires des armées de terre et de mer de 1789 à 1850*, 2 vols, Poignavant, Paris 1851

Muir, Rory *Salamanca 1812*, Yale University Press, New Haven 2001

Naam-Register der Officieren van de Koniglije Hollandsche Armee over den Jare 1808

Nafziger, George *The Bavarian and Westphalian Armies: 1799–1815*, RAFM, Cambridge 1981

— *The Armies of Westphalia and Cleves-Berg 1806–1815*, privately published, 1991

— *The Armies of Germany and the Confederation of the Rhine 1792–1815. Vol. 1: Anhalt, Frankfurt, Nassau, Hesse-Darmstadt, Mecklenburg, and the Saxon Ducal Houses*, Privately published, np 1993

— *The French Army: Royal, Republican, Imperial 1782–1815. Vol. 3 The cavalry, artillery & train*, Privately published, Pisgah 1997

Napier, William F. *History of the War in the Peninsula and in the South of France*, 6 vols, Constable, London 1993

Naylies, M. de *Mémoires sur la guerre d'Espagne: pendant les années 1808, 1809, 1810, et 1811*, Chez Magimel, Paris 1817

Ogier d'Ivry, Henri P. *Historique du 9e Régiment de Hussards et des Guides de la Garde*, Jules Céas, Valence 1891

References

d'Ollone, Charles *Historique du 10e Régiment de Dragons*, Berger-Levrault, Paris 1893
Oman, Charles *History of the Peninsular War*, 7 vols, AMS Press, New York 1980
Parquin, Charles *Napoleon's Army*, ed. B. T. Jones, Longman's, London 1969
Pascal de Julien, Pierre *Galerie historique des contémporains, ou nouvelle biographie*, 8 vols, Aug. Wahlen, Brussels 1822
Pawley, Ronald *Mounted Grenadiers of the Imperial Guard*, Osprey, New York 2009
— *Napoleon's Mounted Chasseurs of the Imperial Guard*, Osprey, New York 2008
— *Napoleon's Polish Lancers of the Imperial Guard*, Osprey, New York 2007
Pelet, Jean *The French Campaign in Portugal, 1810–1811: An account by Jean Jacques Pelet*, ed. Horward, Donald, University of Minnesota Press, Minneapolis 1973
Petre, F. Loraine *Napoleon's Conquest of Prussia – 1806*, Arms and Armor Press, London 1972
Place, Rene de *Historique du 12e Cuirassiers (1668–1888)*, A. Lahure, Paris 1889
Quintin, Danielle and Bernard *Dictionnaire des colonels de Napoleon*, S.P.M., Paris 1996
Reiset, Marie-Antoine *Souvenirs du Lieutenant Général Vicomte de Reiset: 1810– 1814*, 2 vols, Calmann-Lévy, Paris 1901
Rocca, Albert Jean de *In the Peninsula with a French Hussar*, Greenhill Books, London 1990
— *Mémoires sur la guerre des Français in Espagne*, 2nd Edition, Jules-Guillaume Fick, Geneva 1887
Saint-Cyr, Gouvion *Journal des opérations de l'armée de catalogne, en 1808 et 1809*, Chez Anselin et Pochard, Paris 1821
Saint-Just, V. de *Historique du 5e Régiment de Dragons*, Librairie Hachette, Paris 1891
Sarrut, Germain and N. Saint-Edme *Biographie des hommes du jour*, 2 vols, Paris Henri Krabe, 1836
Sauzey, Camille *Historique du 19e Regiment de Dragons 1793-1913*, privately published, Paris 1945
Sauzey, Jean *Les Allemands sous les aigles françaises: le Régiment des Duchés de Saxe*, Libraire Militarie R. Chapelot, Paris 1908
Sauzey, Jean *Les Allemands sous les aigles françaises: les soldats de Hesse et de Nassau*, Libraire Militarie R. Chapelot, Paris 1912
Savin de Larclause, Charles *Historique du 11e Régiment de Dragons*, L. P. Gouraud, Fonenay-le-Compte 1891
Ségur, Phillipe de *An Aide-de-Camp of Napoleon: Memoirs of General Count de Ségur*, Worley, Chippenham 1995
— *Napoleon's Russian Campaign*, Time-Life Books, Alexandria 1980
Sherer, Moyle *Recollections of the Peninsula*, Spellmount, Staplehurst 1996
Six, Georges *Dictionnaire biographique des généraux & amiraux français de la Révolution et de l'Empire (1792–1814)*, 2 vols, Librairie Historique et Nobiliaire, Paris 1934
Smith, Denis *The Prisoners of Cabrera: Napoleon's forgotten soldiers 1809–1914*, Four Walls Eight Windows, New York 2001
Smith, Digby *Napoleon's Regiments: Battle histories of the regiments of the French*

Army, 1792–1815, Greenhill, London 2000

— *The Greenhill Napoleonic Wars Data Book*, Greenhill Books, London 1998

Southey, Robert   *History of the Peninsular War*, 3 vols, John Murray, London 1827

Staub, André   *Histoire de tous les régiments de Hussards*, Martin-Beaupré, Paris 1867

Suchet, Louis   *Memoirs of the War in Spain, from 1808 to 1814*, 2 vols, Worley Publications, Tyneside 1986

Susane, Louis   *Histoire de la cavalerie française*, 3 vols, Librairie J. Hetzel, Paris 1874

Tascher, Maurice de   *Campaigning for Napoleon: The diary of a Napoleonic cavalry officer 1806–1813*, ed. Rosemary Brindle, Pen and Sword, Barnsley 2006

Thiébault, Paul   *The Memoirs of Baron Thiebault*, 2 vols, Worley Felling Publications, 1994

— *Relation de l'expédition du Portugal faite en 1807 et 1808*, Chez Magimel, Anselin et Pochard, Paris 1817

Thomas, J.   *Un régiment rhénan sous Napoléon Premier. Historique du Régiment de Cavalerie du Grand-Duché de Berg*, Vaillant-Carmmane, Lille 1928

Thoumas, Ch.   *Les Grands cavaliers du Premier Empire: Première Série Lasalle, Kellermann, Montbrun, Les Trois Colbert, Murat*, Berger-Levrault, Paris 1890

Tomkinson, William   *The Diary of a Cavalry Officer in the Peninsular War and Waterloo: 1809–1815*, Frederick Muller, London 1971

Van der Aa, Abraham and et al.   *Biographisch woordenboek der Nederlanden, bevattende levensbeschrijvingen van zoodanige personen, die zich op eenigerlei wijze in ons vaderland hebben vermaard gemaakt*, 12 vols, Van Brederode, Haarlem 1862

Vane, Charles W.   *Story of the Peninsular War*, Henry Colburn, London 1848

Vernon, Gay de   *Historique du 2e Régiment de Chasseurs a Cheval*, Librairie Militaire, Paris 1865

Vigneron, Hippolyte   *La Belgique militaire*, E. Renier, Brussels 1856

Vingtrinier, Aimé   'Le Général Maupetit', *Mémoires de l'Académie des Sciences, Belles-Lettres et Arts de Lyon*, J. B. Baillière, Paris 1896, pp. 97–116

Vivian, Richard H.   *Richard Hussey Vivian: A memoir*, Claud Vivian (ed.) Ken Trotman, Cambridge 2003

Vossler, Heinrich   *With Napoleon in Russia 1812*, Folio Society, London 1969

Warre, William   *Letters from the Peninsula, 1808-1812*, John Murray, London 1909

Wellington, 1st Duke of.   *The General Orders of Field Marshal the Duke of Wellington in Portugal, Spain, and France, from 1809 to 1814: in the Low Countries and France in 1815; and in France, Army of Occupation, from 1816 to 1818*, ed. John Gurwood, 2nd edn, Parker, Furnivall, and Parker, London 1847

Wolf, A.   *Historique du 10e Régiment de Chasseurs a Cheval*, Librairie Militaire de L. Baudoin, Paris 1890

Worley, Colin   *An Atlas of the Peninsular War: 1808–1814*, Worley Publications, Felling 2000

Yvert, Louis   *Historique du 13e Régiment de Cuirassiers 1807-1814–1891 a Nos Jours*, Imprimerie Garnier, Chartres 1895

Internet references

Broughton, Antony 'French Chasseur-à-Cheval Regiments and the Colonels Who Led Them: 1791 to 1815' *The Napoleon Series* www.napoleon-series.org November 2000, accessed 14 February 2010

— 'French Dragoon Regiments and the Colonels Who Led Them: 1791 to 1815' *The Napoleon Series* www.napoleon-series.org August 2000 accessed 5 February 2010

— 'French Hussar Regiments and the Colonels Who Led Them: 1791 to 1815' *The Napoleon Series* www.napoleon-series.org August 2000 accessed 28 February 2010

— 'French Infantry Regiments and the Colonels Who Led Them: 1791 to 1815' *The Napoleon Series* www.napoleon-series.org December 2001 accessed 8 February 2010

— 'French Light Infantry Regiments and the Colonels Who Led Them: 1791 to 1815.' *The Napoleon Series* www.napoleon-series.org June 2002 accessed 1 February 2010

Challis, Lionel S. 'Peninsula Roll Call' *The Napoleon Series* www.napoleon-series. org January 2009 accessed 3 February 2010

Nafziger, George *Nafziger Collection* www.cgsc.edu/carl/nafziger.htm (U.S. Army Combined Arms Center 2010)

'French Army & the Armies of Client States Dispositions: 10 September 1810'
'French Army & Mobilized Forces of Client States: 15 October 1811'
'French Army of Catalonia 14 January 1814'
'French Armée du Centre: 17 July 1812'
'French Army of Spain 1 September 1813'
'French Army of Spain 16 January 1814'
'French Cavalry in Southern France April 1814'
'French Forces Drawn From Spain for 1814 Campaign in France January 1814'
'French Units Ordered from Spain to France: June 1813'
'Reorganized Army of the Pyrenees: 10 March 1814'

Senior, Terry J. 'The Top Twenty French Cavalry Commanders: #20 General Edouard-Jean-Baptiste Milhaud' *The Napoleon Series* www.napoleon-series.org August 2002 accessed 8 July 2011.

Timmermans, Dominique *Les Monument de l'Empire* napoleon-monuments.eu/ nd accessed 2010

Index